To

DELIVER
THEIR SOULS

THE DIARY OF A
YOUNG RABBI
DURING THE
HOLOCAUST

EMANUEL FRIEDER

In loving memory of my dear parents,
Rabbi Pinchas and Sarah Frieder,
and the entire families of Czechoslovak Jewry,
including many of my relatives,
who perished at the hands of the Nazi oppressor.

Rabbi Abraham Abba
Frieder

Thoughts from the Son

From an early age I remember my Father, the Rabbi Armin Frieder, leading the congregation in Nové Mesto, Slovakia. I remember him sitting on a chair near the ark where the synagogue's sacred Torah scrolls were kept facing the bima (altar). I would sit on his lap or dangle around his legs while he prayed. He was an important man, and I was beloved by the Jewish community because I was his son.

On September 9, 1941, the wartime Slovak Republic approved a code that stripped us Jews of our civil rights, right to work, and freedom of movement. My Father, a born leader and activist, tried to influence government officials to repeal the deportations mandated by these government decrees. Although my Father saved many lives, nevertheless, the Jewish community of Slovakia was shattered.

Jewish children, like me, were no longer permitted a public education. There were streets on which non-Jewish children would throw stones and verbally harass Jewish children simply because we dared to walk on the public street. I learned at a young age where it was safe and where it was less safe in my neighborhood.

As the war progressed, I saw my Father less and less. My Father devised a plan to try to protect my Mother, my sister Gita, and me. Thus, we left my Father and Nové Mesto. Sadly – although this word doesn't describe the depths of this sadness - my Mother and Gita were killed. I remained in the mountains hidden in plain sight by Paulina and Josef Strycharsyk, a righteous couple who harbored me.

I was 8 years old when I returned from hiding. My Father died a year later. How much can such a young child remember of his Father? The thing I remember most about my Father: he taught me that our days are numbered and that a day without learning is a wasted day. In his honor and memory, I've tried, my whole life, to learn so as not to waste any precious day.

Lately, I've thought a lot about the courage shown by my Father, my Mother, and Paulina and Josef Strycharsyk during a time where the reality and law of the land threatened each of them in different ways. I've thought about the rise of anti-Semitism globally and the need for people and governments to continue to show courage lest we forget.

Thus, in July 2021, I invited representatives from the Embassy of the Slovak Republic in Washington, D.C., to meet me for lunch. Eventually, we were able to meet in person. After introductions and greetings, I appealed to them and challenged the current Slovak government to apologize for the actions of the past Slovak government, which devastated the lives of the Jewish community. One of the representatives promised to take this message directly to the heads of the Slovak government.

This time, good triumphed. I do not know whether my lunch with the Embassy representatives was causally related to the declaration a few weeks later. However, marking the 80th anniversary of the enactment of the "Jewish Code" on or about September 9, 2021, the current Slovak government issued a monumental statement that it "feels a moral obligation today to publicly express sorrow over the crimes committed by the past regime" against the Jewish people.

"Slovakia government apologizes for WWII anti-Jew laws" -- https://tinyurl.com/SlovakApology (last viewed 1/7/2022)

Now, dear reader, thank you for reading this book. I'm certain you will learn from this book, and thereby, honor my Father's heartfelt charge to learn something new every day.

Gideon Frieder

Thoughts from the Grandchildren

Dr. Rabbi Abraham Aba Armin Frieder, during his brief life of less than 35 years, monumentally changed the lives of many, both within and outside his community. Without exaggeration, thousands of lives exist today directly due to his efforts. It is thus not surprising that many books and encyclopedias, both online and in print, describe his efforts; museums worldwide have permanent exhibits honoring his contributions; and locations in multiple countries are dedicated and named in his honor. He has inspired a legacy that hopefully will shine bright into the future. In his honor and spirit of tikkun olam, we republish this biography and write this dedication.

Unfortunately, actions like his remain a necessity even today. Hate crime is increasing worldwide. In the United States, the frequency of hate crime is at a decade-long high. In some parts of Europe, hate crime has more than doubled in the last year. Antisemitism specifically, namely, hate crimes targeting Jews, is ever-present and intensifying. Once considered a safe haven, even in the United States, Jews can no longer expect a "care-free" existence. Results from a 2021 survey recently released by the Anti-Defamation League (ADL) indicate that roughly 63% of Jewish Americans had either "experienced or witnessed some form of antisemitic incident" over the past 5 years. Even with the 4% polling margin of error, that is a "notable increase" from the 54% of similar respondents from a similar survey taken the previous year. More so, although within the margin of error but yet a slight decline from the previous year, still 59% of this year's respondents felt that Jewish Americans today are less safe than they were a decade ago, and 49% of respondents fear "a violent attack at a synagogue". Thus, tolerance, and thus silence, is not an option. From the immortal lessons of and in his own (translated) words, Pastor Martin Niemöller guides us to speak out, otherwise: "…

Then they came for me – and there was no one left to speak for me."

We do, however, share Rabbi Frieder's sense of optimism that there is hope. There are the voices of the righteous who dedicate and risk themselves to help others. Their voices, who never forget and always remind others, inspire us, as lest we forget, we would be doomed to relive the past.

We are thus in gratitude to the Most Rev. Dr. Robert Gosselin, General Secretary for the Continuing Evangelical Episcopal Church, who enabled the reproduction of this biography; he is one of those, unfortunately too rare, who are forever speaking.

Gony Frieder Goldberg, Tally Frieder Balakirsky, & Ophir Frieder (Grandchildren)
January 2022

Foreword

The story of Slovak Jewry, a Jewish community of long standing, occupies a special place in the history of the Holocaust. Slovakia had both a very Orthodox Jewish community, comprising several generations of disciples of the Hatam Sofer of Bratislava (Pressburg), and a Zionist community, comprised of secular and religious Jews. The Zionist community included people aspiring to live by Jewish tradition and *halakhah* while interpreting Judaism in a way more compatible with the intellectual climate of the first half of our century. Rabbi Abraham Frieder, the central figure of this book, was one such man.

After the treachery of 1938-1939, in which Slovakia's southern and eastern realms were wrested from her and, with their substantial Jewish population, given to Hungary, and after the declaration of an independent fascist clerical Slovak state (March 14, 1939), the Jewish population of Slovakia was reduced to approximately 90,000. The Slovak government was extremely anti-Semitic and corrupt. A regime totally dependent on Nazi Germany, the government passed harsh legislation against the Jews, culminating in the publication of the Jewish Codex of 1941, based on racist principles and aimed at stealing the Jews' property. By then initial contacts had begun between Slovak leaders and the upper echelons of the German Reich with regard to expelling the Jews. Since this would enable them to lay their hands on the Jews' wealth, the Slovaks were interested and, in early 1942, reached an accord with the Germans on the expulsion of the Jews of Slovakia. Initially the plan apparently involved some 20,000 Jews, but before long all the Jews of Slovakia were included, save some specially privileged persons. The first deportations of Jews were brought to the Lublin region, to the Majdanek camp (in the early stages a labor camp, but subsequently a concentration camp and ultimately a death camp), and later to Auschwitz. The young men and women left in the camp and not sent directly to the gas chambers were essentially the first group of Jewish inmates at Auschwitz. Thus, insofar as they have survived, Slovak Jews are among the earliest witnesses to life in this camp.

A desperate attempt was made to save the remaining Jews in Slovakia. Gisi Fleischmann, head of WIZO before the war, together with Rabbi Michael Dov Weissmandel, son-in-law of the illustrious Rabbi Ungar of Nitra, founded a group calling itself the "Working Group" (or the "Clandestine Council" as Weissmandel referred to it). The group established contact with Eichmann's man in Bratislava, the S.S. officer Dieter Wisliceny, to bribe the Germans to stop the deportations. The deportations were indeed halted temporarily in July, and again for an extended time beginning in October 1942. The cause of this respite in deportations is a subject of debate, yet it is clear that the "Working Group" believed the ransom they paid the Nazis to have been the decisive factor.

Hoping to halt the deportation of Jews from other parts of Europe to Poland, the group embarked on the "Europa Plan" - a second, more ambitious attempt to pay off the Nazis. These negotiations, a subject of sharp controversy, were conducted from November 1942 through late August - early September 1943, but in the end came to naught. Rabbi Frieder was an active participant in these negotiations and all that surrounded. This, it must be said, was the first, and one of the few, attempts within Nazi-controlled regions to do more than save individual local Jewish communities, trying, rather, to rescue all the Jews of Europe. The spiritual strength to undertake such an endeavor as this came from the surviving remnant of Slovakia's small Jewish community, strategically placed by fate.

The leaders of the Jewish underground were involved in other rescue operations, as well: smuggling Jews across the border into Hungary, rescuing refugees from the ghettos of Poland, saving some of the 30,000 Jews who remained in Slovakia after the halt in deportation in October 1942, and supervising three special labor camps which were established to save Jews from deportation. Rabbi Frieder was a key figure in all these undertakings, especially in establishing the central refugee home, Ohel David [Tent of David].

The journal which Rabbi Frieder kept as these events were taking place provides an important perspective on these developments, reflecting the vantage point of an alert observer and a learned and active man. This testimony, as any other, has its subjective aspects. This journal, however, reflects the perceptions of a central figure, one of the most important actors in the tragedy of the Jews of Slovakia, and therein lies its special merit. Rabbi Armin Frieder's brother, Mr. Emanuel Frieder, the Hebrew translator and annotator of the manuscript and the moving force behind the publication of this book, deserves the special gratitude and appreciation of all who are concerned with the history of the Holocaust.

Yehudah Bauer

Preface

This book is comprised of two parts: the first is based on the diary of Rabbi Abraham-Abba (Armin) Frieder; the second a sequel about Slovak Jewry after the war.

The original diary, written in German and Slovak, is close to 800 pages long. It begins with a description of Rabbi Frieder's activities in 1933, when he began his career as a young rabbi in Zvolen and later in Nové Mesto and Bratislava, and continues with an account of the years of oppression and Holocaust during Nazi Germany's domination of Europe. During the latter period Rabbi Frieder kept a record of developments in his own community, as well as events which left their mark on the life of Jews throughout Slovakia. He committed to writing précis of his sermons and political speeches. His diary comprises a four-volume book of memoirs, entitled *Aus meinem Leben* (My Life), including documents, reports, pictures and illustrations from the same period.

The book gives detailed accounts of conversations and meetings between Rabbi Frieder and various figures in the Slovak administration, whose actions affected the lives of the Jews of Slovakia and often determined their fate. The diary also covers his activities in the underground "Working Group" and his encounters with prominent figures in this group.

Although the author's style is occasionally metaphorical and not devoid of soulful outpourings, at times discretion dictated a more oblique mode of expression. The facts mentioned in the book, especially the dates, numbers, and details concerning deportations of Jews to death camps, are based on reports of the Jewish Center from the time of the Holocaust itself.

The diary is an original document of great significance. Through his extensive involvement in the central bodies of the Zionist movement, in the Central Jewish Bureau, in the Yeshurun Federation of Jewish communities, and in the Working Group, where he labored indefatigably to save Jewish lives, Rabbi Frieder was party to these dramatic developments. Thus, his diary serves as a primary source on these events. The chapters on the period of the Holocaust were written by Rabbi Frieder out of historical awareness, as a testimony and memorial, to fulfill the biblical verses: "Remember what Amalek did unto thee" (Deuteronomy 25:17), and "Write this for a memorial in the book, and rehearse it in the ears of Joshua" (Exodus 17:14).

While serving as principal of the Jewish school in Nové Mesto, from the autumn of 1939, I followed the multi-faceted activities of my brother and assisted him in writing and collecting his materials. Later, when I sat down to edit his manuscript and prepare it for publication, on the one hand, I found it necessary to sift through a vast amount of material, selecting essential passages and often abridging detailed descriptions. On the other hand, occasionally I deemed it necessary to expand upon the text, explaining the historical setting of Rabbi Frieder's activities and going into greater detail on the laws and decrees promulgated against the Jews of Slovakia and important events to which the diary only alluded obliquely – all to present a more complete picture of the ·times. These passages, written by myself, are presented in a different typeface. The marginal notes, as well, are my own additions.

The second part of the book, "Slovak Jewry after the War," written entirely by myself, sets out to describe the post-war history of Slovak Jewry. During this period, after the passing of my brother, I served as chairman of the Central Union of Jewish Congregations in Slovakia. This part of the book is based both on personal memories and archival material and minutes of Jewish organizations from 1946-1949.

I hope that the book as a whole, while not purporting to be an objective history, will contribute to the study of the Holocaust suffered by the Jews of Slovakia and to preserving the memory of what was once a great Jewish community but is no more.

Emanuel Frieder

Part One

My Life

The Diary of Rabbi Frieder

5693 - 5705

(1933 - 1945)

Introduction

(By Emanuel A. Frieder)

Abraham-Abba in His Father's House

The city of Prievidza lies near the springs of the River Nitra, after which the provincial capital is named. The surrounding mountains are rich in coal and curative springs; and the pleasant climate, beautiful landscape, and deciduous and evergreen forests of the region attract many tourists to the area.

Jewish habitation in the area apparently dates from the end of the 17th century. The first Jews to arrive here were a group from Moravia, permitted to settle in the villages of the area in exchange for a fee for protection by the local ruler, who dwelled in Bojnice. The largest concentration of Jews during that period was in the village of Nováky, where the settlers established a Jewish community providing all the necessary services and institutions: a synagogue, *beit midrash* (house of study and prayer), ritual bath, and cemetery.

At a later period, the Jews were also permitted to take up residence in the district city of Prievidza. By the beginning of the twentieth century the Jewish community there numbered close to 400 people, about ten percent of the population. The community had its own elementary school, synagogue and cemetery, and used the bathhouses in Bojnice as their ritual bath. In 1910 my father and teacher, A. Pinchas ben Isaac Jacob Frieder, of blessed memory, was chosen to serve as teacher, *shohet* (in charge of the ritual slaughter of kosher meat), and spiritual leader of the congregation. My father, a graduate of the Bonyhád and Pressburg *yeshivas* (Talmudic academies), was strict in leading the congregation in the Orthodox spirit. Apprehensive about the assimilationist practices being introduced in liberal circles and firmly believing that keeping the commandments was an inseparable part of belonging to the Jewish people, he fought against all change in matters of religion.

My mother, Sarah (née Messinger), a woman of noble temperament, succeeded marvelously well in caring for the needs of the family, even in times of trouble and hardship, such as when my father fell prisoner in the First World War and was away from home for a long time. Her third child, Abraham Abba-Armin, was born on June 30, 1911. Having had to grow up without a father at home, he became acquainted with hardship from an early age. When he was seven, he witnessed the pogrom which broke out the day the Czechoslovak Republic was proclaimed. On that day, October 28, 1918, Jewish houses and stores were plundered and two Jews – Julius Kováč and his brother Heinrich Cohen – were killed. These experiences left a deep impression on the young Abraham-Abba, who was destined to stand in the breach, defending Jewish rights in a heroic battle against anti-Semitism.

Abraham-Abba studied in the local Jewish elementary school, where the language of instruction at first was Hungarian and later, after the establishment of the Czechoslovak state, Slovak, which the local teachers were required to learn in intensive language courses. Jozef Sivák, later appointed Slovak Minister of Education and noted for his great assistance to the Jewish people during the Second World War, was the superintendent of schools for the Ministry of Education and Culture.

Abraham-Abba's fifth year of schooling was spent in the state-run gymnasium, where he evinced great interest in studying Latin. At the same time, he acquired the beginnings of his religious education from his father, who spent the afternoon hours teaching him Bible, Mishnah and Gemara. When our father decided that his sons must learn in a more intensive fashion, he transferred us to the small *yeshiva, Mahazikei Torah,* in Topolčany, the neighboring district city, known for its Jewish educational institutions. Several dozen lads, ten years and older, studied in this *yeshiva.* The students came from all ends of the country, mostly from poor families, and received their meals from well-to-do members of the community, each day in another house. The meals were nutritious, although sometimes the circumstances under which they were received were somewhat uncomfortable. *Mahazikei Torah* had four classes. Abraham-Abba and I were in the second class, studying under the famous teacher, Rabbi Chaim-Dov Fürst, a graduate of the Pressburg and Frankfurt am Main *yeshivas.* Using progressive teaching methods, Rabbi Chaim-Dov Fürst imparted to his pupils a knowledge of basic Hebrew grammar, cantillation of the Bible, and love of the Torah and its language. He insisted that his pupils translate the Torah into literary German. He prepared Abraham-Abba, a beloved pupil, for his Bar Mitzvah ceremony and maintained that the youngster had latent talent as a public speaker and orator. We studied in this *beit midrash* another two years – in the third class with Rabbi Ben-Zion Braun, and in the fourth class with Rabbi Pinchas Deutsch. Upon concluding our studies in this class, our ways parted. I continued my studies in the Sered *yeshiva,* under Rabbi Moses-Asher Eckstein of blessed memory, while Abraham-Abba went to Bratislava, where he studied at *Yesodei Torah* under Rabbis Goldstein and Petenyi, and in the Pressburg *yeshiva.* Eight years he poured over his studies with diligence and talent, and at the end of 1932 three distinguished and learned rabbis gave him a permit to officiate as rabbi, pending his full ordination.

Abraham-Abba aspired to be a rabbi. From an early age he spoke at community and family events in Prievidza and in time developed into a successful orator with a reputation in the surrounding area.

The "status quo" congregations[1] in Slovakia, affiliated to the Yeshurun Federation of Jewish congregations, suffered a severe shortage of rabbis due to a shortage of appropriate institutions for training them. The rabbinical seminaries in Vienna and Budapest were now beyond the borders. Abraham-Abba's religious and secular education made him well qualified to lead one of these congregations. Indeed, he began his rabbinical career in Zvolen, continued in Nové Mesto, and finished in Bratislava. He was a fighter, a man of principle, and a God-fearing Jew. In all the congregations where he served as rabbi he fought against assimilation, instituted various corrective measures, and called for a return to rabbinic Judaism and national-religious Jewish identity.

His true greatness was revealed in the time of the Holocaust.

---

[1] Congregations which followed Jewish religious law but did not affiliate themselves with the Central Orthodox Bureau.

Chapter One

Zvolen

(5693 - 5697; 1933 - 1937)

*"Come, ye children, hearken unto me;
I will teach you the fear of the Lord."*

(Psalms 34:12)

I. Shepherding His Flock

For years the Jewish community of Zvolen had been seeking a rabbi who, among his other qualifications, could serve as a religious and Jewish studies teacher in the state schools and could deliver lectures in Slovak.

In 1932 the Jewish community advertised an opening for the position of Chief Rabbi. Although I was not yet fully ordained as a rabbi, my friends and acquaintances urged me to apply. The board of the community invited me for the Sabbath of *Shemot,* the first scriptural reading from the Book of Exodus (December 1932), to give a sermon in German to the congregation and a speech in Slovak to the youth.

Quoting from Psalms, "Open Thou mine eyes, that I may behold wondrous things out of Thy law," I began a sermon in German which won the hearts of my audience. My speech in Slovak was originally scheduled for the *minhah* (afternoon) service of the youth, but I abstained from participating in this service because it had a mixed choir of young men and women. Therefore, I consented to lecture only after, and not during, the service. In my lecture in Slovak, which lasted nearly two hours, I established close rapport with the youth. I felt my chances of being awarded the position of Chief Rabbi were good, and that this day was likely to mark a turning point in my life, a beginning in my career as a public figure.

Several weeks later I received a letter of appointment, signed by the president of the community, Eugen Schlesinger, and his vice-president, Bartolomej Reinl, in two versions – one Slovak and the other German – perhaps an indication that the affairs of the community were handled in both languages. My election was approved by the national office in April 1933, and the installation ceremony was held on August 27, 1933.

The congregation, whose official name was Židovská náboženská *obec* (Jewish Religious Community), was not designated as a neologist (progressive) community, like many other congregations in the country; however, a number of assimilated Jews with reform inclinations sat on its board, and they demanded that the installation ceremony be held in the manner to which they were accustomed. I, however, had decided to lead my congregation according to the custom of rabbis in Orthodox congregations and refused to wear the officiating garb customary in neologist congregations, insisting instead on wearing a *tallit* and a black velvet *yarmulka* (skullcap) at the ceremony. Likewise, I flatly objected to a mixed choir and organ accompaniment and gave official notice that if my demands were not met, I would not accept the position. In the end they conceded.

The installation ceremony was attended by Jewish delegations from the surrounding towns and Jewish communities, and received news coverage in the daily press under the headline: "Zvolen Becomes the First City in the Country to Elect a Slovak-speaking Rabbi."

II. Activities in the Zvolen Community Religious Rulings and Corrective Measures

Years without religious leadership had turned the Zvolen community into a liberal, secular congregation, neglecting Jewish values and leaning towards assimilation. Its religious institutions did not function as they ought to have, and the *hazzan* (cantor) and *shohet* (butcher), influenced by the general secular atmosphere in the community, did not always act in conformance to the *halakhah,* religious law. This compelled me to begin reorganizing the community, bringing it closer to its Jewish roots. One means to this end was to found a chapter of *Herut,* an association open to all members of the community and aimed at teaching Jewish history, culture, and values through lectures, plays, classes, and other cultural activities. A rich library of books on Judaism was established. Eugen Schlesinger was elected honorary president of *Herut,* and Dr. Moritz Reisz and Alfred Grünmann vice-presidents. Mrs. Irene Gerson was treasurer of the association, and Mrs. Deborah Ernst and Dr. Aladar Sós were its secretaries. I was placed in charge of coordinating and running cultural activities.

Being young and energetic, I succeeded in winning over the youth in the Jewish community. The weekly classes in religion at school, which previously had been detested obligatory lessons, suddenly became interesting. History and Hebrew language instruction received new impetus and were also offered in the youth club, where teenagers came to hear lectures and participate in singing and dancing. Every

Sabbath, as part of *seudah shelishit* (third meal of the Sabbath, Saturday afternoon), I held competitions at which the young men and women showed off their knowledge of Hebrew and Jewish studies. The youth also greatly enriched their parents' knowledge of Judaism and helped disseminate the wellsprings of Torah.

I was assisted in my work by my two sisters - Rachel-Rosa, who managed the household, and Pirka,[1] then in her last year at the local secondary school and active, with her sister Rosa, in the Zionist youth movement. My varied and intensive activity made itself felt throughout the community and brought a sense of satisfaction and reward. This was reflected in the spontaneous decision of the board of the community to grant me tenure in my position and confer on me the title of Chief Rabbi.

Patiently and gradually, I took charge of the religious affairs of the community, aspiring to impart it an Orthodox way of life. Using gentle persuasion, I enacted various religious regulations in accordance with the *Shulhan Arukh:*

Shehitah (kosher slaughtering of meat) and kashruth: On my initiative one of the two *shohatim* was dismissed, and in his place a new *shohet* and kashruth supervisor was hired to be in charge of the kosher slaughtering of cattle. The other continued in his job as *shohet* only after passing a test and mending his ways. To assure effective supervision of kosher meat, a new central butcher shop was opened and its keys kept in the hands of an authorized *mashgiah* (kashruth supervisor).

Public prayer: Over the years the Great Synagogue had been open for public prayer only on Sabbaths, Festivals, and *yahrzeits* (anniversary of a relation's death) of individual congregants who requested to have a

---

[1] Pirka, born in 1919, completed her studies at the Bratislava Academy and died of tuberculosis in 1941.

minyan (quorum of ten, necessary for public prayer) organized in order for them to say *kaddish* (doxology, often recited as a memorial prayer). I instituted daily *shaharit* (morning) and *arvit* (evening) services. Attendance was rather poor at first, but with the introduction of a lecture series on the weekly scriptural reading it improved, until eventually the services drew about forty people. About twenty-five adults began attending morning services regularly. By the end of my tenure as rabbi the synagogue was too small to accommodate all those who came to services on Sabbaths and Festivals, and we even gathered a *minyan* of men for prayers on public fast days, hitherto almost completely forgotten in the community (save the Day of Atonement). Prayers which hitherto had been abbreviated henceforth were said according to the custom of Pressburg and in conformance to the *halakhah*. A change was also instituted in the manner of calling men up to the Torah. Instead of the synagogue's customary formula, *"Ya'amod ha-rishon, ya'amod ha-sheni"* ("Will the first person please come forward, will the second person please come forward, etc."), the person being called up was summoned by his Hebrew name and the name of his father. This was done with a view to increasing the community's Jewish identity and bringing the congregants back to their Jewish roots.

Morning and evening services were followed by lessons on the weekly scriptural reading, spiced with homilies of the Sages, legends, and parables. The frequency of lessons given in the synagogue increased, as did the number of people who attended them. Jewish holidays were celebrated in full splendor. On every holiday I delivered special addresses to the adults in German and to the youth in Slovak, to refute the anti-Semites' assertion that the Jews were disseminating German and Hungarian culture.

Changes within the synagogue: All the changes were instituted cautiously and gradually, until the synagogue functioned according to original traditional Jewish practice. Even the official robes, which had customarily been worn in the congregation and which originated from a gentile practice, were proscribed, and in their stead the *hazzan* draped himself in a large, unfolded *tallit* (prayer shawl).

One serious problem troubled my peace of mind from the day I entered office - the internal structure of the synagogue, which was not built in Orthodox style. The *bimah* (platform where the Torah is read) was not situated in the center of the synagogue. Instead, it stood near the Holy Ark where, according to the neologist practice, in addition to serving as the desk for reading the Torah, it was also used as the platform for the *hazzan*. Orthodox rabbis forbade Jews to pray in such synagogues and declared them unfit on the grounds that they followed "gentile practice." I brought the subject up in my sermons, at meetings, and in conversation with the beadles and members of the board of the community and pointed out the necessity of making our synagogue a fit place for Orthodox Jews to pray, as well. The boards of the synagogue and of the community, however, did not wish to take a stand on this issue.

Fearing that the board of the community would not approve the changes, I presented them with a *fait accompli* and ordered the furniture and all the necessary renovations according to my own plans and at my own expense. A sharp controversy broke out in the community, and the assimilationists called for a show of opposition by boycotting the inauguration ceremony of the renovated synagogue. However, the first time I came to preach from the new *bimah,* the synagogue was more packed than had been anticipated. I did not hesitate to admonish the supposedly progressive, assimilationist camp, who were moving away from their Jewishness and casting off the yoke of their religion and their Jewish national identity at one and the same time. The sermon had an impact on most of the congregation, and the furor died down. The subject did not come up again in the meetings of the board. It was simply decided that the expenditures should not be reimbursed since "the rabbi acted exclusively on his own initiative." I, however, was overjoyed, for I had achieved the holy goal of standing before my Maker in a house of prayer which was fit for any Jew.

III. Educational and Nationalist-Zionist Activity

After successfully establishing good relations with the principals of the state schools and with the senior teachers in the city, I worked to reduce violation of the Sabbath by the Jewish pupils in these institutions. I saw to it that the schedule of instruction be changed so that only those subjects not requiring writing would be taught on the Sabbath (for I had essentially forbidden the Jewish pupils to write on the Sabbath). On Jewish holidays the Jewish pupils were excused from school.

I held special study groups for teaching the laws of kashruth, and about thirty families in the community decided to keep kosher homes. Special emphasis was laid on learning the laws of kashruth pertaining to Passover, which were not well understood by a large number of women in the community. As part of their activities the women undertook a campaign to refresh the mantels on the Torah scrolls, the cloths for the tables in the synagogue, and the curtains covering the Holy Ark. The men, for their part, saw to a budget for examining the Torah scrolls and repairing the *mezuzot*.

Circumcision ceremonies and bar-mitzvah celebrations were transformed from family occasions into events involving the entire Jewish community. Weddings, which had been held inside the synagogue, as was the custom of the neologists, were henceforth held under the open sky, in conformance to the practice of Orthodox congregations in our country. Changes were also made in funerary ritual, making it conform to the tradition of our forefathers.

Alongside my work in the religious sphere, I fostered nationalist-Zionist activities, instructing the youth in the writings of Herzl, Pinsker, Nordau, and others, and lecturing on historical themes and Jewish philosophy. In response to growing anti-Semitic propaganda I began to publish monographs, articles, and apologetics in the Slovak press.

After the Nazis' rise to power in Germany, despite the steadily worsening condition of the Jewish communities there, the Jews in the other countries of Europe, including Czechoslovakia, did not heed what was happening across the border or pay attention to the fact that their brethren in Germany were being denigrated as belonging to an inferior race. Even complete assimilation into the German people and culture did not stand the German Jews in good stead or save them from persecution.

Most of the assimilated Jews in Slovakia in general, and in Zvolen in particular, especially the younger generation, took every opportunity to proclaim their allegiance to the Slovak people. But they could not conceal their faith and, when asked their religion, involuntarily wrote "Jewish" or, in supposedly more refined language, "Israelite." They aspired to equal rights in all spheres, in accordance with the constitution of the state. This faction in the Jewish community could not understand how I, who had grown up after the First World War, could converse and lecture in the language of the country, as behooves a loyal citizen, yet at the same time could preach Zionism and advocate the movement for Jewish national revival. These youths, more than others, were sorely in need of ideological tutelage. This was provided in evenings of questions and answers, at which I explained my Jewish nationalist outlook.

Sowing the seeds of Zionism and reaping its fruits on the soil of Zvolen was very difficult. Most of the Jewish community was assimilated, and the non-assimilated minority was indifferent to the Zionist movement. Given the atmosphere in the Zvolen community, the existing nationalist and spiritual crisis could be overcome only with the aid of the Zionist idea, which meant fostering the Hebrew language and actively supporting the Land of Israel. Without affiliating with a specific Zionist faction, I offered my services to the Zionist movement and stepped-up activity to spread the Zionist idea. Cultural evenings, held two to three times a week, attracted a considerable fraction of the local Jewish youth. In time, the participants themselves began preparing the cultural activities, and my personal involvement became less necessary. Concomitantly I organized study groups for the youth, for elementary school and secondary school students. Those over eighteen years of age participated in the adult study groups. Lectures in history, Jewish literature and philosophy, and the history of Zionism were held in the evenings. Likewise, classes in the Hebrew language were offered on a variety of levels. These were language courses and preparatory programs for shaping the activists of the Zionist movement, which was later to develop in Zvolen. The students in the upper grades of the secondary school worked for the Jewish National Fund and brought the "blue box" into every home. In 1934 the Jews of Zvolen contributed 60 thousand korunas to the Jewish Foundation Fund. This was considered an impressive achievement, as was the resolution adopted by the board of the community to allocate funds from its budget to the two national funds. Henceforward

Zionist leaders and activists began to make appearances in the city, in settings other than indoctrination gatherings, and elicited considerable public response. All this widely varied activity was coordinated by myself, assisted by my students. When the state-wide Zionist leaders became aware of what we were doing and had achieved in Zvolen, I was requested to appear at public gatherings in other towns throughout the region as the representative of the JNF and the state-wide Zionist movement.

After establishing myself in the community, I decided to marry my beloved Rozi-Rela, daughter of Hermina and Max-Meir Berl of Bratislava, whom I had met when I was studying there and living with my brother Emanuel in a room which we rented from her father. The wedding took place on 8 Elul (August 19), 1934, in the Great Orthodox Synagogue in Bratislava.

IV. "Let thy springs be dispersed abroad" (Prov. 5:16)

Since the "status quo" congregations had no seminary which could train suitable candidates for the rabbinate, the congregations in Kremnica, Levice, Šahy, Banská-Štiavnica, and other towns lacked rabbis. These congregations used to invite me to perform ceremonies and officiate at congregational functions, and several of them elected me to act as their regular rabbi. This connection with many Jewish communities enabled me to develop an extensive cultural program, including a series of lectures, sermons, and speeches. Likewise, I performed marriages and officiated at family ceremonies but would have nothing to do with matters pertaining to the kosher slaughtering of meat, since these matters were not always handled as I would have liked. Therefore, I felt constrained not to accept responsibility for them.

My scope of work increased still further with my election to various local and national bodies. In March 1935 I was elected to the executive committee of the *Marica Slovenská* (Slovak National Institute), Zvolen branch. This appointment was extremely significant, since the very fact of my presence there prevented anti-Semitic outbursts and statements. This institution fostered Slovak culture and on more than one occasion served as an arena for attacks on the Jews, who, since they spoke Hungarian and German, were thought to be disseminating the culture of nations that had enslaved the Slovaks for centuries. Even though the Slovaks were aware of my views, I was re-elected to the committee every year of the period I spent in Zvolen.

In January 1935, at the national conference of the Yeshurun Federation, an organization of traditional Jewish congregations centered in Bratislava, I was elected to the board for a term of three years. During the same period, I was also elected to the cultural committee of the Union of Traditional Rabbis in Slovakia (rabbis of Yeshurun congregations). The chairman of the Union at the time was Dr. Eliezer Schweiger, Chief Rabbi of the Yeshurun congregation in Nitra. In the fall of 1935 (beginning of the Jewish year 5696), after a branch of the Women's International Zionist Organization was founded in Zvolen, broader circles began to evince a change in attitude towards Zionism, whose ideas hitherto had been quite removed from them. Mrs. Eugen Schlesinger, wife a rather assimilationist or reformist, was elected chairwoman of the local WIZO chapter. Mrs. Schlesinger was very active and organized benefit parties for WIZO in the city's Grand Hotel.

At that time Hannah Steiner presided over the national federation of WIZO in Prague, and Gisi Fleischmann was chairwoman of Slovakia's WIZO in Bratislava. Both women expressed admiration for the accomplishments of the Zvolen chapter.[2] In February 1935, on my

---

[2] Cf. letters of the WIZO centers in Bratislava (December 1934) and Prague (January 1935),

initiative, a branch of the Jewish party *(Židovská strana)* was founded in Zvolen. Dr. Paul März, a member of the party's executive committee and a Zionist leader from Moravská Ostrava, appeared at a public rally, and a local committee was elected under my chairmanship.[3]

In March 1935, Dr. Oscar Jeremiah Neumann, a deputy of the Jewish National Fund, visited Zvolen, and it was decided to expand Zionist activities and found a regional action committee for the *JNF* and the Jewish Foundation Fund. During those months we launched a fund drive for Kefar Masaryk, a new settlement site in the Land of Israel, which Slovakian Jewry had decided to establish and name after Czechoslovakia's founder and first President, Thomas Masaryk.[4]

On June 9, 1935, the Zionist movement in my home town of Prievidza celebrated the tenth anniversary of the founding of the local chapter of the *Ha-Shomer Qadimah* youth movement. Youths from the Maccabee chapters in Žilina, Ružomberok, Banská-Bystrica and Liptovský Svätý Mikuláš joined in the celebrations, participating in sports and gymnastics performances.

* * *

---

in the Frieder Brothers Collection, M--5/191-194, Yad va-Shem Archives (henceforth FYVS).

[3] The Jewish Party was a national political party whose activity focused specifically on elections, with the aim of achieving Jewish representation in the principal local and national bodies. In the 1928 elections the party received 45,239 votes in Slovakia, winning it a seat in the Slovak National Council in Bratislava. Albert Gestettner was chosen for the position. Dr. Julius Reiss, a lawyer from Bratislava, was elected to the Parliament in Prague. In 1936 the representatives of the Jewish Party in the National Council were Dr. Julius Reiss and Ludwig Mayer, both from Bratislava. In the municipal elections the Jewish Party won representation on all the local councils of the large outlying cities. According to data from post - World War I years, at the time Slovakia had 138,918 inhabitants belonging to the Jewish religion. Of these, 71,018 called themselves Jews; 29,136, Slovaks; 21,584, Hungarians; 8,738, Germans; and the remainder, foreign citizens and others. Cf. *Židovská Ročenka pre Slovensko* (Jewish Annual of Slovakia), 1940.

[4] Cf. letter of the national office of the JNF in Prague, dated April 29, I 936, FYVS.

The Jewish communities of Slovakia also held annual festive services in the central synagogues on two national holidays: Czechoslovakia's Day of Independence, on October 28, and the birthday of President Masaryk, on March 7. These ceremonies were times of great excitement, for the mayor, representatives of various government offices, the police, and the army were all invited to attend. What impression must this have made on the gentiles? Most of the rabbis did not know Slovak, and only a few could eke out several sentences in broken Slovak. This certainly did not do any credit to the Jewish community. Under such circumstances several congregations requested me to come and speak at their festive services. In 1934 the Yeshurun congregation in the capital city of Bratislava applied to the municipality of Zvolen and the board of the community, on the initiative of State Commissar Dr. Arpad Tauber, requesting that I be released from leading the festive service in Zvolen on October 28, so that I might officiate at the same ceremony in Bratislava, in place of Rabbi Samuel Funk of the Yeshurun congregation, who was not fluent in Slovak.

V. Zionist Activity in 1936

In the fall of 1936 (beginning of the Jewish year 5697) I organized a regional conference of JNF deputies and activists in Zvolen, sponsored by the national office of the JNF. I succeeded in persuading the chairman of the Jewish community, Dr. Moritz Reisz, who was not a Zionist, to deliver the benediction at the conference. Dr. Reisz also listened to Dr. Oscar Neumann's lecture about the Land of Israel and the projected fund-raising drive, "The People in Need." The central office of the Jewish National Fund in Prague expressed its appreciation of the fund-raising work which obtained several grants for the JNF. In my lectures I tried to introduce the idea of Zionism into those communities where the Jews hitherto had been indifferent to "The People in Need."

At the invitation of the local branch of the Zionist movement in Nové Mesto on the Vah, headed by Alexander Wohlstein, I appeared there in May 1936. Upon finishing my talk, as I bid the Jews of Nové Mesto "see you later in the Land of Israel," a lone voice was heard rising above the din of applause: "But until then, see you again in Nové Mesto." I did not understand the purport of his words until Desider Reich, secretary of the Zionist movement in the city, approached me and explained that the gentleman intended to express his wish for me to accept the position of rabbi in Nové Mesto. Indeed, later Alexander Wohlstein sent me a letter expressing his admiration and requesting that in the future, as well, I come and encourage the Zionist movement in its work.

* * *

The first conference of the World Jewish Congress was held in Geneva from August 8-19, 1936. I wished to meet the leaders of the Jewish organizations around the world, from the Diaspora and the Land of Israel, who were to participate in this important congress. Since I was a correspondent for Jewish and non-Jewish daily papers and on the staff of a literary periodical, I was known in the government press office and recognized as a journalist. A document signed by Stephen Wise and Aryeh Kubowitzki, leaders of the congress, certified my participation in the conference as a journalist.

In Geneva I met Jewish journalists from all over the world, heard talks by representatives of Jewish communities in Europe and America and by leaders of the *yishuv* (pre-State Jewish community) in the Land of Israel, representing all the circles and parties of the entire, broad spectrum of the Jewish public – save Orthodox Jewry, which had not joined the congress because a Reform rabbi, Dr. Stephen Wise, headed it. The conference participants spoke Hebrew, Yiddish, and other languages. The discussions, which went on day and night, were on a high level. Dr. Nahum Goldmann, the life spirit of the congress, made a powerful impression. The congress demonstrated the international organizational strength of world Jewry and the vitality of the Jewish people.

Returning from the congress full of experiences and with a strengthened sense of Jewish national identity, I visited the Jewish communities of Slovakia and reported on the condition of Jews around the world. My reports aroused great interest everywhere.

At the World Jewish Congress in Geneva, I chanced to fall into conversation with representatives of the World Mizrachi[5] movement, whose motto was "Torah and Work," i.e., to build the Land of Israel according to the Law of the Jewish people.

This motto essentially expressed my views, as well; although from an official, organizational standpoint I was not affiliated with any specific faction of the Zionist movement.

Due to my ideological identification with this movement, I decided to work on behalf of religious Zionism in Slovakia, which suffered a lack of spiritual leadership, because many Orthodox rabbis were afraid to support it publicly; for they feared such a step might well lead to their excommunication. Indeed, young rabbis who at first supported the Mizrachi had been forced to change their position because of pressure by the ultra-Orthodox establishment.

In my conversation in Geneva, in which Dr. Ladislav Rosenzwieg

---

[5] The Mizrachi movement developed in Slovakia even though the leaders of ultra-Orthodox Jewry strongly opposed any Zionist movement, including a religious one - which perhaps they opposed even more vehemently. The centers of the movement were in Košice and Bratislava. The first world conference of the Mizrachi movement, held in July, 1904, convened in Bratislava, the city of the Hatam Sofer, who, as we know, supported the *yishuv* in the Land of Israel. And in this city, not without serious controversy, a religious Zionist pioneer movement, with all its branches, was born.

(Rosen-Zvi) of Nitra participated as well, I proposed that the World Center of the Mizrachi establish a Zionist *yeshiva* in Slovakia which, in addition to teaching religious subjects, would also provide a general education and train spiritual leaders for the Jewish community and the Zionist movement. Such an institution had been my dream since my youth, from the time my father, much to his disappointment, had been unable to realize his aspiration of giving his sons an education in Torah and worldly subjects, such as was offered in the educational institutions of the *Adat Yeshurun* congregation in Frankfurt am Main, under the direction of Rabbi Dr. Jacob Hofmann. The Mizrachi delegates at Geneva listened to my proposal and promised to give it consideration. In September 1936, the executive committee of the Mizrachi organization in Czechoslovakia requested me to draft a detailed program for founding the *yeshiva*. At the appointed time I submitted a proposal projecting a *yeshiva* that would serve as a *beit midrash* and dormitory for young men, 18 and older, who had shown their ability in independent *gemara* (Talmud) study. The program of study would last four years. It was suggested that around twenty young men be accepted into the first class, and that each successive year another class of like size be added. As for the curriculum, I proposed it include close study of tractates and questions in Talmud and its interpretation, *posekim* (rabbis who ruled on questions of Jewish law), *Shullhan Arukh* (Joseph Caro's 16th century code of Jewish practice) with commentators, Bible, Hebrew language and grammar, history of the Jews, and Jewish literature and philosophy. I also suggested that study groups be organized to prepare participants for the state matriculation exams. When I appeared before the executive committee of the Mizrachi, I stressed the need to establish a *yeshiva* which would serve as a Jewish school, training graduates who would become the leaders and active figures of the Jewish community, men who would understand the changing times and pressures of modern life, but who also would fight the spread of assimilation by disseminating among

Jewish communities the notion of a return to Zion. I also expressed willingness to assume responsibility for running the dormitory.

The *yeshiva,* however, never came into being. For political reasons the Mizrachi was hesitant about placing me in charge of the *yeshiva,* claiming that they must also penetrate into extremist Orthodox circles.

VI. In Essay and Deed

Embittered that my plans for a *yeshiva* had not come to fruition, I nevertheless continued my wide range of activities in the surrounding towns, especially on Sundays.

After three years as rabbi of the congregation, I proposed that the synagogue which had been built 40 years earlier be renovated. The president of the congregation, Dr. Moritz Reisz, took up the idea and, with money raised specially for the purpose, had repairs made in the plaster and paint, inside and out, so that as the High Holidays approached the synagogue stood in full glory. On Rosh ha-Shannah 5697 (1936), I inaugurated the renovated building, whose facade proudly bore the Tablets of the Covenant and the inscription, "This is none other than the house of God."

* * *

A festive athletics convention was held in Bratislava's municipal theatre to mark the fifteenth anniversary of the Maccabee sports association. The Maccabee and Bar Kokhba sports associations participated in the games. I was invited to the opening ceremony and in my remarks lauded the success of Maccabee in bringing the youth into the Zionist movement, uniting them under the motto of a "healthy soul in a healthy body." The theatre was packed, and among the guests were representatives from the government, the municipality, and the army.

The convention prompted further development of sports departments associated with chapters of the Zionist movement in Slovakia.[6]

* * *

I wrote many articles in German for the *Allgemeine Jüdische Zeitung (General Jewish Newspaper)* and on various occasions also contributed to the Slovak literary paper, *Pero (Pen)*, edited by A. Nacin. When this paper published several anti-Semitic articles by Vladimir Vladkin, in which he attacked the Talmud and poured out his wrath on the Jews in general, I published a series of articles in response, refuting his biased claims and prejudices. When Vladkin persisted in responding, I proved that he was drawing his ideas from Rohling's well known anti-Semitic work, *Der Talmudjude (The Jews of the Talmud)*. My rebuttals apparently hit the mark, for Vladkin ceased his polemical dispute, remarking that he wished to remain silent now, "until the next provocation."

In 1934 I published a pamphlet in German, entitled "Sin - The World of Jewish Thought of Solomon Judah Ibn-Gevirol," based on my lectures in a seminar on this 11th century Spanish Jewish philosopher and poet. Six months later I published a monograph on Maimonides, in Slovak, entitled "Maimonides – 800 Years after his Birth." This booklet, the first Slovak work to appear in Jewish philosophical literature, was enthusiastically received by enlightenment circles in Slovakia.

---

[6] The Jewish sports center in Bratislava was founded in 1912 as part of the "Love of Zion" movement, headed by Samuel Bettelheim. A Maccabee sports association was founded by Hugo Brief and Dr. Joseph Knapp in 1921, by the Makabe'ah sports club, which specialized in soccer and athletics. The athletics section developed into a separate Maccabee association. The Bar Kokhba association, founded in 1929, focused on swimming. Jewish youth in Czechoslovakia showed great interest in physical education, and Maccabee associations functioned in most of the outlying cities. Sports conventions were held on national and international levels

Likewise, I wrote an essay in Slovak entitled "Maimonides and Masaryk," and in 1935 I translated the prayer book into Slovak. I applied to the *Matica Slovenská,* the Slovak National Institute, which handled the dissemination of Slovak literature and culture, and requested them to publish this *siddur,* the first Jewish prayer book with a Slovak translation, but the manuscript was returned with the comment that the Institute does not publish religious books. Nevertheless, they viewed publication of such a prayer book as very important and asked me not to give up searching for another publisher. However, due to its economic unprofitability, no publisher was found willing to print the book. Therefore, we reproduced translations of the more important prayers and published them in a supplementary booklet for teaching Jewish liturgy as part of the religious instruction curriculum in the state schools. Subsequently a complete prayer book translated by Rabbi Eliezer Schweiger was published in Nitra.

Encouraged by the success of the pamphlets, I began writing a *History of the Jewish People* in Slovak, along with my brother Emanuel, who helped me greatly in producing the work. The Academia Publishing House in Bratislava published Part I, which was received very enthusiastically by religious teachers in the secondary schools. Due to political developments and vicissitudes of fate, the remaining parts were never published.[7] In the introduction to this book I wrote: "These very days Jewry is entering a new era. We are witness to a unique development in the history of mankind. A people scattered throughout the world, living dispersed among the gentiles and speaking seventy different languages, is aspiring to unite, to gather itself together and settle in its ancient homeland, and to speak its own tongue."

In all my activities I was guided by the principle neither to

---

[7] They remained in manuscript form at the *Nekudah* publishing house in Mukatevo, in Carpatho-Russia, a region which was severed from Czechoslovakia in 1938.

hide my opinions nor disown my Jewishness, even when acting as the representative of the Jewish community in national Slovak institutions in Zvolen. For example, at the founding meeting of the *Slovenská Liga* (Slovak League), where the main speakers of the organization, known for their anti-Semitic vituperative, voiced attacks on the Jews, I arose against the attackers and refuted their words, pointing out the Jews' loyalty to the state as citizens seeking its welfare and growth. Whenever necessary, I also appeared in municipal and district offices to defend the rights of Jewish citizens.

Even my opponents in the community, led by Dr. Igor Schlesinger, Dr. Zigmund Oppenheimer and Daniel Kemény, who for ideological reasons opposed my activities in the nationalist and traditional-religious spheres, began to respect my firm position and faithful adherence to my views.

* * *

Žilina, a major city and cultural center and seat of the regional governmental bureaus, was the first large Jewish community officially to invite me to be its rabbi. The Jewish community there numbered approximately 1,500 people. The Yeshurun congregation in Bratislava, where I had officiated at festive services a number times, also invited me to be their guest over the Sabbath and address the congregation. Neither of these congregations, however, held much attraction for me. I did not wish to join the Yeshurun congregation in Bratislava, officially called the Congress Congregation, because of its neologist character and because I did not wish to offend the. chief rabbi of the community, Dr. Samuel Funk, on whose territory I would have been stepping. He was an observant Jew, a diligent man of learning and an excellent orator, and attracted large audiences to his sermons, which he delivered in German. He fought hard against the neologist innovations which his congregation wished to introduce, but was not adequate to the task; for he faced a powerful opposition that did not appreciate his personality, which could be likened to a fine bottle of old wine.

Nor was I enthused by the Žilina congregation. It was headed by the elderly rabbi Dr. David Friedman, who ran it according to the school of thought of the rabbinical seminary in Budapest, the seminary for neologist rabbis, and had a clearly neologist character.

My aspiration was to work in a congregation which observed the Jewish traditions and had a strong core of leading families with a national-religious sense of identity. Nevertheless, I opened negotiations with the Žilina congregation, which invited me for the Sabbath of the scriptural reading of *Toledot* (autumn 1935) to be the guest of the community and to address the adults and youth. Protracted and trying negotiations ensued, ultimately only to reach a dead end because of my flat refusal to comply with the demand of the leaders of the congregation that I wear a robe and folded *tallit* during the services, and because of my refusal to give advance promise that I would request the consent of the synagogue council and the board of the community before making any change or emendation in the prayer ritual. On March 25, 1936, I gave final notice that there was no point in continuing negotiations, since I would not agree to dictates from the leaders of the community which contravened my ways, the ways of the *halakhah,* traditional Jewish law. Indeed, my close associates and even my wife urged me to accept the position and contribute to the religious life of the community, but I could not do something which went against my world outlook. Neologism aims at assimilation, whereas my belief was that we must revive authentic Judaism, based on the *halakhah* as it was revealed to Moses at Mount Sinai. It was my father and teacher who guided me and encouraged me to reject the offer to serve as rabbi in Žilina, saying: "You are destined to serve as rabbi in Neustetl (Nové

Mesto), not Žilina."

* * *

My father always gave wise advice. In May 1937, the head of the congregation of Nové Mesto, Julius Löwinger, wrote to me in German, requesting that the "Rabbi do us the honor of being our guest for the month of July and give a series of lectures as a candidate recommended for the position of chief rabbi of the community of Nové Mesto." He also wished to know whether I had documents ordaining me as an Orthodox rabbi.

I accepted the proposal with composure, hoping and praying that I would be privileged to serve in the congregation of the author of *Ohel David* and to work in the spirit of its author Rabbi David Deutsch, in conformance to his principles and religious rulings.

I accepted the offer and informed the leaders of the Jewish community of my credentials: a permit to officiate as rabbi, issued by Orthodox rabbis, and a doctorate from the faculty of philosophy at the Komensky Slovak University in Bratislava, where I had submitted a doctoral dissertation in philosophy.

The suggestion of electing a chief rabbi in Nové Mesto roused interest and great controversy in the community. Those opposed to the position - wealthy assimilationist Jews led by Hugo Tauber - maintained that for budgetary reasons the office of *dayyan* (rabbinical judge), held by Rabbi Joseph Weiss, should suffice and that there was no need to lay out an additional 30,000 korunas per year. In a newsletter published in German these circles pointed out the difficult financial situation of the community and called on the members of the community to oppose appointing anyone to this office. The opposition was joined by the *dayyan* himself, who requested the intervention of several rabbis, including Dr.

Samuel Funk of Bratislava and Rabbi Pinchas Keller of Trenčin, who appealed to me not to accept the office of chief rabbi on the grounds of the commandment not to "move your neighbor's landmark" (Deut. 19:14), i.e., not to encroach upon your neighbor's territory. I rejected their petition, for this community previously had had a rabbi and *dayyan* serving at the same time. My candidacy was supported by the youth, members of the Zionist movement, and wealthy religious families. The ranks of supporters were joined essentially by all the members of the board, led by the chairman, Julius Löwinger, a highly respected and esteemed wise, elderly man of conscience, who enjoyed the trust of the entire community. He always kept the good of the community in view and, seeing that the youth were enthusiastic, supported my candidacy.

As the moment of decision drew closer, the controversy between the two groups became a veritable election battle. At a stormy general meeting on August 29, 1937, I was elected Chief Rabbi of Nové Mesto.

I was overjoyed to be appointed at the age of 26 to the Chief Rabbinate of a community where famous rabbis and *geonim* had served, and was firmly resolved to continue leading the community in their spirit, the spirit of our ancestral Judaism.

The High Holidays and Festivals of the beginning of the Jewish year 5698 (1938) passed in a state of elation. My sermons in the synagogue in Zvolen were marked by words of parting, hope, and prayer that the youth and the members of the congregation would continue in my footsteps, upholding my actions and rulings. The festive atmosphere of the holidays and *Simhat Torah* was compounded by a joyous family event - on Thursday, the 25th of Tishri, 5698 (September 30, 1937), our first son was born. The way the leading families of the community shared in our joyous occasion and the presents which they bestowed upon us, along with words of appreciation and regret at our decision to leave the congregation, were true testimony to the exceedingly great affection which I and my family had been privileged to receive.

We named our son Chaim Eleazar and, as was the practice among Jews in the Diaspora, gave him an additional name - Gideon. The name Chaim Eleazar was given after the *Admor* of Munkács, Rabbi Chaim Eleazar Shapiro of blessed memory, who had befriended me despite his vehement opposition to Zionism and notwithstanding my being a Zionist rabbi in a non-Orthodox congregation. Our friendship was forged when the *Admor* spent a summer in the health resort of Sliač, near Zvolen, and I assisted him with official arrangements there.[8] The *Admor* died on the 2nd of Sivan, 5697 (May 12, 1937).

* * *

On October 31, 1937, the Zvolen Jewish community held a general meeting, chaired by Dr. Moritz Reisz. The participants in the meeting paid tribute to the late President of the Czechoslovak Republic, Prof. Thomas Masaryk, who had recently passed away. In his opening remarks Dr. Reisz announced my appointment to the position of chief rabbi of Nové Mesto and expressed his appreciation for the four years I had served as chief rabbi of Zvolen, which until my arrival had been a neglected community where anyone was free to do as he pleased. Full of emotion, the head of the community bid me farewell in the name of all and wished me success in my new situation. Greatly moved, I responded with words of thanks for the pleasant reception I had enjoyed both from my friends and from my ideological opponents.

---

[8] When asked in wonder by of one of his inner circle why he associated with the rabbi from Zvolen, in view of the fact that the latter was a Zionist, the *Admor* is said to have replied that Zvolen's rabbi was destined to rescue Jews in a time of trouble. Hassidim have said that Gideon-Chaim Eleazar was miraculously saved during a German air attack on the Banská-Bystrica Mountains by the merit of the *Admor*. Today Gideon is a professor and dean in Syracuse University, Syracuse, New York.

On the last Sabbath of 1937 I took leave of the congregation in a sermon which I delivered during the *musaf* (additional) service.

Chapter Two

Nové Mesto on the Vah

(5698 - 1938)

"Return to the stronghold, ye prisoners of hope;
And I will stir up thy sons, 0 Zion!"

(Zechariah 9:12-13)

I. Activities in the Community

The installation ceremony was held on Sunday, 29 Tevet, 5698 (January 2, 1938). A delegation from Nové Mesto met me at the train station in Žilina, and from there we continued together by train to Nové Mesto. When we arrived at the train station, I was greeted by representatives of the community and the Jewish organizations, led by Julius Löwinger and Mrs. Janka Spitzer, who greeted us in the name of the women and presented my wife a bouquet of flowers.

After a short ceremony the many guests set out in a long automobile procession to the center of the city, which was decorated with the Slovak national flag and with blue and white flags for the Land of Israel and a gate of honor bearing the greeting "Welcome" in Hebrew and Slovak. The sides of the street were lined with members of the Maccabee association, dressed in uniform, and school children waving flags.

At the entrance to the synagogue, I was received by the beadles, the *dayyan* Rabbi Joseph Weiss, who delivered a short welcoming speech in Hebrew, the board of the community, and rabbis from other Jewish communities of Slovakia. The leader of the congregation opened the ceremony in the synagogue and wished me success in my work, that I might continue in the glorious tradition of the community, where illustrious rabbis had served.

The inauguration speech was delivered by Dr. Eliezer Schweiger, Chief Rabbi of Nitra and chairman of the Union of Traditional Rabbis of the Yeshurun congregations. Then I spoke. The ceremony in the synagogue concluded with the singing of *Ha-Tikvah*[9] and the Czechoslovak national anthem.

Afterwards parties were given in my honor by the board of the community and the local Zionist organization.

The first place I went in my new community was the old Jewish cemetery, to prostrate myself at the graves of the *geonim* (illustrious rabbis) Rabbi David Deutsch and Rabbi Joseph Weisse, and of the other rabbis and *dayyanim* who had been active in the community. I prayed that their merits would stand me in good stead as I began along my way. The next day I visited the most important institution in the community – the Jewish elementary school on Rabbi Weisse Street, across from the Great Synagogue. The school, which had two levels of classes, was maintained by the Jewish community and was under the supervision of the Ministry of Education and Culture. The two teachers were considered employees of the community but received their salary from the government. An additional sum was paid them from the community budget for extra hours in Jewish subjects, German language instruction, administrative work, and the like. The teachers had a strong Jewish-nationalist and Zionist sense of identity, and were

---

[9] *Ha-Tikvah* became Israel's national anthem. (Translator's note.)

devoted heart and soul to their work. I spoke with the schoolchildren and, after explaining the meaning of the greeting *Shalom* (peace, hello, goodbye), asked them to use this greeting both at home and in the street. From then on *Shalom* became a popular greeting among the Jewish public, for the youngsters spread it around and vied with one another to be the first to greet their fellows with *Shalom.*

Visiting the school brought me special pleasure, for Zvolen did not have a Jewish school. But there was a fly in the ointment. The children sat in class bareheaded, as was the custom of Jews living among the gentiles. I wanted the school of the Jewish community to fulfill its role and educate our children towards Jewish consciousness and faith in the spirit of traditional Judaism. Therefore, I demanded that the pupils cover their heads, not only when studying Torah and religious subjects. The head of the school agreed in principle but proposed that such a change in the social mores be brought up for discussion in the community's education committee. After long debate and discussion in committee, the proposal was adopted, and henceforth our children attended the Jewish school with *yarmulkas* (skull-caps) on their heads. This was only the first step, for I knew that much remained to be done in the sphere of religious education.

Next, I visited the butcher shop to examine the provision of kosher meat. I was greatly disappointed to see the owner of the butcher shop and the *mashgiah* placing a stumbling block before the blind: kosher and non-kosher meat were sold in the same store. The butcher himself removed the forbidden sinew from the hindquarters of the meat, and the shop functioned without regular, authorized supervision. I immediately demanded that the situation be remedied, despite exception taken by the butchers. One section of the butcher shop was made kosher and separated, then locked and bolted shut, with the key entrusted to the *mashgiah* in charge. The two *sohatim* were obliged to oversee the kashruth and to open and shut the butcher shop according to a regular schedule. Some members of the community found it difficult to adjust to the new order, which compelled them to do their shopping at fixed hours. In time, however, the patrons themselves demanded that the *mashgiah* be present and even submitted complaints to the rabbinate if he was not.

Hand in hand with instituting a new order in matters concerning commandments between man and God, I went to see the institutions dealing with commandments between man and man. The largest and most important of these was the Adolf and Helena Baiersdorf Jewish Hospital and Home for the Aged.

I was shocked to find this relatively large institution in a frightful state of neglect. It was inconceivable, I told myself, that twenty poor, elderly, and sick people should be left in dank, moldy rooms, reeking of filth. The condition of the elderly was deplorable. The institution had no kitchen, and food was provided by charitable families who sent over meals every day. The chairman of the Baiersdorf Foundation was Hugo Tauber, a leader of the opposition in the community, who had objected to my election as Chief Rabbi. Therefore, the matter called for delicate handling, in order not to arouse opposition from the outset. Yet it was clear to me that the institution could not remain in its deplorable state. Hence, I waited for an opportune moment to realize the objectives of the institution as originally envisioned by its benefactors.

Samuel Alexander Weiler, the secretary of the community, kept the by-laws of the Jewish community's charitable funds and associations in the offices of the community. I studied these by-laws and met with the beadles and leading workers in each and every association: the Rabbi Joseph Weisse *Malbish Arumim* Association (for clothing the poor), *Ner Shel Shabbat* (Sabbath Candle, for providing poor Jews with the means to celebrate the Sabbath), *Menahem Avelim* (for consoling mourners), *Bikkur Holim* (for visiting the sick); the *Sandak* Association for helping poor new mothers, the Bing and Engelsmann Foundations, and others. All these institutions and associations had one common goal: to keep the commandment "that thy brother may live with thee" (Lev. 25:36). Therefore, I thought that perhaps all the philanthropic institutions of the community should be united under a single umbrella organization, a sort of welfare department, which would provide social services and address itself to social problems. The current events and political situation, which were aggravating the hardship and suffering amidst the Jewish community, proved the necessity of preparing the tools to attempt to meet the growing threat.

I proposed various changes and reforms, which were adopted without dispute, since they were desirable for the proper functioning of community life. R. Benjamin Sichermann was taken on as a new *shohet,* a new Torah scroll acquired, and old Torah scrolls which were in use were inspected and repaired. Changes were made in the synagogue to make it conform to the norm in Orthodox Ashkenazi synagogues. Services were held according to Ashkenazi liturgy and Orthodox practice. The Mishnah Society *Beit Midrash* was renovated and enlarged to accommodate the larger number of people who now attended prayers to listen to the Torah lessons given between the afternoon and evening services. All these changes were made with the approval of all the leading families. There were four areas in which I succeeded in introducing changes only after an argument and public dispute with the leading figures of the community:

A. Holding wedding ceremonies outdoors, in conformance to Orthodox practice. The subject was brought up for discussion before the board of the community because the leader of the community did not consent to changing the current practice. My stand was clear: in matters of religion and religious law the rabbi is the highest authority, and there must be no deviation from Jewish custom. The fight was not easy, but in view of my intransigence on this matter of principle, the corrective measure was adopted.

B. Proscribing baking what were known as *reib matzas*. These are small, thick matzas, long proscribed in most Jewish communities because of the chance that, due to their thickness, the dough might ferment while being baked.

C. Prohibiting the process necessary to make the hindquarters of animals kosher to eat. To do so the forbidden sinew must be removed by porging, a process which requires great expertise and, due to a lack of trained porgers, was proscribed in Austria-Hungary many years ago. The local butcher and his supporters opposed this proscription, leaving me no alternative but to shut down the butcher shop. From then on, kosher butchers in Nové Mesto, as well, have carried only the front quarters and have sold the hindquarters to gentile butcher shops.

D. Removing the flowers from graves and ceasing their cultivation in the cemetery. This directive of mine roused great excitement and strong opposition among some of the community. The beadles of the *Hevra Kadisha* (Jewish burial society) had been influenced by several wealthy widows who objected to uprooting the flowers, and were hesitant to carry out my directive. Therefore, I gave notice to all the dignitaries of the community that if in two days' time the flowers, which had no place in a Jewish cemetery, were not removed, I would personally see to their removal. This action caused quite a storm of protest, but the furor soon abated.

On every new issue I addressed the public from the synagogue pulpit, and, with the aid of Heaven, my requests were granted. Even when I requested that during services the men in the congregation wrap themselves in large *tallitot* instead of wearing folded *tallitot* like scarves around their necks, which had been their custom until now, they complied unanimously. I was especially pleased by this accomplishment, for thus the last token of a neologist synagogue was erased, and the synagogue took on the coloration of a traditional Jewish house of worship, fit for any God-fearing Jew.

* * *

Concurrently with my religious and social activity in the community, I outlined annual programs which included regular weekly lectures and a monthly cultural evening or panel discussion on Jewish affairs. Likewise, Sabbath eve parties in the Jewish school were planned by the youth themselves, Bible lessons were offered, and Hebrew language study groups were held.

The work was intensive and aimed at all levels of the community, and the participation was high. Especially active were the youth, with whom I maintained close and friendly relations, and in whose conversations and gatherings I frequently participated.

At a meeting chaired by Julius Löwinger and attended by Dr. Isaac Rosenberg, as well as community leaders and authors, it was decided to found a Jewish newspaper in Nové Mesto called *Židovské Noviny (The Jewish News)*. At the meeting I explained the need and importance of publishing a Jewish organ in Slovak, and on May 20, 1938, the first edition appeared. The paper was financed almost entirely by the Jewish community of Nové Mesto, which allocated 40,000 korunas for the purpose. I contributed a column to the paper, entitled "Glancing at the Past," presenting chapters of Jewish history. My efforts to publish a book on the history of our people having failed, I tried to use this column to give the readers a Jewish education and to strengthen their consciousness, faith, and sense of belonging to the Jewish people. The government banned the paper on September 27, 1939.

II. Political Developments in Europe and the Worsening Plight of the Jews

In 1938 Nazi Germany stepped up her war preparations and embarked on a policy of expansion and "bloodless" annexation. The same year marked the beginning of a worsening in Nazi policy towards the Jews. On November 9, *Kristallnacht,* many synagogues were burned throughout Germany and Austria, thousands of Jewish shops and businesses were pillaged and destroyed, 91 Jews were slaughtered, and a wave of ruthless anti-Semitism began, manifest in violent acts of terror throughout the state.

Earlier, on March 13, 1938, the Nazis took over Austria. The *anschluss* immediately brought anti-Semitic legislation in its wake. Jews were victimized without restraint. Great numbers were thrown in prison, and forced emigration and expulsion were instituted.

The Germans in Czechoslovakia's Sudetenland sought to subvert the state and called for annexation of the region to the Third Reich. Encouraged by the Germans to seek independence, the Slovak nationalists in the *Hlinkova Slovenská Ľudová Strana* (Hlinka People's party) first demanded autonomy. Thus, Czechoslovakia underwent a rapid process of splitting from within, leading to ruin from without.

On September 29, 1938, the infamous Munich Pact, in which Britain, France, and Italy agreed to German annexation of the Sudetenland, was signed. On October 6, 1938, the Slovaks declared their autonomy and established a national government headed by the Catholic priest, Dr. Jozef Tiso. Hungary laid claim to the southern part of Slovakia, which had a large Hungarian minority, and in the Vienna arbitration, on November 2, 1938, the Germans agreed to this annexation. In December 1938, Carpatho-Russia, too, was annexed to Hungary. The Slovak nationalists were greatly disappointed to see their new state thus carved up. A scapegoat was immediately found: the Jews, who were largely Hungarian-speaking, were blamed for this national disaster. Thus many "Magyar Zhids" living in the new border regions were expelled across the border into no-man's-land, to live without a roof over their heads to shelter them from the wind and snow of the bitter cold winter. The heads of the Jewish community, shocked at this cruel act, immediately used every means to alleviate the plight of the exiles and to transfer them to places of residence.

A new and tragic chapter began on March 14, 1939, when the truncated and divided Democratic State of Czechoslovakia surrendered to the Germans. The German army occupied Czechoslovakia unobstructed and set up the Protectorate of Bohemia and Moravia. The leaders of the Slovaks – Tiso, Tuka and Mach – gladly did the Germans' bidding and established an "independent" Slovak puppet state under the patronage of Nazi Germany.

On August 23, 1939, the foreign ministers of Germany and the Soviet Union, Ribbentrop and Molotov, signed a non-aggression pact, and on September 1, 1939, with Hitler's invasion of Poland the Second

World War broke out, in the course of which Nazi Germany continued to subjugate nations and conquer almost all of Europe.

III. Organization of the Jews in Autonomous Slovakia

With the declaration of autonomy in October, 1938, as anti-Semitic instigation steadily mounted, the leaders of the Jewish party in Slovakia assembled for urgent consultations. They feared their party would be outlawed and it would be necessary to establish an umbrella organization comprised of representatives of all the national Jewish organizations and associations in autonomous Slovakia. Dr. Otto Löbel, an attorney from Bratislava, initiated the meeting. The participants in the deliberations accepted my proposal to work in conjunction with the National Bureau of Orthodox Jews, which had hitherto always functioned independently; the new reality made it obligatory to join ranks in a united national Jewish council. Likewise, we decided to request an interview with the Prime Minister of autonomous Slovakia, immediately upon his appointment by the central government in Prague. Dr. Otto Löbel, Dr. Oscar Neumann, Eugene Winterstein, and myself were chosen for the delegation.

Dr. Tiso received our delegation the day after *Simhat Torah* 5599 (October 18, 1938). The delegation conveyed to the Prime Minister the loyalty of the Jewish population and its preparedness to obey the laws of the state and its new government. A number of fundamental questions were clarified at the interview, and it was agreed to establish a new central organization for the Jews of Slovakia, called the *Židovská Ústredná Úradovňa pre Slovensko – ŽÚÚ* (Central Jewish Bureau of Slovakia).

In November talks were opened with the deputies of the Orthodox Bureau in Bratislava, with the aim of arriving at a joint. platform and united representation which would protect the rights of Jews before the authorities of a hostile regime. I, too, participated in one of these meetings and contributed my efforts to bringing about unity.

Nevertheless, the negotiations failed due to the fundamental opposition of the chairman of the Orthodox Bureau, Isidor Pappenheim, who had served in this office since the passing of his predecessor, Rabbi Kalman Weber of Pieštany. The leaders of the Central Jewish Bureau, fearing a deterioration in the condition of the Jews, tried to convince him that unity was the imperative of the hour, but Pappenheim, the elderly activist, was not prepared to cooperate with "neologist" Zionists and even spoke out rather bluntly.

Therefore, the Zionists began acting without the representatives of the ultra-Orthodox *Agudat Israel*. A vast amount of work awaited, and the volume grew from day to day. Nationwide organizations and institutions joined the Central Jewish Bureau, among them many Orthodox congregations, helping cover the expenses of running the organization. All the Zionist organizations and Jewish communities affiliated with the Yeshurun Federation, and a large number of Orthodox congregations recognized the bureau and cooperated with it, contrary to the stand of the large Orthodox communities of Nitra, Topolčany and Bratislava. At times the two organizations worked side by side on the same issue, but sometimes they worked at cross purposes. Such a condition being baneful, another attempt was made to achieve unity or coordination, but in vain.

The Central Jewish Bureau became a reality and a factor recognized by the authorities. The bureau opened its offices on 3 Ventúrska St., in two rooms on the third floor, and three months later, by the end of 1938, could have used a premises six rooms larger.

Having joined the board of the Central Jewish Bureau in the fall of

1938, after the Jewish New Year, 5699, henceforth I had to divide my time between community activity in Nové Mesto and national activity in Bratislava and, as necessity dictated, in other cities of Slovakia, as well.

Chapter Three

From Hatred to Persecution

(5699 - 5701; 1939 - 1941)

"In the siege and in the straitness,
wherewith thine enemy shall straiten thee in thy gates"
(Deuteronomy 28:57)

I. Political Developments in Slovakia

By October 6, 1938, when the fateful meeting of the directors of the Hlinka People's party convened in Žilina, the extremist wing, headed by Dr. Ferdinand Durčanský and Alexander (Šaňo) Mach, demanded the establishment of an independent Slovak state. But, after the extremist Karol Sidor went over to Jozef Tiso's faction, the more moderate elements had the upper hand and at this point contented themselves with declaring "autonomy," which later received legal ratification in Prague. Although the moderates appeared to have won, the key positions in the apparatus were controlled by the extremists. Dr. F. Durčanský was appointed Minister of Justice, and the propaganda apparatus was entrusted to Š. Mach. Both men received their education in the most dangerous hothouse of anti-Semitism in Slovakia, the dormitory of the Svoradov University in Bratislava, and viewed political anti-Semitism as one of the more popular and effective means of winning the massive support of the Slovak people.

The extremist Slovak intelligentsia, a young generation of Jew-haters and organizers of demonstrations and riots against the Jews, came out of Svoradov. This was the training ground for the reserves of the party's activists, the disseminators of racism and political separatism from the Czechs.

On October 16, 1938, Dr. Durčanský held talks with Hermann Goering about establishing an independent Slovak state and promised him he would solve the Jewish problem in Slovakia according to the German method. The other parties to this conversation, which took place in Goering's residence, included Dr. Arthur Seyss-Inquart, leader of the Austrian Nazis, Franz Karmasin, leader of the German party in Slovakia, and Šaňo Mach. The latter saw to it that all the media in Slovakia disseminated incitement against the Jews, "those pathetic Zhido-Bolsheviks who are threatening the entire world."

In the famous Žilina agreement of October 6, most of the parties gave in to pressure from the Hlinka People's party and united with it. The autonomous government outlawed the Social Democratic party, the Communist party, and Beneš' National Slovak party. The organs of all the factions, which united and continued to appear, disseminated venomous anti-Semitic propaganda, and under their impact Slovakia essentially adopted an openly anti-Semitic policy.

The *Hlinkova Garda - HG* (Hlinka Guard) and the *Freiwillige Schutzstaffeln - FS* (Voluntary Defense Squad), the armed bodies of the People's party and the Carpatho-German party respectively, launched into violent terrorist action against the Jews, attacking Jews in the streets and on the trains, organizing boycotts of Jewish businesses, plundering and confiscating Jewish property. All these actions enriched the Guardists (members of the Hlinka Guard), and lust for gain-enticed masses of people of dubious character to enlist into the Hlinka Guard, where they could then plunder, rob, and extort at will.

Behind all this lay the instigation of the German political secretariat which, beginning October 14, 1938, operated in conjunction with the Slovak Prime Minister's Office, under the leadership of Franz Karmasin. Durčanský quickly drafted a special law against the Jews, and on December 6, 1938, the representative of autonomous Slovakia in the central government in Prague, Karol Sidor, called for enactment of a national law to solve the Jewish question following the example set by Germany. His proposal was accepted in Prague, and henceforth the extremists in Slovakia began demanding immediate exclusion of the Jews from economic life. On March 5, 1939, ten days before Hitler's army invaded Bohemia and Moravia, Durčanský submitted a bill to the Slovak government, similar to the Nurenberg Laws.

On March 14, 1939, the autonomous parliament proclaimed an independent Slovak state, and from that point on developments came in swift succession. The authorities removed all restraints, leaving no one to halt the process of dispossessing the Jews. Indeed, the more moderate elements in the government still believed that for the good of the Slovak economy one should not expel all the Jews from every sphere of economic and social life. However, such people as Tuka, Durčanský, Mach and the younger generation, who had adopted the principals of National Socialism, insisted on an extremist approach and called for immediate transfer of all Jewish property to Christian Aryan ownership and the fastest possible solution of the Jewish question by immediately ousting the Jews from economic life and excluding them from the general life of society. Henceforth the two official organs of the Slovak state, the legal code and the official newspaper, published close to three hundred and fifty laws, directives and edicts against the Jews.

On April 18, 1939, an edict was promulgated defining the term "Jew" and setting a quota on the number of Jews allowed in certain free professions. For lawyers a numerus clausus of 4% was set, and all the rest were expunged from the list. All Jewish notary publics were dismissed from office. Jews were allowed to serve as correspondents only for Jewish papers. In a similar manner Jews were removed from state institutions, from local government, and from other public offices.

On June 20, 1939, an edict was issued giving certain authorized bodies (provincial and local government offices, in cooperation with the Hlinka Guard) legal power to appoint Aryan trustees and managers in industrial, manufacturing, and commercial enterprises. These managers, called Aryanizers, essentially took over factories and property previously under Jewish ownership.

Other edicts and decrees divested the Jews of the right to run pharmacies, required Jewish landowners to register their agricultural assets, and transferred Jews in active military service or in the reserves to special labor squadrons. Later a regulation was issued divesting of their military ranks all Jews discharged from compulsory service or in reserve units.

An edict dated June 1939 restricted the number of Jews permitted to engage in medicine to 4%. Employing Jewish doctors above this quota was permitted only if necessitated by the public interest. All remaining Jewish doctors lost their licenses to practice medicine.

Persecution of Jews was generally done under the guidance of dozens of German advisors attached to Slovak government offices. Thus, the number of laws and edicts against the Jews increased from day to day.

II. Activities of the Central Jewish Bureau[10]

The pro-tern board of the Central Jewish Bureau decided to convene a conference of all the organizations and communities affiliated with it. Over 350 delegates from all the national Jewish organizations and from most of the Jewish communities participated in this conference, which was held in Žilina on January 22, 1939. The 200 guests included observers from Orthodox congregations and the two federations of Jewish congregations that were not officially participating in the conference.

At the close of the meeting a declaration was issued proclaiming the Central Jewish Bureau to be the supreme institution of the Jews of Slovakia. The representatives of the Orthodox Jews at the conference called on all the organizations of devout Jews to join the Central Jewish Bureau to unite the ranks of Slovak Jewry and bolster their strength.

The conference found that the principal problems facing Slovak Jewry were Jewish unemployment (in the private sector, commerce, industry, and the free professions), and refugees. Therefore, a recommendation was made to assist the unemployed by finding new work for them and integrating them into economic life, by extending aid to the jobless, by organizing vocational retraining courses and establishing training centers in crafts and agriculture, and by encouraging refugees and unemployed to emigrate.

To implement these recommendations, it was proposed that the social services in each Jewish community be coordinated according to guidelines from the Central Jewish Bureau and that these objectives be given top priority.

---

[10] The parts of this chapter written by Emanuel Frieder are based on minutes of the Central Jewish Bureau, FYVS.

The conference also called for enlarging the Jewish educational system by establishing Jewish schools in every community where the number of school children made this feasible, and called on the various Jewish communities to supply all the means necessary to achieve this goal. Hebrew language instruction was made obligatory in every Jewish school. To broaden religious education in the schools and to increase the number of teachers for religious studies and Judaism, the conference recommended opening teachers' seminars in religion and Jewish subjects.

The conference also stressed the importance of *The Jewish News,* and appealed to the Jews of Slovakia to strengthen and increase the circulation of this paper. With the aim of advocating Jewish religious law and refuting the slanderous attacks on the Talmud which were published in various hostile libelous documents, the conference recommended circulating appropriate propaganda pamphlets.

Lastly, a board of four was chosen and, alongside it, a restricted leadership body and a broader leadership body. The restricted leadership was intended to serve as an advisory body for the board of directors and was to convene at frequent intervals; therefore, all its members were residents of Bratislava. The following were elected to the board: Dr. Otto Löbel, Dr. Oscar Neumann, Eugen Winterstein, and myself. The smaller leadership body consisted of Dr. Bernat Fürst, Adolf Grünberger, Leo Rosenthal, Dr. Sigfried Steiner, and Mr. Weiss. Their deputies were Jacob Berger and Raphael Goldstein. The broader leadership body included those in the more limited bodies as well as the following: Dr. Adolf Süss - Trenčín, Dr. Arthur Politzer - Čadca, Dr. Anton Popper - Prešov, Dr. Alexander Goldstein - Michalovce, Isidor Schwartz - Prešov, Dr. Alexander Márton - Žilina, Rabbi Dr. Hugo Stransky - Žilina. Deputies: Leopold Glück - Pieštany, Ferdinand Eisler - Nové Mesto, Dr. Robert K. Füredy - Bratislava.

At the meeting of the local council of the Central Jewish Bureau, held in Bratislava on February 22, 1939, I reported on an interview with Slovakia's Minister of Education and Culture, Jozef Sivák, regarding the problems of Jewish students and of Jewish teachers who had been dismissed. The minister promised that the teachers would be reinstated in their jobs and that a way would be found to solve the problem of Jewish youth studying in the universities. Our delegation requested that Jewish officials be added to the ministerial staffs to handle the affairs of the Jewish minority, like other minority groups which have representatives in each ministerial office.

Another delegation was granted an interview with Dr. Sokol, chairman of the Czechoslovak Parliament in Prague. The delegation requested that Jewish experts be invited to attend debates on questions concerning the Jews, but it was explained to them that this was impossible due to reasons of parliamentary procedure. The delegation also pointed out the contradiction between the government's avowed stand and the hostile propaganda in the press, which was likely to countermand the government's intentions.

On May 19, 1939, I sent a letter to the Central Jewish Bureau suggesting a program of activities for the cultural department which the bureau had decided to establish at its conference in Žilina. In these difficult times, I pointed out, extensive political activity was not feasible; but it was our duty to join ranks, studying our religious heritage, the Hebrew language, and the history of our people and striving to strengthen the spiritual fiber of our people, which has safeguarded Judaism throughout the ages. Therefore, the cultural department must immediately organize a study group for teachers in Bratislava, to teach them the history of Zionism, basic Hebrew, Bible, religious law, Jewish philosophy, and methodology for religious studies instruction. Likewise, we must prepare a uniform curriculum for the Jewish schools, for all grades. The cultural department must establish a committee for the Hebrew language which shall publish a Hebrew language instruction book for Slovak speakers, shall see to it that Hebrew is a compulsory subject in all Jewish schools, and shall organize Hebrew study groups for youth and adults throughout the state. The cultural department should send lecturers to visit Jewish communities, participate in cultural performances and parties, and assist in organizing cultural activities and study groups in large Jewish centers and summer camps.

The cultural department should try to establish contacts with the Ministry of Education and Culture to look after the problems of the Jewish schools and the teachers employed in them. A secretary should be appointed in the cultural department to run the various committees, and these committees should represent all the Jewish organizations of all Jewish groups.

The cultural department should maintain ties with the Jews in the Land of Israel by means of circulars, pamphlets and leaflets, and by a special column which the Central Jewish Bureau should write for *The Jewish News*. A person in charge of cultural affairs should be appointed in every city. The cultural department should endeavor to assist teachers, rabbis, and spiritual leaders, its objective being to serve as a spiritual-cultural center for the Jews of Slovakia.

* * *

Numerous hardships and threats to the Jews' very right to exist led to a fundamental revision in the structure of Jewish society. It was impossible to know what lay in store or what problems would arise. Despite this, the central organizations of the two main factions of Jews had not yet found a common language, although the Central Bureau never ceased striving for unity and always had this issue on the agenda at its meetings.

The board meetings of the Central Jewish Bureau held in May and June, 1939, discussed the bureau's current endeavors, such as negotiations in London regarding transferring the capital of Slovak Jews who wished to emigrate, "illegal" immigration to Israel, and the condition of the Jewish cooperative savings and loan associations in Slovakia. The board established a committee to handle transference of property via the bureau, and decided to dispatch additional delegations to Amsterdam, Brussels, and London, as soon as possible, to handle negotiations in this regard. It was decided to open an employment service for Jews who had been laid off from work, and to prepare statistics on the condition of Jews in various branches of employment, with special sections on law, medicine, agriculture, office work, trade, and manufacturing. Emphasis was laid on the need for closer cooperation with the Central Orthodox Bureau, with whose assistance vital statistical data could be obtained and common ground found for the two organizations, so that together they could represent Slovak Jewry within the state and abroad. Rabbi Frieder's proposal to establish a cultural department was unanimously accepted. The board decided that the department not handle matters pertaining to religion; these would remain within the exclusive jurisdiction of the two national federations of Orthodox congregations and of Yeshurun congregations. Likewise, the board decided to establish a department for agriculturalists as part of the Central Jewish Bureau.

A committee for vocational retraining was established, and reports were submitted upon conclusion of the first series of courses in electricity and electronics, shoemaking, and painting, in which 51 people were retrained.

The courses for women – literature, baking, sewing, cosmetics, and cooking – had an enrollment of 159. The board decided not to work together with the bureau for emigration which had opened in Bratislava and which handled the emigration of craftsmen and people in industrial vocations.

* * *

At the June 6 meeting of the bureau, Rabbi Frieder reported on the activities of the cultural department. By June 1939 the department had accomplished all its plans and was about to open a short, five-week seminar for teachers in Bratislava, whose objective was to train Hebrew teachers for Jewish schools in various Jewish communities.

Dr. Isaac Rosenberg reported on his trip to London and Holland, the purpose of which was to arrange assistance for emigration and to establish commercial ties for transferring property belonging to Jewish émigrés. In England he had no success, for all the Jewish organizations and committees were working on behalf of the Jews of Germany. In Holland, on the other hand, he met with Jews who showed understanding and sympathy for the Jews of Slovakia, and he also found the commercial possibilities there greater. In Belgium, too, prospects were good. Success was possible everywhere, provided representatives from Slovakia were sent to lay the groundwork for the emigration and transference of property.

On June 24, 1939, a memorandum on vocational retraining, emigration, and transference of Jews' property was sent to offices of the government, requesting them to assist the Central Jewish Bureau in planning and implementing Jewish emigration.[11]

---

[11] See appendix for quotes from this memorandum.

III. The Ohel David Old-Age Home in Nové Mesto

Even though work in the Central Jewish Bureau took up many hours of my week, I continued performing my duties as rabbi of Nové Mestto. I spent two days a week in Bratislava, while the rest of the week, and of course the Sabbath, I devoted to current work in the community, my activities on the Central Jewish Bureau directing and guiding me in this work. I realized that it was none too soon for us to take action to assure that in the future, as well, Jews not be left to go hungry or without a roof over their heads. My plan was to turn the Baiersdorf Old Age Home into an institution which would aid any Jew suffering hardship. In the small and modest auditorium of the Mishnah Society which the author of *Ohel David,* the venerated Rabbi David Deutsch of blessed memory, had established to teach Judaism to all, I began publicly voicing my idea. I secretly vowed that if, with God's help and by the merit of the great rabbi who had taught here, I succeeded in realizing my plan, I would name the new institution Ohel David after this venerated rabbi.

My appeal to the community was received seriously. I succeeded in persuading a number of magnanimous individuals to contribute to this holy cause, and by the end of one week 30,000 Slovak korunas had been raised. Large sums were donated by the brothers Samuel and Dr. Leopold Reiss, and inspired by them, Eduard Krauss donated all his wealth to maintaining and enlarging the old age home and established a fund in his name. The elderly leader of the community, Julius Löwinger, who himself made a considerable contribution towards establishing the institution, enlisted with youthful enthusiasm to head a special finance committee which continued to raise money so that construction work could be started immediately.

The cornerstone laying ceremony was held on the 22nd of Sivan

(June 9, 1939), in the decorated courtyard of the Baiersdorf Home and was attended by most of the Jewish community, as well as many Christian residents and delegations from the surrounding area.

Thanks to Moritz Beck, who volunteered to oversee the construction work, we completed the building in half a year. Many Jews of all ages enthusiastically lifted a hand to help in the work. Many were already out of work, and there was a feeling that time was running out. Only the poor received wages. Despite the heat of the summer months and the volunteers being unaccustomed to physical labor, everyone worked industriously and accomplished a great deal. Especially noteworthy was the volunteer effort of the youth. By Hanukkah the home was ready.

On Hanukkah 1939, in an hour of distress for their people, the Jews of Nové Mesto gathered in the synagogue of the old-age home for *minhah* and *arvit* services, to give praise and thanksgiving and celebrate the inauguration of the renovated Ohel David and Baiersdorf Home.

I was elected chairman of the board of governors of the Baiersdorf Foundation and of the board of the Ohel David Home and shelter.

A local committee of the Joint was also established under my leadership and participated in maintenance of the institution. With the assistance of activists in philanthropic institutions, an effective and well-organized program of community social work came into being and won high acclaim. In the first month of its existence, Ohel David served over 7,000 meals to the needy, free of charge. The Ohel David soup-kitchen was managed with devotion by Moritz Beck, who volunteered his services for free.

IV. Activities of the Jewish Organizations in 1939[12]

In June and July, 1939, the members of the board of the Central Jewish Bureau lobbied in various government offices on behalf of Jewish pharmacists and holders of tobacco franchises, most of whom were war invalids. The members of the bureau contacted persons in the administration who were making policy on the Jews and submitted them a memorandum on Jewish emigration and a proposal concerning possibilities of transferring Jewish property.

Foreign Minister Durčanský assured the delegation that he would see to the opening of a Slovak legation in Jerusalem. As for their request that representatives of the Jews be included in deliberations concerning their own fate, the minister replied that he would present the proposal to the government. The delegation also paid a visit to the Ministry of Economics.

On the initiative of government circles, a group of jurists led by Dr. Winterstein prepared a proposal for a government decree regarding the organization of the Jews and their representation. The first draft was brought up for debate by Dr. Alexander Wasservogel on July 27, 1939. Dr. M. Mayer and Dr. V. Steiner prepared proposals of their own for further debate. Likewise, Dr. Veilchenfeld, the representative of the Jewish Agency, drafted a proposal for establishing a company for property transference, which he wished to submit to the Ministry of Economics for study and approval.

Circular no. 7 of the Jewish Bureau, sent to the Jewish communities in July 1939, attests the varied activities of the bureau.[13] Training centers: The plan to establish training centers for immigration to the

---

[12] Based on protocols and circulars, FYVS.
[13] See FYVS.

Land of Israel became a reality. The bureau obtained a license from the Ministry of Interior to set up 20 training centers throughout Slovakia, ten of which were for agricultural training, 3 for building and road-paving, 4 for construction work in cities, and 3 for miscellaneous works. Around five hundred young men and women prepared themselves for immigrating to the Land of Israel by vocational retraining and spiritual preparation. The bureau also tried to persuade the authorities to consent to release several Jewish farms to help in agricultural training.

Summer camps: A permit was obtained to run summer camps for Jewish youth. In these camps, too, an organizational framework for vocational training was formed. That summer close to 1,550 youths were served by eight camps, functioning in the lap of nature. Acting on their own initiative and at the request of local councils, the Jewish Bureau's officers and leaders lobbied government bodies and interceded on the Jews' behalf both in economic affairs and in matters of professional status and problems of employment. Numerous requests came in daily from all parts of the state to intercede with government offices on such issues as residence and visiting permits, work licenses, and the like. This work comprised a large part of the bureau's undertakings.

The by-laws of the Zionist Organization of Slovakia *(Ústredný Sväz Cionistický - USC)* were ratified by the national government. The branches of the movement received guidelines for their activities from the organization's center in Bratislava.

The weekly *Jewish News* was the only Jewish organ published in Slovakia which any efforts were made to maintain. No organized work could conceivably be done without this means of communication. The local councils and the Jewish communities were called upon to support the paper morally and financially. The paper's circulation reached 3,000 copies. The legal section marched with the times and published laws and ordinances pertaining to the Jews, along with commentary and explanations. The paper also published news from the Land of Israel and information on the life of the Jews in the Diaspora. In addition, it had a section on the weekly Torah portion and current interest articles. With the aim of strengthening ties with the Land of Israel, preparatory work was done towards opening a branch office of the paper in Tel Aviv.

In that period, when political activity had become no longer feasible, the Central Jewish Bureau established a cultural department which had already gone into in high gear.

That summer (1939) a teachers' seminar was held in Bratislava, and its participants, 20 teachers from all ends of the state, received enrichment studies in Hebrew language and literature, Jewish and Zionist history, Jewish philosophy, and Bible.

The department prepared to publish Hebrew language instruction booklets and selected excerpts from Hebrew literature, translated into Slovak. A chorus was organized and was about to begin a tour of the Jewish communities, to perform Hebrew songs and passages of Jewish music. The Central Jewish Bureau's cultural department recommended that cultural departments be established as part of the community activities of the local Jewish councils.

The Central Bureau established a committee comprised of experts in exporting Slovak products for the purpose of transferring Jewish property. This committee-maintained contacts with the Slovak National Bank and various other governmental bodies.

Brief Reports of the Central Jewish Bureau (from one of its circulars)

- With the approval of the authorities, the bureau is organizing a group of property-less émigrés. Preparations for their departure are proceeding apace.

- Government sources have given our representatives assurances that Jewish loan associations will continue to exist.

- Negotiations are under way with authorized government circles for the discharge of Jewish soldiers wishing to emigrate.

- We have applied to Jewish welfare institutions abroad for support of the needy and of émigrés.

- Updated statistics on the Jews of Slovakia are in preparation; detailed questionnaires have been circulated for the purpose.

- In the near future we shall hold special consultation days in outlying cities; please send suggestions on the matter.

- Many Jews have recently been dismissed from their positions and offices and have become jobless. Therefore, the need was felt to organize employment services throughout the state. Employment bureaus will be opened everywhere shortly, through advertisements in *The Jewish News,* in the Work Wanted section.

- We intend to organize groups of workers according to vocation: merchants and small industrialists, members of the free professions and academicians, farmers, clerks, office workers, etc.

- Registration of the assets of Jewish companies which have been liquidated: According to the government order of June 1, 1939, number 125 in the Slovak law code, the assets of liquidated companies revert to the state of Slovakia. The state is responsible for the company's debts at the level of the active assets of the company. According to this order a fund shall be established from the assets of these companies to finance cultural and philanthropic activities of the nationality to whom the company belonged (according to our interpretation, this also applies to the Jewish nationality).

The Zionist Organization in Slovakia

With the declaration of an independent Slovak state in March 1939, the Slovak Zionist movement's ties with the Zionist centers which remained in the Protectorate of Bohemia and Moravia were severed. The leaders of the movement in Slovakia immediately requested the Slovak government in Bratislava to ratify the by-laws of the Central Zionist Organization. The by-laws were ratified by the government authorities in the summer of 1939.

Even before receiving ratification the movement did not cease its activities; quite the contrary, due to the needs of the hour and the political situation, the movement redoubled its efforts. Henceforth its activities also had legal sanction and proceeded at full pace.

Dr. Robert Füredy headed the Zionist Organization, and Dr. Oscar Neumann was its general secretary. Three factions were organized under its umbrella: Maccabee, the movement of the General Zionists, led by Rabbi Frieder; *Torah va-Avodah,* which belonged to the Mizrachi movement and was headed by Dr. Zigmund Steiner; and *Ha-Oved,* of the *Eretz Yisrael ha-Ovedet* movement, under the leadership of one of its members, Dauker. The Zionist youth movements were Young Mac cabee (1st youth division), *B'nai Akiva* (2nd youth division), and *Ha-Shomer ha-Tzair* (3rd youth division). *He-Halutz, He-Halutz ha-Dati, Ha-Oved,* and *Ha-Poef ha-Dati* were involved in organizing pioneer and professional retraining programs to prepare people for immigration to Israel.

The following institutions operated under the aegis of the Zionist Organization: the Jewish Agency's Land of Israel Office, directed by Leo Rosenthal, the Jewish National Fund, and the Palestine Foundation Fund.

There was full cooperation and coordination between the Zionist Organization and the board of the Central Jewish Bureau, whose members were also leaders of the Zionist movement.

Dr. Oscar Neumann and Gisi Fleischmann went to Paris and London on behalf of the movement's rescue operations to look into the possibilities of *aliyah* and emigration to lands across the ocean. They visited the diplomatic missions of North and South American countries and other countries; but no state was willing to open its doors to Jewish immigration. They negotiated with various Jewish international aid institutions such as the Joint and Hicem. The Jews of England and France were prepared to run a fund drive to help support refugees and to establish a mutual aid society to this end; but beyond this, the legation did not achieve its objectives. Efforts to organize an exodus of the Jews of Slovakia by train, during the period when the government was still in favor of emigration, also proved unsuccessful.

The Revisionist movement in the new Zionist Organization, led by Nathan Beck, had the following groups operating under it: the *Berit Trumpeldor - Betar* youth movement, *Berit Nashim Le'umiyot,* and the *Yavneh* students' organization. Their main office was in Bratislava and their larger branches primarily in eastern Slovakia.

Other National Organizations

Agudat Israel firmly established itself in all the large ultra-Orthodox communities. The national office in Bratislava was headed by Dr. Karl Rosenbaum, and its secretary was Y. Goldstein. The chairman of Young *Agudat Israel* was Aladar Porges. This movement invested great effort in educating children in *Talmud Torah, Mahazikei Torah,* and *Yesodei Torah* schools, where pupils studied until the age of 14 and then continued in *yeshivas.* The girls learned in *Bet Ya'akov* schools. With the rise of the Nazis to power in Germany, the movement began to concern itself with the commandment of settling the Land of Israel according to Jewish law, and a *Yishuv* ("settlement") Fund was established to finance the religious settlement effort of *Agudat Israel.* Representatives of the *Agudah* worked together with Hicem and the Joint in the fields of social work and emigration. Hicem's office was headed by Gisi Fleischmann. A union of Jewish teachers formed in Slovakia to help establish and maintain Jewish schools. The chairman of the organization was the principal of the Jewish school in Prešov, Isidor Schwarz. Other principals working with him included Arpad Sebestyén and Y. Neumann from Bratislava, and Alexander Mittelmann from Piešťany.

The teachers' union published several booklets edited by Isidor Schwarz, mostly stories of Jewish folklore written in Slovak, as reading material for pupils in the Jewish schools. They also published a newsletter called *Chronica*. All the Jewish teachers and nursery-school teachers in Slovakia were members of the union, and it handled their professional problems.

V. The Condition of the Jews in Late 1939 - Early 1940

During the first year of rule by the People's party, headed by clerics and devoted supporters of the Catholic Church, the local authorities made haste to expel the Jews from vital branches of the economy, primarily through use of its operational arm, the Hlinka Guard. Initially, however, the central authorities were inclined to proceed somewhat cautiously, so as not to paralyze the economy. The first to be hit were Jewish officials in public service jobs, lawyers, and doctors. In commerce, which was mostly in Jewish hands, Aryanization had been proceeding under other guises since June 1939. The Jews were not yet explicitly mentioned in the edict regarding the appointment of temporary trustees and managers "to look out for the economic and public interest" in industrial enterprises, manufacturing, and commerce. In practice, however, the edict was only enforced with respect to Jewish businesses, and control over these enterprises was transferred to "temporary management," which generally came from the ranks of the Hlinka Guard and understood nothing about business management. On December 21, 1939, another edict was published, explicitly limiting the number of Jews in economic positions. Thus, the purge of the Jews from the economy was now backed by official legislation.

Outrageous propaganda against the Jews goaded Jew-haters to acts which had no foundation in the law, and shortly the Jews were expelled from all offices and positions in which non-Jews were interested.

Many of the Jews' Christians neighbors, seeing that they could inherit the property of the Jews easily, without investing the least effort, overnight were turned by their avarice into grasping predators.

When the Nazis first took over in Germany and Austria, they established institutions there for the emigration of Jews. Many Jews moved to Slovakia and remained there. A similar atmosphere of emigration and exodus now seized the Jews of Slovakia, as well. The youth, and even the middle-aged, wished to go to Israel or emigrate elsewhere, if only to get out of Slovakia; and they prepared themselves emotionally and physically for this move. They studied Hebrew and English and took vocational retraining courses. Tens of thousands of Jews wanted to leave; but generally, there was nowhere for them to go.

The inveterate split between the Jewish factions and the poor relations between the Orthodox *Agudah* camp and the Zionist camp worked to the Jews' disadvantage. The competition between the two centers of activity, each trying to help its own confederates and accusing the other of impairing its functioning, was most detrimental.

The Bratislava office of the *Aliyah* Division of the Jewish Agency for Israel acquired only around ten immigration permits for veteran Slovak Zionists and their families. In view of the great demand, this was a ridiculous number. However, all protests and lobbying proved fruitless. On the other hand, Hicem and the Joint helped many Jews emigrate to various countries. But the possibilities for Jews to find a place in countries of the free world were limited, especially in the wake of the endless stream of Jewish émigrés from Germany, which began in 1933 and was followed by a similar exodus from Austria.

The committee for transferring property, operating under the Central Jewish Bureau, found an opportunity to export sixty million Slovak korunas worth of tobacco and prepared plans for exporting tens of millions of korunas worth of paper fiber and other products. Dr. Isaac Rosenberg worked as the bureau's representative in this area in Holland. Minister of Commerce Medrický and Minister of Finance Pružinský approved the export plans and property transfers. With the cooperation of the Governor of the National Bank, the Jewish lobbyists succeeded in forming correct relations with these official economic circles. Thanks to these relations, foreign currency was allocated to pay passage for organized Jewish groups fortunate to leave Slovakia, and for a delegation of Slovak Jews to attend the 21st Zionist Congress, held in Geneva from August 16-25, 1939. The war broke out six days after the congress adjourned. The delegates from Slovakia were Dr. Oscar Neumann, Zigmund Klinger, Dr. Ladislav Rosenzweig, Dov Berthold Weiss, Jacob Berger and Abraham Ben-David. This was the last international meeting between representatives of Slovak Jewry and representatives of Jews from other lands before the Holocaust. Dr. Neumann and his colleagues tried to look into the possibilities of *aliyah* for the Jews of Slovakia, but without success.

During this period many Jewish refugees from neighboring European countries were captured by the police and concentrated in the Červený Most (Red Bridge) camp, on the outskirts of Bratislava, where the Slovaks drafted them into hard labor gangs, kept under heavy and strict guard. Five months later they were transferred to the Patronka camp, to a building which had formerly been an arms factory. The Jewish community worked hard to aid these refugees and alleviate their plight.

Under the aegis of the Orthodox Bureau, whose general secretary was Heinrich Schwarz, Aaron Grünhut and Ludwig Kastner organized the illegal immigration of approximately 450 Jews from Slovakia, mostly from Bratislava, to Israel. On July 3, 1939, they set sail along the Danube in two steamboats – the Yugoslavian *Czar Dushan* and the

Hungarian *Queen Elizabeth* – bound for Varna. Around 800 refugees from the Patronka camp also joined them.

The convoy proceeded slowly until it reached Bulgaria. There the authorities refused to give the boats right of passage. After many hardships the passengers were taken to the Solina detention camp, and two weeks later were put on board another boat – the *Naomi-Julia*. The passengers, who now numbered 1,366 people, included around 300 members of the *Betar* youth movement. They saw to order and discipline among the passengers, who due to their great suffering and hardship in the journey had begun to despair of ever reaching their destination. However, on September 19, 1939, the *Naomi-Julia* reached the territorial waters of the Land of Israel. It was captured by a British warship, and only after great efforts and a difficult struggle did the British give in and agree not to turn the boat back to the high sea. Weary and exhausted, the immigrants were taken off the boat and imprisoned in the Sarafand detention camp. A month later they were released.

To the great disappointment of dozens of families, another emigration project for Jewish farmers to settle in Canada, organized by Salomon Gross from Trnava, fell through because of the war when the project was already at an advanced stage. At this point the Nazi authorities were still interested in ridding themselves of the Jews by means of emigration, and Bratislava, located on the banks of the Danube, became an important crossroad of emigration and illegal immigration to Israel from Nazi-conquered lands.

Each convoy of illegal immigrants and each ship that worked its way through the stormy waters, in both senses, has a fascinating story. The *Katina* left Brno on January 18, 1939, and discharged its passengers on the shores of the Land of Israel after three months of wandering. Approximately 400 illegal immigrants from Czechoslovakia left on Passover, 1939, aboard the *Colorado-Atarto,* and safely arrived off shore from Shefayyim on April 23, 1939. The *Pruso/a,* carrying 700 immigrants from Czechoslovakia and Rumania, set sail for the Land of Israel on May 25, 1939. Many groups of immigrants were delayed in setting sail due to difficulties in taking their fare out of Slovakia. Fare for passage was obtained by property transfers. Goods of a Slovak Jew were sent abroad, and the payment for them was deposited in a bank in London. One group of immigrants who set out from Bratislava on May 18, 1940, on board the *Pancho,* arrived in the Land of Israel after four years of wayfaring, hardship and suffering. Groups of "illegal" immigrants who were delayed in Bratislava were assisted by Jewish organizations and communal institutions that saw to their welfare.

The conquest of Poland brought a rise in the number of refugees concentrated in the northern Slovak Jewish communities of Čadca and Žilina. Representatives of the Jewish Bureau succeeded in persuading the government to consent to these refugees remaining in Slovakia until they could continue their journey, and Jewish institutions saw to their food and shelter.

Negotiations for the Polish Jewish refugees to remain were handled by Dr. Winterstein. Heinrich Schwarz, who was on good terms with Dr. Koso, also worked towards this end. To the government's assertion that allowing foreign Jews to remain would be a burden on the local Jews and would be detrimental to them, Dr. Winterstein responded that the foreign Jews would not be a burden because the Joint would support them with foreign currency. It was ascertained that within the span of several months the Slovak National Bank received 30,000 dollars from the Joint for supporting these refugees, and the Governor of the Slovak National Bank, interested in this revenue, was supportive of the idea. At the meeting of the board of the Central Bureau on February 6, 1940, Dr. Winterstein reported the good news that he had obtained an entrance permit for the inmates of the Sosnowice camp in Poland; they were housed in the Vyhne camp, supported by money from the Joint.

In contrast to this success, at one of the bureau's meetings Dr. Winterstein had to report that the journey of a group of immigrants from the Maccabee movement, organized under the aegis of the bureau and the Zionist Organization, had failed. The exodus of 700 people, most of them youngsters who had been prepared for *aliyah,* had been meticulously planned. A contract had been signed with a Yugoslav government shipping company, which dispatched two ships to the Danube port of Bratislava. The people were taken on board the ships and awaited rite of passage through Yugoslavia, but the Yugoslav government refused to grant it. After intervention by the Ministry of Foreign Affairs and other Slovak governmental officials proved to no avail, the immigrants were compelled to disembark. They were held in the Vyhne camp, and the Jewish community saw to their needs. This was a bitter disappointment for people who had left their homes and liquidated their sources of livelihood, and now faced an uncertain future.

In February 1940, an emissary from Poland, by the name of Moses Merin, presented himself to the delegates of the Jewish Bureau, allegedly speaking in the name of 1,600,000 Jews from Warsaw and Katowice. He presented a plan for transferring Jews from Poland through Slovakia to the sea, and requested help from the Central Jewish Bureau in his contacts with the Slovak authorities. The board promised to render all possible assistance to the emissary, but it was an enormously difficult mission.[14]

---

[14] The account of Merin's visit comes from the minutes of the Central Jewish Bureau of

VI. The Zionist Movement in 1940

In the last two months of 1939 I visited the Jewish communities of western Slovakia – Hlohovec, Nitra, Piešťany and Bánovce – on a lecture tour to explain the activities of the Central Jewish Bureau and the Zionist Organization and discuss the political situation. The communities were requested to contribute their share in supporting the central organizations of Slovak Jewry and the cultural activities of these organizations. The cultural department planned to publish a series of five books; the first, *Stories of the Land of Israel,* was already in print. At the end of September 1939, the government shut down *The Jewish News,* but steps were immediately taken to publish a new weekly called *The Way,* owned by the Zionist Organization and edited by Dr. Oscar Neumann. In this paper, as well, I continued publishing articles on Jewish topics in a weekly column entitled "The Jewish Calendar."

In winter camps for youth, organized by various Zionist parties, I lectured on the Bible and the Oral Torah. I also participated in seminars on Jewish philosophy run by the Maccabee movement, *B'nai Akiva,* and *Ha-Shomer ha-Tzair.* I taught Judaism in all the youth movements, regardless of their ideological affiliation; for in this respect, they were all the same in my eyes. In *Zprávy (The News),* a periodical published by Maccabee and the General Zionists, I wrote articles on the Bible and the Mishnah and Talmud, which were used as a focus for discussions in the movement's clubhouses.

In January 1940, I received an interview with Minister of Education and Culture Jozef Sivák. Among the topics we discussed were the possibility of paying a special stipend to rabbis to supplement their salary, the problem of their nationality, the status of Jewish teachers, and governmental support for Jewish schools. The minister expressed

February 27, 1940, FYVS.

his willingness to help to the utmost.

The first Zionist congress in independent Slovakia convened in an atmosphere of great political tension, with new edicts that essentially denied our right to exist being published every other day. The congress was held from May 12-13, 1940, in the Jewish school in Liptovský-Svätý-Mikuláš. Each Zionist faction was allowed thirty delegates. An atmosphere of good will surrounded the deliberations, and the Zionists of Slovakia felt exultant.

As chairman of the congress' cultural committee, I brought the following recommendations before the plenum:

1. The objective of our cultural work should be to strengthen our members' nationalist consciousness and give it more content by enriching our members' knowledge. This objective should be achieved by teaching Jewish nationalist values from the past and the present.

2. Educational work should be based on appreciation of the spiritual and ethical world of the Bible.

3. Our cultural work must be directed towards practical Zionism.

4. The congress should stress the pressing need to study Hebrew as a fundamental requirement of cultural-educational activity in the Zionist movement. To this end a special committee, which would maintain contact with the Association for Dissemination of the Hebrew Language in Bratislava, must be established in each branch office.

5. The congress calls for establishment of a seminar to train Hebrew teachers to work in outlying cities.

* * *

The congress elected Dr. Oscar Neumann chairman of the Zionist Organization of Slovakia. I was elected to the executive committee, as well as the cultural committee and the central *Shekel* (Zionist movement membership) committee. The deliberations of the congress were fruitful; ruffled feathers were smoothed and misunderstandings were cleared up. Much of the credit for these accomplishments may be attributed to the general secretary, Dr. Desider Ehrenfeld.

* * *

During the congress a national council was elected for the Maccabee association of the General Zionist movement, henceforth known as Group A. It convened in Nitra under the leadership of Zigmund Klinger, on May 26, 1940, and elected its officers. I was elected to the larger directorate and participated in many meetings in a variety of branches. At the first meeting of the new leadership, I was elected chairman of the central cultural committee of the Zionist Organization. I requested that the publications of the various factions be submitted for review by the committee to prevent publication of things which had nothing to do with Jewish culture.

* * *

Group A of the General Zionists (i.e., Maccabee in Slovakia) ran a summer camp and seminar in the town of Lubochňa, in July 1940. (Group A was a group of comrades who acted as an autonomous faction within the larger setting of the General Zionists.) Since there were differences of opinion within the faction, it was decided to convene the larger national council, on July 14, within the context of the seminar in Lubochňa. These deliberations, which I chaired, were the most explosive I have ever witnessed, especially when it came to formulating an agreement. Julius Fleischhacker, speaking for Group A, and Dr. Winterstein, for the General Zionists, were the leading spokesmen in the conference's heated debates. We finally managed to come to an agreement outlining a joint plan of action, and, with our differences smoothed over, the conference ended on a peaceful and amicable note.

* * *

In the summer of 1940, on the initiative of Joseph Weiser and Alexander Schwarz of Bratislava, a group of teachers organized a preparatory committee to establish a Department of Zionist Education *(Cionistický Skolský Odbor)*. I was asked to head the department but decided not to accept the offer because I was opposed on principle to any divisiveness and fragmentation in the Jewish camp. I asserted that if the teacher's organization was not sufficiently Zionistic, the Zionist teachers should try to bring an ideological impact to bear on the course of events within the union. This was not the time for in-fighting and fragmentation, but rather for unity and mutual friendship. The leaders of the Zionist teachers agreed with me that it was preferable to initiate separate activities than form an opposition group against the teachers' association. With the aid of the Zionist Organization, plans were made to publish a Hebrew grammar book for Slovak-speaking students in the Jewish schools and a Zionist pedagogical periodical. The initiators requested me to contribute articles to the monthly.

* * *

On September 25, 1940, the Zionist Organization issued one more circular winding up the campaign of the Zionist *Shekel*. The circular stressed that the number who contributed to the drive was growing from year to year, and that this was a sign that Zionism was reaching the hearts of the Jewish masses in Slovakia, who were convinced that Zionist fulfillment was the correct and best way to solve the problem of Jewish life in the Diaspora.

As chairman of the General Zionists, concurrently I issued a detailed circular on the activities of the secretariat in Bratislava, including a section relating to the possibility of *aliyah,* in which the following was said: "Despite the great difficulties involved, we can bring you the good news of a possible way to immigrate to Israel by train, through Hungary, along the Constantinople-Syria line. The journey takes about three and a half days. Immigration permits are available for students, women farm hands through WIZO, and property owners. Anyone interested should apply immediately to the Land of Israel Office in Bratislava, Ventúrska 3."[15]

The circulars mentioned were the last ones openly issued by the Zionist Organization in Slovakia. A government edict of September 26, 1940, out-lawed all the Jewish organizations and shut down their offices, and on October 22, 1940, the only Jewish weekly, *The Way,* was banned. The Zionist Organization went underground.

---

[15] Announcing an overland route for immigration to Israel was intended to encourage people to make every effort to leave Slovakia. In actual fact only isolated individuals managed to leave, and they faced a way fraught with obstacles. The Mediterranean became a war arena and its ports were closed. Transit papers for overland travel became unobtainable, and virtually all hopes of immigrating were defeated. Nevertheless, the movement of "illegal" immigration by boat continued. Here we must mention the *Patria,* a deportation ship carrying "illegal" immigrants from the *Pacific* and the *Milos,* which was blown up on October 25, 1940, and sank with over 200 immigrants on board; and the *Struma,* which sank with 768 passengers, of whom only one was rescued. Immigrants from many countries of Europe, including Czechoslovakia, were aboard these boats.

VII. Lobbying by the Jewish Bureau Until it was Shut Down

In January 1940, the Central Jewish Bureau published a newsletter to the Jewish communities briefing its readers on a number of subjects and new laws and edicts. Circular no. 10, which was six pages long, reported on interviews with ministers and efforts by members of the Central Jewish Bureau to lobby government and other offices on behalf of Slovakia's Jews who applied to the Bureau from all parts of the country. The number of appeals approached 700 per month. The circular announced the opening of various departments within the bureau: culture, vocational retraining, *aliyah* and emigration, and legal advice. The circular wrote that a committee of jurists would handle requests for assistance and would also answer inquiries addressed to it through *The Way* with respect to the following questions: citizenship, residence permits, taxes and social insurance, import and export licenses, passports, counseling and information on laws and edicts against the Jews. The circular stated:

> In any instance in which an injustice has been done you, if it is a matter of principle, apply to our office. Regarding personal matters apply to a lawyer. You may also apply to us concerning labor camps. The practice of drafting Jews for labor, which has been instituted in several localities, is against the law, and the district offices have been notified accordingly. Reporting to civilian labor camps is not yet in force. Reporting to military labor camps should be done only pursuant to an appropriate order from the National Department of Defense. Jews planning to leave will be discharged in the event of emigration.

We are studying the government's proposal regarding Jewish factories and Jewish laborers in other factories. We have obtained the consent of the authorities to the temporary release of agricultural land for the purpose of running agricultural *aliyah* training programs on farms. Instructions for drafting an "Aryanization" contract are appended herewith. We have seen to it that the Jews who were dismissed from their jobs in the Social Insurance Institute have been reinstated in their positions. We are seeing to the issuance of new work permits for rabbis and *shohatim.*

The circular was signed by Rabbi Frieder, Dr. Max Mayer, Dr. Oscar Neumann, Dr. Vojtech Winterstein, and Dr. Ludevit Cohen.

Rabbi Frieder prevailed upon the Ministry of Education to approve a request by the Orthodox community of Michalovče for a government stipend and obtained the ministry's consent to parallel classes of Jewish pupils remaining in the general public school for the coming school year.

In October 1939, labor camps for Jews were established under the Ministry of Interior. Management of the camps was entrusted to a central parity committee of six, two from each central organization, i.e., from the two federations of Jewish communities and from the Central Jewish Bureau. The communities participated in 50% of the budget of the camps. The camps had a technical department, a department for economics, for medical services, and for nutrition. The inmates of the camps worked eight hours a day, five days a week, excluding Saturday and Sunday. The workers were up to 45 years old. Oscar Krasniansky was charged with responsibility over the camps, and life in them was managed according to the principle of autonomy. Jews were employed in work on railroad tracks, sewage systems, etc., in the following places: Saint Peter, Račisdorf, Smrekovice, Nitra, Zbehy, Vyhne, Svätý Jur, Oremov Laz, Zohor, Láb, Degeš, Ilava, and elsewhere.

On March 4, 1940, the Ministry of Interior reiterated its consent to run classes for vocational retraining and to establish crafts and agriculture centers for Jewish youth in Slovakia. Centers for studying agriculture were opened in Nitra and Oravský Podzámok. Study groups for radio and film technicians were organized by Mr. Politzer, an engineer, and six-month courses for nurses were organized in the Jewish hospital with the assistance of Dr. Oesterreicher and Dr. Neumann.

Difficulty arose maintaining the refugee camps in Patronka and Slobodárna, since the Joint had stopped its support due to lack of money, and the number of refugees was steadily increasing. A request came from the Jewish community of Berlin to take in some seventy pioneers and find place for them in the *aliyah* training programs in Slovakia, so that they could continue from here along their way to the Land of Israel with *Aliyah bet* (the movement of "illegal" immigration). The Central Bureau obtained temporary residence permits for them to participate in the training programs and also saw to their passports, in the same way as these were obtained for the residents of the Vyhne camp.

Circular no. 11, the last circular of the Central Jewish Bureau, came out in July 1940 and contained information on the new edicts and laws which had been promulgated and on the possibilities of alleviations in certain instances. The first section explained edict number 130/1940, dated May 29, 1940, regarding the temporary arrangement for compulsory labor by Jews and gypsies, who were required to report for labor for the defense of the state instead of regular military service. The term of service was set at two months. Whoever paid per diem expenses of 500 korunas could have his service shortened to one month. For a ransom of 3,000 to 18,000 korunas, depending on the economic status of the applicant, one could be exempted from serving altogether. Requests were submitted to the Ministry of Defense. A head of family who was drafted for labor could request support for his dependents at the rate of 8 korunas per person per day. The circular also cited other details about this new decree.

Regarding Aryanization the circular continued:

> We have submitted memoranda and deliberations are now being held on the various clauses. We maintain that restricting Jewish workers to four percent of the total employed in an enterprise essentially amounts to a "nil quota." We have requested that the Aryanization law not be applied to enterprises serving Jewish needs. Likewise, we hope to be permitted to work in the manufacture of medicines and pharmaceuticals, gathering medicinal plants, etc. We are appending explicit instructions with interpretation and guidance regarding everything related to the law's implementation. We have received numerous applications, especially with respect to employing Jews over the quota of 4%. We have been assured that the law of "Jewish enterprises" will not apply to the Jewish credit and loan associations; these must submit requests to the provincial and district offices. Consult us before submitting your requests.

Various other announcements appeared in the circular, including announcement of the initiative to establish a fund for poor and needy Jews in Slovakia; the possibility of organizing *aliyah* preparatory programs and vocational retraining courses for groups and individuals; requests for commercial agents and workers in the private and public sectors to organize under the aegis of the Central Bureau; steps taken to exempt philanthropic endowments, real estate owned by the Jewish communities, and lands worked by *aliyah* preparatory groups from the agrarian reform law; handling the acquisition of work permits for Jewish doctors, and treating poor Jews free of charge, on a volunteer basis; providing legal protection for refugees in the Bratislava and Vyhne camps and for Jewish refugees wherever they may be.

The circular was accompanied by a 19 - page booklet further explaining the Aryanization law. Little did the leaders of the Central Jewish Bureau whose signatures were affixed to the circular imagine that they had signed the last circular which this office would ever issue; for, on September 26, 1940, all Jewish organizations were outlawed.

VIII. Laws and Decrees in 1940

Slovakia's *Gestapo,* otherwise known as the *ústnedňa štátnej bezpečnosti - ÚŠB* (Center for State Security) was established in January 1940. The agrarian reform law, designed to solve the social problem of farmers "hungering for land," was promulgated on February 22, 1940. In actual practice, the only action taken was to expel the Jews of Slovakia from agriculture, although they possessed only 101,410 hectares of land, comprising 6.3% of the agricultural and forested land of the state. These lands were now listed in a compulsory register and were expropriated, but only a small fraction – about 2.8% – was distributed among applicants. The rest of the land, such as the large estate of Eugen Orenstein, a Jew from Sered, was given to public bodies. Approximately 820 hectares were given to the education fund of the Catholic Church.

On April 25, 1940, law 113/40 regarding Jewish enterprises and Jewish workers in other enterprises was published. This was the famous Aryanization law which stipulated that by the end of 1940 the number of Jewish laborers shall not exceed 25% of the total number of senior laborers, and that subsequently this figure shall gradually be reduced to 10%. A quota of 4% of the total employed in any enterprise was set with respect to all other types of employment. Prior to this, a regulation was issued forbidding the closure of Jewish businesses without justification. In addition, an economic bureau was opened in the Prime Minister's Office with an advisory body "for solving the Jewish question."

On June 19, 1940, an edict was issued forbidding kosher slaughtering of beef, sheep, and goats, and forbidding the sale of kosher-slaughtered meat. The national union of sheep growers sent a memorandum to the Ministry of Agriculture requesting permission to slaughter sheep, and Jewish intercessors also appealed to various offices. Among them was Rabbi Frieder, who appealed to the minister of education and culture, requesting that the vulnerable heart of the Jewish religion not be threatened, but at this stage only kosher slaughtering of fowl was guaranteed. In October 1940 an amendment to the law was obtained, permitting kosher slaughtering of beef, but only for export.

On July 28, 1940, Slovakia's leaders, Tiso, Tuka, and Mach, attended what became known as the "Salzburg talks" with Hitler and Ribbentrop, in Hohensalzberg. In these secret talks the Slovak statesmen accepted all Germany's dictates. Durčanský was dismissed from all his positions in the government, Alexander Mach was appointed Minister of Interior, and Prime Minister Tuka took over the portfolio of the Foreign Ministry as well. His German counterpart, Ribbentrop, notified Killinger, the new German legate in Bratislava, of the appointment of German advisors to all government offices, and on September 1, 1940, the SS officer Dieter Wisliceny entered office as Germany's advisor to Slovakia on Jewish affairs. This marked the beginning of the Jews being purged from their positions in all walks of life, at a whirlwind pace and with great thoroughness. Dr. Isidor Koso, who served in the double role of director general of the Prime Minister's Office and of the Ministry of Interior, was highly instrumental in this process. Koso was a radical Jew-hater as well as a sly, double-faced careerist, who maintained ostensibly "correct" relations with the Jewish leaders, especially the general secretary of the Orthodox Bureau, Heinrich Schwarz, and Dr. Winterstein of the Central Jewish Bureau. These two central bureaus of Slovak Jewry had still not found a common tongue, and, due to stubborn disagreement over who would be the primary spokesman of the delegation, their representatives appeared separately for interviews with government leaders. This situation continued until August 8, 1940, at which time Dr. Neumann and Dr. Mayer were delegated to talk with Dr. Kondor, chairman of the Yeshurun congregations, and propose that the leaders of the Jewish communities be called together for an urgent meeting. Dr. Kondor invited the representatives of the Jewish communities for August 15. Preliminary consultations were held with Rabbi Frieder, Dr. Winterstein, and Dr. Neumann, who insisted on the necessity of uniting forces. The leaders of the Jewish community expressed their unqualified support and relayed this decision at the meeting of the Yeshurun congregations. Thus, at long last, a draft agreement was formulated among the three organizations, according to which a representative body of 12 people would be established: 5 Orthodox, 5 representatives of Yeshurun congregations, and the two chairmen of the Jewish community federations. Dr. Winterstein and Dr. Neumann of the Central Jewish Bureau were among the Yeshurun representatives. Several days later Dr. Kondor announced that the Orthodox federation had accepted the proposal. The Central Jewish Bureau would continue functioning, and important political and economic questions would come under the jurisdiction of the joint representative body. Political work would be directed by Heinrich Schwarz, Dr. Kondor and Dr. Winterstein. Current affairs would be brought up for discussion in committees led by members of the joint representative body. The board of the Central Jewish Bureau ratified the proposal on August 27, 1940, and decided to present it to the larger committee for their approval.

Augustine Morávek, a corrupt man and one of the most radical anti-Semites, was made head of the Economic Office and Advisory Committee of the Prime Minister's Office. Prompted by Dr. Koso, the office began issuing far-reaching edicts at an accelerated pace, even exceeding the guidelines of the political leadership. The worsening condition of the Jews found expression in two edicts, promulgated on August 30, 1940: No. 203/40, regarding obligatory registry of Jewish property, pursuant to which every Jew and every Jewish legal body was required to declare their belongings of value, and another edict which forbade Jews to acquire a secondary education, even through private lessons. Diplomas given Jews by foreign schools were not recognized. Henceforward Jews were only allowed to study in elementary schools which were maintained at the expense of the Jewish communities.

An order of September 3 forbade Jews to employ Christian (Aryan) household help under forty years of age. A household was considered Jewish if one of the spouses was a Jew. Other edicts required the Jews to turn in whatever passports and driver's licenses they held. In addition, the law protecting tenants from eviction was declared no longer applicable to Jews.

* * *

According to the last minutes of the Central Jewish Bureau, dated

September 3, 1940, Dr. Winterstein reported to the board meeting on the agreement establishing a joint representative body and the joint delegation's first visit to Dr. Koso, who demanded that by September 9 he be given a detailed list of all Jewish organizations, the purpose of their activities, their membership, etc. The board decided that the secretaries of the Bureau, Dr. László and Dr. Cohen, would visit the Jewish communities to give them information on the new laws and decrees. It was the mockery of fate, for Dr. Koso was to use the list of Jewish organizations, which he requested from the newly formed joint representative body, to announce their liquidation and to place these organizations outside the law. The Central Office for Economy (Ústredný Hospodársky Úrad – ÚHÚ), subordinate to Prime Minister Tuka, was established on September 18, 1940. Its first head was Augustine Morávek, already infamous as the head of the Economic Office mentioned above. This office coordinated all the Aryanization of Jewish property in Slovakia. Morávek removed the Jews from economic life and even exceeded his authority in all that concerned "solving the Jewish question" in Slovakia. Regulations and orders against the Jews were promulgated one after another, two to three a week.

IX. The Government Establishes the Jewish Center

Edict no. 234, promulgated on September 26, 1940, banned all Jewish organizations and associations and transferred their property to the Jewish Center (Ústredňa Židov – Ž), a body which the government established as the exclusive institution representing and coordinating all affairs of the Jews and placed under the supervision and authority of the Central Office for Economy. The Jewish Center was required to bring the directives of the government to the attention of all the Jews, by means of its branch offices in outlying cities, and to publish these directives in a paper entitled Véstník (The Herald).

The government-sponsored Jewish Center was headed by the Jewish Elder *(Starosta)*, Heinrich Elhanan Schwarz. He was the secretary of the national Orthodox Bureau, and had good relations with Dr. Koso and various government offices. Schwarz had thus far maintained an independent policy, without including the representatives of the Central Jewish Bureau in it. He will surely prefer to staff the new organization with members of his faction, thus leaving me no alternative at this stage but to accept the verdict and confine myself to work in the community.

I continued to function in my capacity as rabbi of the Jewish community of Nové Mesto and remained on the outside when it came to central public activity. My time could thus be devoted to scholarly work. I completed my dissertation, "The Philosophy of Ethical Values," and resubmitted it to the university; but due to anti-Jewish legislation, I could no longer take the doctoral exams in philosophy. During this period the central Zionist Organization published a booklet which I wrote in Slovak, celebrating the 900th anniversary of Rashi's birth. For the anniversary of the founding of Ohel David I published a booklet containing a monograph on the *gaon* Rabbi David Deutsch of blessed memory, as well as a report on the activities of the institution and the progress of the Adolf and Helena Baiersdorf Foundation. A series of articles which I wrote on Jewish ethics appeared in *Židovská Kultúra (Jewish Culture)*, a periodical published by the Jewish Center. Many other of my philosophical essays were never published due to conditions of the times; still they served as material for lectures in study groups and seminars.

* * *

Heinrich Schwarz now set up the board of the Jewish Center and appointed department heads: Arnold Kämpfner, for the social department; Géza Friedländer, finance; Mikuláš Eichner, education and culture; Salomon Gross, work and construction; Dr. Ernst Abeles, emigration and vocational training. The office-holders from the Yeshurun congregations were Dr. Arpad Kondor, deputy Jewish Elder, Dr. V. Winterstein, general secretary, and Dr. Eugen Forbat, statistics. Later on, a department for converts was added as well. The Center operated according to by-laws established by the Central Office for Economy and received its budget from the property of the Jewish organizations which had been transferred to the authority of the Jewish Center.

From the day Morávek was appointed head of the Central Office for Economy until the end of 1940, approximately 50 edicts and orders against the Jews were promulgated on his and Dr. Koso's initiative.[16] All the steps which were taken against the Jews, purging them from economic life, humiliating them, and depriving them of rights, were vested in the law. The Slovaks robbed and plundered lawfully, and expropriated fixed and moveable assets: jewelry, valuables, furs, tools and technical instruments, suits, and housewares. Entire families were evicted and transferred from city to city, from one region to another, all under the law and with the encouragement of the government, whose objective was to transfer all that the Jews possessed to Aryan Slovaks. The President, Father Dr. Tiso, explained the government's stand in public assemblies throughout the country. In a mass demonstration in the village of Višňové, in September 1940, Tiso said the following with respect to the Jewish question:

> We are criticized for taking radio receivers away from Jews. Well, what of it! There are more important

---

[16] During Morávek's entire term of office, until the end of June 1942. approximately 210 such edicts and orders were promulgated, and in the duration of the Slovak Republic, 1939-1945, a total of 351.

things than radio receivers. People come to us with complaints that we are taking away their shops, their enterprises, and contend that our actions do not behoove the Christian religion. And I say to you that it is very Christian. For we are taking what the Jews took from our people. Their leader Moses commanded the Jews that on the Jubilee Year all property shall revert to its original owner; but the Jews appear to have forgotten this law! According to the Talmud a Jew who cheats a gentile is doing the will of God, and therefore it is a religious commandment to cheat him. Know, my brothers, we are only taking what is rightfully ours. Our policy is based on the Christian principle of brotherly love. We shall yet give the Jews an opportunity to do honest work.[17]

In Bánovce, Tiso's parish, he personally saw to distributing the Jews' property among his sister and friends. Following the President's example, Morávek also amassed a fortune from bribes and corrupt dealings connected with Aryanization.

In this depressing atmosphere, with the acts of the authorities foreboding nothing but evil, Elhanan Schwarz, the first Jewish Elder, tried to fulfill his difficult role responsibly, trusting in the Lord, praying and hoping that he would succeed in frustrating or postponing the evil decrees which the local authorities passed against the Jews of Slovakia, and was prepared to put up a fight and not follow orders which were likely to place Jewish lives in jeopardy.

* * *

In my first conversation with Schwarz, I tried to ascertain the

[17] Published in *Slovák*, September 25, 1940, p. 4.

possibilities for continuing Zionist activity, and to my pleasant surprise he showed understanding and willingness to come towards us, the Zionists. Following this conversation, Elhanan Schwarz, Dr. Winterstein, Dr. Neumann, Dr. Porges, Dr. Moses Dachs, Leo Rosenthal, Gisi Fleischmann, and Ben-Zion Gottleib met in the apartment of my father-in-law, Max Berl, for consultation. Since the resolutions which we arrived at were not actually implemented, I called a second meeting, this time in Nové Mesto, during the intermediate days of Passover, 1941. Aside from Schwarz, several prominent Zionist figures also attended the second meeting: Zigmund Klinger, Gisi Fleischmann, Dr. Porges, Mr. Horn, and Dr. Süss. We agreed to establish a department for Zionist activity within the context of the Jewish Center. We were all pleased, and Schwarz promised to present the matter to the authorities for their approval.

The Jewish Eider's courageousness was his undoing. First, he was arrested; then the department heads Arnold Kiimpfner, Géza Friedländer, and Dr. Winterstein were taken for interrogation. Schwarz never returned to office. After being tortured in prison, he fell ill and was sent to the hospital. From there he was smuggled out to Budapest, where he was hospitalized in a Jewish hospital. His wife and three children traveled there after him. Elhanan Schwarz died in 1944, after a long and severe illness (see p. 150).

Morávek appointed Arpad Sebestyén, principal of the Jewish school in Bratislava and a man who aspired to fulfill the wishes of his superiors, to replace Schwarz as Jewish Elder. We did not trust him, and thus our efforts for concerted action by all groups came to nought.

X. Decrees and Pogroms in 1941

The government apparatus worked rapidly, issuing decrees and paving the way for the isolation and destruction of the Jews through more and more extreme legislation. Laws which at first appeared moderate were amended to be more extreme, extending their validity and accelerating their implementation. For example:

In April 1941 a new proclamation was published by the Ministry of Interior with respect to the establishment of work centers and work gangs in conjunction with the Ministry of Defense. Compulsory labor in time of emergency ostensibly applied to all citizens, but special work centers were established for the Jews, who had been expelled from economic life.

In several provinces Jews were ordered to wear a yellow ribbon three centimeters wide on their left sleeve whenever they were on the street or in a public place.

In Bratislava and other cities Jews were forbidden to live on streets named after leaders of the Nazi regime. At a subsequent stage, several months later, they were forbidden to live in certain neighborhoods. Special conditions and time limits were set for abrogating rental contracts with Jews, and evacuations were implemented within one or two months. Following this, having been shunted out of economic life, the Jews were forced to leave their homes in the capital by the end of 1941. The number of evicted reached 10,000, and a special department of the Jewish Center saw to it that Jewish families were moved to the eastern borders of the state, to cities with a large Jewish population capable of taking in the dispossessed families. Nové Mesto was one of the communities which became a city of refuge for the Jews of Bratislava.

On July 15, 1941, the Ministry of Interior issued proclamation number 275/41, restricting the freedom of movement and social contact of Jews throughout the state. Entering public parks and bathhouses, shopping in the marketplace before 10 a.m., being out of one's house after 9 p.m., and having social contact with Aryans were forbidden. Two months later Jews were forbidden to go to public places and places of entertainment.

Beginning in October 1941, restrictions were placed on the Jews' use of the trains; henceforth they were only permitted to travel third class, in special compartments marked "for Jews." A month later, Jews were forbidden to leave their place of residence without a special written permit; special permits were only granted to Jews who were economically important or held a special office.

Anti-Jewish legislation that year reached a climax on September 9, 1941, with the publication of an extreme law (number 198 in the Slovak statutes) dealing with the Jews' legal status. This law, known as the *Židovský Kodex* (Jewish Codex) consisted of 270 articles and comprised all the laws promulgated thus far against the Jews, in addition to several new edicts, including one which made it compulsory for all Jews throughout the state to wear a yellow badge, and another which imposed forced labor on every Jew from age 16 to 60. The principal change introduced by the law was a new definition of the term Jew, which was now cast in a racist way, similar to the Nuremberg laws. The Slovaks were proud of this law and boasted that their anti-Semitic legislation was the most "sophisticated" in all Europe, even superior to the laws issued by the Germans, the creators of Nazi ideology.

* * *

Things began happening at a rapid pace, the declared objective being to purge the Jews from all influential positions in the life of the state. The new Jewish Codex compiled all the laws against the Jews in the severest way. (The statute itself was number 198, which in *gematria* (assigning numerical values to the letters of the Hebrew alphabet) is צחק, meaning "laughed"; and the number of its articles was 270, in *gematria*: רע, "evil." It is difficult to comprehend how, despite everything, Judaism continues to survive.) A branch office of the Jewish Center was opened in each of the larger Jewish communities, including Nové Mesto, and I was appointed to the local council. Given the circumstances, marked by rapid changes, I applied myself energetically to local work in the community. Countless appeals and requests demanded my attention daily. Here the head of a family had his source of livelihood wiped out and needed help, there several difficult social cases arose. Applications for ransoming prisoners and cases of Jews being evicted from their apartments were always on the agenda. Requests were submitted for exemption from labor camps, on the one hand, and for work permits, on the other. Travel permits were requested and applications were submitted to take in relations from another city or to be included on the list of people being supported by charity, stipends, or free meals in Ohel David. Countless other problems constantly arose, due to the severe legislation which restricted the Jew's right to live and exist. A new view of life, new concepts, assorted new documents, papers, and permits, all lent expression to the hardship of the Jews.

And when all our fellow Jews are in straits, with no possibility of alleviating their plight, there are always some malcontent and quarrelsome individuals who will get up and complain and never be satisfied, sometimes out of jealousy and wanton hatred. There were also destructive elements, and it was difficult to protect oneself against them. An interesting social manifestation in time of trouble was that good friends became foes, while yesterday's adversaries became sympathizers. The criterion of friendship was sometimes the size of the benefits which one could attain. There were disappointments and situations which caused me disillusionment, sadness and dismay; but these were not decisive and did not affect my position. The reward and satisfaction which I derived from my work, being able to serve the public and sometimes make a great hardship small, or a small hardship even smaller, thus reducing people's suffering, gave me strength.

I did all I could to prepare for the difficult times that lay ahead. By a miracle we managed to maintain the soup kitchen and Ohel David Home, which now had to sustain 230 people who had been left without livelihood, providing them three meals a day.

Soon another hardship beset us: the Jews of Bratislava were evicted from several quarters of the city. The word *judenrein* began to be heard abroad and became a common watchword. The work was exhausting; every day shipments of Jews arrived from Bratislava, and we had to find homes for them among the Jews of the city. Although no one was willing to volunteer his apartment, no Jew remained without a roof over his head; everyone received a room, even if rather cramped. Nor did anyone suffer starvation; we saw to it that the refugees were taken in and provided sustenance.

* * *

Three sick young members of my community were hospitalized in sanatoria for tuberculosis patients in the Tatra Mountains. I approached several magnanimous and wealthy Jews who were regular contributors to philanthropic institutions and requested them to help cover the hospitalization expenses. Men also donated to this worthy cause when they were called up to the Torah in the synagogue. Thus, the patients regained their health.

The fourth sick person under my care was my sister Piroshka (Pirka), who was taken ill after finishing her studies at the teachers' academy. She had a strong religious-nationalist identity and put her heart and soul into learning to teach, but she never had the privilege of teaching our young Jewish children. She was hospitalized in the Zontag Sanatorium for over a year, and was taken in the prime of youth, at the age of 21, on the tenth of Tamuz, 570I (July 5, 1941). She was buried in Prievidza. I dedicated my short book, *Sh'arei Rahamim* (Gates of Mercy) – prayers and religious practices concerning the sick and the mourner, with commentary and German translation – to the memory of my two sisters.

In these times of hardship and oppression, as the number of unemployed steadily increased and numerous people turned to me in their distress, I attached great importance to my work strengthening faith and trust in God, and fortifying people's souls so that they would not suffer emotional collapse.

In time I again had the opportunity to be active on the national level in a central capacity in the Yeshurun Federation, in which certain personnel changes had occurred: several Zionists had joined its institutions and had had a considerable impact on the federation. Dr. V. Winterstein was appointed secretary of the federation. Although the influence and importance of the central organizations of the Jewish communities had waned since the establishment of the Jewish Center, in the realm of religious affairs these bodies continued functioning as before. After eight years as rabbi, I was elected to the board of the Yeshurun federation as the rabbis' representative, replacing Rabbi Marcus Eckstein of the Yeshurun congregation in Košice, which had been annexed to Hungary. Politically this was not an influential position, but I expected it would enable me to have an impact in the realm of religion and faith. According to its by-laws, in theory the Yeshurun federation followed the *Shulhan Arukh*. This, however, had to be instituted in practice, as well. This holy objective guided me in my future activities in my new position.

I officiated as rabbi in Zvolen for four years, and now another four years of service were drawing to a close in the Jewish community of Nové Mesto. I intended to continue being active here as long as I could serve the community and as long as the public was in need of me. When we live to see better times and the oppressive, evil decrees are annulled and salvation comes, I hope to realize my Zionist aspirations to immigrate to the land of our forefathers and settle there, to bind my life with Zion and Jerusalem, so that my descendants will not be raised in the Diaspora, but in liberty in the Land of Israel, as the free children of a liberated people.

I prepared the members of my congregation, as well, for a life of freedom in the Land of Israel. I explained to them that we must cease wandering from dispersion to dispersion; we must terminate the era of exile and live as an independent people on our own soil in our promised land, so that we shall not always be the object of hatred and attack. We shall put our energy and our talents at the service of our people and shall build something for ourselves. Perhaps we shall have the opportunity of proving through our lives and our work, through our creative spirit, that we are a people worthy of having been chosen the people of the Torah. After the war, perhaps we shall realize that we do not belong here, on foreign soil, but there, in our ancient homeland, in the land of Divine revelation, the land of the Prophets who left their mark on eternal values. If these notions penetrate our souls and we are blessed with being able to realize our aspirations, we shall learn that the pain and suffering were not in vain, that our lives had meaning.

I finished my four years of work in Nové Mesto with a sense of satisfaction that I had been able to work in a variety of areas and accomplish certain things. I look to the future with hope and prayer for redemption and salvation. The vision of our Prophets and our Torah are eternal, and as long as we adhere to the values of the Torah there shall be life for our people. Guardian of Israel, guard the remnant of Israel, that Israel not be lost. Grant that we come through this period of suffering cleansed and purified.

Chapter Four

Persecution and Expulsion

(5702 – 1942)

> *"They have said: 'come, and let us cut them*
> *off from being a nation; that the name of Israel*
> *may be no more in remembrance'"*
> (Psalms 83:5)

I. Rumors of Expulsion

Nineteen hundred and forty-two began with new worries. The authorities continued to publish laws and directives which increasingly limited the freedom of the Jews in various walks of life. Organizational changes were made in the structure of the Jewish Center. Dr. Winterstein and Dr. Kondor were removed, and, in compliance with the wishes of the authorities, the new Jewish Elder turned the Center into an organization blindly implementing the tyrannical regime's directives. This development brought these two leading figures back to work within the Yeshurun federation, and henceforth they stood at its head.

On January 30, 1942, the heads of the Yeshurun federation and myself were received by Minister of Education and Culture Jozef Sivák and talked with him about preparing a new curriculum for the Jewish schools, one of the educational objectives being to prepare the youth for *aliyah*. The minister agreed to appoint Jewish supervisors for the schools of the Orthodox and Yeshurun congregations. We requested endorsement to open a Jewish school in Prešov and schools in the labor camps, to be maintained by the central organizations of the Jewish communities and by the Jewish Center. The minister was in favor of our suggestion that the teachers be considered public servants and that they be exempt from obtaining work permits as stipulated in the Jewish Codex. We brought up the problem of the financial situation of the Jewish communities, which were not capable of paying the teachers their full salary, and the question of social security deductions and transferring these payments to the Ministry of Education. The issues of using nationalized Jewish property for maintaining the schools and prohibiting school facilities from being expropriated for other purposes were also discussed. Likewise, we requested that the equipment for physical education which had been taken from the gymnasiums be returned. In these and other issues which we raised the minister showed complete understanding, requested that they be presented in writing, and assured us of his support.

On February 20, 1942, Yeshurun issued a circular to the Jewish communities presenting information on education and Jewish schools, social work, and fund-raising for the needy. It also provided instructions and explanations relating to all that concerned the real estate of the Jewish communities, exempting community workers from forced labor, obtaining permits for rabbis to travel within their provinces in performance of their duty, etc. The circular was signed by Dr. Kondor as chairman and Dr. Platschik, general secretary.

The two central organizations of Jewish communities agreed to establish a Cooperation Council, but its founding was delayed due to the illness and death of the chairman of the Orthodox Bureau, Isidor Pappenheim. It was agreed that the representatives of the two community bureaus would meet every so often to discuss current issues.

Bratislava became a very unpleasant city in which to live.

Demonstrations against the Jews abounded and generally concluded with attacks, abuse, and desecration of synagogues and houses of study. Graffiti and inflammatory posters appeared on walls and Jewish shops in the city; and there were even cases of murder. The Jews of the community were seized with horror when the Jewish old-age home was cruelly taken over and the elderly forcefully removed. Several days after the elderly had been transferred to wooden huts in the former Patronka factory, the huts were set on fire and the feeble old men and women fled for their lives, denuded of everything. Those who instigated the incident and set fire to the huts were never discovered. Everyone was free to do as he pleased whenever it concerned the Jews.

The chairman of the board of governors turned to me with a request that Ohel David take in twenty of the elderly from Bratislava. Around the time, Rabbi Zevi Perls, the elderly rabbi of Kitsee, who had been expelled from Burgenland and had remained with his wife on board a towboat until the last of the refugees with him on the boat had found a place of refuge and roof over their heads, also sought refuge among us. All in all, our institutions took in 25 people. I met these elderly individuals at Nové Mesto's station and accompanied the rabbi, along with the other elderly, to the old age home (which was destined to give cover and shelter to many more refugees).

One weekend in February, 1942, on my way home from Bratislava, I chanced to ride the train with Salomon Gross, who lived in Trnava. Gross served as deputy Jewish Elder in the Jewish Center, alongside an ineffectual Jewish Elder, and it was he who essentially ran everything there. In the fall of 1941, Dr. Géza Konka was appointed head of the 14th Department of the Ministry of Interior, which had been established with the averred objective of "solving the Jewish question." In this coincidental conversation I tried to ascertain what sort of person Dr. Konka was and what his attitude and approach were to all issues concerning the future of the Jews. Gross refrained from answering outright, but implied that he feared very severe decrees were in the offing. Did he mean labor camps? Far worse than that, he answered, but did not wish to elaborate. I understood that he did not trust me. After all, I belonged to the enemy camp. This conversation greatly perturbed me, causing me inner anxiety, for our circles had not yet gotten wind of this.

Several trying days elapsed. Then, on the night of February 25, at 2 a.m. Wednesday morning, I heard loud knocking on the gate of our yard. Ludevit and Heinz Tauber had come to call me to an urgent meeting in Bratislava, which had been convened in view of the government's plan to expel all the Jews of Slovakia to Poland. Heinz Tauber had nothing to add; he delivered the bad tidings and continued on his mission to Trenčin. I took the first train to Bratislava and went to the offices of the Jewish Center, where representatives of the Jewish communities were assembled: from the Orthodox Bureau – Raphael Levi from Bardejov, Arnold Kämpfner from Bratislava, Salomon Gross and Geley from Topolčany, and Weiss from Nitra; from the Yeshurun congregations – Dr. V. Winterstein, Dr. O. Neumann, Dr. Kondor, and myself; and non-affiliated personages – Dr. Fleischhacker, Dr. Tibor Kováč, and the architect Ondrej Steiner. The meeting was chaired by Dr. Winterstein, who reported on the government's plan to expel all the Jews from Slovakia. The 14th Department had been established in the Ministry of Interior for this purpose, to handle all matters concerning the Jews, to prepare statistical data on all the Jewish communities of Slovakia, and to operate according to a set program: first the youth would be deported, then the adults with their families, until all the Jews were transferred. No exceptions would be made; everyone would be expelled. We sat there in shock, fear and terror written on every face. Everyone understood the meaning of this terrible decree: expulsion – exiling the Jews of Slovakia to Poland, which was under Nazi control. One could hope that this far-reaching plan – to expel 90,000 people, with all the enormous difficulties inherent in such an undertaking – would be foiled by organizational and technical difficulties. However, it was clear that we could not rely on hopes and miracles. We decided to take action in all directions, without delay, and to lobby all possible bodies to avert the decree. A committee of six was set up, three from the Orthodox Bureau: Raphael Levi, Salomon Gross and Arnold Kämpfner, and three from the Yeshurun Federation: Dr. Winterstein, Dr. Kondor, and myself. This committee of six enlisted a group of people with connections and good relations in various government circles and delegated them the task of exploiting their contacts according to a carefully charted plan of action. We decided to work on a number of fronts:

1. The community associations and unions of rabbis would submit memoranda to the President.

2. An appeal would be submitted to all economic institutions, stressing the damage that would be caused the Slovak economy if reckless and hasty removal of manpower from all areas were implemented.

3. An appeal would be submitted to the clerical leadership and the Christian orders, requesting their intervention for humanitarian reasons, to prevent untold suffering and disintegration of family life and to protect the rights of man.

The committee delegated me to submit the memorandum to the President in the name of the rabbis of Slovakia.

To work effectively we required information on the government's secret resolutions, but our intelligence resources were as yet undeveloped. In the context of his work in the Jewish Center, Steiner had managed to establish contacts and good relations with the circles involved in planning the operation. He reported to us on developments and on every stage of preparation, which was proceeding apace in the 14th Department of the Ministry of Interior. Jewish clerks from the statistics department of the Jewish Center had been transferred to the staff of the 14th Department to expedite the work. The danger mounted from day to day.

On February 27, 1942, I had an interview with Minister Jozef Sivák, in which I learned many details. I realized that the situation was extremely grave: they wished to wipe us out. The Slovaks, of all people – a nation with a Christian tradition – had decided to bring calamity upon us and destroy us. The minister revealed to me that the decision to deport the Jews had been made in a conversation between Prime Minister Dr. Vojtech Tuka and German Ambassador and Advisor to the Slovak Government on Jewish Affairs SS Hauptsturmführer Dieter Wisliceny.

Sivák's disclosure shook me to the core. Tears burst from my eyes; I could not retain my composure. The minister was also choked with emotion and, so he said, even wished he could help; however, all affairs of the Jews were under the jurisdiction of the Minister of Interior, who was of the same mind as Tuka that Slovakia must be "cleansed" of Jews. Sivák was at a loss to suggest an indirect contact or means of exerting influence on these persons. I entreated him, saying I could not leave his office with empty hands, that the committee of six had not lost hope or given up its expectations of tangible assistance from the sympathetic Minister of Education. Was the government aware, I asked, that transporting ninety thousand despairing people, innocent of any crime, in time of war, to a ravaged country suffering under a hostile regime, meant utter ruin? After further thought the minister advised me to turn to Mrs. Baleg, the owner of the pharmacy in Bánovce, who was often visited by President Tiso. Perhaps she would be able to persuade him to grant me a secret interview. He also recommended appealing to the head of the Jesuit order, the President's confessor, and to the Papal nuncio, the representative of the Vatican. After this conversation, which lasted two hours, I hastened to report to the committee of six.

Oscar Horvát, one of the leaders of the Nové Mesto Jewish community, also attended the committee meeting, at which I reported everything without embellishment. My voice was choked with emotion. We all were moved to tears. For the first time I saw Dr. Winterstein, strong man that he was, crying as well. His response shall remain engraved in my heart forever: "Full of dread, I awaited the Rabbi's report; 1 had hoped he would speak with the optimism which has always characterized him; but now we have heard that the situation is extremely grave and that we must redouble our efforts and take action without a moment's delay!"

II. Appeals to Church Leaders and the President

We agreed that the following day, the Sabbath, I would go with the Jewish Elder to the head of the Jesuit order in Slovakia, who was in constant touch with the Vatican. He received us cordially, and after opening remarks by the Elder, who rambled aimlessly, his words developing into a pointless discussion of theological problems of the Church, I took the floor and addressed the issue of the danger hanging over us and requested that the priest intercede on our behalf with the President and the Vatican. I asked him to consider the problem from the angle of a Catholic Christian. As an officer of the Church, he certainly could judge the significance of the Inquisition in the history of Christianity. So many apologetics were published in an attempt to cleanse the Church of this dark blot; and now a state which is based on the Christian tradition has arisen, a state which could have been a pride and glory to this tradition, but instead, by abusing the Jews and expelling them, is likely now, in the twentieth century, to renew the blot of the Inquisition. My words apparently had a strong impact on him. He sent a special emissary to Rome with a detailed report, and instructions came back from there to the nuncio. We rejoiced. A ray of hope sparked in our hearts. We hoped that the intercession of the Catholic Church would have an effect. This, however, proved a short-lived illusion. The nuncio was coolly received by the Prime Minister and presented him the stand of the Holy See and his request. Dr. Tuka's answer was brief and adamant: no intervention in the internal affairs of Slovakia. The Vatican responded by recalling its nuncio to Rome. Favorable to us as this gesture of protest may have been, it did not suffice to avert the evil decree.

Various bishops and heads of orders and abbeys were approached by other important persons, but they all turned the supplicants back empty - handed and did not even issue one sympathetic epistle on the subject. Their evasive responses were a disappointment to us all. The official senior clergy, the leaders of the Catholic Church in Slovakia, did nothing on our behalf. I approached the Evangelist bishop, Dr. Osuský, in his private apartment in Bratislava and requested him to exert influence on the Evangelist minister of defense, General Čatloš, to oppose expulsion of the Jews, also so that the manpower who were eligible for the draft not be reduced. The courteous bishop listened to what I had to say with great interest and responded that he personally was opposed to all religious discrimination, to any law which drew a distinction between one man and another; but that as an Evangelist bishop, lacking any political influence, he was not able to bring us deliverance. Moreover, so he said, he had no contact with General Čatloš, did not know him personally, and could not make me any promises in this regard. He advised me not to waste my efforts appealing to the clergy, who would not save us and would not lift a finger, but said we would do better to appeal to political bodies, since the problem of the Jews was a political problem. Developments proved him right. Although there were some liberal and tolerant clergymen who were willing to help us, such as Father Pozdech of Bratislava, the religious establishment in Slovakia remained either hostile or at best indifferent.

Thus, we launched intensive activity in the offices of the government, despite the secret police, who embarked on a policy of harassment and molestation, which started on the Sabbath of the special scriptural reading (preceding Purim and commemorating the Jews' victory over tyrants who sought to wipe them out): "Remember what Amalek did unto thee" (February 28, 1942).

After the two federations of Jewish communities submitted their memorandum to the President, a hunt for the authors was initiated on the pretext that the memorandum had been reproduced without advance permission. Dr. Winterstein was arrested and the offices of the Yeshurun federation were searched. When nothing was found, he was released. The memorandum had been reproduced by Salomon Gross' son, Andy. As soon as the Sabbath drew to a close, I hastened over to Andy in Trnava to coordinate things with him and brief him in the event that he might be interrogated.

On March 1, 1942, I went to Bánovce. My first stop was the home of the leader of the Jewish community, Ernst Munk. I disclosed the purpose of my visit to him: an interview with the President. A courageous under - taking, he said, and wished me success.

Dr. Tiso's mother lived in the town of Velká Bytča. After many entreaties and supplications, the leaders of the Jewish community obtained an important letter from her to the President, in which, so they said, she requested her son to prevent the expulsion of the Jews. The President loves his mother dearly and will do whatever she asks, the naive Jews added. I took the letter to present it as a recommendation and give regards from his mother. However, I did not know what was written in it and was full of misgivings. Mrs. Munk offered me a room to rest in. It was then that I transgressed a ban of Rabbenu Gershom and opened the letter and read it. This is what it said: "My dear son, the Jews leave me no rest, but continually exhort me, crying and requesting that I write to you. Therefore, I am writing: Do as you wish and as you see fit. If you are able to and so desire, help them. Do not be angry at me for writing you this, but they would not leave me alone the entire day and begged that I write to you. Kisses, yours, Mother and Father." This was the important letter which reputedly was to help the Jews. I ripped it up and destroyed it.

The time came for me to call on Mrs. Baleg, the pharmacist. She received me according to the laws of etiquette, and when I began talking about the subject for which I had come, she showed understanding and good will and promised to relay my wishes. She suggested that I return for another talk in the afternoon. I did as she said, and the conversation was to the point and quite long. In Bratislava the Jews impatiently awaited my return. R. Raphael Levy of Bardejov, a wise and devoted man, greeted me with the words: "The eyes of all Israel are upon thee."[18] I reported in detail on my conversation, and we agreed that I should submit a memorandum in the name of the rabbis. At the appointed time, Sunday, the 19th of Adar (March 8, 1942), in Bánovce, I submitted the following memorandum to the President:

Bratislava
March 6, 1942

His Excellency
President of the Republic of Slovakia

---

[18] Kings I 1:20. Translator's note.

Bratislava

In deep distress we, the rabbis of the Jewish communities of Slovakia, turn to you, Mr. President, as the religious leader, as the supreme judge and legislator of this state, in supplication. We have heard the terrible tidings, although not yet officially confirmed, that offices of the government are planning to expel the Jews, men separately and women separately, to countries further east. This decree, which under the law can be given any name and can be accounted for by any motives and justifications, under the present circumstances is tantamount to the physical annihilation of the Jews of Slovakia.

In despair we cry out to you, Mr. President, the supreme judge of this state, confident that His Honor, as well, believes in the Supreme Judge who is above him, and as servants of Almighty God we humbly request in our straits: hear our voices and answer us, for we are in great distress. Did not one God create us, and do we not all owe a final accounting to Him? Have mercy on us, on our families, on our wives, on our men, our children and our elderly, who pour out their hearts with tears and pray to our Father in Heaven for salvation. Hoping for His mercy, we place our fate in your hands.

For many years now we have been persecuted by the heavy hand of the law. Believing ourselves innocent of any crime, for two thousand years we have silently born our suffering, born the heavy yoke of a life of hardship, of attacks on our honor, our property, our health, without crying out. But such a harsh decree, so unjust and cruel as the one which threatens to descend on us, strikes fear and terror in our hearts; and eighty thousand Jews cry out in mortal dread for aid and deliverance, for such calamity as this has not befallen us in the thousands of years of our existence.

Mr. President, tens of thousands of Jews will make do with the meagre bread that they earn by the sweat of their brow and by any hard labor that be required of them, but we entreat you, Mr. President, let these poor people live and remain with their families, in their homes.

"Before the Lord, for He is come to judge the earth; He will judge the world with righteousness, and the peoples with equity,"[19] we, too, entreat you, Mr. President, Father and servant of God, please harken to the voice of the eighty thousand miserable beings who fear for their lives and the lives of their dear ones.

Most respectfully
yours,A. Frieder In the
name of the Rabbis of Slovakia

I thought that on reading these words, written from the heart, even a person with a heart of stone would be moved. But regretfully, I did not leave from the interview with the President with the feeling that my words had touched his heart or were likely to change anything.[20]

The following day, March 9, 1942, at the meeting of the Working

---

[19] Psalms 98:9. Translator's note.

[20] Rabbi Frieder's sense of discretion, perhaps also. his disappointment, prompted him to refrain from recording details about the course of his unofficial interview.

Group, I reported to my colleagues on the situation, and on March 11, I requested an interview with Minister of Education Sivák. However, when I realized that all our efforts were coming to naught, I returned to work within the community, after an absence of close to a fortnight. During these days, of course, anyone who thought he might be effective at averting the decree volunteered his services. Such thorough work was done that Dr. Koso, Director of the Ministry of Interior, remarked that he had never witnessed such rapid and extensive organizational action, involving so many eminent people – politicians, economists, and other influential persons from all walks of life. But all was in vain. The Jews' ill-wishers had the upper hand. Any hope of the decree being reversed proved false.

III. Prayer and Fasting to Avert the Decree

On Thursday, the 23rd of Adar (March 12, 1942), I returned home from Bratislava early, for that day had been proclaimed a public fast day. Between the afternoon and evening services I addressed hundreds of fasting congregants. I advised the youth to marry, because single women would be the first to be expelled. The public notary made it possible for me to issue official marriage certificates forthwith, and from Friday to Sunday I held 45 wedding ceremonies for young couples. A large number of them were saved from death. I also announced an important sermon which I would deliver in the synagogue on the Sabbath of *Parashat ha-hodesh* (preceding or coinciding with the 1st of Nisan, the month of Passover), which fell on March 14, 1942. I knew that it would be hard to speak in public, before a large audience, for although people were already talking in the streets about expulsion, officially it was still a secret and discussion of the subject was forbidden, since this would arouse panic in time of war. Nevertheless, I felt that it was my moral obligation to counsel people how to act and what to do in the face of coming developments.

I was fully aware of the likely consequences of my sermon, but decided nevertheless to take the risk and speak out, for the threat to life was imminent and the sacrifices which would be exacted from the public would be great. Deeply troubled and full of anxiety, the public awaited this Sabbath. Before the *musaf* service the synagogue was packed tight; more people had come than for the *Kol Nidre* service. A rush of emotion seized me as I walked up to the pulpit, making it hard for me to begin my speech. This, I felt, was the last time I would address this large audience; yet I took control of myself and said:

> "I have called you together to talk with you, with all the tribes of Israel – Priests, Levites, and Israelites – who all stand on a single foundation: the Torah. The letter *shin* which stands out on the phylacteries placed on the forehead has three crowns, resting on a single base. But on the other side of the phylacteries the *shin* has a fourth crown, also attached to the common base. We have mentioned three tribes, but there is another tribe which has left the common base, has run away from it, has disowned it. These are the converts away from Judaism, of whom it is said: "A Jew, even if he has transgressed, remains a Jew." This time we have all one thing in common; we are all Jews, with one law and one decree threatening us all. It is this decree which I wish to talk about, this decree of the government to deport the Jews to Poland. Jewish leaders from all circles have tried to avert this evil decree, but to no avail. Since I see no chance of reversing the decision, we must know that we are facing one of the more difficult periods in our history, a new chapter in the annals of expulsions of the Jews. This time, however, we shall be expelled as

slaves to a foreign land, and who knows if we shall return and see our loved ones again. To begin with, we shall lose our daughters, and after them, our sons. As families are broken apart, the rest – men, women, and children – will be deported, as well. More than once have the nations of the world sought to destroy us, to annihilate us by expelling us from one exile to a more difficult exile, fraught with danger. What did our forefathers do before they went into exile? I shall read you from a history book (at which point I opened the prayer book and pretended to read): They tried to flee to neighboring countries where this danger did not threaten, they hid, they went underground and disappeared, they did not register in any census and did not report to any authorities; they hid silver and gold, jewelry, precious stones, and diamonds in their clothes, in their shoes, in their housewares. They tried to find protection and obtain exemption from the decree, or slipped away from joining those going to the vail of grief. They did all they could to transfer their wealth into light-weight, valuable, movable possessions, to support them in their hour of need. If we have learned to understand the past, let us make inferences regarding the present. It appears that those who crossed the borders to the nearest country did best. My dear ones! Perhaps you do not fathom my words; perhaps I have caused you heartbreak; perhaps your illusions have been dashed by the bleak picture which I have presented you. But this is how I perceive the situation and the hopelessness of our position. You might say: No law has been issued yet, no regulation or directive; it is inconceivable that this will happen to us. Would that I be mistaken, would that I be proven wrong. Act prudently, and instead of criticizing, take action today and tomorrow! We are speaking of saving lives, saving human beings. He who saves one Jewish life is as if he had saved an entire world. Perhaps it is decreed from Heaven that it be impossible to save the commonality – therefore, save yourselves, each and every individual. I have said trying things this Sabbath, after the blessing for the new month, perhaps for the last time in this synagogue. "I call heaven and earth to witness against you this day, that I have set before thee life and death, the blessing and the curse; therefore, choose life, that thou mayest live, thou and thy seed" (Deuteronomy 30:19). Therefore, choose life – follow the path of salvation and redemption, for life and not, God forbid, for death; for a blessing and not a curse. Fathers and sons, my pupils and my teachers – if you be fated to walk along a way full of obstacles, stumbling blocks and injuries, along the road of harsh exile, may the Omnipresent have mercy on you and guard you against all hardship and suffering, and save you from all pestilence and illness, and may you be blessed with the priestly benediction: May God bless you and keep you..."

The congregation rose and, with tears in their eyes, received my blessing, many of them perhaps for the last time. Overwrought and depressed, they left the synagogue, many of them with harsh criticism on their tongues, displeased with the hard things I had said and which I ought not to have known, ought not to have uttered. They were of the opinion that my duty was to assuage people, not to reveal the bitter truth. Despite these differences of opinion, I felt satisfaction at having had the fortitude and strength to reveal that which I knew, to give my congregants guidance and perhaps even save some of them from death.

I invited the rabbis of the Yeshurun congregations to Nové Mesto for Sunday March 15, 1942, to report on the situation and discuss our present and future plans for work in the community. The meeting was attended by rabbis Dr. Eliezer Schweiger from Nitra, Dr. Armin Dušinský from Trnava, Pinchas Keller from Trenčin, Israel Berkovič from Ilava, and the *dayyan* Deutsch from Liptovský-Svätý-Mikuláš. After the report I requested that the rabbis warn the public of the imminent calamity; we must give them advice and guidance, and do everything possible to save whomever we could, following the example I set in my own congregation. The rabbis listened in trepidation to my candid remarks, without expressing their approval; perhaps they lacked the courage to accept my suggestions. The meeting proved a disappointment. I was sorry to behold aging and weary spiritual leaders, failing to stand up to the test of the hard times. That Sunday I performed weddings for fifteen young couples. Addressing all the couples together, again I pointed out the gravity of the situation and reiterated my advice concerning our future. Thank God, I was able to save some young people from being among the first deported.

* * *

On Monday, March 16, 1942, I went to Bratislava. I told my colleagues in the Working Group of my activities in the community, and they agreed with everything I had done. At six p.m. I officiated at the wedding of my sister-in-law, Margareta Berl, to Rudolph Spielman in the Great Synagogue on Jews' Street in Bratislava. At seven p.m. we sat down in my father-in-law's house for a modest wedding dinner. At eight o'clock we were taken by surprise by a young man who entered and asked: "Is Mr. Frieder here?" I arose and identified myself. He immediately identified himself, as well, as a secret policeman and led me off to the police station. Here my personal data was taken down, and, without a word being said to me, I was put into cell 16. The police escorted me down four stories, where I was received by a bald man with a raging countenance, who shouted and hurled curses at me and took all my personal effects, even my eyeglasses and suspenders.

IV. Under Arrest

According to my fellow inmates in cell 16, I entered the place with a sense of calm. Here I found a motley crew: four men suspected of being communists and three suspected of engaging in terrorist activity. I was the eighth detainee. One of the eight was a Jew by the name of Brunner who had been in prison for eight months and had not yet been interrogated. We talked all night long, and although the wooden planks of the bed were downright painful, I managed to bear up. I saw to it that my wife not be overwrought. I thought with concern about my public work. What charges were being brought against me? I firmly resolved to take all responsibility upon myself and not involve another soul, be he Jew or Christian. Another day and night elapsed. Meanwhile I waited, wondering anxiously what crime I had committed, wherein I had sinned. It was not until the afternoon of Wednesday, March 18, that I was brought in for interrogation. The session lasted four hours. At first, I was treated with unbridled contempt, but as the investigation continued, I managed to mollify the interrogator's gruffness, and he lowered his voice. Many hard questions were thrown at me: How did I know about the deportations? Who had revealed the information? What was the meaning of so many marriages? Why had I aroused nervousness and panic in my public addresses? Why my frequent trips to Bratislava?

What did I do in Bánovce? Whom have the Jews bribed? Whom had I bought off, and at what price? And many more questions in a cross-examination whose purpose was to confuse me and expose inconsistencies in my account. To begin with I proclaimed that I felt no guilt and that what I had done had been within the context of my duty as a rabbi and Jewish leader. My people were in danger, and it was only natural to take action to rescue them. I, too, did nothing more than perform my duty without transgressing the laws of the state. This activity calls for frequent trips, lobbying, and talks in various offices. Most of his query I answered in the negative: no bribes were given, and nobody would have accepted one. Money cannot solve such a problem. If we could but cancel the decree, we would be willing to place all our belongings at the disposal of the authorities in a legal manner. I learned of the deportations from the Jewish Center; I had been informed of them in my capacity as a representative of the Yeshurun federation of Jewish communities.

Tired and drained, I returned to my cell. Some new detainees had arrived in the meantime. Unlike us, however, they had not been arrested by the Center for State Security, but had been brought in by the police for minor felonies. By then we were ten. It was heartening to know that I was under arrest as a Jew who was working faithfully for the weal of his community. For the sake of the Jewish people, for love of the Jews, I was willing to suffer even a period of arrest. My only concern was for my family, for during the interrogation they had threatened to arrest my family and relatives.

On Thursday, March 19, more detainees arrived. It was a Christian holiday, and some people had been arrested for disturbing the peace. One of them, named Mach, a barber by profession, said he had read in the paper that the rabbi of Nové Mesto had been arrested on charges of disseminating false rumors and engaging in subversive activity against the state. I introduced myself and asked him to tell me more, but he had nothing to add. I wanted to know what charges were being brought against me.

On the morrow, Friday, I was interrogated again and reconfirmed my previous testimony and deposition. Threats were made to transfer me to the Ilava prison. That Friday a Jew who had been arrested in the passport office was brought wailing into our cell. He was Mr. Zobel from Nitra, a well-informed man who told me about the great excitement my arrest had caused among the Jews. Further, he told me that my wife was in Bratislava and, along with all my friends, was working for my release. As several details were clarified, I became somewhat reassured. I was confident that my friends would do everything possible to obtain my release. In general, the mood in the cell was good. I was well liked by my fellows because I gave them hope and good humor. I was also in a position to help them. I received food from outside and could share some of it among them. Meanwhile four more Jews were put under arrest – clerks from the statistics department of the Jewish Center, who were temporarily employed in the 14th Department of the Ministry of Interior and had been arrested when they tried to conceal their files. They informed me about what was going on in the outside world. Saturday and Sunday passed without incident. On Monday morning, March 23, eight more Jews were brought into our cell. They were prisoners from Ilava[21] who were destined for deportation in the first shipments. This was quite a distressing shock. It had been a trying day. The devils were carrying out their villainous designs!

That Monday I realized that all our work had been in vain. The demoniacal dance had begun. The goose-steppers were continuing their foul deeds, taking our men, the best of our youth. Strong young

---

[21] The Ilava prison generally held political prisoners, among them many Jews.

men, the pride of our people, were taken as sacrifices; masses of the sons of Abraham were bound to the altar. I lost control of myself. On Tuesday night I had a nightmare which made me go wild. In my dream I saw my wife dressed in black, looking pale and depressed. With tears gushing from her eyes, she handed me a 50-kilogram bundle, the amount of possessions each deportee was permitted to take, for I was to join the Ilava inmates and be deported with them to Poland. I screamed in terror until the fellow beside me in the cell awakened me.

Tuesday, March 24, my interrogation continued. It was intimated that if I would reveal several things I would be released. Therefore, they were giving me time to think and advised me to give precedence to my own affairs and the affairs of my family over everything else. I remained silent, making no response. Worried and downcast, I returned to my cell. This cell, which was designed for six, now had 24 inmates. There was no room to turn around and no possibility of lying down on the boards.

Before noon the following day, Wednesday, I was interrogated again, and at four p.m., after 9 days of detention, I was released. Immediately I telephoned my wife, who was overjoyed. By six o'clock I had consulted with the Working Group and by 8 o'clock I was on my way home. Dreams, it is said, do not speak the truth; but, as my friends confirmed, at home I found out that there was an underlying element of truth in my dream. Indeed, plans had been made to deport me and orders had already been given to my wife to prepare me a package of 50 kg. of personal effects. How joyously surprised everyone was that instead of being sent to the gathering point at the Sered camp and from there on to Poland, I arrived home, back into the lap of my family and my community. From the beginning, it turned out, orders for my arrest had been sent to the Nové Mesto police, with instructions to bring me to the ill-famed Ilava prison. In my absence, my wife had been summoned to the police station and had given my address in Bratislava. Had I been found at home I would have been taken to Ilava and would surely have been up for deportation in one of the first transports. Divine providence willed that I not be taken, so that I could help my people in their distress, in whatever way possible. I secretly vowed to devote my life to assisting my people, helping those who had already been deported to Poland and those who were still here with us. I prayed that I would have the good fortune to survive and keep my vow, to do all that I had taken upon myself. The other inmates in my cell, too, were heartened by my release; my family and parents were overjoyed, and many members of my congregation lent expression to their happiness in "rejoice in trembling." The head of the congregation wished to compose a special benediction, to be sung by cantor Salomon in the synagogue. My mother wrote me an emotional letter, which my father signed with the traditional blessing, "May God grant you peace."

V. "Like sheep to the slaughter"

I was distressed and grieved to learn that during the short duration of my arrest the first stage of deportations had been carried out. On Saturday, the 3rd of Nisan (March 21, 1942), 110 men were taken from my congregation, three days later another four, and on the morrow, Wednesday, March 25, 1942, the day I was released from detention, six doctors were taken. These 120 people were taken to the deportation camp in Žilina, which had been set up in addition to the camps in Sered and Nováky. From there they were shipped across the border, under inhuman conditions. The Special Services Section *(Oddelenie pre Zvláštné úkony)* of the Jewish Center, headed by Karl Hochberg, came into operation and had a marked impact. Photographs have captured scenes of the roll-call of the candidates for deportation and preserved them for posterity. Jewish and non-Jewish officers decided how many people would be deported and selected the specific persons. Where to, and why? These questions had no answer. The Jewish officers selected a thousand victims. Each was allowed to take 50 kg. of personal effects. In a preliminary check of the deportees the Huns took away their valuables and helped themselves to anything else which they fancied. Bundles in hand and sacks over their shoulders, the deportees marched along, as dozens of police and armed Hlinka Guards stood over them and goaded with sticks those who lagged behind, unable to keep up the rapid pace to the train station. Thus, under heavy guard, decent, upright human beings marched heroically, heads held high, towards their bitter fate. All were taken – the sick and the healthy, whether or not they held protection papers which were supposed to exempt them from the decree of banishment. No exceptions were made.

Freight cars intended for livestock – cars without windows, toilets, or running water – awaited them at the train station. Forty people were packed into a car, along with two pails, one for tending to one's needs, the other for water. Thus, they traveled packed together, men and women, elderly, children and babes, in conditions of terrible crowding. To work – that was what they generally said. The cars were locked shut, and only near the exit could the exiles breathe a bit of fresh air. A Jewish doctor, also a deportee, traveled with them, shut up in one of the cars. This was the "medical service" for a thousand people, including babies of one week and elderly of 95 years. Thus, the Children of Israel journeyed from the exile of Slovakia to another, more difficult exile. And these were the deportations which left Slovakia in March 1942[22]:

Transport I – 8th of Nisan (March 26), young girls aged
   16 and up were deported from the gathering point at

---

[22] The details of the deportations are based on notes in the diaries of Rabbi Frieder.

Poprad.

Transport 2 – 9th of Nisan (March 27), young men and doctors were deported from the deportation camp at Žilina.

Shipment 3 – On *Shabbat ha-Gadol* (the Sabbath preceding Passover), 10th of Nisan (March 28), young girls were deported from the Patronka gathering point in Bratislava.

Transport 4 – 12th of Nisan (March 30), men and boys from the Sered camp were deported.

Transport 5 – 13th of Nisan (March 31), men and boys from the Nováky camp were deported.

Inside of a week, around 5,000 young men and women, the future of Slovak Jewry, were shipped off and had disappeared; no one knew where they had been taken, where they were, or what fate had befallen them. Only later did we find out that the young women reached Auschwitz and the young men were taken to the vicinity of Lublin.

Among the exiles were 120 men from Nové Mesto, who had been taken, as I mentioned earlier, while I was under arrest. Two days after my release, on March 27, 1942, the decree fell on the young women. One hundred and twenty young women from our community were on the list of candidates for deportation. The list was sent from Bratislava, and its implementation was entrusted to the Hlinka Guard. The task of rounding up people for the transport, or the hunt – *Chytačka* – as we later called it, was directed by the District Commissioner. I had connections with both bodies. Thus, when the circular instructing these bodies to carry out the deportation reached me, I managed to interpret its clauses in such a way to have only 27, instead of 120, girls sent to the Patronka gathering point. This was some consolation. We did our utmost to make it easier for the girls; still, it was like a funeral for the living. The same day another ten men were sent from our city to Sered. All in all, the number of Jewish souls leaving Nové Mesto in March came to 203. It broke everyone's spirit; yet this was only the beginning.

Deportations in April

April was an especially sad month for the Jews of central Slovakia. In 15 transports, 15,899 Jews were deported. A new procedure was now instituted in the deportation campaign. The 14th Department sent experts to the large communities to be in charge of rounding up transports there. Jews from neighboring towns, as well, were brought to these concentration points, and from there were sent in freight cars directly to Poland. Only a few were sent to Žilina to stand in reserve to fill out the shipments, each of which numbered a thousand or more human beings. Deportations were accelerated and executed in great haste. The Special Services Section of the Jewish Center, headed by Karl Hochberg, made its contribution to expediting the transports by dedicatedly preparing precise statistical data for the German adviser. I was opposed to such exaggerated obedience to the directives of the Jewish Center. Consequently, a controversy erupted between myself and the head of the Jewish Center's branch office in Nové Mesto, for I refused to comply with his orders to carry out meticulously the directives he received from Bratislava.

On the intervening Sabbath of Passover, April 4, 1942, the local authorities submitted questionnaires to the branch office of the Jewish Center, adding the urgent directive that all the Jews in the city must fill out the forms immediately. I understood that the questionnaires were for the purpose of deportation and advised people to refrain from filling them out. The chairman of the local Jewish Center maintained that he was responsible for execution of the instructions; hence the bone of contention between us. Those who listened to me remained in Nové Mesto, for it turned out that the questionnaires that were handed in were tantamount to death sentences; based on them troops were sent from house to house, rounding up people for deportation. On the eve of Passover (April 1, 1942), 29 males were collected in Nové Mesto. On the morrow, the first day of Passover, another 30 men were rounded up, and the Sabbath, April 11, the eighth day of Passover, 341 people were deported – entire families, including children over 16 years of age. Dr. Anton Vašek, the new supervisor of the 14th Department, instituted this new procedure in which entire families were deported.

The large deportation from Nové Mesto and its environs

The most terrible period for our city began on April 23, 1942 (7th of Iyar, 5702). That day a group of people arrived in Nové Mesto and, on the basis of the questionnaires the Jews had been required to fill out, methodically set about rounding up entire families, from young to old. The large scale rounding up of 679 human beings from Nové Mesto and the surrounding area lasted until April 26. The victims were joined by families from the cities of Pieštany and Hlohovec, bringing the total to 1,004 men, women and children, young and old, who were sent directly by freight train from the Nové Mesto station to Opole, Poland. The organizers who had come from Bratislava were headed by Sharführer SS Slavik, a specialist from the 14th Department, the notary Záberecký, the commander of the Gendarmes, and six Hlinka Guard troopers from the Patronka camp. Six men had also come from the Special Services Section of the Jewish Center, and were joined on the last day by the notorious department head, Hochberg. Hauptsturmführer Wisliceny also arrived before the deportation to receive a report from Hochberg and see to it that the campaign was proceeding as planned.

For four days we all lived as if in a concentration camp. We saw to it that food and supplies were provided for a thousand people, including Jews from the neighboring cities. During these difficult days the head of the local office of the Jewish Center disappeared, as did the Secretary, and did not return to Nové Mesto until six weeks later. I remained alone to see to the enormous task of providing aid. Wherever there was hope of liberating people or of aiding unfortunate souls and alleviating their plight, I tried to intervene. I established an operation headquarters of brave souls, most notably Arthur Marmorstein, and Ilka Horvát and Ella Hammer. I organized a steward service which helped the people greatly. The primary mission which I undertook was to save the largest number of people possible and to rescue entire families, on any pretext or excuse. Thus, I managed to rescue over seventy human beings from the ranks of the deported. Here I became acquainted with the nature of the work being done by the Special Services Section of the Jewish Center. I learned from experience that one must be daring and attempt every possible method of rescue – lobbying, persuasion, prudence, and even trickery. Our work during the difficult days of the large deportation amazed even some of the local Hlinka Guard. I worked three days and nights in the temporary concentration camp in Tauber House, the former malt factory. With the assistance of the dedicated Working Group, we handed out one thousand packages, worth 54 korunas each. From here on in I began to develop connections with other public figures in the local government. In the chairman's absence I essentially ran the affairs of the Jews in the city.

As the number of Jews living in outlying cities diminished, Augustin Morávek, head of the Central Office for Economy, dismantled most of the branch offices of the Jewish Center, leaving only a few offices in the larger cities such as Trnava, Nitra, Trenčín, and Prešov. We were attached to the neighboring city of Trenčín, and I was appointed to the board of directors of the branch office as the representative from Nové Mesto.

The following deportations left Slovakia in April 1942:

15th of Nisan – 1st day of Pass over (April 2)	Patronka to Auschwitz, 1,000 people.
16th of Nisan – 2nd day of Pass over (April 3)	Poprad to Auschwitz, 1,000 people.
18th of Nisan (April 5)	Žilina to the vicinity of Lublin, 1,495 people.
25th of Nisan (April 12)	From Trnava, 1,040 people.
26th of Nisan (April 13)	Sered to Auschwitz, 1,000 people.
27th, 28th of Nisan, 3rd of Iyar	Three transports from Nitra to Lublin,
(April 14, 16, and 20)	Lubartów, and Rejowiec, totaling 3,039 people.

30th of Nisan (April 17)	Žilina to Auschwitz, 1,000 people.
2nd of Iyar (April 19)	Žilina to Auschwitz, 1,030 people.
5th of Iyar (April 22)	Sered to Opole, 1,000 people.
6th of Iyar (April 23)	Poprad to Auschwitz, 1,000 people.
7th of Iyar (April 24)	Žilina to Auschwitz, 1,251 people.
10th of Iyar (April 27)	Nové Mesto to Opole, 1,004 people.
12th of Iyar (April 29)	Žilina to Auschwitz, 1,040 people.

The total came to 15,899 human beings. Among the people in the transport from Trnava were my sister Ethel Esther Malka, her husband Ernst Klein, and their daughter Judith, may the Lord avenge their blood.

Deportations in May

In the month of May the Nazi henchmen brought disaster on eastern Slovakia, an area with a very dense Jewish population, where many helpless victims lived in poverty and hardship. In eighteen transports 18,898 human beings were deported, among them some of the people's finest rabbis, scholars, and religious figures. Hard days were upon us, days of mourning. We not only counted the days of the *Omer* (49 days counted from Passover to the Feast of Weeks), but also the thousands of deportees who were sent from rounding up points to the land of doom:

18th of Iyar – Lag ba-Omer (May 5)	Trebišov to Lublin and Lubartów, 1,038 people.
19th, 20th, 21st of Iyar (May 6, 7, 8)	Three transports from Michalovče to Luków and to Miedzyrzec Podlaski, 3,050 people.
25th of Iyar (May 12)	Humené to Chelm, 1,002 people. The same day a transport also left Žilinafor Chelm with 1,040 people

26th, 27th of Iyar, 7th of Sivan (May 13, 14, 23)	Prešov to Deblin and Rejowiec, 3,090 people.
1st, 2nd, 8th of Sivan (May 17, 18, 24)	Bardejov[23] to Pulawy Nalesz6w and Rejowiec, 3,015 people.
3rd of Sivan (May 19)	Vranov to Opole, 1,001 people. edzilaborce to Pulawy, 1,630 people.
9th, 14th of Sivan (May 25, 30)	Poprad to Rejowiec, to Lublin and to Sobibór, 2,000 people.
10th of Sivan (May 26)	Žilina to Opole, 1,032 people.

---

[23] The leader of the Bardejov Jewish community, R. Raphael Levi, by a courageous stratagem succeeded in saving his congregation from being exiled in the first transports by claiming that a plague endangering the entire area had broken out in their midst. During the quarantine which was put on the city many Jews were rescued. When the Secret Police discovered what had been done, the leader of the community was arrested and deported in the first transport, without any possibility of saving him from deportation. Thus, an active community leader, who had also served on the board of the Central Orthodox Bureau, met a martyr's death.

13th of Sivan (May 29)

Spišská
Nová Ves
to Lublin
and Izbica,
1,000
people.

Appointment of national chief rabbis

Organizational changes and new directives came at a fast and furious pace during these days of emergency. The authorities passed a regulation protecting the chief rabbis of Slovakia's capital, who were also to serve as national rabbis of the state, against deportation. This referred to the chief rabbi of the Orthodox congregations and the chief rabbi of the "status quo ante" and neologist congregations, which were united in the Yeshurun Federation. *Gaon* Rabbi Samuel David Ungar, president of the rabbinical court in Nitra, was elected national chief rabbi of the Orthodox community and I was elected national chief rabbi of the Yeshurun congregations. Prior to this, on the 25th of Nisan (April 12, 1942), I had been elected Chief Rabbi of the Yeshurun congregation in Bratislava.

This important and hasty appointment, ratified by all the governmental authorities and Jewish institutions, was made thanks to the energetic activities of Dr. Winterstein and the intercession of Dr. Tibor Kováč, who obtained the necessary papers for the two rabbis from the commissioner of the 14th Department.

The law on forced emigration of Jews

While the deportations were in full swing, after approximately 40,000 Jews had been deported, on May 15 the Parliament of the

Slovak Republic passed Basic Law 68/42 on "Compulsory Exile of Jews," under which Jews could be ordered to emigrate from Slovakia. The following exceptions were made:

1. Whoever belonged to a Christian sect before March 14, 1939.

2. Whoever married a non-Jew prior to September 10, 1941.

3. Whomever the President exempted and granted immunity, and whomever an authorized office gave a temporary permit to continue being active in public or economic life.

The same special privileges were extended to spouses and minors of exempted persons, and in certain instances even to their parents. The law also stipulated that Jews who leave the soil of Slovakia shall lose their citizenship and their property shall be expropriated for the benefit of the state.

Only one representative in Parliament voted against this law in which anti-Jewish legislation reached its peak. The law made it possible for Jews to be uprooted by use of force and essentially constituted a death verdict for tens of thousands of Slovak Jews. After Jews were expelled, the rabble turned to plundering their property, which disappeared over night from the Jews' apartments, even when locked and bolted. And the fascist, Christian-clerical regime granted these acts legal sanction.

The law gave government offices the right to issue certificates of protection against expulsion. The Ministry of Education and Culture was placed over the Jewish communities and by its authority could grant such certificates to holders of offices in the Jewish communities, thus preventing their expulsion. This offered another way of saving hundreds of Jews, and henceforth this activity occupied the two Jewish community organizations.

* * *

Upon publication of the law on compulsory emigration I requested an interview with Minister of Education Jozef Sivák. At first, he was completely unaware that he had the authority to grant papers of protection from concentration and deportation, but after closely reading the law, he immediately agreed to consider the matter. In our conversation we reached an accord that in small communities three or four office-holders would receive such documents, and in larger communities five documents would be issued. Žilina was given seven and Bratislava ten documents. In addition, we found a way to exempt from expulsion beadles and women active in the Jewish burial society, *mohalim* (sing. *mohel*, men who perform ritual circumcision) and scribes, and around twenty Jewish teachers. In this respect the law was issued too late, for we had already lost many rabbis, cantors, *shohatim* and public servants who could have been saved. Nevertheless, this was a small but significant deliverance, for it enabled us to save many people engaged in community work and to assure the continued functioning of the Jewish community. The boards of the Jewish communities were delegated to choose the candidates for immunity papers, no outside interference was allowed, and the papers were issued solely on the basis of the boards' recommendations. In this way I was privileged to help save many lives.

As far as the legislators were concerned, Jews holding protection papers from economic offices were more vital and important. This led us to fear that the local authorities, being evil, would take a hard line and not always acknowledge the validity of the exempting documents held by the workers of the Jewish communities. Therefore, in a subsequent interview with the Minister of Education and Culture, I requested that every time a proposal to rescind a document exempting its holder from deportation was put forward, the office be required to consult us, on the grounds that we were the only ones qualified to make a decision in matters of religion and the needs of the Jewish community. The minister accepted my suggestion. This was a great achievement. I took this ministerial decision as a personal vote of confidence which strengthened my position in the eyes of senior officials, as well. Indeed, the Ministry of Education did not rescind a single document without first consulting me.[24]

Transports continued being dispatched after publication of the Basic Law on expulsion of the Jews. The Ohel David Home now had an important mission to perform in Nové Mesto. After the large deportation it was left with only 24 residents. In time I developed connections and managed to get people out of the Žilina camp on the basis of a document signed by myself, affirming that the elderly had been accepted into Ohel David. Much was done in this regard by the activists Ervin and Iboya Steiner of Žilina. In this manner the occupancy of Ohel David increased to 178. At this stage residents of the home were considered to be protected against deportation, and the "Jew hunters" did not enter the institution without informing us in advance. My private apartment also became an immune "extra-territorial" area; whenever there was a hunt – *Chytačka* – it provided refuge for around twenty locals and families of refugees from Trnava, Bratislava, Bánovce, and Trenčin, who were under my protection in Nové Mesto and in time of danger found hospitality under my roof.

Deportations in June

In June, 35 people were exiled from Nové Mesto, 30 of them on the 21st of Sivan (June 6), 2 on the 2nd of Tamuz (June 17), and 3 on the

---

[24] See appendix.

11th of Tamuz (June 26).

The following deportations were made from the rest of Slovakia in the month of June:

16th of Sivan (June 1)	Poprad, 1,014 people.
17th of Sivan (June 2)	Ružomberok and Liptovský-Svätý-Mikuláš, 1,000 people.
20th, 22nd of Sivan (June 5,7)	Bratislava, 2,119 people.
21st of Sivan (June 6)	Žilina, 1,000 people.
23rd of Sivan (June 8)	Zvolen and Banská-Bystrica, 1,000 people.
26th of Sivan (June 11)	Nováky camp, 1,000 people.
27th, 28th of Sivan (June 12, 13)	Poprad, 2,000 people.
29th of Sivan, 4th of Tamuz (June 14, 19)	Žilina camp, 2,059 people.

The males were deported to the vicinity of Lublin, the women and children to Sobibór. The last two transports in June were sent to Auschwitz.

VI. Organizing the Working Group – The Jewish Underground

Once more we were bereaved. The last deportation took 11,092 people. The Jews of Slovakia sat on their bundles. They saw to it that their backpacks were in good order and could hold the heavy tins of food, and waited apathetically in their homes for the goose-steppers to come and take them. Parents lost their children, drank the poisoned cup, and sat in silence. No one did a thing. There was nothing one could do. Terror reigned. Everyone rejected us. Hunts, deportations – everything was done with great haste, at whirlwind speed. We were downtrodden to the very foundations.

Rabbi Michael Dov Weissmandel, a man of great learning, enterprise, and broad horizons, felt the pain of his people and conceived a plan to bring salvation. To this end he needed the assistance of the shady and dubious Karl Hochberg, the servant of German Advisor Wisliceny. It was he who had to be influenced to stop the deportations. Weissmandel began talking with Hochberg and tried to get close to him by implying that he would be given a chance to cleanse his reputation if he cooperated with the efforts to stop the deportations. Fifty thousand Jews had already been deported, and the remaining camp of 35,000 to 40,000 Jews had to be saved, had to be kept in Slovakia. At Weissmandel's side stood Aaron Grünhut, Hochberg's friend and right-hand man, a man with connections and prospects of influencing him. Unlike Hochberg, Grünhut was a devout Jew, loved the Jewish people, and acted with good intentions, although at times he was criticized for his role. A group of activists organized: Weissmandel, Gisi Fleischmann, Dr. O. Neumann, Dr. Tibor Kováč, Ondrej Steiner, and myself.

Gisi Fleischmann was one of the more important personages, a veteran public worker with experience in central positions; Dr. Tibor Kováč, who came from an assimilated family and was not registered in the Jewish community, arrived at this calling by way of the Jewish Center and performed his public work with faithfulness and devotion. Attorney Kováč had been a colleague of Dr. Vašek in the Law Faculty at the university, and later continued his friendship with Vašek during their joint work in the legal department of the Bratislava Municipality. This friendship now stood him in good stead, enabling him to exploit his friendly relations with his colleague who headed the 14th Department. Under the influence of Dr. O. Neumann, Steiner was drawn closer to the Zionist idea, established a carpentry workshop in the Sered camp, and thus created the nucleus for founding labor camps, which in time became important in saving Jews from deportation. Although the group was very heterogeneous, all its members shared the idea of helping their fellow Jews. At this stage Dr. Winterstein refrained from becoming actively involved, which offended me personally; nevertheless, I felt obliged to keep him informed of developments. The group was joined by Dr. Ernst Abeles, a devoted public worker, who was head of the social work section of the Jewish Center during the time the young women were being deported and applied the law leniently to the young women in the Poprad camp. Dr. Abeles was arrested and held in prison for several weeks, during which time he was severely tortured. Now he was given the task of raising funds for rescue operations on a nationwide scale. Several other people, among them Fürst, the principal of the Jewish school, joined the group to help it in its work.

Each member of the group worked in a specific area: Grünhut was in charge of forming ties with Hochberg so that the latter would exert his influence on Wisliceny; Dr. Kováč was to maintain his connections with Dr. Vašek and try to obtain his intercession; Steiner handled development of the labor camps and was to negotiate with Pečuch, the commissioner of the Ministry of Interior; Gisi Fleischmann saw to raising financial support from various institutions abroad, especially the Joint; and I continued my intercession in the Ministry of Education and Culture and later, along with Dr. Kováč, maintained contacts with the 14th Department and the Central Office for Economy, directed by Dr. Ludevit Paškovič, who replaced Morávek. Paškovič was a key figure in the Central Office for Economy and wielded considerable influence in the government. He was in charge of issuing protection papers to Jews who were integral to the country's economic life. Unlike his predecessor, Dr. Paškovič was a relatively decent human being, and we succeeded in working our way to him as soon as the 14th Department was established. We knew that we must make every effort to obtain access to this important office, an office that would determine the fate of the Jews and where all the adverse and cruel decisions would be made. This was not one of our easier missions, for entry into this office was forbidden to Jews, and it was situated in the building of the Hlinka Guard's high command. The first director of the 14th Department was Dr. Géza Konka, an extremist anti-Semite, who gladly accepted German overlordship and influence and acted as the hangman of Slovak Jewry. He was surrounded by various advisors who had not the slightest notion of humanity or morality. Under their influence Konka issued numerous severe directives and harsh decrees and was the primary cause of the calamity which befell the Jews. His iron-fisted policy as director of the department is further attested by documents rescinding Jews' protection papers.

VII. Vašek's "Scholarly Work"

Konka was eventually dismissed and replaced by Dr. Anton Vašek, a veteran of the Hlinka People's party and other nationalist organizations and a good friend of Minister of Interior Mach. Vašek drank heavily, consorted with women, and spent long nights at the card table; but he also professed to be a man of science. Being in charge of the subject of the Jews, he wished to write a scholarly work on the Jewish problem, in which he could formulate new ideas, shed new light and present new evidence, all with a slant appropriate to the spirit of the era. He sought an advisor to assist him, a man knowledgeable in history, well-versed and expert in the subject. Such a man had to be a loyal and discreet person, a man who knew how to guard a secret, especially the confidential secret that he, Dr. Vašek, never actually wrote the articles and research papers which appeared under his name. Thus, aspiring to prove his scholarly talents, in his search for the appropriate person it occurred to him to invite me for a talk and delegate me to perform this task.

In a long conversation, which he began by talking about the problem of the Jews, I lectured him about the essence of Judaism, its history and philosophy, and the problems of the Jews in Exile. Thus, our would-be friendship began, bringing me into contact and negotiations with him. I had a double objective in this mission: to work on the topic without causing detriment to my Jewishness, thus fulfilling my obligation while remaining clean and not oppressing my people. At the same time, I was aware that I must take into consideration Vašek's position in this period of anti-Semitic rule. These were ostensibly to contradictory objectives. Nevertheless, I firmly resolved to use my connections with him to help the Jews, to soften him and save as many lives as possible, to sway him to alleviate our plight, and especially to persuade him to stop the deportations.

We met twice a week. First, I would hand him the material I had written, then I would humbly submit my requests. I succeeded in arranging many things with him, and even had an attenuating impact on his ideas, which he drew from the unbridled anti-Semitism of the blood-thirsty *Der Stürmer.* One of the most positive actions in which I succeeded during my regular visits with Vašek was to destroy the anonymous letters from informants and slanderers, thus doing away with slanderous reports and false testimony against our men. Dozens of such letters were referred to his office; and when, as happened on several occasions, I remained alone in his room, I read and ripped up the pernicious material, and thus helped many people who did not know, nor could they know, they were being attacked behind their backs. Vašek himself did not take much interest in the affairs of his office and never knew what documents or files were on his desk; nor did his assistants take much care, since most of the letters were anonymous.

When I returned home with my suit pockets filled with defamatory letters and documents, each one of which was likely to claim another Jewish victim, I was glad that perhaps I had succeeded in saving another Jewish life. The "scholarly work" for Vašek worried and disturbed me greatly. He wished to write articles on Judaism, to be published in the most dangerous and anti-Semitic daily, *Gardista*. I faced a difficult emotional struggle. After all, I could not possibly help the enemy and write hateful things about my people, accusing them, defaming them, shooting barbs at them, as the boss intended and expected of me. On the other hand, I pondered, perhaps it was better that he not use articles written in the venomous style of *Der Stürmer* or similar provocative literature, whose impact was far more pernicious and likely to lead to unrestrained incitement. I was determined to maneuver my way out of this entanglement; for in the world of moral values there is no yardstick for measuring degrees of corruptness, since even the slightest deviation from the straight path is considered a blot on one's character. In this respect a trifling amount is the same as a large sum. If so, I must not write even one word which could be interpreted as hurting the Jews; yet, if the pen which appears to downtrodden the Jews is likely to bring compensation in the form of helping the persecuted, if black ink can prevent red blood from being shed, then it is my duty to write; for verbal battering does not hurt to the same extent as the physical blows which are being dealt at us, torturing and afflicting the living body. I explained to Vašek: "You cannot write cheaply. As a Doctor of Law, you must write in such a fashion that every sentence and statement can stand up to scientific criteria. Therefore, every article must be based on scholarly research. This does not mean that we must write sympathetically to the Jews, but that we must not degenerate to the level of the blood-thirsty *Stürmer.*" These words pleased him, and he acquiesced to my proposal that his writing remain in the realm of pure research. In the same conversation I convinced him to make do with the material which I intended to submit to him: "Chapters from the Woeful History of the Jews." Likewise, I advised him to focus his Strürmer work on two plains: the legal and the historic. I suggested that first he publish a comprehensive book on all the laws issued by the Slovak Republic against the Jews. Here I had two objectives in mind:

1. The anthology would provide a document of injustice, preserving testimony of Slovakia's ignominy and the iniquities it did to its Jews.

2. Such a book would sound bombastic but would be like dust thrown to the wind, devoid of any propagandistic value against us, since the laws were known to all and were published to oppress us and cause us suffering; thus, this would be a lesser evil.

Dr. Vašek accepted the idea. Two young jurists, Dr. Juraj (George) Révész and Dr. László, senior officials in the Jewish Center, wrote and edited this 189-page book. Dr. Vašek did not bestir himself much in its publication; even the introduction was ghost-written by me. I noted that the book, *Legislation against the Jews in Slovakia,* was not only a collection of laws, but also a reflection of the feelings of the Slovak people, who wished to pave their way to freedom and independence, unhampered by the influence of aliens.

The book came out before Christmas, 1942, and before it reached the market we bought up a large part of the edition to prevent its becoming widespread among the gentiles, and tried to put as many copies of it as possible at the disposal of Jewish libraries, so that it could serve as an indictment before an international court of justice, when such should arise. From our point of view this work was a positive achievement. It did not harm us. On the contrary, it helped us establish vital connections and take action for the benefit of our people. However, I was still disturbed by the articles which Vašek wished to publish in the *Gardista*. I suggested that he write a historical survey of the marks of disgrace and various humiliating badges which the Jews were required to wear upon their clothes in previous generations, just as was being required today; thus, he would prove his expertise in the history of the subject. I looked for subjects which would not harm us and essentially intended to publish historical works taken from the woeful annals of our people. From time to time I gave him articles on the Middle Ages and on the yellow badge which the Jew-haters of Europe decreed must be affixed to the back of every Jew's garments to humiliate him and discriminate against him. Thus, I satisfied Vašek and for a while had peace of mind myself. Some time later Vašek invited me to Bratislava. I was to report immediately. At this urgent meeting he instructed me to prepare an objective paper for him on the stand of the Church, i.e., the higher clergy and the popes, on the question of the Jews. He needed this study for the Prime Minister, Dr. Tuka. I was perplexed. Since time immemorial the senior clergy had been anti-Jewish, and I did not understand the purport of his request. Yet I could not refuse. Having no choice, I expressed willingness to prepare the paper, but claimed that the preparatory work necessitated extensive study of source material, since submitting a shallow research paper to the Prime Minister, himself a university professor, was out of the question.

This time, prior to Vašek's request, the cultural section of the Jewish Center had also prepared four pages of printed material on the same subject, which in my opinion were dangerous and pernicious. I had difficulty deciding what line of approach should guide me in my work. The answer came to me after an extremely daring operation. I went to the 14th Department after work hours, when I figured that none of the clerks would be in the office. I turned to the janitor who, in exchange for a tip, always treated me courteously, and asked him to permit me to take a look at a letter on the desk of the department director. After telling him some story or other and suitably rewarding him, we went into the director's office and opened his desk. I immediately beheld the Prime Minister's letter, along with a letter from Dr. Jantausch, the Catholic bishop of Trnava. The bishop was sharply critical of the government for including Jewish converts to Christianity among the objects of their attack. He protested against the expulsion of Jews who had adopted Christianity and requested that the Christian Catholic government revise its stand and treat baptized Jews as Christians, protected by the law. Tuka was interested in unconditionally rejecting this approach. He wished to reinforce his position with historical arguments, proving that he was acting in accordance with the opinion of the Church Fathers and the Pastoral Epistles published by the popes in various eras. Dr. Vašek was to prepare the definitive answer which, based on the opinion of great clerical leaders, would come out unequivocally against the Jews.

This made everything clear. Vašek was posing as a scholar before the Prime Minister and, in turn, was relying on my knowledge and requesting me to supply him material against the Jews. The bosses, however, made a slight error, since they had not taken into account the janitor in Hlinka Guard uniform who stood at the gate, ready, whenever it paid, also to serve a Jew. Bishop Jantausch wished to protect only Jews who had converted out of the faith. True Jews were of no concern to him; they could be wiped out and annihilated in concentration camps in the land of doom. Our sages once pronounced a great rule: A Jew, even if he has sinned, is still a Jew. A Jew who has converted to another religion is considered a Jew who has sinned, but the same law applies to him as to a Jew. Yet there is a great difference between this statement and giving priority to converts out of the faith. My primary responsibility was to care for those Jews who have accepted the Covenant, and to try to help save them.

Thus, I set to work preparing a paper entitled: "The Stand of the Church on the Jewish Question." Forthwith, in the introduction, I established the thesis that the popes and senior statesmen of the Vatican treated converts from Judaism as second-class religionists and had more respect for Jews who remained devoted to their religion and true to their faith. The larger part of the work was done by my brother, Emanuel, with my guidance. The paper was prepared in total secrecy. Our secretary typed around 70 pages for us and, fortunately for us, did not take any interest in the typed material or even know what she was typing. This became clear to us one day when she brought us the *Gardista* with Dr. Vašek's article on the yellow badge, which she proceeded to read, not realizing that she herself had typed the article for us the previous week in my office.

My brother, principal of a school in my community, prepared the studies for me and worked diligently over this scholarly work for many months, thus freeing me from excessive cares.

After I submitted our work, Jantausch's proposal was flatly rejected on the grounds that it did not accord with the views of the great Church leaders. Vašek ostensibly proved that the position of the Church has historically been not to make a distinction between Jews who remained in the faith and those who converted. We did not abandon the Jews who had been baptized, and we maintained that they, too, must be protected; but under no circumstances did we favor them, giving them preference over Jews who had not been baptized. As I submitted each chapter or section of the work, I also submitted various requests, which for the most part, were granted. Thus, I managed to free many people who were waiting in the camps for the next transport. We looked for all sorts of excuses and ways of liberating them. I was especially successful at preventing Jews from Nové Mesto from being rounded up and deported. I knew many of them personally and, with the assistance of the local authorities, could find various pretexts and devise sundry ways to obtain their release.

In time I ran into difficult straits once more; Vašek came to me with a request that I write about the "international Jewish organization." I surmised that he had in mind that I disclose the would be "international Jewish conspiracy," which flagrant anti-Semites so often wrote about in slanderous works, and whose objective, presumably, was to take control over the entire world and exploit and enslave all other nations. I wondered whether he would believe me if I were to "reveal" the honest truth that no such international organization exists or ever existed. After wavering back and forth we decided to write about the different trends within Judaism and the various worldwide Jewish organizations, about the Zionist movement and its objectives, about *Agudat Israel* and the Orthodox, and about the American Joint Distribution Committee, which works in every country where Jews are in distress and engages in charity and social assistance to the needy.

The article impressed him, and in one of our meetings he said to me: "Most people use the catchword "international Jewry" pejoratively without having the slightest notion of what it means." I used this remark as an opportune moment to persuade him to alter his views. But it was extremely difficult to totally eradicate the preconceptions of this evil man which were deeply rooted in his soul.

VIII. Abatement of Deportations in July-August 1942

The lobbyists of the Working Group steadily and energetically persisted in their efforts to soften, as much as possible, the hard line of radical elements who were pressing to accelerate the liquidation of the Jewish communities throughout the country. Rabbi Weissmandel was the man who kept things running. He turned to important figures in Switzerland and Hungary, summoned the Jewish community leaders and spurred them on to action. He suggested requesting that the deportations be ceased and that the Jews who were not integrated into the economic life of the state be concentrated in special labor camps whose maintenance would be financed by foreign currency received from abroad. Thus, the camps and their residents would become a factor benefiting the national economy. Gisi Fleischmann had good connections with Jewish organizations abroad and had been assured the necessary financial support. The Jews of Slovakia, as well, were prepared to contribute their share, for vast sums were always needed for various purposes.[25] We influenced the crucial bodies in charge of Jewish affairs, and they began to lend an especially willing ear when Hochberg, too, achieved some success in his lobbying of German Advisor Wisliceny. Chances of the plan succeeding instilled new life and hope in us. As a result of this feverish activity a slowdown became evident in the rate of deportations in the month of July. In contrast to 15 transports in April, 18 in May, and 11 in June, only 5 transports left in July, all of them from Žilina. They took 4,810 people, all deported to Auschwitz, on the 18th and 25th of Tamuz and the 3rd, 10th and 17th of Av (July 3, 10, 17, 24 and 31, respectively). The last transport, which left on July 31, was especially inhuman. It included frail and weary

---

[25] Here, sensing a need for discretion, Rabbi Frieder alluded obliquely to various "purposes and obligations," essentially gifts and bribes given to Wisliceny, Vašek, Koso, and many others, which came to huge sums of money.

elderly who had been removed from institutions and hospitals. This deportation hit us hard, causing great sadness and mourning in the Ohel David Old-Age Home. I was not in Nové Mesto on that unfortunate day, and the District Commissioner was on leave then, as well. When orders reached the district office to send all the elderly to the Sered camp on the pretext that an old-age home would be opened there, the Assistant District Commissioner gave instructions to evacuate all the elderly from Ohel David. I was called back home urgently, only to find the old-age home surrounded by dozens of police. There were 74 residents in the institution that day. Through great effort I managed to save 45, but to my great dismay the other 29 were forced to set out on their fateful way. They left the institution on the Sabbath of the reading from the Prophets: "Comfort ye, comfort ye My people," on July 25, 1942.

In Nové Mesto a group of 78 Jews was employed by the Ministry of Transportation laying train tracks. These railroad workers came from the outlying cities of Topolčany, Nitra, Trnava, Pieštany, and Vrbové. Orders arrived on July 16, 1942, to disband the group and round up its members for deportation. In the end, 34 of them were exiled and 44 were saved. On the Ninth of Av (July 23) another nine people were exiled. On the 17th of Av (July 30) a large-scale hunt was made throughout the country; in Nové Mesto 4 people were rounded up.

Our good relations with official bodies in the district increased our influence. The Working Group continued its activity and attained considerable achievements. In August drag-nets were laid for Jews who tried to hide and avoid being deported, and in these searches many Jews were caught, seized, and rounded up. The Aryanizers and extremist proponents of total extermination of Slovak Jewry did not rest. However, in August, following five months during which approximately 55,000 of Slovakia's Jews were deported, there were no deportations and not a single Jew was transferred across the border into Poland. Many of those who remained actually succeeded in smuggling their families into Hungary. In the nationwide searches which were held on the 27th of Tamuz (July 12) and the 7th of Elul (August 20), 32 Jews were caught in the district of Nové Mesto, primarily from the villages, and were concentrated in the Sered camp.

IX. The Struggle Against Conversion

The life of the Jews was very difficult and full of tension. It was no surprise that every rumor circulating abroad immediately found willing ears. When the deportations stopped, a rumor circulated that Jews who converted to Christianity would not be rounded up or exiled. The Basic Law of May 15, 1942, regarding deportation of Jews stipulated that Jews who belonged to the Christian religion as of the day Slovakia declared her independence, i.e., March 14, 1939, would not be deported. Now several circles began spreading rumors that anyone who baptized himself as a Christian would be protected. The source of these rumors, regretfully, was Bratislava's Jewish Center itself. We had degenerated to such a sorry state that officials of the central Jewish organization were seeking refuge under the wings of Christianity. How sad and typical it was that the officials of this organization, established by the government and employing converts with well-placed connections, were the ones to disseminate this new formulation, which actually influenced many Jews to give up their religion out of despair. I am not referring to proper Jews who held forged Aryan papers, but to people who were duly baptized and converted to Christianity as Catholics or Evangelists. Converting to Christianity, which at first was seen as a life saver, became a mass psychosis, and thousands were confounded and converted. In my sermons I came out strongly against this manifestation. Of course, no one ruled out the possibility of obtaining forged certificates from various churches, confirming baptism before the date set by the law. If such certificates could save lives, and the holder of the certificate was not baptized but rather lived as a Jew, in such circumstances, when it was a question of survival, of maintaining the Jewish religion, I felt I had no alternative but to advise everyone: in this hour of emergency and danger, save your lives; be good Jews in your hearts and souls, but carry Aryan papers in your pockets.

However, there were cases of pathetic, confused people who actually underwent baptism, without this step providing them any protection against deportation. There were also instances of Jewish community leaders, having fallen victim to this psychosis, converting without officially resigning their positions. Some even continued to hold protection papers from the Jewish community. In our battle against such manifestations, we issued a circular to the communities of the Yeshurun federation and also sent personal letters to many fence-sitters to strengthen their spirit and their Jewish consciousness. These letters were written on the initiative of Dr. Winterstein and were drafted by him.[26]

At the end of August, we also sent a questionnaire on behalf of the Chief Rabbinate to all the Yeshurun congregations, with the aim of collecting information on the membership of these Jewish communities, their public workers and condition, and their office-holders with protection papers from the Ministry of Education and Culture. The large deportations had drastically diminished the size of these Jewish communities, and, with the rise in the number of converts who cancelled their affiliation with the congregations, the number of Jews was further reduced, especially in neologist congregations. The Nazi press reacted quite unfavorably to conversions to Christianity.

---

[26] See appendix.

The papers attacked the converts and pointed out the futility of their deeds.

X. The Last Deportations in 1942

At the end of August, Alexander Mach, the minister of interior and commander-in-chief of the Hlinka Guard, ordered all white protection papers[27] rescinded by September 15. According to his plan, 15 deportations were to leave in September, taking a total of 15,000 Jews. The remaining Jews were to be rounded up and expelled at a later date. To implement this expulsion, directives cancelling the protection papers were sent to all ministers. In an interview granted me by Minister of Education Jozef Sivák, I was given the opportunity to read the fateful letter.

Once more we faced a grave situation, fraught with danger. The members of the Working Group immediately launched intensive action, interceding with Wisliceny, Vašek, Paškovic, Karva, Sivák, and others. Prospects arose of reducing the number of Jews who would be fired from their jobs and would have their papers rescinded. Instead of deportation, which meant annihilation, we proposed that the Jews be sent to do useful work in camps in Slovakia. We were only partially successful and could not prevent the deportations altogether. In the middle of the High Holidays, 1,992 Jews were deported from Žilina to Auschwitz, 991 of them on the 7th of Tishri, 5703 (September 18), and 1,001 on the Day of Atonement (September 21).

After a lull of a month, on the 9th of Mar-Heshvan (October 20), another 860 patients were removed from hospitals and institutions for the mentally ill and deported. They were gathered in Žilina and cruelly expelled to Auschwitz. Twenty-five members of the Nové Mesta

---

[27] Every Jew who was employed received a white document temporarily certifying that the expulsion edicts did not apply to him.

community were deported in these transports; 9 on September 18, 2 on September 29, 5 on September 30, and 9 on October 7.

All in all, in 1942, 58,600 Jews were deported to Poland in 57 transports. Approximately 30,000 Jews remained scattered in various communities throughout Slovakia, several hundred of them in work camps. Our youth and pioneers, those who hoped to rebuild our homeland in the Land of Israel, are no longer with us. They were exiled to the death camps, as testified by letters and eye-witness accounts.

Chapter Five

Rescue Operations

(5703 - 5704; 1943 - 1944)

"To deliver their soul from death, And to keep them alive in famine"

(Psalms 33:19)

I. Cries for Help from the Land of Doom

By June 1942, an anonymous young Jew from central Slovakia, from the vicinity of Svätý Kríž, a town on the Hron River, managed to escape from the Lublin-Majdanek camp and write a 36-page printed letter testifying to what was happening to the Jews. The young man told of his travails since 1941, when he volunteered for physical labor, of his exile, and of his tribulations in the Majdanek camp, which were marked by a madness unlike anything known thus far.[28] He succeeded in reaching Slovakia and was immediately forced to cross the border into Hungary, where he disappeared and has not been heard of since.

The extent of the tragedy and the life of suffering and torment, which were nothing but a protracted dying prior to physical extermination, are reflected in the various letters, notes and messages which reached us in sundry ways, even by special non-Jewish messengers. We were shocked to the depths of our souls, for we realized that this was the most tragic era we had known in all the years of our Exile.

---

[28] A copy of his testimony is in FYVS. It also appears in L. Rotkirchen, *The Destruction of Slovakian Jewry,* Jerusalem, 1961, pp. 166-204 (Hebrew).

Below I cite the original text of a letter which reached me through Anna Gleich of Michalovce.[29] She received the letter from a friend of hers who was exiled. It was written in Hebrew, in Latin characters. In an accompanying letter Anna Gleich requested that it be brought to the attention of the authorized bodies:

> We are aware that you surely know nothing of the hell we are in. Only a few of us remain of the original ones. We were not taken to a work camp, but rather to a death camp. We wish to tell you all the terrible truth of our lives. There are Jews from all over Europe here. For two years, day and night, transports bringing tens of thousands of Jews have been arriving; but only a few of them come to the camp. Elderly, children, and mothers, even young men and women, are all thrown like animals into a vehicle and driven straight to the slaughter. The torment and pain are so great and long until they throw one into the fire. Worst of all is death. But who knows if my life in the camp is not even more bitter? We work half naked, they whip us, and our guards' dogs attack us. When we go out to work, we never know if we shall return. We sleep in cold, lice-ridden pens, and because of this disease is rampant. There is no medical care, nor any medicine. Every day hundreds of dead lie in front of the tents. People die of lashings, disease, and starvation. We no longer feel anything. We are no longer human beings; they have made animals of us. Not only Jews, but thousands of Aryans, as well, live and die thus. It is impossible to feel for a person who has not lived here. Our souls are filled with bitterness and despair beyond those which

---

[29] All the letters are in FYVS.

words can express. During the roll-calls, held from midnight until dawn, many fall down, never to rise again. Even the healthy are taken to the slaughter. We are beholding the end of our people. We do not want to die this way. We have absolutely no possibility of forbearance. They have separated us from the entire world. This is the first message we have sent. If you receive these words and have any answer, we await your response in consternation. If you cannot give us any tangible aid, at least send us words of comfort to fortify our souls. Please remember that young Jewish men and women are waiting here for a sign of life from their more fortunate brethren.

Take heart and have courage!

Another letter, from Rejowiec:

My dear ones,

We have written to you many times but, to our sorrow, have received no response. We are living on a farm and working in a barn. Out of three thousand, only we three families remain along with our wives and children. All the others were evacuated on August 9, 1942. Philip and his two brothers-in-law were here, too, as well as my mother- in-law and father-in-law, Sari, Yehudah, and his wife. But, to our great distress, all of them have gone. Sister-in-law Hermine and the two children died here, we are sorry to say, as well as her mother. Please tell my sister-in-law's brother, a soldier in Láb, called Lemel Liling, to say *kaddish* for his mother, who also passed away on August 9.

Your father and brother were in uk6w, near Lublin, this summer. Also, your mother has passed away. I have not received thousands of greetings, but if you wish to send me something, write only to the following address: Čap Bronislav, Rejowiec Farm, Chelm District, Lublin Province. He is the man who runs the farm and will surely give me anything you send. Send everything only from Poland. Please destroy this letter immediately because of the address; but please send something quickly and a lot – the more the better – for the two girls have already ceased receiving their 20 decagrams of bread (which are the wages for our work), and therefore the two children are in great danger. Please send as large a sum as possible, and post haste. If you can send anything to Hungary, to M. Leib Kleiman, Harshpalave, p.o. Siliwa, then clothing and undergarments would be a great help, for our clothing is ragged and worn. Your clothes already fit Blanca well, and Adolf's, me - so skinny have we become. Only what remains on our bodies is left us. We have sold everything else. If you can, three pairs of shoes for Blanca and the girl, and a suit for Bony. From there I will receive everything from my good friend who is going there for three weeks. How are Seren and Edith? Regards to everyone.

Joži.

These letters were proof of the deceitful acts of the Nazis, who were interested not in labor but in extermination. Under the name of "Work Service" and the watchword "Labor makes Free," the sadistic murderers sought to cover the blood of men, women, and children, young and old, which was being shed like water. Majdanek and Birkenau became death camps for the Jewish people. The letters which arrived via messengers from our brethren who were exiled from Prešov and Michalovče to ghettos in Poland cried out for help:

October 18, 1942 (written in Hungarian):

> ... To my great sorrow I must bring the bitter tidings that while I was at work my wife and children were taken in the transport... my coat, suit, and shoes were stolen...

October 18, 1942 (written in Slovak):

> ... I beg of you, save my life, for I remain alone, naked ... I am starving and shivering with cold. Help me!

November I, 1942 (written in Hungarian):

> ... Meanwhile summer has come. All the Jews have been evacuated from here. I alone am left. I am again in camp. I remain without anything. I have lost everything. We fled early in the morning, as we were, with only a single garment on our backs. I would like to go on living, but have little hope. Do something for my sake! Does the government know that we are being wiped out, that they have murdered some five hundred of us from the 15th transport? Is this why they brought us here? ...

November 1, 1942 (written in Hungarian):

> I no longer see for tears, and no longer feel anything for suffering and pain. But I know that I must get out

of this hell-hole of destruction … The 15th of October was the most terrible day of my life. I am here, but my wife, my children, and the rest of my family were all transported across the Bug River to an unknown place. But what is important is that they were taken alive. The evacuation claimed many victims, took many lives… The second evacuation was on October 27, and then they took whoever was left. Ever since, I have been living the life of a dog, if it can be called life at all. I have been robbed of everything… Help me!

November 1, 1942 (written in Hungarian):

… I no longer have anything to sell and remain completely naked. Remember me, that I may have the strength to pull through everything. Wednesday, they stole even my last ragged scraps of clothing from me, after I went out to work, leaving me here with only the clothing on my back…

November 2, 1942 (written in Hungarian):

… I wish to inform you, to my great sorrow, that I alone remain… If only you can, please help me, but quickly, else it will be too late… I can hardly believe that I am still alive and that I can write to you, my dear parents, because I do not want to remember that fateful Thursday. It was a veritable Holocaust. There was an evacuation, but fortunately for us, we were not at home. They began in the afternoon. Only a very few of us Jews remain. It was not an evacuation like the deportations which we had at home. Here they murdered. I cannot even describe how they slaughtered children and old folk, and how the bodies remained scattered along the roadside like flies. Imagine, there were 400 dead... No one is ever seen on the street; everyone is afraid to go out... We were put into a single room. There were 240 of us... Children were left without parents, and parents split from their children, women from their husbands and men from their wives; they took them to some unknown place. By a miracle of Heaven, somehow, we few have survived.

November 2, 1942 (written in German):

. . . My dear Mommy and my Ervinka were deported last week to an unknown place. We are left without money or clothing, naked, for during the evacuation they stole all we had. All that was left us were the clothes on our backs...

* * *

These letters reached us by messengers who told us of more atrocities. In the Working Group we resolved to organize and seek a way to help our exiled brethren in their great hour of need. One day a Polish officer by the name of Iwanowski arrived, carrying letters from the region of Opole and Lubartów. He was a valiant and sharp young man, ready to transfer money and valuables to the deported. He performed his missions faithfully, yet I feared he was not sufficiently cautious and discreet and that one day he would most likely fall into the hands of the police and place our safety in jeopardy, as well. Yet the motivation to help suffering people living in sub-human conditions was stronger than any misgivings we might have had, and we continued working through him.

One day Iwanowski was caught by the Center for State Security and handed over to the *Gestapo* for interrogation. His arrest oppressed me greatly. I knew that he carried papers of a double-agent: of the American and the German intelligence services. He also had on his person a notebook of addresses and notes, in which my name, too, surely appeared; letters to and from the deportees; photographs of deported persons; and other incriminatory material, perhaps even valuables. I was further disquieted to learn that he was later executed in Hamburg.

* * *

Aside from Iwanowski, we had a number of other couriers who were willing to take things to Poland to help the deportees. The evening after the Day of Atonement I listed and arranged gold jewelry, watches, valuables and letters to be transferred to the deportees. A meeting was planned with two German couriers, for the following day, in the home of R. Shelomo Stern of Bratislava, a philanthropist and activist who was devoted heart and soul to philanthropic work. My wife and Oscar and Ilka Horvát also lent a hand. To be safe, Ilka took the bag of valuables home with her so that Oscar could give it to me in Bratislava.

The following morning, the 11th of Tishri (September 22, 1942), three men showed up at my home. They were investigators on behalf of the Ministry of Finance in Bratislava and had come to arrest me. After a thorough search of my house, which lasted four hours, they found receipts for the sum of 65,000 korunas which had been sent to Poland. During the investigation in the police station, I declared that I had not committed any criminal offense, that I had only forwarded the money of Jews who had been deported. My motives were commercial,

I had not smuggled out foreign currency, and was only fulfilling my moral duty to help the deportees in their hour of distress. I had acted in my capacity as a National Chief Rabbi of the State. I was held under arrest in Bratislava for three days, then, after lengthy negotiations, was fined 150,000 korunas.

In these days of deportation, this was considered a very favorable end to the episode of my arrest. Such instances illustrate what the Sages' meant when they said no harm comes to a person sent to perform a good deed. Fortunately, we managed to salvage the jewelry, and no one else was implicated in the episode, since I had taken all the blame upon myself.

Now I could continue working with redoubled energy, and once again couriers traveled to and from Poland. Concern for the well-being of the deported and anxiety about their fate occupied us greatly. Dozens of letters and appeals from relatives, seeking information or a way of helping their dear ones, passed our way.

Three hundred young men, soldiers doing their compulsory service, most of whom had become orphaned or lost their dear ones, were in work camps in Zohor and the neighboring village of Láb. In a moving letter, expressive of these boys' closeness to their families and their yearning for a sign of life from them, Oscar Zlatner appealed to me on behalf of his comrades, who were "in need of a fatherly word," requesting that I come visit the camp and bring them encouragement.[30]

In October and November, couriers continued to be sent to Poland's ghettos, where Slovak Jews were living too, until Holocaust descended on the ghettos, and their residents were evacuated and sent off to the valley of death, whose location was unknown. The couriers reached Opole and Lubartów during the very days of the deportation.

[30] See appendix.

Regretfully, we received no word from them or confirmation that the money we sent arrived, nor did they ever return to us. With the couriers who never returned I had sent various valuables and 120,000 korunas in cash to Opole, 111,000 korunas and some valuables to Lubartów, and a total of 16,000 korunas to other labor camps -- Kazimierz Dolny, Ostrów-Lubelski, and Kamionka.

I do not know if our people received the money; the fact is that I never received any acknowledgement or news from them, and from that day on we have had no contact with the Lublin region. Be that as it may, I managed to send money and gold with a railroad worker, twice to Majdanek and once to Birkenau. From both I received acknowledgements, one of them written by a resident of Nové Mesto whose handwriting I recognized.

II. Raising Funds for Rescue Operations

Thanks to the efforts of the Working Group, no transports left during the winter of 1942-1943. Government circles promised us that this respite would continue until March 1943. A vast fortune was needed to finance the activities of the group and to cover its large obligations, and this presented us with a problem of raising money. The few Jews who remained were indeed willing to contribute their share, but most of them had lost their sources of livelihood and became impoverished. Therefore, we decided to send emissaries to Hungary to request aid from our brethren there.

Gisi Fleischmann and Dr. Ernst Abeles were sent to Budapest, where the Joint, under the management of Slovak-born Joseph Blum, was still functioning, as were other philanthropic institutions, the Land of Israel Office, and embassies of Western states, and where Jewish community life was still intact. Our emissaries equipped themselves with letters of appeal and introduction to the two Jewish community organizations in Budapest. In my official capacity I appealed to the Chief Rabbi Dr. Benjamin Fisher. Appeals were also made to circles of converts since under Slovak law the deportation edict also applied to converts in Slovakia.

Benefactors of the Jewish community and eminent wealthy Jews received the delegation with proclamations of sympathy and solidarity, but did not follow up their words with deeds. Wealthy converts from Judaism looked on passively. What kinship did they feel with the converts in Slovakia or with the Jewish people in general? They had long since severed all ties with Judaism. In this respect the visit proved very disappointing. Nevertheless, Gisi Fleischmann, a devoted woman with experience in public and social work, succeeded on other fronts. She established personal contacts with various circles who were likely to come to our aid. She relayed information to them on the condition of the Jews in Slovakia, Poland, and Frankfurt-Bohemia-Moravia, and also sent reports and appeals for help abroad, to Switzerland and the United States. Joseph Blum, director of the Joint in Budapest, was active in this work on behalf of Slovak Jewry and helped the emissaries from Slovakia. This was the primary accomplishment of the delegation, which, while it did not succeed in raising money from the Jews of Hungary, did succeed in convincing the Joint in America to grant us minimal sums of money, via Switzerland, to enable us to meet our obligations through the winter months.

With the means at our disposal, we were able to improve relations with the 14th Department and the Central Office for Economy, and found ways of getting people out of the Žilina transit camp. In this manner we managed to liberate entire families and single individuals, who were returned to their homes or referred to Ohel David.[31]

As we kept a vigilant eye on developments in the camps and in the government offices in charge of Jewish affairs, 1942 drew to a close. This was one of the darkest and saddest years in the history of our people in their 2000 years of exile. The Nazis' objective was to kill and annihilate all the Jews in the countries which they took over. We were aware of this and continued our efforts to save people, to help as much as possible, and to maintain contact with the deportees.

The Jewish year 5703 being a leap year, we issued a circular from the Chief Rabbinate proclaiming *selihot* (penitential prayers, recited on fast days and in time of trouble) to be recited during the first eight weeks of scriptural readings from the Book of Exodus.[32] We also proclaimed a public fast day on the 23rd of Tevet, which coincided with the last day of the secular calendar year, and on the 13th of Adar I, in the hope that "perhaps He will have pity on a poor and needy people, perhaps He will have mercy. . . for repentance, charity, and prayer avert the evil decree." We added special prayers for "our brethren in the land of doom, who are in great trouble and captivity. May the Omnipresent have mercy on them and bring them out of trouble to ease, from darkness to light, from bondage to redemption." I requested

---

[31] Among the people rescued was R. Samuel Reich, chief rabbi of Vrbové, one of Slovakia's greatest rabbis and a man who did much for his town in the field of public works, as well (including establishing a school and, by his lobbying, getting a railroad laid to Vrbové). Despite his many merits he was taken to Žilina. Upon his release from the camp, he went to his son-in-law, Rabbi Isaac Nagel, in Prievidza. (Rabbi Reich and his wife immigrated to Israel in 1949. He died in Jerusalem).

Other people whose release Rabbi Frieder obtained from the Žilina camp included the rabbi of Kurima, R. David Weiss, who moved to Bardejov, and the young rabbi Arnold Levi and his parents from Bratislava, who were taken in by Ohel David. Rabbi Levi later worked as the spiritual counsellor of the old-age home and wed Friska Spiegel, a schoolteacher and daughter of R. Abraham J. Spiegel of Nové Mesto, who also was among those whom Rabbi Frieder succeeded in liberating, along with her family, from the Žilina camp. After both families were saved from deportation, Rabbi Frieder officiated at their nuptials, to the joy of the remaining Jews in the community.

[32] In a leap year, very pious Jews fast on the Mondays and Thursdays before the Sabbaths of these Torah readings.

that charitable contributions be sent to the Jewish hospital, which had been transferred from Bratislava to the vicinity of Sered and was desperately in need of aid.

III. Concluding a Decade of Service

The secular New Year of 1943 began on the eve of the Sabbath of the scriptural reading of *Shemot.* On this Sabbath, ten years earlier, I gave my first sermon in Zvolen and was hired as rabbi of the community. Now I had completed five more years of work in Nové Mesto. It was not a fit time for celebrating, yet I felt a spiritual need to give thanks to God for helping me and giving me the strength to work. This was an opportunity to look back and take stock, and to involve the public in the joy of performing good deeds. I planned a *siyyum,* a celebration to mark completing the study of the six orders of the Mishnah, and also invited friends of mine from the Orthodox congregation, with whom I was on good terms and had a common language, so that all those who followed the Torah in the city would study and prepare for the *siyyum* which I planned to hold during *se'udah shelishit* on the Sabbath of *Shemot.*

These plans did not remain a secret, and when I entered the dining hall of Ohel David, I found it handsomely decorated with a large wreath hanging on the wall, with the letter *yod* (numerical value of 10), designating a decade, in its center. After the completion of the last tractate and a sermon on current affairs, a festive meal was served to the 150 participants.

The vice-chairman of the congregation, R. Moses Samuel Rosenberg, delivered several words of congratulations and appreciation and then handed me a certificate – drafted by him in a traditional and eloquent style and written by a scribe on proper parchment – containing the charter of the Eshel Abraham Society, named after myself and affiliated with the Ohel David Old-Age Home.

* * *

On *Tu bi-Shvat,* 5703 (the Jewish New Year for trees; January 21, 1943), the Working Group held a festive meeting in Bratislava, attended by Dr. Winterstein, Dr. Neumann, and Gisi Fleischmann, at which it was announced that a grove would be planted in my name in the Land of Israel. To this end a Golden Book was made for registering the names of donors.

The very thought that a grove of trees planted in my name might grow in the Holy Land, the object of my yearning and the land for whose rebirth I had been working, was deeply moving.

IV. Labor Camps for Jews in Slovakia

When the Slovak government was formed in the spring of 1939, Jewish soldiers were removed from their units and put into work-gangs in the context of the army. In the summer of 1940 Jews of working age were drafted for two months of compulsory service, during which time they were required to work on projects vital to national defense, such as paving roads, building railroads, digging trenches, etc.

In 1941 Jewish forced labor in labor camps was placed under the jurisdiction of the Minister of Interior, who in turn entrusted the task of organizing the camps to the Jewish Center. All Jews who had been laid off from their jobs were required to work in these camps. Engineers and technicians did preparatory works such as building barracks for single individuals and families and seeing to supplies, acquisition of materials, tools, machinery, etc. On orders from the Ministry of Interior, the Jewish Center carried out all the organizational work for building the Šúr canal in western Slovakia and the Stražké-Prešov railroad line in the east, as well as other construction projects. Besides these two large projects, the Jews carried out works to harness the water of the Morava, Nitra and other rivers. Private construction firms executing public works for the state employed many Jews through forced labor.

Once the infrastructure was established, enterprises using forced labor began to be organized to do public works for the state. During the winter of 1941-1942 the Ministry of Interior prepared a bill requiring every Jew who did not have official certification of employment in a place recognized by the government to work in one of the forced labor plants. The plans provided that these enterprises be managed by a central institution, in accordance with the principles of state-run enterprises. The Jewish Center prepared all the proposals and plans for their organization and economic and technical implementation, and submitted them to the government offices. Implementation of the plans began in early 1942, after their approval by government offices. Residential buildings and workshops were built so that production work could be started. The plan to concentrate the Jews in labor camps on Slovak territory, however, was never implemented. Extremist elements in the government and in the nationalist Nazi movement accepted the Germans' advice to wipe out the Jews, getting rid of them once and for all by deporting them to Poland on the pretext that they were being transferred to an autonomous Jewish region where they could support themselves by their own labor. During the months of deportation, the Nováky and Sered camps served as concentration camps, and the danger of being deported to Poland hovered over the heads of everyone in the camps, including the camp workers. This made the Jews afraid to enter the labor camp.

The Jews began operating the workshops and tried to prove their efficiency and produce high quality products. Other family members were employed in small plants and given productive work in accordance with their capabilities, in order that they not be left sitting idle. It should be noted that the Jewish Center and the labor camps did not receive budgetary or other material support from any governmental body, and that all the preparations and work organizing the camps was done by the Jews, on their own. Large orders placed by various economic bodies made it feasible to open the plants. Thus, in Sered, Nováky, and Vyhne, three permanent camps began to function. Each had a large central factory alongside a number of smaller plants. The main factory employed skilled workers, men and women, while the subsidiary factories employed the rest of the camp's residents.

The Ministry of Interior took charge of all the camps through a government commissar, appointed to direct and supervise all the camps. Each camp was headed by a local commissar, charged with running the camps financial affairs and overseeing the work. The Jewish Center in Bratislava, which followed the instructions of the government commissar and was under his supervision, helped organize and establish the camps.

Life in the camps was managed on a communal basis. In exchange for their labor the inmates received housing, food, and clothing. Social services were established, including a clinic employing Jewish doctors, a kitchen, a bakery, showers, a laundry, a barbershop, and shops for repairing shoes and clothing. Educational institutions were opened, as well, including a nursery school, kindergarten, and elementary school under the supervision of the Ministry of Education and Culture. Lectures and vocational enrichment courses were offered in the evenings. Special attention was given to vocational retraining of non-vocational workers. Social life and culture were not overlooked in the planning, either; a library (under the supervision of the camp command) was established and musical performances, theatrical productions, and the like were produced.

The Sered Labor Camp

The main factory in the Sered camp was a carpentry employing approximately 160 carpenters and equipped with modern, sophisticated machinery. Self-made carpenter's benches, each with the necessary tools, stood in large, well-lit shop rooms. The machine room had all sorts of saws and planes, lathes, presses, and equipment for making and drying plywood, as well as all the tools necessary for processing wood to manufacture high quality furniture and wood fittings for construction work. The carpentry shop produced wooden stairs for the government's campaign to build "a thousand houses for workers" and supplied all the carpentry work and interior wood furnishings needed by the hotels owned by the central management of the state-run spas in Slovakia. The carpentry also supplied furniture and woodwork to the Ministry of Economics, the state forestry departments, the police, and export agencies. A division specializing in a unique process for manufacturing wooden shoe soles received an order for exporting 250,000 pairs of soles to various European countries. Large revenues made it possible to develop and expand production by 300,000 korunas and assured full employment for a long time to come.

Other orders from the carpentry shop included dozens of furniture suites for hotels, thousands of beds, couches, sofas, wardrobes, restaurant tables, etc.

Alongside the carpentry shop was a workshop for manufacturing wooden toys, which were ordered in large quantities by retail shops and exporters. Hobby-horses, wooden dolls, bowling balls, animal figurines, various games, as well as rolling-pins, hammers, and hangers were among the high-quality products of the workshop and were in great demand.

Among the other workshops in the camp was a cement factory which produced concrete pipes of various diameters and supplied sewage pipes to the General Construction Corporation. Attempts were made to produce cinder-blocks as a substitute for bricks. A smithy produced hundreds of wheelbarrows for companies working on the sewage and drainage project. The women worked in women's confectionery, glove manufacturing, hat production, weaving screens, and spinning wool.

Other workshops sewed men's suits, uniforms for the army and the police, cotton shirts, work smocks, aprons, ear muffs, pillows, covers for straw mattresses, and the like. Orders for these products were marketed to private retailers and various government offices, including the Ministry of Defense and the police, whose orders came to 1,300,000 korunas.

The Nováky Labor Camp

The Nováky camp employed about 350 tailors, seamstresses, and needleworkers in women's confectionery, the main factory there. The workshops, equipped with the latest machinery, were very productive. They produced uniforms for the police and for other public bodies, suits and coats for men and children, and workclothes. As order increased, special departments were opened for producing shirts, underclothes, nightwear, and aprons, men's hats, various sports clothes and headwear, and scarves and gloves for soldiers.

Boilers for central heating and hot water were produced in the smithy. These products contributed greatly to the construction sector of the national economy, since such boilers were not produced anywhere else in Slovakia. The branch of smithwork for construction produced iron window frames and railings, gates, and iron wheelbarrows. The tinsmithy's workshop produced 20,000 items for bee hives, hundreds of chimney-pots, sinks, containers for coal and oil, and pumps for oil and other fuel. A workshop for cardboard products employed approximately 100 people. Here boxes for packing dishes, clothing, shoes, jewelry, shaving equipment, etc., were produced. They also produced suitcases, various types of mirrors, albums, office supplies, and bound books. The plant filled orders for 5,000 pocket mirrors, 70,000 cases for square batteries, 600,000 cases for round batteries, and 1,500 boxes for flatware. The leather goods and fabric department produced handbags, bookbags, wallets, knapsacks, suitcases, leather watchbands, and the like.

The department for handicraft products made brushes and various sorts of brooms, hand-knit scarves, vests, ear muffs, and other assorted handicrafts.

The Vyhne Labor Camp

The residents of the Vyhne labor camp were employed primarily in construction work on government spas on the site, and worked under the supervision of the construction department of the Jewish Center. In the first stage of construction a large swimming pool and dressing room, a restaurant, and playing fields – a sort of sports and recreation center – were built. Stage 2 included plans to demolish the old buildings on the site and built a central hotel there. Family members of the men working in construction were employed in various branches of production similar to the enterprises in the Sered and Nováky camps: garments, leather goods and furs, knit products, and screens. This camp, too, had workshops equipped with sophisticated equipment and machinery and enjoyed great demand for its products, since everything it made was of high quality and good taste.

The workshop for leather goods used scraps from the leather

industry to make handbags and bookbags, and along with the furrier's department produced gloves, vests, and jackets with combinations of leather and fur.

On the initiative of several experts living in the camp, a factory for chemical products was established, as well. It produced soap paste, laundry detergent, various types of vaseline, wax for sleds, soda crystals, paste for floor, cleaning powders, etc. Its principal customers being government and public enterprises, the plant's products were in great demand.

Agriculture in the Camps

The Sered and Nováky camps also had small agricultural enterprises. Every tillable plot of land was utilized or growing crops, and a livestock farm was established for raising cows, goats, sheep and hens. Enterprising women developed an angora wool industry based on rabbits which were raised in the camp. They sheared the wool, spun and died it, and knit high quality products.

In November 1942, the three camps together housed approximately 2,200 people – 750 in Sered, 1,200 in Nováky, and 250 in Vyhne. Many trained craftsmen arrived at the camps, bringing with them not only their vocational expertise but also the tools of their trade, which they placed at the disposal of the generality. For most of the residents the camps were cities of refuge, hopefully saving their lives until liberation should come.

The camps proved themselves and were an important factor in the economy of the Slovak state, at the service of the Germans. The leaders of these two nationalities, however, were more interested in adhering to their plans for "a final solution of the Jewish problem" than in utilizing the cheap man-power provided by the labor camps, and hence they preferred to deport the Jews. During the hiatus in deportations the Jewish leaders all agreed on the necessity of strengthening the status of the camps and improving their efficiency to prove to the authorities that great benefit could be derived from the Jews by employing them in productive work for the benefit of the state and its economy. On the other hand, not a single free person was interested in living in a labor camp which overnight could turn into a camp for rounding up and deporting Jews. Those who entered the labor camps were for the most part defenseless people who had been purged from the labor force and did not hold a job or protection papers.

Rabbi Frieder's activities in the camps

The following letters bear testimony to Rabbi Frieder's activities in the labor camps during the early months of 1943:

The Jewish Council in the Nováky Labor Camp
January 2, 1943

Dear Mr. Armin Frieder, National Chief Rabbi, Nové Mesto,

The Ministry of Interior has informed our management that the Rabbi has been appointed spiritual leader of the labor camps. We are glad of this appointment, for it is what we hoped for, and wish the Rabbi much success in fulfilling his duty. We shall be very pleased if the Rabbi set a date for visiting us at his earliest convenience.

On behalf of the Jewish Council,
Emanuel Fürst

Management of the Sered Labor Camp for Jews

February 23, 1943

In response to the Rabbi's letter of the 15th of this month, we grate fully acknowledge receipt of the books and parcel sent to the *Hevra Kadisha* (Jewish burial society). Likewise, we were very happy to receive the shipment of geese. We wish to take this opportunity to inform you that the commissar of the camp and our organization coordinator shall pay a visit to the Rabbi on Tuesday, the 26th of this month, in Nové Mesto. We shall arrive in the morning by the express train. We request that the Rabbi be at home on this date and thank the Rabbi again for his generosity. We close with the blessing of peace, in the name of the management.

Weiner, Organization Coordinator

The Jewish School in the Sered Labor Camp

January 2, 1943

We received the shipment of books containing a history of the Jews, books for youth, 24 story-books for children, and 15 picture-books for nursery school children. Thank you for your efforts and encouragement in helping raise the standards of teaching and education in our school...

K. König, Principal

The Jewish Council in the Nováky Labor Camp
April 22, 1943

We hereby acknowledge receipt of the shipment of *matzas,* for which we thank the Rabbi heartily. We are very glad that by the Rabbi's generous help most of the inhabitants of the camp shall be able to observe the laws and customs of the Passover festival as far as possible.

Emanuel Fürst

In the following letter, Moses David Reisner of Bratislava, a resident of the Sered camp, writes to Rabbi Frieder regarding a "wave of conversions to Christianity":

Reverend Sir, National Chief Rabbi, allow me to draw the Rabbi's attention to an important matter affecting our life and survival in the camp. I am not sure the Rabbi is aware that there is a movement here actively working for conversion from the Jewish faith, a movement which is supported by certain circles. On the second day of the Christian holiday of Easter, the Evangelical priest from Trnava was here and addressed the congregation which were assembled, and took the occasion to baptize two camp residents who had converted.

Yesterday the commandant of the camp, Vašina, published the following announcement: "Since it has become known to me that many among you are interested in converting to the Christian religion, you are requested to sign up with Dr. J. Grál by the 30th of April."

We have the clear impression that the commandant wishes to promote the matter. Rumors are circulating that the government and the Christian Church have reached an agreement providing that anyone who converts is immediately protected against deportation, since he is under the protection of the Church. News of a mounting wave of conversion to Christianity outside the camp, as well, has been influencing apathetic individuals, who do not care one way or the other; and the danger of their falling into the hands of active converts from Judaism, who are veritably hunting souls to convert, is very great. Several months ago, His Reverence the Rabbi came here and preached candidly and persuasively. Forgive me, Rabbi, if I say that it is essential His Reverence visit here and give another sermon to calm the people and help settle the minds of the perplexed.[33]

* * *

Rabbi Frieder also received many letters from children in the camps, including a letter from the student council of the Sered camp school, dated February 1, 1943, thanking him for a shipment of books and fruits for *Tu bi-Shvat* (the Jewish new year for trees).

---

[33] After the war M. D. Reisner, a survivor of the Holocaust, was active in the Bratislava Jewish community and in the Central Union of Jewish Communities. He immigrated to Israel and is now living in Bnai Braq. The first line of his letter was written in Hebrew, printed in Latin characters; the rest was written in German. It was not dated.

The Bar-Mitzvah boys in the camps thanked Rabbi Frieder for the valuable gifts which each of them received: phylacteries, a prayer book, and a watch. "I promise to remain true to the Jewish tradition, in the spirit of our forefathers, and to the ideals to which the Reverend Rabbi has devoted his entire life," one youngster wrote from the Nováky camp. Another youngster wrote: "I wish to thank the Rabbi and promise to be a good and upright Jew." Helena Vogel, a teacher in the nursery school in the Nováky labor camp, wrote a moving letter on March 23, 1943, describing the reaction of the nursery school children when she gave them the parcels of presents – books, toys, and educational games – which arrived for them.

* * *

I paid frequent visits to the camps. This meant traveling back and forth between Bratislava and the labor camps and spending several days a month in the camps. Thus, I established good relations with the Jewish management as well as with the administration working on behalf of the government. This public activity called for a supreme emotional effort to overcome the social problems and not disappoint the expectations of the inmates. The camps were indeed supplied with installations and machinery, and various institutions tried to ease the life of the residents. Nevertheless, the inmates remained shut in the camps like prisoners and slaves, dependent on the whim of the commissar, the strict commandant, who had no consideration for the needs of the workers living in the camps. We must add the fact that the Jewish administration, as well, did not always live up to the test. Perhaps they are not to blame, since their authority was quite limited and even the slightest accomplishment could only be achieved with difficulty. Yet one could say that the members of the Jewish administrative staff were not noted for their devoted service.

Whenever I returned from visiting a camp, it took me several days to overcome the emotional suffering and depression which the visit brought upon me. I saw the problems and tried to help. I did all I could. When the opportunity to lobby the government commissar in the 14th Department presented itself, I tried especially hard to get rid of informers and sycophants in the camps. Yet all this was but a drop in the bucket, a small fraction of what was necessary and required, of all that we would have liked to do but could not do; for the labor camps henceforth became institutions which, operating under sanction of the law, turned free human beings into captive slaves, depriving them of all their rights and freedom.

The infirm, elderly, and sick in the camps were in a sorry state, for there was no one to care for them. Those who were capable of working were required to engage in productive labor; non-productive invalids were left to care for themselves. At an opportune moment I brought the matter up in the Ministry of Interior, where I disclosed the "secret" of the existence of Ohel David and proposed that the institution take in the elderly from all the labor camps, free of charge. In exchange I requested that the institution receive official recognition and that all its residents be guaranteed protection by the authorities. This proposal was fraught with danger, especially since the "bunker," i.e., the shelter for many "illegal residents," would henceforth become a public institution under government supervision, with all entailed thereby. With the assistance of my friends, especially Ondrej Steiner, and thanks to my connections with local and central government circles, we succeeded in bringing these negotiations to a satisfactory conclusion.

On February 2, 1943, the government commissar in charge of the Jewish labor camps, acting under the Ministry of Interior, published an edict establishing a central old-age home in the Nováky Jewish labor camp to house the all the Jewish camps' elderly residents who were unable to work. Until this old-age home was built, the elderly were to be transferred temporarily to the Jewish old-age home in Nové Mesto. The Jews transferred to Nové Mesto would still be registered on the lists of the camps from which they came. This directive would not affect the status of the current residents of the old-age home or the status of the institution itself.

The edict appointed me chairman of the board of directors of the Adolf Baiersdorf Foundation, and by virtue of this position I became director of the old-age home and in charge of implementing administrative matters pursuant to carrying out this directive. According to the edict the district office in Nové Mesto was officially to supervise the institution and to run the files and registry of residents who would be transferred from the labor camps to the old age home. The edict also stipulated that the labor camps must inform the district office in Nové Mesto of every resident who is transferred and must enclose each one's personal card with all the data on the person transferred.

This development enabled us not only to take in people from the labor camps, but also to release them on the basis of certificates of release that I obtained from the 14th Department or on the basis of documents attesting leave for illness and recuperation. In the next stage I obtained papers for many non-protected Jews throughout the state, certifying that they were residents on leave from the old age home in the camp. Thus, Ohel David succeeded in protecting many Jews who essentially lived at home and generally were taken in by relatives, or who fled to Hungary.[34]

---

[34] See letters in appendix.

V. The Minister of Interior Threatens to Expel the Remaining Jews

On February 7, 1943, a national conference of the Hlinka Guard was held in Ružomberok, the metropolis of Catholic nationalism, known as the "Mecca of the Slovaks" since it was the burial place of the priest Hlinka, founder of the People's party. The commander-in-chief of the organization, Minister of Interior Alexander Mach, proclaimed in his address: "Jews, whether or not they have converted to Christianity, whether or not they hold one or another type of certificate, all come under the same law. March will arrive, and then April, and the transports will roll." This radical speech aroused panic among the Jewish public.

By now we knew that our lives were at stake; we knew that deportation to the land of doom meant death, and we were firmly resolved not to sit at home, waiting like sheep to be taken to the slaughter. We immediately went into action, using all the means and all the avenues open to us, to save the remnants of the Jewish people, to deliver them from death. Dr. Kováč and I lobbied Vašek, while I continued my efforts to sway Minister Sivák. Ondrej Steiner appealed to Dr. Koso, Gisi Fleischmann to Margit Šlachta, a high-ranking nun who wielded great influence in Budapest, and various other persons appealed to the senior clergy of the Catholic Church. People with influence in economic affairs lobbied Imrich Karvaš, the president of the National Bank, and talks were also held with the German advisor Wisliceny.

On March 8, 1943, seven bishops published a Pastoral Epistle in which, citing the constitution of the state, for the first time they stated their unequivocal position that all residents, without distinction of origin, nationality, religion, or profession, shall enjoy personal freedom and protection of life and property. In the epistle, read in Catholic churches on the 21st of March, the bishops came out against a policy which punishes people without taking them to court and without proving their guilt. Of course, they stressed the duty to accept converts to Christianity into the lap of the Church. Great importance attached to the response made by the political secretariat of the Vatican, which relayed its stand against deportation of the Jews orally, through Slovakia's ambassador to the Vatican, Karol Sidor, who transmitted it on to Slovakia's president and prime minister. On May 5 an epistle (number 2731/43) was also sent in the name of the "Political Secretariat of His Reverence," reiterating the secretariat's stand and expressing the hope that the government of Slovakia would cease the deportations.

At the meeting of the cabinet, Minister Sivák and Dr. Karvaš lived up to our expectations. They were the primary spokesmen against the minister of interior's proposal regarding deportations and strenuously objected to their being renewed. The decision came out in our favor. Mach's proclamations remained an expression of his own personal desires. This time we won the difficult struggle, and the rounding up of Jews which the Ministry of Interior had been talking about gradually slowed to a halt, leaving the extremists to make do with publishing venomous propaganda articles in all the papers, first and foremost the organ of the Hlinka Guard, the *Gardista,* and with issuing a number of police orders further restricting personal freedom.

Exemption cannot be had without a price

Daily cares were compounded by a non-routine disruption. On March 5, on the eve of the Sabbath of *Parashat Shekalim* (the Sabbath immediately preceding the month of Adar), I was examining the financial books of Ohel David when two men suddenly entered my office and introduced themselves as customs inspectors from Liptovský-Svätý-Mikuláš. After a thorough search through my house, I was arrested without knowing the reason why. Tension ran high. Late in the evening we reached Mikuláš, where the leaders of the Jewish community, Gustav Haas and Kopstock, awaited me. Haas had even managed to arrange hotel accommodations for me and hosted me in his home. My investigation was over on Monday. I was accused of violating currency regulations in connection with the campaign which we ran to benefit the deportees from our city, but for lack of evidence was only fined 15,000 korunas and, after this sum was paid, was released. Gustav Haas and his brother Bendo did a lot to help me, and I was glad to see that Mikuláš was blessed with such excellent workers for the Jewish community. In comparison to the importance of the charitable work we were doing, the fright which I suffered was certainly quite tolerable.

VI. Life in the Jewish Community in 5704 (1942-43)

As Passover drew near, we faced the problem of supplying *matza*. The authorities assured us they would make it possible for *matza* to be baked, but as the time drew nigh, our foes turned the matter into a political affair, and baking *matza* was forbidden.

In March, the Ministry of Interior published an edict forbidding Jews to change their apartments or leave them, or to be outside their homes from 6 p.m. to 8 a.m. The purpose of this directive was to make it easier to round up Jews and deport them. During the period of the counting of the *omer,* from Passover to the Feast of Weeks, evening prayers are recited after dark. Therefore, we requested that this directive be repealed or amended to enable us to hold public services. We were given assurances, but they were not kept. Certain bodies were doing everything they could to disrupt our community and religious life. Things depended primarily on the local authorities.

In Nové Mesto I managed to obtain special permits allowing Jews to be abroad during curfew hours, when going to or from the synagogue. One could say that the burden of the directives against the Jews was on the whole lighter in our community. We managed to lead a relatively normal community life and keep the commandments, including eating *matza* on Passover.

Festive Opening of the Tribe of Simeon Yeshiva

Although a number of Jews converted – most of them for appearances' sake or out of weakness, hoping that this act would spare them from being deported – I can say that those who remained true to our faith continued with greater fortitude in their traditional way of life in the spirit of our ancestral Jewish heritage.

In the synagogue every Sabbath I gave a sermon on topical subjects. Most of the city's Jews, legal and illegal residents alike, including the Orthodox, came to hear my sermons.

On the morning of Sivan 22 (June 24, 1943), the anniversary of the death of Rabbi David Deutsch of blessed memory, we held a commemorative celebration in Ohel David, and on this occasion I officially opened the Tribe of Simeon Yeshiva, named after the last rabbi of the Orthodox community in Nové Mesto, Rabbi Simeon Schreiber, may God avenge his blood. A group of twenty young lads, living in the city under my protection, formed the founding nucleus of the *yeshiva*. The students of the Tribe of Simeon Yeshiva engaged primarily in Torah study, but within this context also were active in philanthropic work and charity on behalf of their fellows – children and youths who were living in our city and whose parents had been exiled, leaving the children with no information on the fate that befell their parents. The lads collected around 5,000 korunas every month from various donors and saw to it that these orphans had bread and butter for their supper.

Notwithstanding the restrictions and harsh laws of these difficult times, social life developed within the Jewish community. Life generally proceeded with a sense of partial relief; the terror of deportation and its accompanying emotional tension had eased up slightly. Yet concern for the fate of the deportees weighed down upon us beyond bearing. When a letter arrived from one of them, we all rejoiced at receiving a sign of life, yet on the other hand we were saddened and depressed, for every card which reached us either openly mentioned or allusively referred to mass death and destruction, to starvation and infectious disease.

Our constant torment and depression leave us no rest. In the terrible straits in which our deported brethren find themselves we must give whatever we can; this is the command of the hour, how else are we to stand erect in the trial of history? Only knowing that we did all that was within our power can justify our existence. Only thus can we be a people aspiring to rise on its feet and stand strong with revitalized strength, when the hour of redemption and rebirth comes for the Jewish people.

In Ohel David

The summer passed without mishap. Our activities focused on aiding our fellow Jews in the community's institutions, in the state, and in the land of doom, whence we received reports which brought our hopes of saving large numbers of Jews to naught. The New Year of 5704 approached, and with it came a time for reckoning. Therefore, I assembled the board of directors of Ohel David to report on the many good things this institution had done for the community and for the Jews on a national scale.

The meeting of the board of directors took place on August 29, 1943. As chairman I delivered a comprehensive report. Among the points mentioned were the official visits by representatives of the government authorities: the notary Pečuch, government commissar of the labor camps; Dr. Vašek, head of the 14th Department; and the commissar of the Jewish hospital in Bratislava, which had been transferred to the Sered camp, who came accompanied by the director, Dr. Fehér. The three visits passed without misadventure and the visitors found the institution to be in fine condition. A vegetarian kitchen was established to enable residents of the Ohel to buy food supplies on the site, without having to go in to town.

The institution cared for 216 people, five were on legal leave, another 16 people outside the Ohel were under its protection, and 77 people came to us from the labor camps. In addition to these people, approximately another 400 people throughout the country held papers of our institution and were protected by virtue of being under our aegis.

Later in the meeting the question of the ownership of the institution came up for discussion, in the wake of recent laws. I expressed the opinion that it would be more advantageous for us if the property were formally transferred to the ownership of the Jewish Center, in accordance with the law. My position was accepted.

Adolf Biermann delivered the financial report and made note of the expenditures associated with the Passover festival and with taking in people from the camps. Revenues came from various sources – monthly contributions by members of the community, donations made in the synagogue, and payments by the residents.

The quality of the food was criticized, and some people suggested that it be improved for those residents who paid for their keep. The complainers maintained that young people who do not do a thing receive second portions of food. In my response I noted that during the months of danger a few rich residents had been accepted to the institution and were perfectly happy then, but that now they were complaining and demanding superior food. Under my leadership the institution would be run according to the commandment "that thy brother shall live with thee," with no distinction between rich brethren and poor. If several dissatisfied rich residents wished to vacate their quarters and enable us to take in their poorer brethren who are in need of our aid, I would not object. With God's help, we would maintain the institution even without paying residents, but we shall keep to the principle of equality and shall improve the food as far as is within our reach. The young residents "who do not do a thing" are a valuable asset of the Jewish people, diligent *yeshiva* students who are studying Torah in the Tribe of Simeon Yeshiva, which provides their additional bread from its own budget and gives monthly stipends to needy residents. A resolution was adopted to bake bread in the institution itself and to increase the ration to 300 grams per day per person.

In my concluding remarks I thanked those present for enabling us to fulfill our historical calling of saving Jews from danger and requested that all constructive forces band together so that we shall be able to continue maintaining the institution, which is a pride to our community and its leaders.

The birth of a son brings a righteous man to our city.

In the month of Elul (September), as the New Year was approaching, a son was born into the family of Alexander Bernfeld, leader of the Orthodox community. His circumcision ceremony, admitting him into the covenant of the Patriarch Abraham, was held on the 5th of Elul, 5703 (September 5, 1943), in the Orthodox synagogue. National Chief Rabbi Samuel David Ungar, who was the *mohel,* and his son-in-law, R. Michael Dov Weissmandel, participated in the ceremony. It was a joyous day for all the Jews of the city and for the Tribe of Simeon Yeshiva. In a festive meal celebrating the circumcision, attended by many guests, Rabbi Ungar delivered a speech of Talmudic argumentation, homilies, ethics and spiritual awakening. In his profound sermon he also mentioned my public activity and wished me success in continuing my work on behalf of the Jewish people. I took these remarks as a compliment, for I had not expected to receive open, public acknowledgement from the lofty personage of the Nitra Rebbe, the official head and celebrated leader of the Orthodox Jewish community. Rabbi Weissmandel expressed appreciation in his speech, as well. For myself, this was an opportune moment to voice my stand on Jewish values as I understood them and was enacting them in practice. It was a day of spiritual elation. After the ceremony the Rebbe and his party visited Ohel David and my home. By this noble deed Rabbi Ungar publicly expressed his friendliness towards me, which gave me a sense of satisfaction. Thus, fortified by the encouraging words of one of the great Jews of our generation, we approached the days of *selihot* (penitential prayers recited from before the New Year and until the Day of Atonement). In our thoughts and hearts we carried the hope and faith that the coming year, 5704, would be a year of redemption and salvation for us and for all our brethren, the Children of Israel, wherever they were.

VII. The Days of Awe, 5704

Especial emotion filled our hearts on these High Holy Days, Days of Awe that they were. It was awful to see the empty places in the synagogue. It was as if the many people who were missing cried out in an inaudible voice, and we all wailed silently over the blood of our brethren that had been shed, for each empty place in the pews was a reminder: he, too, who is missing, fell victim. Our prayers came not only from the prayer book but also from our inner being, from our bitter fate in the cruelest sense of the word. The prayer *Unetane Tokef* became something we truly experienced. Never had this prayer been so real, so immediate; fear and trembling seized the holy congregation as the cantor intoned in a plaintive wail: "who shall live and who shall die..., who by fire ... who by wild beasts, who of starvation and who of thirst ..., and who shall suffer torment ..., who shall be humbled and who shall be exalted."

When the congregation gathered in the Great Synagogue on New Year's Day, before the blowing of the shofar I said:

> Glancing back and recalling the High Holy Days, taking stock of what has befallen us in the past few years, we see a bleak, sad and woeful picture. These have been days of Judgment, marked by deep concern for our fate and our future, Days of Awe, marked by upheaval. During the New Year of 5700 (1939), when I first stood in this pulpit on this holiday, the war was just beginning. The youth had been called up for army service. The military draft, at a time when Jews were already being deprived of equal rights, was doubly worrisome for Jewish women and mothers. In the sermon which I delivered then, I tried to calm the women and comfort them. On New Year 5701 (1940), during the period when the demoniacal dance against us had already begun, as men and youths were being taken to special labor camps for Jews and the younger generation was no longer present in the synagogue, again I had to find words of comfort and encouragement for the mothers and women worrying for their dear ones. The third New Year, 5702 (1941)

was marked by severe persecution, as the bread was taken out of the mouths of our congregants and the first intimations of deportation began to be heard; and my sermon, too, dwelled on the difficult times. Today we are facing the New Year following our punishment, our affliction, after tens of thousands of our fellow Jews have been exiled to the land of doom, after we have given our sacrifices; and now we must examine our deeds. We stand with burdened, aching hearts, shaken to the core by the Holocaust of our people, unable to express that which is in our hearts. Therefore, my afflicted soul would rather sound its prayer in a still, silent voice, for Thou, Lord of Mercy, shalt well understand my thoughts and the ponderings of my heart.

I was unable to devote the remaining Days of Repentance, between the New Year and the Day of Atonement, to my congregation. Serious worry for our safety and survival again occupied the leaders of the community. On the Sabbath of Repentance, the 14th Department of the Ministry of Interior received a letter signed by Minister of Interior Mach, in which the minister ordered all the Jews of Slovakia, including converts, rounded up into a new labor camp. The great danger was that the order had been given at the behest and consent of the President. The content of the letter was relayed to our colleagues in greatest secrecy. I was immediately summoned for urgent consultations to act swiftly to avert the decree. In previous deliberations I had persuaded the Working Group that any action rounding up Jews should be viewed as dangerous and as a prelude to deportation. Therefore, we immediately prepared for full scale action, as if renewing the deportations was at issue.

On Monday, October 4, 1943, Dr. Kováč and I went to see Vašek to discuss the situation with him. I told Vašek that in my opinion this plan of concentrating all the Jews in a new camp was not feasible, and that I was relying on his diplomatic talents to find a solution so that the plan would not come to pass. He, however, did not accept my position and emphatically declared that we should not expect any help from him in this matter.

His refusal to help us came to me as no surprise, for I knew he had had a falling out with Mach, who had accused him of being corrupt and accepting bribes. Their break had not gone so far as an expression of lack of confidence; but Vašek was waiting for an opportunity to prove his loyalty to the official line and his unqualified hostility towards the Jews.

Vašek's passive stand reinforced my opinion, which I had expressed a number of times in the group's deliberations, that his services bore no relationship to the monthly "obligations" which we undertook towards him. Therefore, I suggested that we discuss the matter openly with Vašek and tell him that we were requesting that he render us a service in exchange for a service. Dr. Kováč and Gisi Fleischmann opposed my proposal. With Dr. Winterstein's encouragement, I requested that the question be reopened. This caused a tense atmosphere, bordering on crisis, in the Working Group. Were it not for the personal intervention of Rabbi Weissmandel, who requested that I change my position and maintain peace within the group, I would have ceased participating in the meetings of the group. Out of a sense of public responsibility and because of the danger which we now faced and which was not to be taken lightly, I retracted my opinion. We put aside our ill-feelings and sat down to do real work.

After Vašek's negative response I requested an interview with

Sivák, and by October 11, 1943, was received by the minister. Our conversation lasted an hour and a half. I laid the entire affair out before him, and again brought up all the problems inherent in the plan and the dangers which we would face if the evil plot were indeed to come to pass. The minister informed me that there had been no debate in the Government on the subject of rounding up the Jews and that he must look into the matter and obtain information from official sources. He suggested that I, too, try to obtain further information and made another appointment with me for the next day. In this conversation we summed up all the details, as well as the plan for appealing to various persons. Emphasis was laid on the especial importance of ascertaining the factors and motives behind the stand which the president of Slovakia had taken. Once more Sivák proved his humane attitude and his unconditional, selfless willingness to help. Other moderate and friendly circles were also invoked and responded promptly. Instead of the Jews being concentrated in a camp, several steps were taken against us by the police: curfew regulations were strictly enforced under threat of violators being sent to labor camps, and laws which thus far had hardly been taken note of were henceforth strictly enforced. Thus, the great woe became a lesser hardship, most heavily afflicting our brethren in the capital, where the harassment was most unpleasant. In the outlying cities the situation was generally tolerable, since the local authorities were more relaxed about carrying out the directives and did not take them seriously. The position of the local authorities was also affected by developments on the battle front.[35] In outlying cities the Jews succeeded in establishing good relations with officials of the local government so that the full severity of the laws did not

[35] In the Casablanca Conference, in January 1943, Churchill and Roosevelt pledged they would wage war on Germany until her unconditional surrender. In May 1943, the Axis forces were defeated in Africa, putting an end to the battle on this front. In July 1943, came the British--American landing in Sicily and the fall of Mussolini. In September 1943 Marshal Badoglio declared a cease-fire. On the eastern front the Germans were defeated in the Battle of Stalingrad (February 1943); from July to August 1943 the German army was in steady retreat; and on August 23, 1943, Cracow was liberated.

make itself felt. In Nové Mesto no action was taken to implement the new directives and we were not harassed. Nevertheless, I requested that our brethren who had recently settled in the city, seeking refuge and protection among us, not be seen in the city streets; for Jew-haters were not lacking and there was no need to attract their attention. In my sermons I stressed that we must realize that the danger of concentration hangs over us like the Sword of Damocles. In our current situation we have no choice but to make do with partial success; the edict was only deferred, not annulled.

On the eve of the Day of Atonement I returned to Bratislava very late, barely in time to prepare for the solemn day. *Kol Nidre* services began at 5 o'clock and were attended by a large congregation.

Very excited, I ascended the pulpit to deliver a rousing speech in the spirit of the hard and fateful times. I expounded the psalm, "A Song of Ascents. Out of the depths have I called Thee, O Lord," as meaning that we, who are in deep distress, call out from the depths of our hearts and souls to the Lord. But "out of the depths" does not only mean from the depths of our souls, but also from any deep place; thus, we cry out from cellars, from shelters, from caves and trenches, from huts and "bunkers." Our call sounds from places of hiding, from the depths of the hearts of people living in the dark underground and unable to come out to the light of day and appear in the synagogue to pour out their hearts. Also crying out of the depths are those Jews who, while they live in the light of day, hold various forged papers, certificates, or documents, and thus, like the Marranos – those transgressors whom a worldly court declared fit for us to pray with – cannot join the congregation in this holy hour.

The following day, before the *Yizkor* memorial service, we communed with the memory of the members of our congregation who had been exiled and had passed away, sacred martyrs of our people. I mentioned the prayer of the High Priest on the Day of Atonement, as he exited from the Holy of Holies safe and unharmed: ." . . and of the people of the Sharon he used to say: May it be His will that their homes not become their graves." We must learn our lesson and know that if, God forbid, danger threaten us again, we must not sit in our homes and wait like sheep to be taken to the slaughter, lest our homes become graves.

The Feast of Tabernacles 5704

On the Feast of Tabernacles, we were able to observe the commandment of dwelling in booths. The problem was where to obtain the Four Species (for the *lulav*). Even Switzerland, Italy and Hungary were without *etrogs* because of the war. We despaired of being able to keep the commandment. Five *etrogs* for a million European Jews were imported into Hungary via diplomatic channels. An argument broke out in Budapest between the two organizations of Jewish congregations, since the neologists also claimed an *etrog* for themselves. When this became known, Rabbi Weissmandel protested, demanding that one *etrog* be given to Slovakia, as well. I appealed to the chairman of the national council of neologist congregations, Samuel Stern, and urgently requested that they make their *etrog* available to the Jews of Slovakia. The holiday came, but no *etrog* arrived. On the second day of the festival, during the Torah reading, an announcement came from Nitra that in the afternoon a *lulav* and *etrog* which the Rebbe was sending to me in Nové Mesto would arrive by car, and that after making the blessing over the *lulav* and *etrog* they were to be returned. The gentile messenger did not arrive with the *lulav* and *etrog* until 3 p.m. A large crowd had gathered in the synagogue, for the Orthodox had joined us, as well, in the hope that everyone would have a chance to take the *lulav* and *etrog* into his hands and bless *shehehianu* (blessing the Lord "who hast kept us in life ... ''").

It was a once-in-a-lifetime experience to see the ultra-Orthodox praying fervently along with our congregation. The union of the Four Species had bound us together, had united us. Immediately after the services we returned the *lulav* and *etrog* to the messenger so that he could take them to the Trnava congregation. Since I wished to bless the *lulav* once more, on the third intermediate day of the festival of Tabernacles I went with my brother Emanuel to Nitra to pray in the Rebbe's congregation.[36]

The Rebbe conferred on me all possible honors during the service and even invited me and my brother to join him in his *sukkah* for breakfast and a pleasant conversation, which lasted close to noon.

These experiences reminded me of my time studying in the *yeshiva* and in the *heder* of my mentor and teacher, Rabbi Ben-Zion Braun, in Topolčany, where I had my first exposure to the atmosphere of Ashkenazi *hassidism*.

VIII. Social Conditions in the Labor Camps

After the holidays I set out on a tour of the labor camps. At well-

[36] Rabbi Samuel David Ungar, chief rabbi of the Orthodox congregations in Slovakia, during those difficult times also extended his patronage over dozens of young men studying in the Great Yeshiva, over talmudic scholars in the *kolel* (talmudic college supported on modest stipends), who found refuge in his court. His love for the Jewish people and its Torah was without bounds. His house was always open, whoever came into his court was welcome, and there was always enough room. He inspired certain members of the community to action, and they formed good relations with the authorities so that the *yeshiva*, which took in dozens of "illegal" people, was not touched. It was for good reason that the Rebbe's kingdom was dubbed the "Vatican." On the Rebbe's mission and inspiration, his son-in-law, the *gaon* Rabbi Michael Dov Weissmandel, one of the mainstays of the Working Group, worked with great devotion and close cooperation with Rabbi Frieder. Rabbi Weissmandel not only worked energetically to save Jews in Slovakia, but also saw to it that the large Jewish community in Hungary, which had not yet been hit and was still complacent and even apathetic, be warned of what was transpiring beyond its borders. He initiated the Europa Plan, which he wrote about in his book, *Out of the Straits* (1960), and sent letters, reports and appeals abroad, together with other members of the Working Group. Rabbi Samuel David Ungar of Nitra passed away in the "bunker" in the Banská-Bystrica forest, on the 9th of Adar, 5705 (1945), and after the war was laid to rest in his own city.

attended meetings I discussed all the problems troubling us and the inmates of the camps. They told me about life in the camp and its impact on the individual. The people were generally very tense. Living in camp for a prolonged period, under a rigid regime which restricted personal freedom, was a heavy burden.

I found the situation especially difficult in the Sered camp. Having to live together under conditions of extreme crowding and under constant tension and uncertainty regarding the future in many instances led to loss of moral restraint, to letting one's desires run wild, and to sexual licentiousness between lonely older women and unbridled younger men. Sometimes these women got into trouble and needed surgical care. The day I visited the camp an unusual wedding was held between a young 22-year-old man and a 34-year-old woman. This was not, to be sure, the first time such a thing had ever happened, nevertheless it was characteristic of social life in the camps. Each camp also had a group of people who adhered to the commandments of the Jewish tradition, but they had little impact on the rest of the society. How to remedy the situation was beyond my ken, as well. It was clear that simply by preaching I could not succeed in arresting the moral degeneration which had set in.

The Jewish Center had a section in charge of labor camps, called the Central Bureau for the Labor Camps of the Jews of Slovakia. The bureau was headed by Dr. Oscar Neumann and Ondrej Steiner. With the approval of the government's commandant of camps, in April 1943, the heads of this bureau established a public council for economics, culture, and social life. As a member of this council, I was in charge of cultural and social affairs. I visited the camps regularly, spending a day or two in each camp, as needed, studying the social problems and cultural activities of the camps at close hand and listening to the wishes of the inmates.

On one of my visits to Sered I begged the inhabitants of the camp to be patient with one another, to behave in a brotherly and kindly way so that life would be easier and not encumbered with additional hardships. I said to them:

True, life is not easy, but we must think of the vast numbers of our brethren who have been cruelly expelled from the camp and today, a year later, most likely are no longer among the living. They were ostensibly transported to labor camps, but what kind of camps were these? Even if conditions were a thousand times worse there than here, it would still be considered paradise. Do not look at those whose lot is easier; look at the reality with patience and understanding, until salvation comes. I am convinced that one day, when the story of the Holocaust of the Jews of Central Europe goes down in history, the labor camps of Slovakia, with all the bad in them, with all the pain and suffering in them, shall be seen as bright spots in the gloom of these dark ages, the history of our times. We are not yet capable of comprehending or appreciating the significance and importance of the camps. Central European Jewry, to our great distress, is being annihilated, is perishing off the face of the earth, and you here shall be a center which, God willing, will be saved; you shall be the core out of which a new Jewish community will grow. You shall hopefully have the good fortune to leave this life of exile and immigrate to the Land of Israel, there to restore our days as of old. Your hands, skilled in creative work, shall rebuild the land of our forefathers – may it be reborn speedily in our day.

The Vyhne camp pulsated with Jewish life. Its first residents came from the Sosnowice ghetto in Poland. Although many of them were expelled again during the mass deportations, a core nevertheless remained. These were good Jews, deeply imbued in Jewish tradition and culture. Later they were joined by Jews from Slovakia who had a different mentality, different ways of life and thought. This occasionally led to differences of opinion and even outright conflicts and fights between the two groups. The Polish Jews, however, had the upper hand, which proved to be for the good of the camp. Their camp also had a group of religious Jews from Topolčany, who contributed greatly to the social life there. The decorated *sukkah* which they built in honor of the holiday was proof of their adherence to the commandments of the Torah, even under the difficult condition of life in a labor camp.

In the evening, at a general meeting, I tried to encourage the camp residents and expressed my appreciation of their efforts. I praised those who were upholding the faith, most of whom came from Poland, and who were occasionally attacked by the assimilationists, who drew a distinction between the Jews of Eastern and Western Europe. The activities of the Ostjuden, as they were derogatorily called by the assimilationists among Slovak Jewry, were contributing greatly to the proper functioning of community life, strengthening Jewish identity, and safeguarding morality and the Jewish tradition in the closed society of the camp. I added further:

> We are being smitten by our enemies, and their hatred
> for us abounds. Therefore, brothers and sisters, you
> are afflicting yourselves with jealousy and intolerance,
> sometimes bordering on wanton hatred, presents an
> incomprehensible and intolerable situation. I beg you, let
> there be no strife between you, for we are all brethren[37]
> in distress, in suffering, and in sadness; and we must be

---

[37] Cf. Genesis 13:8. Translator's note.

forthcoming towards one another and unite in a covenant of brothers – like David and Jonathan, who were devoted to one another heart and soul – for the sake of life and peace over the entire House of Israel.

These words were well received, and on the morrow, after talks with members of the Jewish management and the camp commissar, I left the Vyhne camp, intending to visit Nováky, the third camp, in the near future.

Questioned by the Center for State Security

Following the dispatch of aid packages to the deportees, an activity which necessitated contact with many people, it was reported in the German Embassy and in the Center for State Security that Dr. Kováč and I were disseminating rumors of atrocities concerning the fate of the people deported to Poland. The military attaché at the embassy requested that the political and state security institutions investigate the matter.

Detectives of the secret police came to my home and questioned me at length. In the end I succeeded in convincing them that it was an altogether unfounded case of slander and cleared myself of all guilt. We understood that henceforth continuing the mission would be more difficult; yet, despite everything, we knew that we must continue to take action. We tried to continue our activity under the greatest secrecy. Nevertheless, at times there were leaks due to indiscretion on the part of several of our collaborators, who did not guard their words and occasionally, without meaning to, let slip information about which it would have been better to remain silent. Henceforth we must be more careful and take greater precautions.

Being on the black list of the German police is not the most pleasant thing, nevertheless I remained optimistic that I would be able to overcome this obstacle, as well. In the meantime I established good relations with Dr. Paškovič, chairman of the Central Office for Economy, and obtained from him a considerable number of certificates of protection and labor permits for Jews who were living in "bunkers" or in other underground conditions. This only helped isolated individuals and families, and not the vast number of Jews. Nevertheless, every individual is a part of the generality of the Jewish people, whom we must try to save. In my lobbying I was guided by the principle that the generality needs the individual and the individual needs the generality.

IX. The Koso – Gisi Fleischmann Affair

On Friday, the first day of the month of Mar-Heshvan (October 29, 1943), I was notified by telephone that the secret police, i.e., the Center for State Security, was looking for Gisi Fleischmann. In the afternoon Gisi herself told me that "the same people who held the Rabbi on account of the refugees are looking for the mother of Lizi and Juci (the names of her daughters)." I immediately passed the message on to Rabbi Weissmandel, who played a key role in the rescue operation of saving Jews who had fled from Poland, to prepare him for what was in store.

Early Saturday morning I received a telephone call from Bratislava in which I was informed that Gisi Fleischmann's presence was a danger to her person, and that I must immediately go by car and bring her back to Nové Mesto. I was shaken by the message but realized clearly that I could not go there, for if Gisi was in danger and could not remain in Bratislava, then my safety in the city was uncertain, as well. I decided to request Oscar Horvát to go on the mission in my stead. He had a certificate of protection from the president of Slovakia and on more than one occasion had shown his willingness to help out in time of need. Moreover, one could count on his resourcefulness. I hurried over to him and he agreed to carry out the mission as requested.

As I was returning home from the synagogue after the *musaf* service, an official from the district office intercepted me clandestinely and informed me secretly that several minutes ago an order for my arrest had arrived from the Center for State Security with instructions to transfer me to Bratislava. Arriving at home, I found a policeman awaiting me. He was surprised when I asked him whether he had come to arrest me. I "sent" him home, intimating to him that he should fib that he had not found me in. Then I went to Horvát, who immediately set off in his car for Bratislava. I remained in his home until his return the same evening. Meanwhile Dr. Steiner came from Bratislava to inform me that Dr. Tibor Kováč, Marcus Fürst, and Leo Rosenthal had been arrested, and that I was being hunted for, as well. The people who had been arrested were being held hostage until Gisi Fleischmann was found. I was very concerned for Gisi's fate, since arresting hostages intimated a serious accusation. Feverish work began in Bratislava. I decided not to report to the police until the situation became clear. Dr. Winterstein, Alexander and Iluš Adler, and Alexander Eckstein worked intensively and successfully, and thus Dr. Winterstein received a secret report on developments:

The wife Ministry of Interior Director Koso had been caught on the border between Germany and Switzerland by German security and customs officials, who found on her person a note from Gisi Fleischmann. Since the note was written in code, Mrs. Koso was arrested on suspicion of espionage. The authorities were looking for Gisi Fleischmann so that they could use her testimony to prove that the suspicion of espionage was totally unfounded.

The situation was very grave. There had been no espionage here, but there had been a violation of foreign currency regulations in which a senior official had been involved, and the affair was likely to get us into trouble. We had to stage a money transfer, purchasing Swiss marks in exchange for Slovak korunas, and make the entire affair look like a financial transaction. Various stories were fabricated and material evidence manufactured, a veritable feat of cleverness worthy of King Solomon. Four days later, on November 2, 1943, after everything had been prepared, Gisi Fleischmann reported to the police.

The police transferred her to the German Embassy, where she was interrogated for five hours and, after giving testimony, was released. The following day I, too, reported to the police and was released with the other hostages.

The entire episode filled us and senior government officials with fear and terror. Nevertheless, we not only survived it unscathed but even emerged somewhat strengthened vis-a-vis certain circles to which we had not had access heretofore, for they now realized that we were trustworthy and reliable partners.

* * *

Upon conclusion of the Koso affair, in the wake of which Koso was dismissed from office, Prime Minister Tuka published an announcement including the text of the note: "Mr. Schneider's trip has been postponed. Please receive the bearer of this note well and help her in the visit with the uncle." Signed Ella. In the interrogation Mrs. Koso admitted that she wished to put her son in a dormitory in Switzerland and, since she was afraid the amount of foreign currency allotted her by the National Bank would not suffice, intended to avail herself of the assistance of the addressee to receive a loan of 5,000 Swiss francs from him. It turned out, Dr. Tuka stated, that Mrs. Koso had connections with a certain Jewess, who had written the note to a certain Jew in Switzerland. She was punished for illicitly having contacts with a Jewess, and legal proceedings were instituted against her for foreign currency violations.

The Koso affair had far-reaching repercussions and set off various rumors and accusations of corruption. The investigation was reopened, and on January 13, 1944, Gisi Fleischmann was arrested again.

X. Personnel Changes in the Jewish Center

In the wake of the Koso – Gisi Fleischmann affair the question of reorganizing the Jewish Center became an issue once more, especially the problem of dismissing the current Elder, Arpad Sebestyén. We had often conferred among ourselves and agreed that this man, who had failed and was leading the public into error, should be replaced. Back on December 5, 1942, after Hochberg and his colleagues were arrested, the head of the Central Office for Economy offered me the position of Elder. The members of the group were actually in favor of the offer, yet I asked myself whether I could drag Sebestyén's sinking cart out of the mud. When Dr. Winterstein pressed me to accept the position, I made my acceptance conditional upon the following terms:

1. That all the informers be ousted from the Jewish Center and from all public work and be transferred to labor camps.

2. That the Jewish Center be thoroughly reorganized, from management to clerks.

3. That only Jewish clerks who had not converted be employed in the Jewish Center. Converts would be transferred to the Ninth Department, which handled the affairs of converts to Christianity.

4. That the salary of officials be raised to a level enabling them to live without having need of private business or payoffs.

I knew from the outset that these conditions could not possibly be met and would prevent me from receiving the position. When the head of the Office for Economy continued pressing me in this regard, I decided to follow a policy of postponement and delay. Eventually things reached an extreme; it was manifestly proven that Sebestyén was doing the unspeakable, and serious accusations were being made against him. Now, when he failed to keep his mouth shut even in the Gisi Fleischmann affair and told the police things which put our work in jeopardy, we reached the conclusion that the time had come to get rid of him, for the Jewish Center had acquired a bad name and had become the most accursed Jewish institution. In order that it not remain in its current state, as an organization serving the government, it had to be headed by an honest man, a man with clean hands and a pure heart,[38] a man from the board of the Jewish Center who was acquainted with affairs there and who would act justly and courageously and not betray his people or misuse his office. Without asking the person concerned, I decided to go to the officer in charge and recommend our comrade Dr. Oscar Neumann, former chairman of the Zionist Movement and the Jewish Center's board member in charge of labor camps, for the position of Elder. I claimed that Dr. Neumann, who was known for his diligence and devotion, had the necessary talents to qualify him to head the Jewish Center. This recommendation was accepted by all the bodies concerned.

Dr. Kováč suggested that Arpad Sebestyén submit a request for sick-leave from which he would not return to office, and that at this stage Dr. Neumann be appointed deputy. Since Kováč was a sober-

---

[38] Cf. Psalms 24:4. Translator's note.

minded, rational man, we accepted his suggestion and rejected the proposal advanced by others to oust Sebestyén openly.

Thus, it was that the head of the Central Office for Economy summoned the Elder in the presence of Dr. Kováč, notified him that he must submit the request, and confirmed Dr. Neumann's appointment. On this occasion Sebestyén praised himself as being the most qualified and appropriate person to fill the office, and said that he was not in need of sick-leave. Therefore, it came as no surprise to us when, under the influence of his friends, instead of submitting a request for sick-leave, he sent the head of the Office for Economy a long memorandum enumerating his accomplishments as the captain of the Jewish ship, which he claimed to have navigated flawlessly, with "inspiration from on high," for the past two and a half years. And if some fault or shortcoming was now found in him, he wished to defend himself openly and correct the errors while continuing his work as Elder. The chairman of the Office for Economy, however, had resolved to fire Sebestyén from office if the latter refused to submit a request for leave. Paškovič even saw to it that the Elder be apprised of his position. Having no alternative, the Jewish Elder appeared before the chairman, carrying two requests of different content in his pocket, intending to use whichever one necessity dictated. Parting from this highly respected office was not easy for him.

On December 7, 1943, two letters were received from Dr. Paškovič. One confirmed Sebestyén's request to take sick-leave for an unspecified period of time and notified him of the cancellation of his rights to intervene in or manage the affairs of the Jewish Center. The second letter informed Dr. Oscar Neumann of his appointment to the position of Elder of the Jewish Center, with all the authorities, rights, and responsibilities placed upon him by article 5 of the by-laws of the Jewish Center. Sebestyén was severely shaken and had a hard time bearing this humiliation, but our group received the decision with considerable satisfaction.

On December 13, 1943, the leadership of the Jewish Center issued two circulars to its branch offices and agents in the outlying cities; in one of them Sebestyén announced his departure on sick-leave, and in the other Dr. Neumann announced his pro-tem entry into office. Dr. Neumann wrote that he was open to public criticism and even welcomed it, and promised to remedy wrongs within the limits of feasibility. As for criticism which was only an expression of hard feelings caused by temporary circumstances, he requested that people understand that we are living in very difficult times and must solve hard questions which call for restraint and self-control, and swift, sensible judgment. Our people are living under constant tension. Therefore, we must try to overcome the many difficulties besetting us; we must help one another, and do that which is imposed upon us with united forces and good will. "I ask for the support and cooperation of all circles of Slovak Jewry," Dr. Neumann concluded, "and am convinced that in this hour each of you knows his particular responsibility and obligations towards the larger Jewish public."

XI. Towards the End of 1943

Saving the burial ground of the Hatam Sofer, of blessed memory

The Bratislava Municipality planned to pave a road through a tunnel, routing it through the old Jewish cemetery, where the graves of a number of righteous Jews, *geonim,* and holy persons lay. The Jewish burial society and the rabbinical court were called upon to tackle this difficult problem, and the Jewish community confronted the fact that the authorities were planning to do away with the cemetery. The rabbinical court gave instructions for removing the bones. Each grave was carefully opened and the bones gathered in a cloth bag, which was then placed in a small wooden coffin. The coffins were buried in a common grave, with a layer of soil scattered between one coffin and the next.

The small plot of graves belonging to saintly Jews and *geonim,* first and foremost the resting places of the Hatam Sofer and Rabbi Akiva Eger, caused the community especially great concern. The rabbinical court ruled that these graves must not be touched and that everything must be done to save them and leave them in place. It was during the days of *selihot* of "Monday, Thursday and Monday." Thus, the rabbinical court of the Bratislava Jewish community decreed the second Monday a day of public fasting and prayer to avert the harsh decrees. On the 24th of Mar-Heshvan, 5704 (November 22, 1943), in my community, as well, we undertook a day of fasting and prayer for the souls of these saintly Jews.

As evacuation of the rest of the graves was proceeding, our efforts to save the graves of these righteous Jews bore fruit, thanks to the intercession of a brave woman by the name of Iluš Adler-Bondy, who managed to obtain six months postponement for clearing away the graves.

A heavy financial burden fell upon the Bratislava *Hevra Kadisha,* which was obliged to cover the enormous expenditures. Therefore, on the 2nd of Kislev, 5704 (December 8, 1943), in a special circular I appealed to all the Jewish communities throughout the state to view the undertaking of evacuating and maintaining the graves as a holy mission of all Slovak Jewry and to contribute generously by imposing a special tax or by paying a direct grant to the *Hevra Kadisha* of Bratislava, which had performed the task these past days.

The first contribution came from my second congregation, the

Yeshurun Congregation of Bratislava, which assumed 10,000 korunas of the expense – a sizable sum in these days of economic hardship and destruction of Jewish communities. We hoped that all the Jewish communities would follow their example.

Of course, postponing the date for evacuation of the graves was only a temporary solution. The big question still remained: would the authorities let our great Torah scholars rest in peace in their graves until they arise to meet their fate at the End of Days, or would they force us to uproot the bones of the deceased *geonim,* as well, as they have uprooted our living brethren from their homes?

I was in Bratislava on Tuesday, December 14, 1943, when news came informing me of the passing of Rabbi Pinchas Keller, chief rabbi of Trenčín, and requesting me to deliver the eulogy at his funeral. Rabbi Keller, of blessed memory, studied in *yeshiva* together with my dear father, who told me of his learnedness. Several hours before his death he wrote me a letter asking me to be his spokesman and to see to his affairs as the local Rabbi. At the funeral, attended by a large number of people, considering the fact that Jews were forbidden to travel without a special permit, Rabbi Schweiger of Nitra, Rabbi Lichtenstern of Žilina, Mark Griinsfeld, editor of *The Herald,* and Dr. Frankel, the head of the congregation, took their final leave of the deceased. Rabbi Pinchas Keller, a student at the Pressburg Yeshiva, who continued his studies in Germany, spent his entire life fighting a spiritual conflict. A God-fearing man who remained true to the principles of traditional Judaism, he went to serve in neologist congregations in Yugoslavia, and since 1928 officiated in Trenčín, where he tried to reduce the neologists' influence and to abolish the innovative changes they had introduced in Hungary. He was by nature a fighting man; yet he had a quiet, pleasant manner, was good-hearted, just and true. He became very embittered when he failed in his mission and calling as a spiritual leader. He had left three congregations, one after the other, before he was hired in Trenčín, although there, too, people made his life bitter. In eulogizing him I noted his lofty traits of character, his faithfulness to his principles, and his continual battle to uphold the commandments of the Torah and the tradition of our forefathers against the inclinations of assimilationists. Rabbi Keller, of blessed memory, was also a man of letters and wrote many articles in the Jewish press, under the pen-name Pinchas Martef.[39]

After Rabbi Keller's death I obtained a certificate of protection for his widow from the Ministry of Education and Culture.

Discovery of valuables in the Vyhne camp

I spent several days of the Hannukah festival in the Vyhne camp, with my family. In a pleasant atmosphere, the Jews from Sosnowice, the residents of the camp who were true to the Jewish faith and nationality, warmed themselves by the light of the Hannukah candles and listened to a series of lectures which I delivered after candle-lighting. It was sad, in contrast, to see the behavior of several Jews who had converted to Christianity and on the "Holy Night" went to church for mass.

A very interesting story was told by Smorgoński, an engineer and former head of the Sosnowice group in Vyhne. He disclosed to me that two youths from the Sered camp, Juraj Cohen and Eugen Rosenbaum, who were working in the camp as plumbers, had found a treasure of jewelry and valuables in a water pipe and had handed their find over to him. From the initials, IF, which were inscribed on a silver cigarette box, he surmised that the treasure belonged to Ferdinand Immergut, one of the Jews from Sosnowice, a jeweler who had been deported.

---

[39] His pen-name, Martef, means basement or cellar, i.e., an underground name. Translator's note.

Smorgonsky gave me the treasure trove to use it to help save the Jews of Poland.

I did not want to accept the valuable jewelry into my exclusive personal possession. Therefore I requested Mr. Funk, an expert in jewelry, to weigh and assess the value of each and every piece in my presence, and then, in the presence of the head of the Jewish council, Mr. Wildman, and his deputy, Mr. Einhorn, to wrap everything in a package and take it to Bratislava, where he would hand it over to the members of the Working Group.[40] Upon my return from Vyhne I reported the episode to the Working Group and we decided unanimously to stow away the treasure as received, for the time being. Who knows how many such finds, which could have served the needs of the community, have fallen into evil hands? I praised the camp inmates for their probity.

* * *

Being in Bratislava again, I tried to do something on behalf of the Jews who had been working in plants belonging to Germans and whose employment had been terminated, and who consequently had lost their certificates of protection and were subject to deportation to labor camps. Regretfully, I did not succeed in this mission. I managed only to bring one family to Nové Mesto on the pretext of their being elderly. Several others were admitted to the hospital through other people's lobbying. The majority of them, however, were forced to go into the labor camp. Whenever the gentiles have a disagreement between themselves, they take it out on the Jews; this is characteristic of our times. Any struggle, hostility, or competition in the end explodes over our heads. This applied to the fight between Mach and Vašek, too.

---

[40] Each one of the persons present received a list of the items: 39 rings. weighing 80.5 grams, 95 earrings – 92.5 grams, 10 chains – 105 grams, 29 pendants – 17 grams, 3 gold coins – 33 grams, a small woman's gold watch and 6 silver spoons, as well as 317 zloti, 29 US dollars, 11 pounds sterling, and 2,5000 korunas of the Protectorate.

In the last two weeks of 1943 a fourth wing was opened in Ohel David. The number of camp residents who were transferred to us was constantly on the rise and now had reached 120. Prefabricated huts had to be built to take them in. I was extremely concerned with raising funds for this. We had undergone difficult trials in the past two years. It is painful when at times our efforts bear no fruit. On the other hand, when I walked through the clean and neat rooms of Ohel David, people thanked me for the kindness which had been done them, and it felt pleasant to be reassured that life has purpose, benefit, and hope, even in the hardest of times. Would that we be able to overcome all our difficulties!

The convention of Ha-Shomer ha-Tzair

Members of the *Ha-Shomer ha-Tzair* youth movement approached me with a request to enable them to hold a meeting in Nové Mesto on the last night of 1943. After a hiatus of two years, they had decided to reconvene and discuss the current situation and future plans. The convention was held clandestinely, in contravention to the law, which forbade conventions in general and those of Jews and illegal organizations in particular. I consented without a moment's hesitation and helped them run the convention. Among the participants – 18 youths from all over the country, including the work camps – were a pioneer who had been rescued from Poland, the land of doom (Heike Klinger), and a member of the movement who arrived from the Protectorate of Bohemia and Moravia (Efraim Neumann).

The convention began at 9 p.m., and the discussions lasted through the night, until 2 p.m. the next afternoon. I took part in two conversations which evoked great interest. It was a very pleasant experience for me to see these wonderful youths evincing such courage and adherence to the ideas of the movement. These lovely youngsters arrived without travel permits, certificates of protection, or other documents. The members from the labor camps went to even greater risk and sneaked out of their lock-up through hidden openings, all because of their strong desire to participate in the discussions of the movement's plans for the near future. Although there is a great distance between my views and theirs, I listened with elated spirits to the words of these youngsters, who were instilled with a deep Zionist Jewish identity and who ran their discussions almost exclusively in Hebrew. In my conversations I talked about the political situation and reported the latest information on the suffering and despair, the destruction and annihilation, of our brethren, and on the efforts which were being made, and must be made, to save those still alive. My audience listened attentively to my review of the situation, which included sketching lines of action in anticipation of possible future developments.

I parted from the youngsters with much emotion, firmly believing that a people with such ardent youths shall succeed in coming through the hard times, and that our enemies shall not succeed in their designs to wipe us out. The [movement] is indeed a hope and a future for the Jewish people.

Chapter Six

The Fight for Survival Reaches
Its Climax

(5704 – 1944)

*"And there shall be a time of trouble, such as never was since
there was a nation even to that same time"*
(Daniel 12:1)

I. Meetings and Consultations

I called a meeting of the principles of the Jewish schools to
discuss the status of Jewish teachers and the problems they faced,
for Sunday the 6th of Tevet, 5704 (January 2, 1944). The meeting
convened in Bratislava and was attended by Dr. O. Neumann, the
Jewish Elder, Mikuláš Eichner, the chairman of the department
of education and culture in the Jewish Center, Professor Beck,
his assistant, the principles from the Jewish communities of
Bratislava, Topolčany, Nitra, Trnava, and Banská-Bystrica, and
several teachers.

The meeting evoked great interest but also aroused debate
and apprehension among the teachers. I was surprised to learn
that the teachers' ranks included certain converts to Christianity
who, instead of hiding silently in the wings, dared to speak out

and openly criticize and attack activists working for the Jewish teachers' survival and the betterment of their condition. One of the sad signs of our times is that educators who have abandoned their faith continue to teach our Jewish children.

I opened the meeting with a report on my talks with representatives of the Ministry of Education and Culture, foremost with Minister Sivák, who asked me to inform him who represented the Jewish teachers in Slovakia and what my stand was regarding the salary of these teachers and the budget it required. I responded that I had no intention of representing the teachers and promised the minister that I would give him an answer to his questions after consulting the relevant persons.

It was decided that the authority to represent the teachers and to handle all their affairs would be delegated to the pedagogical-didactic committee of the Jewish Center, led by the principles Neumann, Weiner, König, and Beck from Bratislava, Herlinger from Trnava, and Mittlemann from Trenčín. After a lengthy discussion of the financial situation the committee decided to send a memorandum to the heads of the Jewish communities, explaining the teachers' difficult straits. The memorandum explained that now that the government subsidy on which the teachers' salary had been based was been cancelled, responsibility for the teachers' salary fell on the communities employing them. I noted with regret that the discussion was held on a disappointingly low level.

On January 5, after a long hiatus, I invited the General Zionists to discuss the question of electing a delegate from the Zionist Organization of Slovakia to attend the convention on *aliyah* to be held in Constantinople. The executive committee, representing three parties, *Eretz Yisrael ha-Ovedet,* the Mizrachi, and the General Zionists, each with three people on the committee, was responsible for electing Slovakia's delegate. The first two parties had already selected their candidates: Moshe Dachs for *Eretz Yisrael ha-Ovedet,* and Ben-Zion Gottlieb for the Mizrachi. At the meeting we put forward the candidacy of Oscar Krasniansky, whom the executive committee later chose as its delegate to the convention.

II. I Shall Recall the Distress that Befell Me in the Month of Tevet

Several seemingly quiet weeks elapsed, and life proceeded peacefully. But in these times, there is no such thing as a happy life, untroubled by evil rumors or worrisome and even horrifying tidings. This week I visited the Sered camp to see how our brethren were faring. I was worried by articles which had appeared in the Nazi German paper, *Grenzbote,* sharply attacking us – the Jews – and the labor camps. They were particularly angry about the Sered camp having printed greeting cards for the New Year for Aryan factories, in contravention to the law, and were especially irate that the graphic design on the greeting cards used a symbol closely resembling their own.[41] Who knows what hardship and torment these men of evil shall bring upon us because of this innocent act.

Thursday, on my way home, rumor reached me that Gisi Fleischmann was being hunted in Bratislava. My wife Rosa met me at the Nové Mesto train station and, to my dismay, confirmed the bad news, which I had so much hoped was false. She told me that Vojtech had called her and, speaking in Hungarian, had said the following: "Our sister Naomi has been invited to the Adler family." According to our code this sentence meant: Gisi Fleischmann has been arrested by the Center for State Security. My telephone call to Dr. Winterstein that

---

[41] See photograph.

evening provided me with no further information. Everything is still under a veil of secrecy. From his words I was led to understand that I must remain at home until further notice.

* * *

On Saturday, January 15, 1944, our group found out that Gisi had been arrested on account of the former accusation against her, and that there was a good chance the affair could be finished off and her file closed. On Sunday my wife went to Bratislava to obtain information on developments but returned with no further news. I decided to go to Bratislava the next day, despite warnings that I not go. There I found out several unpleasant details. Government circles had reopened discussion of the affair involving money transferred to Switzerland by Koso's wife and therefore were interrogating Gisi Fleischmann again.

* * *

This blow was followed by yet a harder one. We found out that the cabinet was scheduled to deliberate the Jewish question on Thursday, January 20. The invitation which we obtained to this meeting proved that we are always on the agenda. Our men also learned of a visit by the personal emissary of German Foreign Minister von Ribbentrop to President Tiso and Prime Minister Tuka, in which he emphatically demanded that deportation of the Jews to Poland be resumed. The warning light went on and terrible fear descended upon us, but we were not intimidated. We had to do our utmost to foil the evil design.

On the morning of Tuesday, January 18, the secretary of the Orthodox Bureau, Dr. Grünblatt, relayed to me in a choked voice that the ministerial advisor, Revucký, had notified him that I must report to the Ministry of Education and Culture for an urgent talk with Minister Sivák punctually at 10 o'clock. Sivák informed me at 11 a.m.

that a cabinet meeting had been scheduled for the same day. He also confirmed the rumor about the emissary's visit and the latter's demand. In a comprehensive discussion I analyzed the situation and presented several reasons for not going ahead with the dangerous plot. I told Sivák that we now knew beyond the slightest shadow of a doubt that "leaving for work in Poland" meant deportation to the death camps. Even in the 1942 deportations it was explicitly stated in letters to the high command of the Hlinka Guard that the Jews were leaving for labor camps, but they were all deported to their death.

Secondly, I pointed to the policy in Hungary, where the authorities were following an obvious course of alibi politics to improve their position and prospects at the peace table, after the war. Why was Slovakia following a policy which was diametrically opposed to her own interests?

Thirdly, I mentioned the memorandum which Kirschbaum, the Slovak ambassador in Bern, had sent the Foreign Ministry, in which he informed the government in the name of the nuncio, Ritter, that Slovakia was sullying her name and making herself detested among the nations of the world by the brutal way in which she was handling the Jewish question. Minister of Interior Mach responded personally to this memorandum, writing that Slovakia had been forced to transfer the Jews to Poland due to German pressure and that now she had not the slightest intention of taking strong measures against the Jews. Let Mach's actions bear up his words!

Fourthly, I mentioned the letter which the political secretary of the Vatican sent the Foreign Ministry on behalf of the Pope, censuring the stand of the Slovak government and defending the rights of man, including the Jews.

Fifthly, I appealed to the emotions of the minister, who was a devout Christian, saying that it was clear now that deportation meant murder. Does anyone wish to stain his hands with the blood of innocent human beings, young and old, shed for no reason?

In conclusion, I asked the minister to talk with the minister of finance and relay to him the arguments which I had presented. Sivák promised me he would make every effort and requested me to call him at 1 p.m. That I did, but even at 2 p.m. I could not reach him at his office. At three o'clock I called his home, and his wife informed me that the minister had not yet returned from the meeting. At 4 o'clock the situation was the same. Half an hour later Sivák called to set a meeting with him at 6 p.m. In the meantime, no one from our Working Group had managed to obtain any information whatsoever. Extremely tense and depressed, we decided to meet for consultation at 7 o'clock in the evening, after I should return from my meeting with the minister of education.

* * *

Sivák told me that the debate on the Jewish question had lasted four and a half hours and had been declared secret. The prime minister reported that the Germans were calling for deportation of the Jews, and the minister of interior joined in this request and proclaimed that he was prepared to send five transports in February and the remaining Jews in March. He spoke bluntly and came out sharply against the Jews and asked the rest of the ministers to go along with him. At the end of his remarks the minister of interior declared that the president was also in favor of handing the Jews over to the Germans. After Mach spoke, Minister of Finance Medrický requested the floor and presented economic arguments against the proposal advanced by the minister of interior and the prime minister, and requested that they change their stand. Minister of Transportation

Stano concurred with the previous speaker's opinion, for similar reasons. The next to speak was Sivák, who used all the arguments which I presented him and even added some reasons of his own, declaring that he was flatly opposed to the worthless proposal and requesting that it be removed from the agenda. Sivák told me further that before the meeting he had managed to talk to his two colleagues, Medrický and Stano, who were equally convinced of my well-argued position.

The last to speak was Karvaš, president of the National Bank, who participates in cabinet meetings and has a vote. He joined the opposition to the proposal, arguing that it was detrimental to the state for economic reasons, and put forward a motion of his own: If the government must do something against the Jews, let it take security measures against those Jews who are causing harm politically, by concentrating them in work camps. The ministers of finance, defense, and justice abstained from voicing an opinion. Four ministers came out against the motion to deport the Jews and two in favor. Thus, a resolution was passed that the minister of interior should issue a circular to the district commissars, calling upon them to prepare in utter secrecy, in cooperation with the police, the Hlinka Guard, and the Hlinka People's party, an accurate list of all the Jews, who for this purpose were to be divided into three categories:

A. Politically dangerous Jews;
B. Neutral Jews, who. are not undesirable;
C. Desirable Jews who are essential to the state's economy.

The lists were to be prepared by February 7, 1944, and relayed to the 14th Department via the secretariat of the Ministry of Interior. There the lists would be reviewed and the immunity status of the Jews checked, after which various offices would receive recommendations to cancel protection papers or to extend their validity, as appropriate. Only then would the Jews whose protection papers were abrogated be concentrated in labor camps. At its meeting the cabinet also discussed a query which Karvaš addressed to the prime minister, requesting to know the truth of the Koso affair, which had gained such notoriety. The minister of interior responded by hurling insults and accusations at Koso and dubbing his wife a "secretary of the Jewish Center," who had connived with the "accursed Jewess" Mrs. Fleischmann, and claimed that both women together had bribed the entire Ministry of Interior. He announced that Gisi Fleischmann had been arrested for interrogation and would not be released "until I know what mess I am in." This was a very painful and dangerous question, one likely to spell disaster for Gisi Fleischmann, who would suffer from the very fact of the matter being discussed in this forum in which the minister of interior had lost his composure.

The conversation with Sivák lasted until close to nine o'clock, making my colleagues in the Working Group wait for me in tense forbearance close to two hours. Overall, we had reason to be pleased with the government's resolutions, yet we dispersed in low spirits because of the straits into which our colleague, Gisi Fleischmann, had fallen.

Henceforth our endeavors focused on two levels. On the one hand, we worked on the 14th Department to prevent any worsening in the status of the Jews. On the other hand, we were occupied by our concern for Gisi's fate. Dr. Kováč managed to soften Dr. Vašek's position in a téte-á-téte with him, and in a subsequent conversation to which I was privy, as well, we received several reassuring promises from him. Yet how could we help Gisi, caught between the hammer and the anvil? Alexander Adler and his wife Iluš, our excellent liaison people, worked day and night in the secret police, while Ernest Wintner, an activist from the Sečovce Jewish community, interceded with one of the leading figures in the Center for State Security, Peter Starinský (whose wife was Wintner's "aryanizer"). Kováč worked on Dr. Vašek, and I on Paškovič. director of the Central Office for Economy. Still there was no change in Gisi's situation, although we had hopes for a turn for the better.

* * *

Upon visiting the Nováky camp I received complaints about the iron fisted and cruel attitude of Švitler, commissar of the camp, who was abusing the residents and treating them most brutally. I brought the matter up before Pečuch, the commissar in charge of all the camps, and requested him to fire Švitler. Pečuch made a thorough investigation of the matter, however Švitler managed to defend himself successfully and remained in office, keeping the upper hand. Irate at me, he rebuked me and tried to put a wedge between me and the Jewish council in the camp. In this, however, he did not succeed, for Dr. Mandler, chairman of the Jewish council, visited me in Bratislava and suggested searching for a way to appease this heathen man. Ondrej Steiner did the job and closed the affair. Let us only hope that Švitler, too, learned a lesson.

"A time to be born, and a time to die ... a time to mourn, and a time to dance" ... "To every thing there is a season, and a time to every purpose" (Ecclesiastes 3). The time has come to put aside for a moment our secular, public tasks, and to attend to the needs of the Jewish community that are connected to the religion and the faith. For I am not only a public activist, at times successful and at times unsuccessful, at times with the upper hand and at times not; I am also a rabbi, rejoicing over the newborn and eulogizing the dead. "Death and life are in the power of the tongue" (Proverbs 18:21) and a rabbi uses his tongue on joyous and mournful occasion, at circumcision ceremonies and at funerals.

On the 24th of Tevet, 5704 (January 20, 1944), Heinrich Stahler, chairman of the *Hevra Kadisha* and *Gemilut Hassadim* (Jewish burial and philanthropic societies), was laid to rest. He worked as Isidor Engel's right-hand man when the new Jewish hospital was being constructed in Bratislava. Both men belonged to the group of moderate Orthodox Jews who called themselves "whites," as opposed to the extremist group of staunch, uncompromising "blacks." Both groups were constantly vying with one another for control of the Jewish community's affairs and its public institutions. At the age of 15, when I was a student in the *yeshiva,* every Friday night I dined as a guest of Isidor Engel and his family. I recall, while seated at his table, every now and then hearing him complain to his wife about inside attacks directed against him. I did not understand what it was about at the time, yet I sensed that he was in the right. Isidor Engel worked industriously at his life's calling – building the Jewish hospital, the only one in Czechoslovakia which ran according to Jewish law. He served as chairman of the hospital's board of directors for years, from the hospital's establishment until the day of his death, and now his close friend, Heinrich Stahler, who continued in his footsteps and saw to the maintenance of this philanthropic institution through the hard times which have come upon us, had passed away. As the chief rabbi of the Yeshurun congregation in Bratislava, I took my leave of this eminent man by eulogizing him and expressing appreciation for his good deeds. Nor did I refrain from mentioning the fruitless struggles which at times take place between groups of people who hold the same philosophy and ideals and who, in principle, have no differences between them, and only the name tag affixed to their faction separates them and hampers them from working for the common goal shared by all – justice and charity.

* * *

Generations pass and generations come. On the Sabbath of the scriptural reading of *Va'era,* on the 26th of Tevet (January 22), we celebrated the circumcision of Ezra, son of Dr. Israel and Piri Ganz, who honored me with the role of *sandak* (Godfather). Since our numbers have become so decimated, every joyous family occasion has become a joyous event for the entire community.

Our joys, however, are never complete. There is always a reminder of the destruction that has befallen our people. As I was holding the newborn in my lap, Arthur Marmorstein, a devoted activist in the community, came up and whispered to me that the police had received a writ to interrogate a woman by the name of Horečná, who had been arrested in Bratislava. This was none other than a Jewish woman by the name of Schramm, whom we had given "Aryan" papers to save her life. She had been caught holding the forged documents from Nové Mesto. And little Ezra was screaming in pain, for he had just been circumcised and for the first time in his life was experiencing the pain of being Jewish. We must congratulate this youngster on having been admitted into the covenant of our forefather Abraham.

* * *

On Monday, the 28th of Tevet 5704 (January 24, 1944), I went to Bratislava. Mrs. Horečná-Schramm, who was being detained on Goering Street, told me that in her interrogation she testified to having received her papers in Nové Mesto from George Berger. In such cases every detail is important to know how to settle the affair. It seems that from here she will be transferred to the Sered camp.

III. Community Life Continues Even in Time of Stress

The Gisi Fleischmann affair keeps us in a state of constant tension and alert and is very wearing. The entire staff is working hard on the case, but to no avail. Koso has been fired, and rumors are abroad that he will be transferred to the Ilava prison on orders from the Minister of Interior. It is feared that Gisi will also be locked up in this ill-famed prison. Actually, orders had already been issued to transfer the "Jewess" to Ilava, but our vigilant comrades, first and foremost Ernest Wintner, who is on good terms with Peter Starinský, director of the 16th Department of the Center for State Security, managed to get this plan changed, and thus on January 28 Gisi was taken to the Nováky labor camp. She was brought in under a different name and confined in a solitary room, closely guarded by jailors, under the harsh conditions imposed on criminals. Fortunately for us, Ondrej Steiner was in Nováky the same day and saw to it that all the severe instructions regarding a close guard on the "Jewess Goldfinger" would remain only on paper and that in actual practice, except for her isolation, they not be strictly enforced. Gisi is very tense, despairing and nervous, and writes us melancholy letters. As things have turned out, however, this place of detention is the best solution. We hope that she will rejoin us in the near future.

* * *

Still feeling for Gisi's suffering, a new trouble came upon us, one which was likely to put all the members of our group behind bars.

We heard that Karl Hochberg, former director of the Special Services Section, who was incarcerated in Ilava, had suddenly been taken to the Center for State Security. We knew why his interrogation was being renewed.

Immediately after giving his first deposition Hochberg had told one of the jailors, the keeper of the keys, that soon the latter would be very busy since "approximately 20 Jews will be arrested shortly." The jailor, who was on good terms with our men, brought this malicious comment, so characteristic of Hochberg, to our attention. Hochberg's interrogation took place under veil of secrecy, leaving us in the dark. We were left guessing, while everything remained uncertain. Did his interrogation have to do with Gisi Fleischmann? Perhaps Koso was plotting to land a blow on some other people's heads? Did the Minister of Interior wish to cleanse his ministry of corruption, using Hochberg for this purpose? We were perpetually tormented by these questions, which kept coming into our minds. On Wednesday a bit more light was shed on the picture. Our comrades found out that something was afoot against the German advisor, Wisliceny, and that Hochberg could reveal a lot and add fuel to the fire. As far as we were concerned, this was ostensibly a reassuring report, for the issue appeared to be one of strife and quarrels between Slovaks and Germans. and becoming embroiled in a struggle between two rival groups was none of our concern when the ground was about to be pulled out from beneath our feet. Nevertheless, our friends decided to relay this information to Wisliceny to persuade him to take action in such a way that the Slovaks would not have new grounds for trying to undermine us. The entire affair continued to occupy us, and we tried to preclude dangerous developments.

Recently the Jews of Michalovce, on the eastern border of Slovakia, now very close to the battle-front between Germany and Russia, sent me a letter expressing the worries of the Jews in their city. This is the gist of what it said:

> Rumors are circulating in Michalovče about a danger that the Jews will be rounded up one day soon. We live in a state of fear like the panic at the time of the deportations to Poland in 1942. In our state of despair, we appeal to His Reverence the Rabbi, calling for help and asking you to save us and our children.

> We would also like to know if the decree of concentration is a general one. We are left here with a community of around 700 Jews, with our numbers steadily diminishing as many move to other places, and approximately 180 Jews in labor camps. Our request is that the Rabbi try to minimize the number of people who will be forced to leave the city, to assure the survival of our community and its institutions.

Aside from letters of this type, requesting thorough and comprehensive handling, I have been receiving many letters from various people, requests for aid, and letters of thanks.

On February 1, on orders from the Ministry of Interior, all the Jews in the city were registered, whether or not they had converted to Christianity by the date stipulated in the law, or were part of a mixed marriage, or held sundry protection papers such as those issued to doctors, engineers, and others who are active in economic life. Every Jew must carry a document proving his right to reside legally within the territory of the Slovak state. This registry classified the Jews according to three categories. Although the classification was secret, we managed to disclose several useful details and thus were able to affect the classification process in our favor.

* * *

My holding a central position in public affairs has had an impact on the life of my community. Various edicts and directives have restricted the lives of the Jews considerably, yet their survival depends on the local authorities. In some cities the Hlinka Guard has been especially strict about carrying out orders, which has made the life of the Jews more difficult and has led to frequent outbursts by hostile elements. In Nové Mesto the authorities have treated us very leniently. This was a great achievement on the part of the activists in my community, who succeeded in establishing connections in the city council, the district office, the police, and other offices. Were it not for this we would not have been able to expand Ohel David and take in dozens of Jews from outside the institution.

Thus, our community has become an important Jewish center in the state, a place with an active Jewish life and culture. Torah lessons, study groups, lectures, meetings, ceremonies, and philanthropic activities have been the hallmarks of our community life and have united the members of the community.

IV. Efforts to Help Children in the Camps

In February, I went on another round of visits to the labor camps. Rumors of the government's deliberations on renewing the transports have terrified the inmates of the camps, and many of them are still very agitated. They do not sit back tranquilly like fools, but ask what will become of them as the battle front approaches. The horror stories about the fate of our brethren who were deported to Poland have magnified the panic, so that many people have begun running away from the camps. The commissar's reaction has been to institute a more severe regimen, and this deterioration in conditions has further reinforced the fear and increased the number of people fleeing the camps, thus creating a vicious circle.

I could not condemn the flight from the camps. Whoever is brave enough and wishes to try to save his life in this way, I wish him every success. We cannot know what the next day has in store for us, and it is our interest to reduce the number of people concentrated in the camps. I hoped to temper the commissars' reactions and to reduce the suffering of the camp inmates. First, I visited Sered, where the fabrication of rumors was farthest from reality and most developed. Results were quick in coming. In a talk with the commissar, I succeeded in cancelling several regulations and putting through a number of palliative measures; although who knows for how long, for the man is not stable. The second, and more serious, problem concerned the health of the adolescents. Many youngsters who entered the camp healthy and strong had grown weak and were suffering from pneumonia. In consultation with the heads of the Jewish councils in the Sered and Nováky camps, we arranged for Dr. Frisch, head of the department of health in the Jewish Center, to appeal to the director of the health division of the Ministry of Interior, Prof. Sovik, and to do everything to assure that the youngsters receive the necessary treatment for their speedy recovery.

* * *

One of the laudable campaigns undertaken by my community was the practice of sending parcels of fruit for *Tu bi-Shvat* and *mishloah manot* (traditional presents) for Purim to children in the work camps, a practice instituted since the establishment of the camps. This campaign was initiated by my brother Emanuel, the principal of the Jewish school. The school children drew pictures of various fruits on construction paper and offered them for sale "by the pound." Assisted by the parents' committee, they then used the proceeds to send parcels – fruits for *Tu bi-Shvat* and *mishloah manot* for Purim – to every child in the schools of the Sered, Nováky, and Vyhne labor camps. As the number of children in the camps increased and the price of fruit and other foods rose steeply, the principle appealed to all the Jewish schools throughout the country to participate in this worthwhile, educational project.

V. Hungarian Passports and Current Problems

Many Jews in Slovakia acquired Hungarian passports to attest that the holder of the passport was a foreign national, not subject to the emigration law. Many documents were needed to obtain a passport. Aside from a birth certificate and marriage license, proof of having paid taxes, and a document from the district office certifying that the holder of the passport had resided in Hungary from November 2, 1928 until March 1, 1939, one also needed confirmation from the local council in Slovakia that during the above-mentioned period the person was registered as a foreign national and confirmation from the Ministry of Interior that his request for Slovak citizenship had been denied.

About nine hundred Jews managed to obtain these papers in various and sundry ways. In the wake of the recent registry of Jews these passports were discovered, and authorities in the Ministry of Interior, the Center for State Security and the Treasury mounted an attack against this corrupt dealing, charging the holders of the passports with financial crimes and accusing them of forging documents. They not only stood in great danger of losing more than they had hoped to gain, for the interrogators were likely to compete with one another in imposing strict fines, but also were in danger of being thrown into work camps as criminals, pursuant to the special directives in time of war and emergency.

Rabbi Michael Dov Weissmandel, having being under arrest as an activist suspected of financial violations, handled this affair very successfully, for during his detention he had reached an understanding with Kukula, head of the investigation department of the Ministry of Finance, which he now put to use on the passports issue. Weissmandel successfully negotiated a compromise with Kukula, settling on a total fine of four hundred thousand korunas. This was a satisfactory solution, and only left the problem of bringing it to the attention of the 900 passport holders, who had to pay their share of the fine. This was the first time the Jewish Center had officially cooperated with the Working Group. The Elder, Dr. Oscar Neumann, issued an urgent circular on February 4, 1944, in which he requested all those in charge of the Jewish Center's branch offices throughout the country to present, within three days' time, a list of all the holders of Hungarian passports so that, by paying the collective fine, these people could be released from the legal proceedings which had been instituted against them. It was noted that whoever's name did not appear on the list risked having the authorities lodge legal charges against him for financial crimes. Thus Dr. Neumann made the Jewish Center a positive organization, serving the Jews of Slovakia, and not simply acting as a middleman passing on to the public the directives of the government, which were generally to our detriment.

* * *

Meanwhile, there has been no progress in Gisi Fleischmann's case. She is in solitary confinement in the Nováky camp, and although we are in constant touch with her and she is not suffering physically, nevertheless all our efforts on her behalf have been to no avail, since her position is tied to Dr. Koso's fate.

On February 11, 1944, the Sabbath eve of the scriptural reading of *Jethro,* Zvi Fehér came from Bratislava to see me in my home on business of the Working Group and to inform me of plans afoot to seize 22 Jews in Kežmarok to send them to labor camps. Karol Záberecký, the chief secretary of the 14th Department of the Ministry of Interior, was in charge of the operation, and the Group was requesting that I take action to cancel the evil designs of the informers. A meeting with him was set for Saturday night, in the Jewish hospital in Sered, since Záberecký was also the government commissar in charge of the hospital. The outcome of the talk with Záberecký was quite positive. Although he could not cancel the entire plan, since the directive had come from the Ministry of Interior itself, Záberecký nevertheless promised me he would only send 10 cables and that he would make it possible for me to forewarn the victims. In the end, not a single Jew from Kežmarok was sent to the labor camps. In our talk we also reached an accord on another subject: a number of people who were proper Jews in every respect had obtained baptism certificates from a place whose registry books had been burned. The president of Slovakia had gotten wind of this, and his office had issued strict orders to round up the Jews who held these forged papers and to put them in labor camps. Záberecký now promised me that he would not rush to carry out the order and would try to let the affair be forgotten. Should he be forced to take action, he would take 15 names of people holding forged papers off the list, and would give me advance notice of the names remainmg.

This indeed was a good conversation for the Saturday night after the reading of *Jethro,* a fine beginning for the week. How Jethro, Moses' father-in-law, rejoiced for all the goodness which the Lord did to Israel, and said: "Blessed be the Lord, who hath delivered you out of the hand of the Egyptians, and out of the hand of Pharaoh" (Exodus 18:10)! Rashi interprets "out of the hand of the Egyptians" to mean "a hard nation" and "out of the hand of Pharaoh" to mean "a hard king." I, too, rejoiced, for even though the nation is hard and the government hard, blessed is the Lord who has delivered this people out of the hand of the Egyptians!

* * *

On February 2, 1944, the Central Office for Economy decided to reopen the Jewish Center's branch office in Nové Mesto and appointed me to serve as *prednosta* or supervisor. I had long expected a branch office to be opened. While I had no personal aspirations to be the Jewish Center's man, the fact that henceforth I could act in an official capacity, demand certain rights, and defend the Jews in the name of an official office had general and legal significance. The building housing the office of the Jewish Center also housed the third branch of the old-age home, which actually had many young residents, Torah students, whose presence there was "illegal." Therefore, I attached great importance to obtaining the official stamp of approval of the Jewish Center and the building in which it was housed. Notice of the office's opening was sent to the district office and the police. Dr. Isidor Ganz served as secretary of the Center.

VI. Facing Judgment on Earth and Judgment in Heaven

The codex on Jewish affairs and other laws passed earlier stipulated that, immovable assets of Jews or Jewish associations shall be transferred to state ownership. By a notice of the government (no. 238, dated October 31, 1941), everything pertaining to this matter was under the jurisdiction of the Central Office for Economy. This office was left to decide whether these assets should be sold or should remain under state ownership and be managed by Aryan directors. Under this law the property of the Jewish communities was expropriated, as well, leaving them without any revenue from real estate and housing, which made their, financial situation very grave. Our jurists pointed out that the Jewish communities did not come under the category of Jewish associations and that therefore transferring their property to state ownership was unlawful. However, the prudence of appealing against application of this law to the immovable property of the Jewish communities was questionable.

Dr. Winterstein was opposed to submitting an appeal, partly for political reasons. The communities, however, found themselves drained of all their resources and at the point of complete financial collapse. Several Jewish community leaders maintained that the Supreme Court of Slovakia thus far had been strict in upholding the law and that one could expect it to rule objectively on this question, as well. I felt out the Central Office for Economy on the issue and sensed that the time was right to take care of this important matter. In numerous conversations with crucial people, I succeeded in softening their position and understood that if we were to begin legal proceedings now we would not encounter strong opposition on their part.

We proposed that the Yeshurun congregation in Liptovský-Svätý-Mikuláš submit an appeal to the Central Office for Economy. After this office rejected the appeal, we would have the legal opportunity to turn to the Supreme Court of Justice to resolve the issue, once and for all. We were extremely happy when the Supreme Court found "in the name of the Republic" (no. 6-1943/228, dated December 17, 1943) that the Jewish communities are not "Jewish associations" and therefore are not subject to the law on transference of their property to state ownership. The court heard the case in open session, with Justice Karšay presiding and Justices Cserhelyi and Stefánik sitting beside him on the bench. May it go down in history as a merit to these people that they did not pervert justice for the persecuted in their quarrel against the rule of despots. This ruling reached us recently, at a time when the Jewish communities were in serious financial distress, for neither the individual Jew, with no source livelihood, nor the public coffers of the Jewish communities, with their many financial obligations, had a cent left. The property which will now be returned will ease the straits of the Jewish communities somewhat.

Before we heard of our victory in the Supreme Court this week, we received the sad tidings of the sudden death of Julius Fleischhacker, a devoted member and activist of the Zionist movement, who was called to stand in judgment before the Almighty on the Sabbath of the scriptural reading of *Mishpatim,* on the 25th of Shvat, 5704 (February 19, 1944), at the young age of 36. Julius Bezalel was always present in time of need, was one of the best clerks in the Jewish Center, and was in charge of social concerns in the labor camps. He loved his fellow man and won many friends.

* * *

The same Sabbath, the week of *Mishpatim,* the 25th of Shvat, 5704 (February 2, 1944), the police raided the offices of the Jewish Center in Bratislava, closed them, and searched the homes of several senior officials of the Center, without the latter knowing what it was all about. On February 22, Elo Gross, a Zionist activist, came to me from the Nováky camp to inform me that Gisi Fleischmann had been transferred under guard to Bratislava. She had in her possession letters in which we reported to her on developments, and, although they were in code, if they should fall into the hands of the interrogators, they were likely to provide incriminating evidence against us. Thus, we felt in danger of arrest. Later we were informed that Gisi would arrive from camp at 5:40, and were requested to wait for her at the Bratislava train station. Oscar Neumann and Elo Gross did so and determined that the guards escorting her were customs officials from the Ministry of Finance. We were somewhat reassured, for the investigators of the Treasury were quite a different lot than the detectives of the Center for State Security, and although Gisi had incriminating letters on her person, the customs investigators were more interested in financial violations and less in political matters. Rakovský, who escorted Gisi from Nováky, gave us further information: Kukula, head of the investigations department, had come to Nováky along with another investigator and taken a deposition from Gisi. After searching her room, they had found a letter from Oscar and Ondrej, and Gisi's response. She had been arrested forthwith and taken to Bratislava.

The next day our team work went into high gear, with Rabbi Weissmandel directing it. Using his great resourcefulness, he managed to replace the letters Gisi was carrying with innocent letters of a friendly, family nature, full of encouragement and hope for her speedy release, for all her deeds were for the benefit of mankind and had no fault in them, nor were they reason for her to be punished. If Kukula were to study the letters, he could conclude from their content that Gisi was innocent. Rabbi Weissmandel negotiated very cleverly with Kukula, and we hoped to obtain Gisi's release in the near future.

* * *

The offices of the Jewish Center, which had been shut down Saturday on orders from Minister of Interior Mach on the grounds of a slanderous report that the Jewish Center was working to subvert the state and was active in hostile propaganda abroad, were reopened four days later. All the accusations were proven to be based on false reports with no bearing in reality.

It was ironic that this, of all institutions, which under Sebestyén's leadership had faithfully carried out the government's directives against the Jews, had now been accused of hostile activity against the state. It is tragic for us that precisely at this time, when under Dr. Neumann's leadership the Center is likely to protect Jewish interests, people are talking of doing away with its offices. Such a decision is likely to hurt the Working Group, now working hand in hand with official persons in the Jewish Center. Šaňo Mach is conniving to transfer the Center to the Sered labor camp, i.e., to concentrate all its officers in a closed camp, thus cutting off their contact with other government offices, gradually making the Jewish Center ineffective, and ultimately doing away with it altogether. Once more we rallied our forces to fight this plan.

I had a talk with Sivák and pointed out the danger inherent in the plan. I also talked with Paškovič, chairman of the Central Office for Economy, who essentially is directly in charge of the Jewish Center. Likewise, all our people with connections with senior officials took action to assure that the institution which the law had set up to serve the authorities would remain in Bratislava. The direction of the extremists in the government, however, did not change. As far as they were concerned, law was of no account, and whatever one hand built the other hand could tear down. All means were justified by the goal – destroying all the foundations of our existence. We shall have to fight dauntlessly and indefatigably to hold our own.

VII. Jewish Community Leaders Come Together

We had long planned to hold a country-wide meeting of the General Zionists in Nové Mesto. The Zionist movement is officially proscribed, as is traveling. Thus, we had to obtain travel permits on the pretext of a legally permissible activity. After a long and difficult search, I finally came up with a way: a convention in honor of the general meeting of the representatives of the Jewish communities in the national federation of Yeshurun Jewish congregations, called for Monday, February 28. The convention of the General

Zionists was called for Sunday, the 27th. Since many members lived in Bratislava, we held the two preliminary consultations in the capital. During these tense days, caution was the command of the hour. I made the members of the movement into delegates of the Jewish communities and had Revucký, advisor in the Ministry of Education, issue travel papers to the congress to all delegates who did not have a general travel permit in their possession. The convention of the General Zionists was attended by 36 people, 16 of them from Bratislava and another twenty from outlying cities.

As chairman of the General Zionist faction, I opened the meeting with an address on the activities of the Working Group and the role played by our members in missions to render aid and rescue people. Dr. Oscar Neumann reported on developments in the Zionist movement and the Land of Israel. An argument broke out between the spokesmen of two groups. Klinger and Krasniansky, speaking for Maccabee, came out against the generalists. Dr. Winterstein, acting as spokesman for the latter, accused Klinger of having failed as chairman of the board of the Land of Israel Office and called for his resignation. The retorts degenerated to personal attacks, which certainly did not raise the level of the discussion. Klinger drew appropriate conclusions, and tempers cooled. Speaking on behalf of the general membership, I expressed appreciation for Klinger's work, his integrity, and his devoted service in office. The subsequent deliberations took place without friction, were to the point, and remained on a behooving level. Some good and important things, but also some critical remarks, were said in the course of the meeting. In conclusion, the participants left the convention feeling good from the very fact of having convened, and took away with them experiences which encouraged us and strengthened our desire to continue the battle.

* * *

The following day was the national meeting of the Yeshurun Federation, in which the chairmen of the Bratislava, Nové Mesto, Trnava, Trenčín, Velká Bytča, Žilina, Nitra, Prešov, Ružomberok, Liptovský-Svätý-Mikuláš, Turčiansky-Svätý-Martin, Banská-Stiavinica and Banská-Bystrica congregations participated.

We discussed the communities' problems of the hour, especially questions resulting from the ruling of the Supreme Court with regard to returning the Jewish communities' immovable assets which had been unlawfully expropriated.

In his address the general secretary, Dr. Julius Platschik, an educated man and a graduate of the rabbinical seminary, praised my activities, saying that "by his initiative and hard work Rabbi Frieder has established a magnificent philanthropic institution, Ohel David; and there, under the aegis of the authorities, he is saving and maintaining the lives of hundreds of people who had lost all hope and now, by his resourcefulness, he is protecting them under the law."

The chief speaker at the convention was Dr. Winterstein, who explained the new legal status of the Jewish communities and proposed lines of action to remedy the injustices which had been done. In my speech I focused on the serious problem occupying our attention today, namely abrogation of the "white" protection papers in the wake of the recent registration of Jews this February, in which they were classified according to the three specified categories. The papers of certain sectors would without doubt be cancelled, and we must take action to cancel phony papers, i.e., those whose holders are not here. We were seeing to the matter, and the prospects of finding a satisfactory solution seem good. In any event, we hoped that there would not be any unpleasant surprises and that we should be able to give advance notice of any steps to be taken by the authorities. The meeting was adjourned with a good feeling, and the participants returned home, hopeful that our efforts would bear fruit.

* * *

Tuesday, the 5th of Adar, 5704 (February 29, 1944), I had an interview with Minister Sivák. We discussed the validity of the documents issued by the Ministry of Education, and I was pleased to learn from the minister that he would not cancel a single document. Every office was busy working on the lists, since the directives stipulated that classification of the Jews and cancellation of their documents had to be completed by March 15 and that the lists must be turned over to the Ministry of Interior by that date. Let us hope that this stage of erasing and abrogating documents also passes without shaking up our communities.

VIII. People No Longer with Us

The seventh of Adar is both the day on which Moses was born and on which he died. As is our custom, on this day I eulogized the rabbis who departed from us in the past year, notably the eldest of the rabbis, Rabbi Zvi Perls of Kitsee, who was interred in our community, Rabbi Pinchas Keller of Trenčin, and the rabbi and *dayyan* Deutsch of Mikuláš. In great sorrow I also mentioned Bezalel Fleischhacker of blessed memory, and we communed with the memory of the tens of thousands of our brethren who lost their lives in the extermination camps. A special memorial prayer was recited in their memory, may the Lord avenge their blood.

That evening I was informed that our colleague and activist, Ervin Steiner of Žilina, had been arrested in connection with rescue operations and aiding exiles. The forces of evil wish to keep us busy performing the good deeds of redeeming captives.

Our sages proclaimed that "when Adar comes in, gladness is increased," but this commandment cannot be realized in the sad days in which we live. Bad tidings continually arrive from all sides. From Budapest we heard that R. Elbanan-Heinrich Schwarz, who served as the first Jewish Elder and as the general secretary of the Orthodox Bureau in Bratislava, passed away on the 9th of Adar (March 4, 1944), the Sabbath of *Zakhor* (the scriptural reading before Purim). H. Schwarz personally coordinated all the political work of the Orthodox congregations, which comprised the vast majority of the Jewish congregations in Slovakia. His funeral in Budapest was attended by many Slovak Jews who found refuge in Hungry.

Heinrich Schwarz was the sacrifice of the community for which he had worked. He fell ill in prison in Bratislava and did not receive the necessary medical care. After being released he was smuggled into Hungary and hospitalized in the Jewish Hospital in Budapest, where he breathed his last. His elderly father, R. Moses Aaron, knew neither of his son's arrest nor of his illness, both of which were kept from him until the day he died. Rabbi Weissmandel was of the opinion that appreciation of Elhanan Schwarz's work should be expressed anonymously. Therefore, I decided to publish a tribute to him in the Jewish paper, *Vestnik,* without mentioning him by name. I did so in an article entitled "Final parting from an unnamed soul."[42]

IX. Deportation Threatens the Jews of Bratislava

---

[42] Heinrich Schwarz left a wife, two daughters and a son. The two daughters, Erica and Vera, immigrated to the Land of Israel with Youth Aliyah before their father's death, and went to school in Jerusalem. When the Jews of Hungary began being deported, his wife Savina returned to the home of her former teacher. Grünsfeld, in Bratislava. In September 1944, she and her son were caught and deported to Auschwitz, never to return. Heinrich Schwarz was a fine person, a benevolent and philanthropic man. In 5707 (1947) the Budapest Jewish community erected a stone over his grave. His father, four sisters, and four brothers and their families were sent to Auschwitz and perished there, may the Lord avenge their blood.

From the beginning of March, we were occupied with problems concerning the new lists. In the cabinet the minister of interior was adamantly demanding that the papers of all Jews in Group A be rescinded. The list from Bratislava had 599 names on it and the list from outlying cities, 160. The capital's list was absolutely absurd, for it included everyone who was not actively involved in economic life or in the labor market. In other words, even one-year-old babies and eighty-year-old grandparents were on the list and, from now on, would be considered politically dangerous to the state! We pointed out the deplorable situation to all the ministries, until Paškovič, the general secretary of the Ministry of Interior, finally intervened and reduced the number to 187. Thus, a total 347 protection papers were subject to cancellation.

First, they began to "take care of" the Jews of Bratislava. Our first objective – to get hold of the lists – was successfully accomplished. In the Ministry of Interior, I managed to get hold of all the lists and annotations from the entire country, thus making the picture clear to all and enabling us to take action accordingly. This, however, was not the end of our worries. On March 4, the Sabbath of *Zakhor* (preceding Purim), all the offices of the Jewish Center were searched by the security forces and then were shut down by the police for five days. The minister of interior was still pressing his plan to transfer the Center's offices to the Sered labor camp. Our entire staff of activists launched into action once more, beginning another round of lobbying in government offices. At first, we were very apprehensive, but our efforts in the Central Office for Economy and the 14th Department softened the stand of the officials in charge, and, although this was essentially a political question, senior officials have begun to be "convinced" that the apparatus of the Jewish Center and its entire office are actually in their hands and serve the purposes of the government. All that remains is for Messrs. Paškovič and Vašek to persuade the minister of interior, too, to give up his idea.

Indirectly, in the course of my conversations with these bodies, we found out the source of the minister of interior's negative attitude towards the Center. The minister, it turns out, was angry at the Jews for submitting him what he felt was an unduly large bill, for nearly 90,000 korunas, for furniture which he had ordered from the carpentry shop in the Sered labor camp, despite the fact that the prices quoted him were by far the lowest, many times cheaper than the market price. Thus, the problem could be easily solved. We submitted a new bill for the sum of 20,000 korunas, through Dr. Vašek, and also paid a like sum ourselves. The Sered camp received the sum originally billed. Moreover, when Vašek saw that the minister's wrath had been allayed, he went so far as to tell us about the minister's difficult financial straits and heavy debts, especially alluding to a bill of 100,000 korunas. Therefore, we worked to calm things down and see to it that the dangerous plan of transferring the Jewish Center's offices to the Sered camp passed into oblivion.

X. Purim with the Nitra Rebbe

Purim fell on Thursday, and after a trying week, I longed for a Godly place. Now, for elevating the soul and strengthening one's trust in the Lord there is no finer place than the court of the Nitra Rebbe, R. Samuel David Ungar. It was a pleasant experience to leave one's dreary, mundane existence and enter another world in which original, Jewish spiritual values are cultivated. An aura of holiness reigned throughout – in the service, the conversation, and the Purim feast. The festive meal began at 2 o'clock and lasted until nearly 10 p.m. The tables were set with delectable things to eat, and the Rebbe graced us with learned remarks, to which we listened in holy reverence. Beside him was the prominent figure of the Csörcs Rebbe, a holy and righteous man. On this day of rejoicing, on which miracles were performed, he did not cease crying over our fellow Jews who are in trouble and captivity and over those who are no longer. His tears and sighs roused all those present, and presently there was not a dry eye among us. Let us pray that our tears ascend to the Holy Throne through the Gate of Tears which is forever open.

Rabbi Weissmandel's warm and friendly reception on this occasion and his effusion of pleasant words, affection and friendship for me and my work gave me great satisfaction, as well as encouragement and hope that by the merits of the righteous we, too, might live to witness wonders and miracles in our day, just like those wrought in days of yore, and that our tears become tears of joy. Would that the saying, "The Jews had light and gladness, and joy and honor," become true for us in our day.

XI. Deportation Still Threatens the Jews

The days following Purim were occupied with preparations for celebrating Slovakia's Day of Independence. The security forces prepared for searches and hunts after suspects and undesirable elements, and in such searches the first victims are usually Jews who are not allowed to live outside the labor camps, i.e., those dubbed "illegals." Searches were held throughout the country, including Nové Mesto, from March 11 to 13. Primarily Jews of this sort have been arriving in our community of late. The police force regional headquarters issued explicit instructions to run two searches of all the branches of Ohel David, to close the city streets, and to enter private residences. We prepared for these days in fearful trembling, worried lest security forces be brought in from outside the city. We were in great danger, for lurking in every street were evil informers who knew the whereabouts of the apartments of the new Jews. This was a difficult trial in our fight for survival. After great effort I managed to persuade the local authorities to warn me in advance when Ohel David would be checked, and was also given a say on which policemen would be chosen to carry out the mission. During the operation I persuaded the police not to enter the Jews' homes, and thus the days of the hunt passed in fear and terror but, thank God, also in mercy and peace.

After Slovakia's Independence Day (March 14, 1944), the Ministry of Interior embarked on a new initiative. In a secret circular to all the ministries it set forth a plan for uprooting all Jews in outlying cities. With the country's present boundaries, almost all our large communities were in border regions, thus the decree entailed the danger that the communities of Bratislava, Nitra, Prešov, Michalovce, Medzilaborce, Bardejov, and other cities would be wiped out. The ministers were requested to state their position.

Forthwith I requested an interview with Minister Sivák and spoke of the dangers inherent in this cruel plan. If you behead a living body, how can the body possibly remain alive? It is not only baneful to the Jews, but also detrimental to the interests of various sectors. Moreover, this plan should also be opposed for reasons of the government's prestige. We discussed the issue in a similar vein in the Central Office for Economy, as well. Dr. Winterstein brought his influence to bear in the Treasury, while others worked on other economic offices. All these offices, with which we are on good terms, came out against the plan, and Alexander Mach's initiative was squelched again.

* * *

Concurrently, the affair of baptism papers in the eastern part of the country was also troubling us. Many Jews in eastern Slovakia held papers testifying that they had converted to Christianity before the date stipulated in the law, even though everyone knew they were good and proper Jews who obeyed the commandments and upheld the Jewish tradition. Eventually directives were sent to the towns of Sečovce, Trebišov, and Michalovce, ordering the arrest of several Jews suspected of forging documents and possessing counterfeit papers. We were seriously afraid that the entire affair would be exposed and would end in disaster. Under these circumstances, the leaders of the Jewish communities mentioned appealed to me to find a way out of the difficulty.

On March 16, at 8:00 p.m., I talked with the head secretary, Záberecký, who was handling baptism papers on behalf of the 14th Department. We agreed on a number of names that would be marked on the list of people holding baptism papers, and that these names could be crossed off if, under pressure from informants, he was forced to issue concentration orders. Of course, this was all done surreptitiously, since the list included names of people who were no longer in Slovakia. Many had left and were either living underground, in labor camps, or in Hungary, or had been exiled to Poland. We also drafted a list of people with baptism papers whom we agreed had to be protected. Should explicit orders be given him to place these people in a camp, he would only do so if the person held no other protection paper such as a "white" card, work license, foreign passport, or other certification from abroad. In exchange for this service, I offered Záberecký the sum of 1,000 korunas for each person saved. Feeling quite satisfied with the agreement, I was glad that I would be able to bring good news to my brethren in the eastern communities of Slovakia.

That night I received a visit from the representatives of the Michalovce, Medzilaborce, Sečovce, Prešov, and Humené communities. We sat up until the early hours of the morning, discussing and deciding on our lines of action. We parted, pleased that we had succeeded in warding off the danger threatening a large number of Jews.

XII. The German Invasion of Hungary

On March 19, 1944, the German army invaded Hungary. This was a severe blow to Central European Jewry. We already knew from experience that the Germans would institute a new order immediately, and we had reason to fear that this development would have repercussions in Slovakia, as well, because the Minister of Interior would want to capitalize on it politically. Indeed, at a meeting of the cabinet on March 21, 1944, Mach took the first opportunity to call for 5,000 Jews to be rounded up in camps, in conformance with the political line of Foreign Minister Tuka, who aspired to a "successful foreign policy." A similar proposal had been brought up for consideration not long ago, and then, just as now, had been vehemently opposed by Minister of Education Sivák and President of the National Bank Karvaš, who were joined by Minister of Commerce Medrický and Minister of Transport Stano. Ministers Čatloš, Pružinský, and Fric remained silent. Thus, our extremist opponents, Šaňo Mach and Dr. Tuka, remained in the minority. At this meeting a question was addressed to the minister of interior, asking why protected Jews holding "white" immunity papers were also being concentrated in labor camps. Mach's response was that, as far as he knew, no such thing was being done. This information having been leaked to me by our friend, Minister Sivák, I took advantage of Mach's statement to help the Jews of eastern Slovakia. In the meanwhile, I found out that the agreement with Záberecký had been short-lived and that during past week 86 rounding-up orders had been sent to eastern Slovakia. This was a severe blow to the Jews living in the east and a bitter disappointment for me. I was filled with pain and anger and oppressed with worry how to right this wrong. Mach's statement, relayed to us by Sivák, encouraged us to take action.

Wednesday was devoted to attempts at intervening with

several bodies on the basis of the minister of interior's statement that "concentration orders had not been sent to protected Jews." From Vašek, Záberecký's superior, we succeeded in obtaining cancellation of the orders which had already been sent to the cities of eastern Slovakia. Dr. Kováč, who worked swiftly and devotedly, performed outstandingly in this operation, and the eastern Jews were overjoyed. I was glad that no disaster had occurred, even though the agreement with Záberecký had been violated. In the evening I had a fruitful talk with Paškovič, in which we decided on our lines of action in the event that it become necessary to do away with and abrogate various protection documents, including baptism certificates, which we all knew were only for appearance's sake.

XIII. A Time for Torah

I spent Sunday through Thursday in Bratislava. On the Sabbath of *Rosh Hodesh* Nissan, after what had been a tense, moving, and tiring week, I held a celebration marking the conclusion of my study of the Mishnah's order of *Moced*. I had taken it upon myself to study all six orders of the Mishnah, and studied at every opportunity, even in the train or in waiting rooms. I am glad I have been able to set aside time for Jewish studies and Torah, and that I have now finished *Mo'ed*, the second order of the Mishnah. This is the offering of thanksgiving which I am able to present before the Rock of Israel, who dealeth kindly with us and is our saviour and protector.

I invited about forty learned Jews and scholars to a festive meal in celebration of this religious event. I began my sermon with thanks to God for enabling me to reach this occasion, on the same day that two years earlier the Holy One, blessed be He, undid the designs of the evil and ruined the machinations of the interrogators of the Center for State Security, who arrested me then with the aim of expelling me to the land of doom, ordering *Sonderbehandlung* or "special treatment" for me, which meant death by suffocation and burning. Here is an excerpt from what I said:

In the order of *Ma'ed* we study tractates about the festivals, holy days and days of remembrance, about the Sabbath and Passover, Sukkot and *Ma'ed Katan* (dealing with the intermediate days of Passover and Sukkot), about *Shekalim* (dealing with the half-shekel tax collected to maintain the Temple and its services), fast days and *Megillah* (dealing with liturgical readings from the Bible, especially the Scroll of Esther, which is read on Purim), and about *Hagigah* (dealing with laws of peace-offerings, the duty of pilgrimage, etc.). We study these tractates to know, perform, and keep the commandments. But today we are at times forced to violate the Sabbath, and we have neither festivals nor *Ma'ed Katan.* Sometimes we lay out vast quantities of money and dwell the entire year as if in tabernacles; we decree fasts upon ourselves and find the Book of Lamentations more relevant to our lives than the tractate of *Hagigah.* We are living in a time of suffering and torment, a time of hardship; and for the most part we are powerless to change the situation and bring salvation. If we instill in our hearts a trust in God, if we set aside time for Torah study and apply ourselves to obtaining wisdom, knowledge, and fear of the Lord – wherein lies all man's wealth and his security – these things shall stand us in good stead in our hour of need. May the Lord deliver us from all hardship and may we live to see the dawning of our freedom and complete redemption, speedily in our day.

After listening to the remarks which my honored father delivered on the question of *hatzi shi'ur*[43] and to the talmudic discussion which ensued, I decided to address this question in my sermon in the synagogue on *Shabbat ha-Gadol* (the Sabbath preceding Passover). Later in the meal, R. Moses Aaron Schwarz, R. Moses Weiss, and R. Moses Rosenberg also spoke. For a brief hour we set aside our daily cares and indulged in the spiritual pleasure of other-worldly thoughts.

XIV. Preparing to Help Hungarian Jewry

The Jews of Hungary, who had been spared the disaster which befell us two years ago and who did not understand our situation, had not prepared in the least for the eventuality that the Germans might invade Hungary and immediately set about "making order" in a radical way. Suddenly they were beset with troubles, like thunder out of a clear sky.

Experienced from our own troubles, we tried to help them and give them guidance. We had connections with Wisliceny, the German advisor who was now appointed government advisor on the Jewish question in Hungary as well. Ondrej Steiner, who succeeded in establishing good relations with him, was the best man for counseling the leaders of Hungary's Jewish community. We decided to sit down and talk with Wisliceny forthwith, and initiated a number of proposals to help Hungarian Jewry. We used our influence to assure that loyal, experienced Jews, who were unimpeachable public figures, be placed on the Jewish Council or *Zsidó Tanács* in Budapest. This service which we performed was very important, since we immediately established contact with them and could help somewhat alleviate their plight. There was also reason to hope that the Germans would not succeed in carrying out their evil designs. For the victorious Russian army was approaching the borders of Hungary, and perhaps the Germans would not have sufficient time to take any drastic steps. Budapest was

---

[43] The religious law regarding half of a specified quantity of something. Translator's note.

attacked from the air several times, and this, too, was likely to have a psychological impact to our benefit.

XV. Ohel David Saves the Lives of Young and Old

Before *Shabbat ha-Gadol,* I called a general annual meeting to report on developments within Ohel David and all the institutions working under its aegis. The meeting took place on Sunday, the 10th of Nisan (March 26, 1944), and was attended by the board of directors and guests from Bratislava, among them Dr. Oscar Neumann, the Jewish Elder, Dr. Tibor Kováč, the general secretary of the Jewish Center, Wilhelm Fürst, the chairman of the finance department of the Jewish Center, Eugen Hegedüs, the head of the Yeshurun congregation in Bratislava, and the leaders of the Nové Mesto Jewish community.

Here is a summary of the 20-page minutes of the meeting, containing the gist of my remarks:

After opening remarks, I communed with the memory of friends, former supporters and residents of the institution, who were exiled to the death camps and ghettos of Poland and wiped out there. Today marks two years since the beginning of the deportations, for the first transport from Poprad to Auschwitz left on March 26, 1942. In the intervening years our institution performed rescue missions far exceeding what anyone ever imagined. Twenty-four hunts to round up people for deportation were held in Nové Mesto since 1942. In all these days of "kidnapping" Jews, the residents of Ohel David suffered only twice, while the other 22 times our institution provided shelter and protected many people in danger of deportation, thus directly or indirectly saving the lives of hundreds of people.

On this occasion I feel a spiritual need to give thanks unto God for His great kindness in saving me at this time, two years ago, from the hand of the enemy, and for delivering me from deportation, which meant certain death. I mention my arrest by the Center for State Security in part because it precluded me from taking steps to minimize the number of victims taken from the residents of this institution, which was practically cleaned out of all its residents at that time. This was the saddest chapter in the history of Ohel David and of Slovak Jewry in general, who sat in their homes, waiting to be taken to the slaughter. Thus, the residents of Ohel David shared the same fate as 60,000 Slovak Jews, expelled in 1942.

In May, June, and half of July of that year, Ohel David was not touched, despite the five big hunts that took place then. However, another difficult and black day came on July 23, 1942. At this time, I would like to tell those assembled here how events developed, what preceded the disaster that befell Ohel David; nor do I wish to hide the fact that I received anonymous letters, at the time, accusing me of sitting helplessly by; and now I turn to this anonymous person, who surely is present in the hall at this moment, for him and all those here to be the judges.

In the middle of July 1942, a cable was sent to all the district offices in Slovakia, announcing that a central old-age home would be established in the Sered camp and that all the elderly and decrepit must be sent to this camp, from which they would not be expelled but would remain in the central home for the aged. Contrary to this directive, not a single elderly person was transferred from Nové Mesto to Sered. The district commissioner found a way out of deporting the elderly, by sending a would-be innocent inquiry to the 14th Department, asking how the law was to be applied to elderly who were already concentrated in an old-age home of their own, since there was no point in their being a burden on the central institution. Somebody saw to it that this inquiry not receive any answer . . .

Later, the head of the district office went on vacation, and his assistant repeated the question by telephone, for no particular reason, simply out of fear, since he had heard that the elderly from several other districts had been sent to the Sered camp. Of course, the answer was yes, they had to be sent; and when he asked how many he must send, the vexed clerk from the 14th Department responded with an unequivocal order to transfer all the elderly to Sered. That day, July 23, 1942, I was in Bratislava and, immediately upon being urgently summoned to the telephone, sought out the district commissioner where he was vacationing. The commissioner instructed his office to hold off with everything until he returned to work and handled the entire affair in person. His deputy, however, was recalcitrant and turned to the 14th Department again, and the latter demanded that all 64 elderly individuals be evacuated to Sered.

When I arrived on the scene at 4 p.m., I found the institution shut and under guard by eight policemen, so that no one could enter or leave the home. We had to prepare a list of the 64 elderly individuals, but, negotiating shrewdly, I stalled at every name and found all sorts of reasons for protecting 35 people. Thus, I reduced the number who had to leave to 29, among them one seriously ill person who passed away in Sered, and Mr. and Mrs. Feldman, whose relatives got them out of Sered and who are residents of Ohel David today. Among the residents who remained here, 23 were poor people, which refutes the shameful accusation that any favoritism was shown the elderly who paid for their keep. Faithful testimony of this was provided by two women who were on the list but whom I rescued at the last minute, as they were packing their bags. They were Julia Just, who to our dismay passed away in the meantime, and Mrs. Josephine Szalwendy, who can testify reliably on what took place. Those were the most tragic days in the history of Ohel David. Our only consolation is that on the scales of justice the balance is likely to be in our favor, contrary to the claims of those who speak ill of us.

In 1943 the occupancy of Ohel David increased from 63 to 182 – almost threefold. By our intercession, 150 people were released unconditionally from the labor camps and were taken in by their relatives. and around 400 elderly individuals, now residing throughout the country, received temporary release papers which they renew periodically.

In the initial stage we took in the new residents in Wing C, which is the renovated building of the Orthodox Jewish community. Changes were also made in Wings A and B, making it possible to find room for another 21 residents. When even more people joined us from the labor camps, we built a fourth wing in an inn which we rented from Michalčik. We put up partitions in this large hall and, although it was an illegal and dangerous act, created rooms for elderly couples who had temporarily settled in the city. Our expenses in all these undertakings came to more than 210,000 korunas and were partially covered by the funds of Ohel David. I can announce with great satisfaction that, despite many difficulties, we met the challenge and succeeded in raising the money necessary to cover our expenditures. Now the institution is carrying out its holy mission in the best possible way. During the past year we served 108,601 hot meals free and 80,677 meals for pay. The cost of running the kitchen, including hosting a festive Passover *seder* and providing dietetic food, came to 496,695 korunas.

Thanks to the release of the private equipment belonging to Dr. Huber, which had been expropriated by the law, we opened a clinic in the institution, and Dr. Huber himself was appointed doctor of the old-age home. X-ray and other examinations are performed by the specialist Dr. Pohr, who has volunteered his services. In the past year there were 13 deaths in the institution.

The residents of Ohel David themselves are active in philanthropic and charitable works. The late Adolf Rakovský established a project to aid deportees to Poland. Every woman has been donating one koruna a week to charity every Monday; in a year over 12,000 korunas were collected. Donations in Ohel David's synagogue this year have come to 6.728 korunas. This is quite a respectable sum, compared to the 18.111 korunas which were donated in the Great Synagogue. Eshel Abraham and the Tribe of Simeon Yeshiva have been performing an active role in the religious and community life of the residents of Ohel David, giving lessons in Judaism and Torah, studying Mishnah and saying kaddish on memorial days, and studying Torah and Talmud in the yeshiva. This fine undertaking has been able to function thanks to the devoted work of the Biermann brothers, Desider as director and Adolf as financial director in charge of all financial affairs.

So much for a precis of the minutes.

XVI. Events in the Spring of 1944

By the end of March, all the ministries finished reviewing the lists of Jews. The ordeal passed without causing great upheaval, since only the papers of people who had disappeared from the scene or who were already in labor camps were cancelled. Due to a misunderstanding, the Central Office for Economy cancelled 11 papers and had actually already transferred their holders to camps, but in the end, we managed to get these people out. Things were more difficult in Bratislava, where the list was handled by a special advisory board. Whenever papers were rescinded, the decision was brought to our attention, and Dr. Kováč or I were able to intervene, generally successfully.

Of the 187 papers held by Jews on list A, 12 were in the name of people no longer alive and 18 belonged to people who were given advance warning that their immunity was being rescinded. This was, in short, the lesser evil to which we had to reconcile ourselves.

At the meeting of the Slovak cabinet on March 31, each of the ministers reported on the results of his investigation and on the protection papers which he had cancelled. The minister of interior was not pleased, for he considered the results extremely poor. In the debate which ensued the moderates had the upper hand, and the minister of interior had to give in. At the meeting the cabinet decided to announce the concentration of 5,000 Jews in labor camps. The announcement was published in the context of an interview with the minister of interior, who proclaimed that now the majority of Slovakia's Jews were concentrated in labor camps and only a small minority was protected by immunity papers issued by the president: Jews who were actively involved in the country's economic life, who had adopted Christianity prior to the date stipulated in the law, or who were partners in mixed marriages. Thus, in a seeming disclosure which actually obscured more than it revealed, even the extremist minister of interior publicly covered up the moderate decision taken by the government.

For us this was an important turn for the better, as evidenced by the fact that we could influence how the problems which we faced in recent months were handled. But this did not mean we could take it easy. Quite the contrary, the situation in the neighboring country was cause for worry and concern, and demanded that we stand on guard.

* * *

The day before Passover I held the traditional *siyyum* (ceremony upon concluding a tractate of Mishnah) with the first-born males of the community, in commemoration of the plague of the first-born, and mournfully recalled the names of those who were no longer with us. It says in Scripture, "The first-born of thy sons shalt thou give unto Me" (Ex. 22:28), but we have sacrificed not only our first-born sons; for every member of the Jewish people is considered by the Holy One, blessed be He, as His first-born, as it is said: "Thus saith the Lord: Israel is My son, My first-born" (Ex. 4:22). We have been smitten by a massive plague of the first-born, far more terrible and extensive than the plague suffered by the Egyptians.

On the first two eves of Passover, I held *seders* in my own home and hosted many guests. During the memorial service on the last day of Passover we were full of emotion, for we already knew the extent of the Holocaust: tens of thousands of our brethren had been burned and had become like the dust of the earth, and their blood was crying out to us from the ground.

* * *

Passover 5704 (1944) went by peacefully, with the stillness that precedes a storm. Reports of the Red Army advancing as far as the border of Carpatho-Russia were coming in from the eastern front. The German army, which invaded Hungary, was deployed as far as the Carpathian Mountains in the north; and it is well known that wherever the Germans set foot the most radical measures were taken against the Jews. Their Hungarian assistants performed this job faithfully. They immediately began rounding up Jews, and thousands of our brethren from Slovakia, who had found refuge in the neighboring land, once again faced the danger of deportation, threatening Hungarian Jewry in general.

* * *

Two youngsters from Slovakia, Alfred Wetzler and Walter Rosenberg (also known as Rudolf Vrba), recently succeeded in escaping from Auschwitz and, after many hardships along the way, managed to reach Slovakia on April 21, 1944. The two had been deported to Auschwitz in March 1942, had worked in the camp's offices, and had managed to write down details and facts about everything that happened to them in the extermination camp, about the fate of millions of Jews from all over Europe, and about the cruel methods of extermination employed in the gas chambers and crematoria. They told stories of atrocities and indescribable suffering, of starvation and contagious diseases, of torture and murderous beatings, of never-ending fear and terror. They had sketches showing the plan of the camps, the various buildings and the purposes these served, the furnaces and gas chambers, and the routes taken by the death trains, which transported the Jews to their slaughter and destruction and not, as the Nazis claimed, to work. When these refugees reached Žilina, Oscar Krasniansky, a representative of the Working Group, took 26 pages of testimony from them, which was typed by Gisi Farkas-Steiner.[44] With the help of diplomats, this testimony, along with another deposition by a Polish refugee of the rank of Major, was sent to Jewish organizations in the free world and to Pinchas Freudiger, the leader of the Orthodox Jewish community in Budapest. Letters from Rabbi D. M. Weissmandel and other members of the Working Group, including a request to blow up the train tracks leading to Auschwitz and the crematorium installations in the camp, were sent along with these documents.

The transcripts of the testimony given by these refugees from the camps were published in the press of the free world, but the train tracks and crematoria were not blown up.

It was during this period that the first details about the extermination camps of Treblinka, Belzec, Sobibór, Majdanek, and Auschwitz emerged in the testimony of other private emissaries.

---

[44] A complete transcript of the testimony is in FYVS, and a Hebrew translation of it appears in M. D. Weissmandel's book, *Min ha-Metzar* (Out of the Straits), New York, 1960, pp. 230-251.

Meanwhile, mass deportation of Hungarian Jews living east of the Tisa River, in the province of Siebenbürgen, and from Carpatho-Russia and Kosiče began. Four trains departed daily, each train with 45 cars, and each car containing as many as seventy-five people – standing, confined in locked cars, without water or sanitary provisions and without sufficient air to breath. Thus 12,000 people were deported every day. Many died en route, during the journey which lasted two to three days, and those who arrived alive were stripped of their clothes and deceitfully put into the gas chambers, where they were suffocated by gas and burned in the furnaces. This was the "final solution," a short and hurried way of solving the problem of the Jews in Hungary's eastern realms.

* * *

Gisi Fleischmann, still in prison, has been suffering great torment; and as long as the Koso affair is not wrapped up there is no chance of her being liberated. On April 22, 1944, Dr. Tuka published a statement on the "Koso incident" in which he summed up that "it has been eminently proven that Koso did not know about the affairs of his wife, who has been fined for her violations, that all the rumors about gold and jewelry being smuggled abroad are unfounded, that the stories about real-estate purchases are exaggerated, and that whatever he did buy he acquired through fully legal means. Nevertheless Dr. Koso could not continue to hold his office, which at times required him to handle similar cases to that of his wife." Thus, the affair was closed, Koso and his wife were "released" from a luxurious sanatorium in the Tatra Mountains, and on the 11th of Iyar, 5704 (May 9, 1944), after suffering four months of detention in various jails, Gisi, too, was released from the Ilava prison. She recovered rapidly, returned to work, and immediately added her name to the other signatories on the letters and appeals sent abroad, calling for help for the Jews of

Hungary.

XVII. Evacuation of the Jews in Eastern Slovakia

The minister of interior invited representatives of the Ministries of Interior, Finance, and Security for consultations on April 27. Security in the eastern realms of the state was the issue on the agenda. Colonel Janeček came out sharply against the Jews, claiming that they were "collaborating with the Partisans, engaging in espionage, and handing over information to the Russians and English," and called for the strongest measures to be taken against them. Šaňo Mach was assertive and precipitous, as usual, and proposed that all the Jews in the province of Šariš-Zemplin immediately be concentrated in camps. Dr. Vašek pointed out various difficulties and succeeded in postponing the decision for several days. When deliberation of the question was resumed, Paškovič, head of the Central Office for Economy, also mediated in our favor, and implementation of the resolution was put off once more.

This time 4,000 people were at stake, for the authorities were demanding the evacuation and concentration of all the Jews in the districts of Vyšný Svidnik, Humené, Stropkov, Bardejov, and Giraltovce, and of about half the Jews in the remaining districts further from the eastern front. When this became known to the Jews living in these five districts, they began fleeing their homes, and the first refugees arrived in Nové Mesto on Saturday night, April 29. Refugees also came to other cities in western Slovakia, but in fewer numbers. I immediately sensed that this development was bound to bring calamity.

On May 3, Pavel Mala, the chief commissar in the Ministry of Interior, sent his representative to the cities of eastern Slovakia to handle the Jewish problem there. We also sent our man, Dr. Juraj Révész, in an attempt to protect, advise, and counsel the Jews. Dr. Kováč and I began negotiating with Dr. Vašek. We proposed transferring the Jews to several central Jewish communities, leaving their "white" protection papers and work permits in their possession and employing them in construction work and agriculture in the *Stavebné družstvo* (Construction Association) and the Agriculturalists' Foundation. Dr. Vašek was favorably inclined towards our proposal.

As the influx of refugees into Nové Mesto increased, a worrisome situation developed. Ohel David was an officially recognized institution and could not be turned into a "bunker" for illegal refugees on such a large scale. Such an action was likely to spell disaster for all the residents of Ohel David. My colleagues in Bratislava were also worried by the situation. I wondered whether Vašek could possibly be addressed on the matter; for I was apprehensive about how he might react. However, when I saw that his position was quite moderate, I took courage and disclosed to him that "a number of elderly individuals have come to the old-age home," and requested his consent to our taking them in. When he agreed, I dared suggest, "Could we not actually take in any Jew over 60 years old, who is evacuated from the province of Šariš-Zemplín?" Happily, his answer was affirmative. At the end of our talk Vašek gave me permission to issue official papers bearing my signature and attesting that the evacuated persons were entitled to leave the province of Šariš-Zemplín and move to the Central Old-Age Home in Nové Mesto on the Vah. In accordance with this decision, Dr. Vašek officially informed the district office in Nové Mesto that temporary residence was legally approved for any evacuated person over the age of 60 who was admitted to the old-age home. This directive, giving Ohel David authority to grant shelter and protection to displaced and evacuated persons, was the institution's greatest triumph.

Thus, the issue was resolved to the satisfaction of our brethren in the eastern part of the state. But this was only in theory, since in practice things developed quite differently. On Thursday, May 4, we were informed that Jews were being seized and rounded up through-out all the districts of Šariš-Zemplín, using the same methods as in the days of the 1942 deportations. The alarm was sounded and cries for help and rescue were sent out by all the Jewish communities in the east. We were taken by surprise and dumbstruck, since we had not had any information about what was going on. We felt betrayed, as if a laughing-stock had been made of us. All that we had agreed and settled upon became for naught, for everything turned out to be lies and deceit. Jews were being seized and rounded up without anyone having given us the slightest forewarning!

The following morning, I hurried over to Vašek, along with Kováč, and asked him to stop the general round-up. But he was angry, flatly rejected our request, and admonished us lest the evacuation fail. We found out that Vašek himself had issued the order for the round-up when no more than five Jews were left in the five districts facing evacuation. To protect his honor and reputation he had given instructions to round up the Jews in all the districts of the province.

We decided to send Dr. Wohlstein and Aladar Vesel of the Jewish Center to help Dr. Révész in his difficult mission. They were joined by representatives of the Jewish communities in the province, whose central city was Prešov, the capital of the east: Dr. Sandor from Humené, Alexander Fuchs from Michalovce, Krautwirt from Prešov, Strauss from Vranov, and Ernest Wintner from Sečovce. Wintner was especially successful and, due to his well-placed connections, was authorized by Vašek to issue travel permits to Jews who moved to the west.

In all, approximately 400 Jews, out of a total of about 2,500 officially registered Jews and others whose name did not appear on any lists, were rounded up from Šariš-Zemplín. Dr. Révész invented the resourceful idea of keeping one representative from each family hostage at the place of concentration, and freeing all the rest. This suggestion was accepted, and Dr. Vašek issued instructions, which had been agreed upon with representatives of the Jewish Center, to assure the orderly and organized evacuation of the Jews from the province.

According to these instructions, all Jews had to leave Šariš-Zemplín province by May 15, 1944. Doctors and Jews in mixed marriages were excepted. People who had been arrested by the security forces were to be released, and only one person from each family would be kept as hostage. The staff of the Jewish Center was responsible for seeing to it that, after shipping all their movable possessions, all the members of the family, including the hostage, were moved to their new destination.

Agents of the Jewish Center had to organize the move of all the Jews, provide them with travel papers from the police, and find places to receive them, according to the following categories:

1. People over 60 years old would be transferred to Nové Mesto or to the homes of relatives.

2. Abandoned children would be evacuated to Nitra or to the homes of relatives.

3. Jews accepted by the Construction Association would be moved to Bratislava.

4. Clerks in ministerial and various public offices would be moved to Trnava, Nitra, Topolčany, and other cities, in accordance with the new work licenses which would be granted them, or would wait until job openings were found for them.

5. Other factory workers would be moved to various places, with a view to finding them work.

6. Holders of protection papers from the president would be moved wherever they wished in western Slovakia.

On May 5, 1944, Dr. Neumann also issued a circular containing explicit instructions to the leaders of the Jewish communities and the Jewish Center, requesting them to assist the evacuated persons, to see to it that they have roof over their heads in their new places of residence, and to help them find work quickly.

The evacuation decree presented us with a very difficult challenge and, thanks to Dr. Révész and Dr. Kováč, the general secretary of the Jewish Center, it remained a decree which the Jewish community, having no alternative, was able to face. Dozens of Jews from "bunkers" benefited from the evacuation. These included Jews who had returned from Hungary, who had fled from Poland, and other "illegal" Jews who had worked their way onto the lists of evacuated persons and now received protection papers and work permits. For these people it was an unexpected change of fortune, as it is said, "out of the strong came forth sweetness."[45] These actions were only possible thanks to the new leadership of the Jewish Center.

But we must not be overly optimistic, for this development posed a problem in the cities which had to take in the evacuated Jews. These Jews have aroused the furor of radical Jew-haters, who have begun inciting, slandering, and provoking us. In the weekly conversation in the 14th Department, Dr. Vašek voiced blunt and serious complaints about the behavior of the evacuated Jews. His strong, biting words set us worrying lest these Jews come to harm.

---

[45] Cf. Judges 14:14, figuratively meaning that good came of evil. Translator's note.

XVIII. Arrests of Leading Figures

On May 12, orders were issued to arrest Dr. Winterstein and to transfer him and his family to a camp. On May 15, a Jewish engineer named Holz, who held an important position in the Ministry of Transport and who cooperated with us, was also arrested. Early in the morning of May 17, the officials in charge of the gathering-point at 6 Goering Street, where people were rounded up before being transferred to work camps, were arrested. On May 17, 1944, the most painful blow of all was dealt: Dr. Oscar Neumann was arrested by the Center for State Security.

Oscar Neumann, the Jewish Elder, was arrested in his office under especially aggravating circumstances, there being secret documents in his pocket, likely to be used as incriminatory evidence of engaging in relations with the enemy, espionage, and treason. We all tried to preserve an outward appearance of calm and, while inwardly fearing and trembling, endeavored to shed light on the great mystery. What had happened to us? Were these arrests all links in a chain, or were they each independent of the other? Did they have to do with events in the east, with leaks, or with informers' reports?

We had neither rest nor repose until the darkness cleared somewhat. Jozef Sivák helped me solve the riddle of the warrant for Dr. Winterstein's arrest. The latter was born in Bánovce, where President Tiso had his parish; and Tiso wished the Minister of Interior to explain to him how it was that this clever Jew was still living freely on the soil of Slovakia. Šaňo Mach immediately issued orders to put Winterstein and his entire family in a labor camp. Winterstein was protected by immunity papers issued by the Ministry of Education and Culture, which provided a good reason for requesting the intervention of Minister Sivák, who promised to use his influence to obtain

Winterstein's release. This was very important to us, for if it were shown that the liberal minister had the upper hand and could overcome his radical colleague, this would be a significant precedent and would open various doors to us in the future. We prayed he would succeed!

Oscar Neumann's arrest was a different, more dangerous business, related to the evacuation of the Jews from the eastern cities. Colonel Janeček, who fervently wished to make a pogrom on the Jews, was noted for his extremism in this regard. This officer from the Ministry of Defense had a brother-in-law by the name of Kočiš, who was a senior official in the Ministry of Transport and a colleague of Mr. Holz.

Dr. Neumann, acquainted with the old-time Zionist, Holz, asked him whether he could request his brother-in-law, the colonel, to intercede on behalf of the Jews. What he wanted was for the evacuation of the Jews to be done in a calm, restrained manner, and not in precipitous haste. The security officer Janeček responded by ordering the immediate arrest of Kočiš and Holz. After two days of interrogation Holz broke down, and in the wake of this Dr. Neumann was arrested. He now bears a great responsibility, since he knows that the closely guarded secret about evacuation of the Jews from the eastern cities was revealed to me by Minister of Education Sivák, and he must not give this away lest everything come tumbling down. We had no doubt that he would hold out, despite all the emotional torture and threats which would be brought to bear against him. Even though he is not fully fluent in the Slovak language, he used his resourcefulness to invent a story about an unnamed Jew who overheard a conversation between senior government officials on the train, and said this was how we received wind of the secret plan to evacuate the Jews. Contact between Oscar Neumann and the members of the Working Group was established by exchange of notes, which was facilitated by the jail wardens.

XIX. A Trying Conversation and an Accidental Encounter

The political situation in the country, meanwhile, has been growing steadily worse. Insurrectionist movements have been organizing underground and have been drawing encouragement from the victories of the Russians, who liberated all of the Crimean Peninsula in May and are advancing westward along a wide front, towards the borders of Slovakia. Attacks against "Jewish parasites, enemies of the state, who are endangering its security from within," have mounted. The press writes incessantly about the "inundation of Jews who have come from the eastern part of the state and are flooding the city streets, dealing on the black market and causing prices to soar, so that the time has come to take care of those who still remain, too."

In this climate I, along with Dr. Kováč and Dr. Révész, had a difficult conversation in Dr. Vašek's office, on May 24. Vašek lost his self-control and, in a burst of fury, even threatened to renew the deportations if places of work were not found for the evacuated Jews. The atmosphere was grim and depressing. To our great dismay, our fellow Jews are not well-disciplined, and everyone does as he pleases, without considering that the behavior of the individual is likely to cause harm and bring calamity down on the generality. We rattled our brains trying to find a way out of the complicated situation. The discussion did not finish the same day, but continued the following day with difficult and wearying negotiations. This time Vašek spoke threateningly and pointed to the deportations of Jews from Hungary. "Twelve thousand Jews are being expelled from Carpatho-Russia every day," he said, "and do not forget that." The talks in the Ministry of Interior continued until late in the afternoon. While waiting at the streetcar stop I had a pleasant experience. A person waved to me from the streetcar. Only after boarding the car and coming closer to him, did I recognize him to be the well-known surgeon Professor Koch.[46] After we greeted each other, the professor said to me: "I am now doing what you have been doing your entire life: I am helping the poor and the persecuted." Mentioning recent developments in Hungary, he continued: "You Jews made great contributions to the spread of Hungarian and German culture, and look what thanks you have received from these two nations? The Germans wiped out the Jews two years ago, and now the Hungarians are doing the same in the most radical way. Look, Reverend Chief Rabbi, as a nation with a Jewish culture of your own, you must have independence, even if you shall be a small nation."

This interesting, Zionistic conversation with Professor Koch took place two days before the Feast of Weeks and provided the point of departure for my sermon on the holiday.

I spoke about the great Holocaust, which we are yet in the midst of, and about Ezra the Scribe, the leader of the Jews, who returned to Zion from Persia in the early days of the Second Temple, bringing nearly 40,000 Jews with him; and I said: "Although we, the Jews of Europe, may appear lost – for death and destruction have been decreed against us – nevertheless there is still hope! It is our supreme duty to produce from our ranks at least a million pioneers, men of valor, who shall immigrate to the Land of Israel and build our new state." Perhaps my listeners were shocked by what I said, yet I believe that even if it be our fate to be diminished to a few survivors, nevertheless they shall form a strong kernel, and from this kernel shall burgeon a new plant, and we shall live and not die; for "They that sow in tears shall reap in joy. Though he goeth on his way weeping that beareth the measure of seed, he shall come home with joy, bearing his sheaves" (Psalms

---

[46] Koch was recognized by Yad va-Shem as one of the righteous gentiles. and in 1974 a tree was planted in his name in the Boulevard of the Righteous Gentiles on Har ha-Zikaron, the Mountain of Remembrance, in Jerusalem. He died in the United States in 1981.

126:5-6).

XX. Plans to Establish Ghettos

I went to Bratislava on May 31, after not having been there for five days, and asked Tibor Kováč what was new. "Everything is o.k.," he answered tersely. The same day we paid a visit to the 14th Department, but Vašek was not in, so Dr. Kováč spoke with the secretary. We received the impression that everything was indeed in order. I suggested to Dr. Kováč that we see the chairman of the Central Office for Economy to try to get some news. Kováč was not enthused by the idea. Yet something prodded me to look into whether some new developments had occurred in the past six days. When we went to see Paškovič, he asked Kováč whether there was anything new in the 14th Department. Having been answered in the negative, he repeated his question in surprise. Then he told us that he had requested Dr. Mála to come up to talk with him, but that the latter had replied that he was busy drafting a plan to establish ghettos and that, at the suggestion of the minister of interior, the plan was scheduled to be brought up in the cabinet for approval that very afternoon. I was shocked at hearing this, and Dr. Kováč was even more surprised, since he himself was in charge of all our lobbying and connections with the 14th Department.

I immediately made a phone call to check if the cabinet was indeed meeting that day, and the fact was confirmed. It became clear that the entire affair was being hidden from us and that things were being done behind our backs. Worried by the bad news, I held a consultation with Dr. Winterstein and Rabbi Weissmandel. We viewed establishing ghettos as a great danger, as a preparatory step before deportation. We knew that every day tens of thousands of Jews were being taken from the ghettos of Hungary to the valley of the shadow of death. We had to do everything possible to prevent ghettos from being established. But what were we to do right now?

It was already 2:45, and at 4:00 p.m. the matter was scheduled to be discussed in the cabinet! Perhaps I still had time to take some action, perhaps I could still manage to talk to some of the key figures, even at this late hour. I decided to call up Minister Sivák, to point out the dangers which lie in store for us and to request that he relay our appeal to the more moderate ministers. Rabbi Weissmandel undertook to talk with Mr. Feuer, who would relay our desires by way of his manager to Dr. Karvaš, president of the National Bank. This failed, since Dr. Karvaš could not be reached.

I hurried to the telephone, but then I hesitated, wondering whether it was correct to turn to the minister in such a manner at this hour, wondering what to say to him and how to say it, there being detectives following us and tapping our telephone calls. Should one take the risk? Oscar Neumann's case proved that it was best to be cautious. All these thoughts and questions flashed through my mind in an instant, but in the end the great responsibility which rested upon me tipped the balance and guided my trembling hand to lift the telephone receiver. I succeeded in reaching Minister Sivák on the phone. I begged his pardon, said that the matter was most urgent, and asked whether I could have a talk with him before the cabinet meeting. It was three o'clock, time was short, and it was not technically feasible for him to receive me. Therefore, I had to state what I wanted over the telephone in a few minutes. This matter which concerned our souls, our lives, which called for careful explanation and analysis, had to be conveyed in several sentences and, at that, not openly but allusively, clandestinely! Deciding to phrase my words briefly, alluding obliquely to the tragic situation, I said: "Tono will come this afternoon and request that we all live together like one family. He told us that things will develop the way they did with your sister. Please try to put it off, and talk things over with our friends." His response was: "I understand. Thank you for your kind attention. See you tomorrow."

With this the short and fateful conversation which concerned our very survival came to an end. I had put things in a somewhat exaggerated way. The interpretation of my words, which were said hastily and mysteriously, was as follows: Tono meant Anton Vašek, i.e., the minister of interior, who seeks to concentrate and deport the Jews; since Sivák's sister lives across the border, in Hungary, the reference to his sister alluded to plans to deport us to Poland, as was being done from Hungary.

As it later became clear to us from a conversation with Dr. Paškovič, Sivák was successful in this mission.

Dr. Kašovič, the director-general of the Ministry of Interior who replaced Dr. Koso in this office, invited Dr. Kováč and myself for a talk, which took place on June 1, and was also attended by Dr. Vašek.

We received the impression that we were dealing with a cultured man, who viewed us as the representatives of a national minority group. He spoke forcefully, to the point, without a word of enmity or hostility, or the slightest hint of anti-Semitism. The atmosphere at the meeting was decent, and even Dr. Vašek behaved with restraint and inoffensive passivity, the few remarks he made being to our benefit. We listened full of tense uncertainty, since we did not yet know what the government had decided; I would only find that out in the afternoon, at my meeting with the minister of education. We were groping in the dark and waiting fearfully, for we were not acquainted with the man and did not fully fathom his words.

We also received a report, relayed to Ondrej Steiner by way of Freudiger, head of the Orthodox Bureau in Budapest, in which

Wisliceny sought to warn Steiner that a hard line would be taken with respect to the Jews of Slovakia and that it would be best for him to disappear from the scene. This information, Vašek's outburst a week ago, and the discussion in the cabinet were signs of unrest which did not bode well. In this atmosphere, Kováč and I sat opposite Paškovič and Vašek for a conversation which was later joined by Révész as well. Paškovič began talking quietly about the evacuation from eastern Slovakia, which had caused sharp reactions. In his opinion, this problem had to be resolved to obviate the need to take stronger measures and cause upheavals as extreme as renewing deportations. The men from the east must work in the Construction Association in Zemanská Kert and in new agricultural units. We must see to it that all of them work, arrange jobs for them, and maintain order and discipline. The present situation was intolerable and its consequences were likely to be fateful for all of Slovak Jewry. He warned us emphatically that the situation was exceedingly grave and that he had no way of knowing or assuring us what the future would bring.

The conversation was lengthy, and on our side, we promised to make every effort to set things in order and to integrate the Jews into the labor force by June 10, 1944. It was clear to us that the proposal to establish ghettos had fallen through, since it was not mentioned at all. We were relieved to know that the ghettos would not be established; this was also confirmed by the most competent source, Jozef Sivák. Thus, we left the office satisfied although aware that a very difficult undertaking lay ahead of us.

XXI. The Situation in Hungary and Renewal of the "Europa Plan"

The sly and two-faced Dieter Wisliceny, who in 1942 commanded the deportation of the Jews from Slovakia and in February 1943 was transferred to Greece, where he, along with Eloise Brunner, orchestrated the deportation of the Jews from Salonika and Macedonia to the extermination camps, is now performing Satan's service in Hungary, but continues to hold his office in Slovakia and from time-to-time visits Bratislava. One such routine visit was made on June 2, 1944.

Our contact, Ondrej Steiner, called on German Advisor Wisliceny the same day, and the latter told him about the swiftly expedited deportation of 240,000 Hungarian Jews, who had been shipped out inside of 20 days.[47]

Wisliceny declared that the Hungarian rulers were putting on more pressure in this regard than were the Germans. The most aggressive person on the Jewish question was Endre László, who was working with unbridled energy to annihilate Hungarian Jewry. This man pays no heed to any obstacles, and if anyone tells him of difficulties, he immediately clears them away, even if it can only be done at the expense of the proper functioning of internal affairs in the state. For example, he had 5,000 gendarmes sent to Carpatho-Russia to carry out the deportation of the Jews from there at a pace unparalleled anywhere else in Europe. This situation, Wisliceny explained, has a bearing on Slovakia's Jewish problem, which is now under discussion again; and that is why he sent his warning from Budapest.

During this conversation Wisliceny disclosed a suspenseful story in which we played roles of whose latent dangers we were not aware. It turns out that the courier who took all our mail abroad was a double agent, informer, and traitor, who, upon receiving the

---

[47] With Germany's invasion of Hungary on March 19, 1944, hunting and rounding up the Jews began. By April 28, 1944, the first transport left for Auschwitz from the Kistárcsa camp, where the Jews who had been caught in the hunts, on the streets, and in public places were being detained. Large-scale deportations began on May 14, 1944.

letters, brought them first to the attention of the Germans and only afterwards relayed them to their destination. Our messenger, whom we called Joži, was a *Gestapo* man. Incidentally, he had been sent us by the World Zionist Organization, with their recommendation as a faithful man whom we could trust. A German intelligence officer by the name of Joseph Schmidt was stationed in Budapest, and all our outgoing and incoming mail passed through his hands.

While our colleagues in Bratislava were negotiating the Europa Plan with Wisliceny, which provided for a complete halt in the deportation of Europe's Jews in exchange for paying the Germans dollars, these proposals, which were brought to Eichmann's attention through Wisliceny, also reached the *Gestapo* man, Schmidt, by way of Joži. Schmidt took up the idea and, after the conquest of Hungary by the Germans, discussed it with Dr. Rudolf Kasztner. Thus, unbeknownst to us, talks were held on this subject in two countries, on two levels, by two separate bodies in the German establishment. In Bratislava, on the initiative of the Working Group, Ondrej Steiner was negotiating with the SS man, Wisliceny, while at the same time Dr. Kasztner was discussing the subject with the *Gestapo* man, Schmidt, without coordinating with us and without us even knowing about their parallel talks.

This double handling of the matter was intolerable. Eichmann ordered Schmidt and Joži arrested, seized all our material, which was photographed and filed, and thus discovered all the cards in our hand. Joži the courier also collected the mail of Moshe Dachs, the representative of the Zionist Organization in Slovakia, and thus our enemies found out about the conflicts and differences of opinion which existed within our ranks. These letters also covered political matters, wind of which reached Berlin and from there was forwarded to the German embassy in Bratislava, to the advisor and investigator of criminal affairs, Wolf. This explains the warning Wisliceny sent Ondrej Steiner, which was not actually motivated by his love of "Mordechai the Jew," but rather by his fear lest the matter work him into a corner. Therefore, coordinating with Steiner, Wisliceny steered matters in the direction good for him, and the wrath of Obersturmbannführer Eichmann abated. The Europa Plan still stands, but instead of dollars the Germans are now demanding materials and goods essential to the economy of the Third Reich, especially every-day consumer products for the civilian population, which is suffering from the massive bombings which have begun over Germany. The Germans have asked for blankets, clothing, vehicles, and various articles for the roofless in the bombed cities.

To this end, Joel Brand was sent from Budapest to Constantinople to buy the goods there.[48] The Germans suggested that the same boats that bring the goods be used to transport the Jews overseas. The Germans were plotting to include the Jews of Slovakia in the Europa Plan, as well. In other words, we, too, were to embark on a long journey, wandering over the seas, at a time when mines, submarines, and powerful fleets of warships were maintaining a hermetic blockade, not allowing anyone to come or go. As we saw it, being thus cast out to sea was equivalent to being deported to Auschwitz or Birkenau, and so we rejected the plan out of hand.

Hence Steiner sought to exclude the Jews of Slovakia from the Europa Plan. As for the Jews of Hungary, he proposed that conditions be eased, deportations ceased, and the search for a solution delayed until after the war. Steiner, an experienced intercessor who was well acquainted with the man with whom he was dealing, forcefully held his own, and, since he had also seen to the economic infrastructure, it seemed that we were in no immediate danger. As for the situation

---

[48] See Judah Bauer, *"Shelihuto she/ Yael Brand* (Joel Brand's Mission)" Ha-Shoah – Hebetim Historiim (The Holocaust – Historical Aspects), Tel Aviv, 1982, pp. 148-191.

in Hungary, I am extremely concerned and very skeptical about all the plans, because annihilating Hungarian Jewry was among the things discussed at the Slovak statesmen's meeting with Hitler and Ribbentrop. Only one thing can save Hungarian Jewry – an unusual development on the battlefront.

XXII. The Minister of Interior's Visit to Nové Mesto

The problem of the Jews from Šariš -Zemplin continued to involve us greatly. This is one of the internal problems which still weighs down on us and has not yet been resolved. As in other cities, here, too, we hear reactions in the street and read them in the press. The locals distinguish between Jews from eastern vs. western Slovakia. The displaced Jews are in a more difficult state, for overnight they became destitute of everything. They have no roof over their heads, and naturally all want to find habitable apartments. The landlords are taking advantage of this and raising rents; and the reaction to this is to blame the Jews for pushing up prices, instead of blaming the Christian landlords. And thus, anti-Semitic propaganda is mounting: the Jews are accused of paying black-market prices and dealing in the black market (for how else can they pay 1,000 korunas a month for a room instead of 200 korunas?). As usual, the Jew is to blame for everything.

Here in Nové Mesto, Ohel David continues to perform its mission, as it has from the day it was founded. We began building huts, at an investment of 1,500,000 korunas, to take in the elderly among the uprooted Jews. We regret to say that people are not evincing a proper attitude towards this philanthropic institution. Many people are shirking their responsibility to participate in the large expense of building the apartments and do not realize that if they do not contribute their share, we shall not be able to keep going. Where are we to get the large sums of money which this enterprise needs daily?

It has come to my attention that, in honor of Minister of Interior Alexander Mach's upcoming visit to Nové Mesto on June 4 to participate in the ceremony of our town becoming a city, hostile circles are planning to launch an offensive, and present various questions against the Jews. To foil these intentions, I visited all the government offices and organizations in the city and requested that the anti-Semitic instigators be removed or shut up. I spoke to the district commissar and the commander of the district police station, as well as the district commander of the Hlinka Guard, and requested them not to allow the state ceremony and fine celebration of the entire town to be turned into an anti-Semitic demonstration. They gave their word, and the visit of this radical, hostile, Jew-hating minister also passed without trouble. Nové Mesto can continue serving as a city of refuge for the Jews of Slovakia, despite the incitement in the press.

Below we cite a passage against the Jews, which appeared recently in a newspaper:

> Inundation by Jews. Our correspondent from Nové Mesto writes: Nové Mesto has always been a city with a large Jewish population. But now when you walk down the street, you get the impression we are living before 1938. Recently Jews have been arriving here from eastern Slovakia and have been pushing housing and food prices up. The price of a liter of milk has reached 6 korunas. Soon nothing will be left on the shelves. The synagogue is overflowing. The populace is angry and embittered. Naturally, this inundation of Jews has an impact on other destructive elements, as well. There

are families here who sympathize with the Jews, and they have been coming out with insults right and left. It is hard to understand them. Sometimes they believe the Jews' propaganda and sometimes they refuse to swallow it. One thing is certain, that when Jews from the east settle here, they descend like locusts on the food products and apartments, and offer high prices for them. We must put an end to this Jewish insolence.

XXIII. Conflagration

The early days of June were full of tension and excitement. On Monday the 5th, the minister of interior appeared in the 14th Department along with the head of the Center for State Security, Dr. Beňuška. This was not a routine call by the heads of the ministry; they had not come to question and investigate Dr. Vašek, who, contravening explicit instructions by the minister of interior not to issue travel permits for any reason whatsoever, had issued a travel permit to a Hungarian Jewish author from Trnava by the name of Egri. A disagreement between Mach and Vašek had blown up into a fight which was likely to weaken the latter's position; and this meant extreme measures would be taken in solving the Jewish problem. When Kováč and I had an opportunity to talk with Vašek, we saw that the roots of the argument went back to deep differences of opinion; thus, the incident was very disquieting. We considered all sorts of suggestions and ways of healing the breach, but none were to any avail in eradicating the roots of the quarrel. The great man had fallen into the fire, and an ill wind was spreading the conflagration to other victims as well. Our colleague, Ervin Steiner of Žilina, informed us the same day that Ost, a clerk in the Jewish Center's Special Services Section, told him he had been questioned by a detective from the Center for State Security and that he had been asked, among other things, to say what he knew about Záberecký, head secretary of the 14th Department, with whom I had good personal connections. Záberecký was one of the people who received a monthly grant from our Working Group and helped me arrange urgent matters at secret meetings in his friend's apartment; therefore, upon hearing this news, I could not sit idle. I decided to pay him a visit in the evening and talk things over with him, because if he were to involve us in the interrogation, things would be likely to develop into a serious matter, harmful to all the Jews. Likewise, I sought ways to prevent the conflagration from spreading. I hope this affair will be set in order, even though relations between Vašek and Mach still appear to be strained.

We are now working energetically to find jobs for the Jews from Šariš-Zemplin, since the date for winding up this operation is approaching; yet no encouraging results are yet to be seen. Due to bad experiences in the past, the Jews are in no hurry to obey orders from the Jewish Center, even though the leadership and personnel in all the departments have changed and there is practically overt cooperation with the Working Group.

* * *

In times of darkness there is always a ray of light. We have at long last received some good tidings to brighten the bleak times in which we are living. On the eve of the Sabbath of *Be-ha'alotkha,* the 18th of Sivan (June 9, 1944), I received a cable from Dr. Neumann: "I came home today. Sincerely, Oscar." While he was in prison, Dr. Neumann, who had just been released, proved his intellectual prowess and moral rectitude. He took all the blame upon himself and stood firm in his cross-examinations by the detectives of the Center for State Security. Vojtech's case has still not been settled. Therefore, I requested an interview with Minister Sivák to remind him that he had promised to repeal the warrant for Winterstein's arrest and release him for the torment which he is suffering. I hope that his case, too, will be settled shortly. The people arrested on Goering Street have not yet been released either, and their case has been further embroiled by the discovery of a network of people in the Czechoslovak underground. Sixty-four people, denounced by a barber in the Karlton Hotel in Bratislava, who informed the authorities about a cell of underground activists, were arrested and interrogated under cruel torture in the Ilava Prison. Ferdinand Hoffmann, director of the manpower division of the Jewish Center, was among those arrested; and all the blame was hung on him. His brother was arrested too, and his arrest led to the arrests of Julius Meir and Smetana. Hoffmann and Meir worked as clerks of the Jewish Center at the gathering point on Goering Street, in the building of the former Jewish Hospital. After being authorized to accept uprooted persons over the age of 60 into Ohel David, I managed to release several of the detainees from the gathering point. I generally arranged these matters with Julius Meir and through him had met the police officer, Pavlačka, with whom I carried on the negotiations. My colleagues cautioned me that Meir was not to be trusted, yet I could not help but let him in on the secrets of my work freeing detained persons. Now that he is being investigated in Ilava, he has shown the weakness of his personality: he has told the interrogators everything he knows. I was afraid things would get complicated and snow ball, but thanks to the connections which our people had in the secret police, as well, we managed to extricate ourselves from this dangerous situation.

On June 12, the 14th Department was handed a report on the integration of the Jews from eastern Slovakia into the labor force. The detailed document was skillfully drafted by Dr. Kováč. Anyone reading it would receive the clear impression of a mission accomplished with relative success. We hope that this affair, which has bothered us for a long time, has been brought to a close.

Commemorative day for the eponym of Ohel David

Tuesday, the 22nd of Sivan (June 13, 1944), was the anniversary of the death of the *gaon* Rabbi David Deutsch, of blessed memory. Nové Mesto has had a longstanding tradition for hundreds of people to visit the grave of this righteous man on this day, to commune with his memory and pour out their hearts in prayer and supplication, asking for salvation and consolation. Since our city has been laid waste and most of the members of our congregation deported, vastly depleting our numbers, and the laws of the state no longer permit one to travel freely from city to city, the number of people visiting the grave of this righteous man has dropped to a mere 10 or 20. This year, however, on the same commemorative day we also held the unveiling of Rabbi Zevi Hirsch Perls' tombstone, and a large congregation from among the residents of Ohel David and the new émigrés came to participate in the ceremony. We prayed at their gravesides, and I eulogized these two righteous men.

May this day, the 22nd of Sivan, be a milestone for us, that we may continue to work in the light shed by these two great and holy men. May their souls be bound in the bond of eternal life.[49]

XXIV. Cancellation of Harsh Decrees

Whenever a dispute broke out in our enemy's camp, in the final analysis it always turned out to be at our expense. The fight between Vašek and Mach ended in a compromise in which Mach had the upper hand and we, of course, were the sacrifice.

On June 14 Vašek called us for an urgent talk. Dr. Kováč, Dr. Révész, and I attended. Vašek read us the new orders and decrees:

---

[49] Rabbi Frieder also died on the 22nd of Sivan, in the year 5706 (1946).

1. The number of workers in the Fond[50] is to be reduced by 50%. Those laid off are to be transferred to a labor camp.

2. The Jews of Slovakia are to be concentrated in ghettos. Jews living in communities of fewer than 200 people are to be transferred to a central ghetto.

3. All Jews wearing a "large star,"[51] in other words all dependents of people holding protection papers, are to be concentrated in labor camps.

4. All Jews over 60 are to be concentrated in the camps' central old-age home, Ohel David in Nové Mesto.

5. All patients in hospitals throughout the country are to be transferred to the Sered Jewish Hospital attached to the labor camp.

6. All protection papers are to be closely reviewed. The holders of papers that are cancelled are to be transferred to labor camps.

"These are the orders that I received from the minister of interior," Vašek said, "and I cannot change anything or help you. I must ask you, as representatives of the Jews, that the Jewish Center carry out all the orders punctiliously, or else a situation similar to the one in Hungary, where the Jews are being deported to Poland, is likely to develop. The situation here is what might be called the lesser evil."

When he finished his words, which were said in a tone to which

---

[50] An association which operated under the Ministry of Agriculture and employed many Jews from Bratislava and the outlying cities. Its employees had immunity against deportation or concentration by virtue of protection papers issued them by the Ministry of Agriculture.

[51] A head of family who held a protection paper, i.e., who was essential to one of the sectors of the economy and society of the state, was obliged to wear a small yellow star. His dependents, who were protected under his papers, i.e., his wife, children, and parents, wore large yellow stars.

we were unaccustomed, we stood in shock, unable to utter a word. My two colleagues were official representatives of the Jewish Center, and perhaps for this reason hesitated to respond. I was in a better position, since I did not belong to the Center. Therefore, I took the floor and said to Vašek:

"Mr. Chief Advisor, what I have to say to you, of all persons, is not easy, since you do try to help us. Yet we cannot carry out these orders. Please permit me, as a representative of the Jews of Slovakia, to declare in your presence that we cannot be obedient and submit to the authorities in this matter. The decrees are exceedingly harsh, and we shall not be able to live with them. What, after all, is the meaning of clause 3? That I, who hold a protection certificate, shall wear a small star, whereas my parents, my wife, and my children will wear large stars; in other words, that you, Sir, by orders from the minister of interior, are demanding that I take my wife, my young children, and my aged parents and lead them to a labor camp? You do know that I would do no such thing to myself and my small family; and therefore, I could not possibly do this to my larger family, the Jews of Slovakia. I, for my part, shall henceforth enlist all my energies and talent to cancel this evil decree.

And what does the second clause say? That Jews living in places where there are fewer than 200 of them will be evacuated and concentrated in a central ghetto. That is precisely what they are doing in Hungary! I see only a small step between a ghetto and deportation. All that remains is to station several SS men and Hlinka Guards there, and the transports will roll. We are not willing to be the murderers of our people!

The fifth clause states that all hospital patients must be transferred to Sered. What this means is taking all the tuberculosis patients, the heart, kidney, and nervous system patients out of the sophisticated and well - equipped hospitals where they are receiving vital care from expert doctors, and transferring them to a small, unorganized and ill-equipped hospital. With what intent – to cure them? Or to hasten their death and annihilate them?

Mr. Advisor, we ask you, we entreat you in every possible way, do not require this of us. Do not hand us such orders, for we shall not betray our people. Our people are being smitten and persecuted to death. Our brethren are being killed in gas chambers and burned in crematoria. We love our brothers, and it is our duty to help them, to save them, not to do the opposite. I, Sir, shall not obey these instructions, even if you take my life. I shall die only once, in this world; but I shall live in the World to Come, in the world of Truth."

Dr. Kováč and Dr. Révész followed suit in the same spirit, each in his own style, also speaking plainly and openly. Apparently, we made an impression upon him, for his response was that he understood the orders were not executable and had no rhyme or reason, but that they came, as he had said, from his superior. Vašek proved his good will, for in this difficult setting, upon my request, he issued an order to free Margit Winterstein from arrest on Goering St. Now it remained for us to extricate her husband Vojtech, who all the while had been hiding in my room in Bratislava, from the danger of being rounded up.

The following day we continued our discussion of the subject in the 14th Department, with Chief Commissar Dr. Mála and Commissar Bučenec and the chairman of the Central Office for Economy, Dr. Paškovič, who agreed with our stand. After lobbying here, we went back to Vašek, encouraged and feeling that our firm stand had influenced him.

The first bombs which fell on Bratislava affected the course of events most of all. On June 16, I remained in Bratislava to handle the grave crisis confronting us and was lobbying various offices when a considerable number of allied planes appeared overhead and bombed the city for the first time. This event presented the authorities with urgent problems, which demanded an immediate solution and, I hoped, had pushed aside further handling of the Jewish question.

I did not even go down to the shelter and did not know what was happening. Only on my way to the minister of education, during a lull between two raids, did I notice the smashed shop windows along Uhorská St., the merchandise scattered over the street, the trucks evacuating the wounded, and the thick column of smoke rising into the sky from the Apollo refinery.

Several houses in the area of the Presidential Palace had been destroyed and public transportation had been paralyzed, because the cable-car lines on Stefánik St. had been blasted out. Thus, I was forced to go on foot. I hurried to see Sivák about the subject worrying us all and about cancelling the arrest warrant against Dr. Winterstein, but the minister was not in. Later on, I reached him on the telephone, and he set an appointment with me for 4 p.m. In the meantime, I realized that the bombing had caused serious damage and that many houses had been destroyed and a large number of people killed. I was afraid the guns would be aimed at us and that we would be the object of attack and the scapegoat, as usual. Therefore, it became all the more important to meet with Sivák, who would be able to foil any proposals the minister of interior was likely to advance in the cabinet meeting which would surely be called in the wake of the massive bombing.

In the afternoon I set out again on foot along the street which had been most badly hit by the bombing and along which masses of people had gathered. Hateful snipes were hurled at me every step of the way. "There goes that Jewish pig, he is to blame for the bombing," someone called out excitedly. I reached the minister's office and found him in a grave, adverse state of mind. I laid my requests before him, and he listened and promised he would not allow us to be victimized.

At 6:15, I hastened to the train station to travel home. Thousands of people – men, women, and children – were there already, all trying to flee from the capital. It was truly dangerous to board the train in such a crush; and I, a thick-bearded Jew dressed in my unique garb, wended my way with difficulty through the shoving crowd, which spared no anti-Semitic quips. I was glad to reach the Leopoldov station. There I promised a taxi driver a special reward if he brought me home by 8:30, before the beginning of the Sabbath. We drove 100 km. per hour, and I arrived home safely, two minutes before candle-lighting time. Indeed, those who are sent to do good deeds are protected by Divine providence. How good it was to be back in my congregation after six trying days of work and to receive the Sabbath Queen in the synagogue and sing Solomon ha-Levy's hymn: "Long hast thou dwelt in the valley of tears. Now shall God's tenderness shepherd thy ways."[52] May the All-merciful grant us a day that is wholly Sabbath and rest!

---

[52] From *Lekha Dodi*. Translator's note.

* * *

On Monday, June 19, I had an interesting téte-á-téte with Dr.
Vašek. I arrived at the 14th Department at 1 o'clock and several
minutes later was received by the head of the department. He was
not in a good mood, had family problems on his mind, and perhaps
for this reason spoke gently. It was an opportune moment to discuss
current problems, the economic situation of Slovak Jewry, and
expected developments in the next few months. In the course of the
conversation, he went over to a personal tone and said, "Mr. Chief
Rabbi, I know that you are essentially the leader, just as Tiso is the
leader by us, and therefore I speak differently with you, because the
entire congregation stands behind you." I immediately demurred
against his statement, primarily because I did not wish to detract from
the rights and importance of Dr. Kováč, who has had great influence
over Vašek ever since their school-days together, and who was the
one who held candid conversations with Vašek. Nevertheless, Vašek
proceeded and said that Dr. Kováč was perfectly just towards me
and acknowledged my priority and leadership. "The same cannot be
said for Ondrej Steiner with his strong ambitions, whose personal
aspirations led him to become involved in public affairs; but even
though he is not the type to be an outstanding activist, he has worked
faithfully and done much for the general welfare." I refrained from
responding to these personal remarks and turned the conversation to
the subject of the deportations. "I believe," I said to him, "that there
will not be any more deportations from Slovakia. This opinion is
based, first of all, on my faith that you Sir, the chief advisor, will not
permit people to be sent to their death. I know you as a decent man
who would not agree to genocide, and you know, as well as I,
that deportation to Poland means annihilation. Sir, there will not
be any deportations, because we shall put up resistance to their
murdering us. All the Jews of Slovakia today know about the gas

chambers, the crematoria, and the death camps. We shall use any means to defend ourselves, even fighting the murderers. If it be decreed on us that we must die, we shall die here, but not in the gas chambers of Auschwitz-Birkenau and other death camps. If we must die, we shall die here in our homes and our cities, and we shall be buried in our Jewish cemeteries according to our custom, in Jewish graves. And the last reason for my opinion is that the government of Slovakia knows by now that the Germans misled them, and they will not agree to death transports. Therefore, I am not intimidated by the specter of deportation."

Vašek agreed with what I said and promised me there would be no more deportations from Slovakia. The very fact of such a long dialogue, of openly exchanging words and opinions, was an important and positive factor, and was bound to have an impact on him and set him thinking about what might be in several months, after the war is over. There is no doubt that people of his type are already beginning to do their soul reckoning.

The following day, June 20, I conversed with the chairman of the Central Office for Economy, Dr. Paškovič, and requested him to complete the stage of integrating the Jews from Šariš-Zemplin into the economic life of the state and to provide them with protection papers. Dr. Paškovič promised to talk with Minister of Finance Medricky, and we agreed between ourselves how the mission would be carried out.

XXV. Repercussions of the Air Raid

After the bombing the authorities wished to place 100 Jews in work gangs clearing the debris. For political reasons the Jewish Center agreed to this plan and sent a circular to the Jewish community, requesting people to come forward for the job. The response, however, was very poor, and this led to harsh criticism from the 14th Department. We were afraid that if the Jews continued avoiding such jobs, this unloyal behavior was likely to have unpleasant consequences. Therefore, we embarked on an explanatory campaign to warn our brethren that their behavior was likely to lead to a new wave of anti-Semitism. I appeared in the beit midrash Yesodei Torah at an information meeting, and, after great efforts, the community succeeded in raising 80 people to participate in these works every day.

The bombing had powerful repercussions and strongly influenced defeatist tendencies among the populace. It not only made a swell in the press, which wrote incessantly about the effects of the bombing and the lessons to be learned from it, but was also felt in lectures and in conversations between friends. Everyone was worried and began fleeing from the capital to the countryside. As we feared, the press began looking for a scapegoat and, of course, immediately pointed the finger at international Jewry. Tido Gašpar, director of propaganda, stated: "The Jews and the Czechs are to blame for it all. With joint forces they are fighting us from without and gnawing away at us from within." Gašpar was a member of the cabinet and took part in its deliberations, and all he lacked was the title of minister. He was the principal ringleader of insults and incitement against the Jews and exceeded all limits in his venomous propaganda.

On June 26, when I arrived at my office in Bratislava, Dr. Neumann informed me that the minister of education and culture was looking for me. Presuming that I was to have an interview with Minister Sivák, I gathered my thoughts and analyzed the political situation.

As I said, Tido Gašpar saw to it that hostile articles were published against us in all the media. He aspired to build a political career and, now that the prime minister was about to be changed, made efforts to exploit the situation and used any means, including the most brutal, to please his masters, the German advisors. That is how I account for the renewal of the strong, hard line against us now. His rival, Minister of Interior Šaňo Mach, also aspires to increase his rank and become Prime Minister, and to tip the balance in his favor he must appear very aggressive, because the Germans weigh and evaluate politicians by their extremism on the Jewish question.

Minister Sivák received me, as I had expected, and in a two-hour talk we brought up various ideas and avenues of action to clear the atmosphere and ward off the dangers threatening us. We agreed on the need to find a way of reaching Tido Gašpar himself.[53] The minister expressed his readiness to talk with the president and suggest ways of calming the air and consolidating the problem of the Jews.

On June 28, I was received by Minister Sivák again. I listened to what he had to say and sensed an inclination towards letting up tension, moderating hostile proclamations, and shelving extremist proposals. But the situation was still grave, and if rapid advance were not made on all fronts, eastern, western, and southern, we would be likely to find ourselves facing serious difficulties in the month of July. Sivák, however, led me to entertain hopes of his succeeding in influencing President Tiso. How could he accomplish this? The President is friends with the priest, Štefanec, who has a parish in Modra, near Bratislava. Tiso often visits his old friend Štefanec, and in the evenings they have dinner, drink, and play cards together. Sivák has also moved to this town recently, and thus he will have the opportunity to participate in these social get-togethers and, along

---

[53] Dr. Neumann writes in his book, *In the Shadow of Death* (Tel Aviv, 1958, p. 171 [Hebrew]), that in a conversation between Rabbi Frieder and Tido Gašpar the latter received 200,000 korunas "for social purposes," in exchange for which he promised to act with restraint.

with Štefanec, might be able to exert influence on the president and change his radical views. We shall see.

XXVI. A New Commissar in the Nováky Camp

June 29 was a Christian holiday and a day off throughout the country, a suitable opportunity for visiting the Nováky camp and checking on the condition of our brethren incarcerated there. On the eve before the visit, the Jewish council updated me on the situation, and I was glad to receive encouraging reports from them.

There is news from Nováky. The commissar of the camp, Švitler, whom I had not succeeded in getting fired, has at long last been removed and has been replaced by police sergeant Gabčan, a man from the old democratic regime, a decent and humane person, who brought a more relaxed atmosphere to the camp, much to the satisfaction of the people there.

The work ethic did not decrease. On the contrary, output went up, and in exchange the commissar allowed the residents of the camp greater freedom of movement. Švitler's idiosyncrasies, which angered and annoyed the residents, his accusations and taunts, which embittered the lives of the Jews in Nováky, were soon forgotten. Švitler, who behaved as a heartless despot, did not distinguish between good and evil, between what is important and what is unimportant; he was only a vexation and was not suited to his job in any respect. The new commissar, in contrast, was magnanimous and understanding of the residents and commanded the camp without hurting the Jews and without instilling fear and terror in them. I spoke with many people, and found that they were calm and that despite being concentrated in a closed camp their lives were relatively quiet, for they were not oppressed by the tension felt outside, in civil life, which could hardly be said to be free. Even the recently constructed swimming pool – and I say this with a degree of reservation, hoping that morality is being upheld – has contributed to strengthening the body, to good health and recreation, and especially to the children's enjoyment of the summer months. In addition to a swimming pool, a *mikveh* (ritual bath) was also built in the camp, upon the request of the religious families and with the aid of Mr. Pinchas Wintner, one of the leaders of the Sečovce community.[54]

I was glad to meet with friends again and with the community in general, who, considering the circumstances, were quite satisfied with their lot and hoped that their liberation and salvation were close at hand. According to the schedule, I was supposed to return home by 11 p.m., but a formation of Allied planes flying overhead disturbed the night's rest, and air-raid alarms stopped the trains, so that my trip from Nováky to Nové Mesto took 13 hours, and I did not arrive home until 7 a.m.

I was glad to see my children, who had just awakened. When they surprised me with greetings for my 33rd birthday, which was today, June 30, I forgot the difficult journey, my weariness left me, and I rejoiced at being in the lap of my family once more.

In the history of mankind thirty-three years are like the wink of an eye, but considering the life of man – as we read in Psalms, "The days of our years are three-score years and ten" (Psalms 90:10) – almost half my life has passed. And if it is true that years which are devoted to faithfully serving the community count doubly, then this calculation must certainly apply to the past few years of my life. In the depths of my soul, I prayed that I would be blessed with the privilege

---

[54] Mr. Pinchas Wintner, a textile wholesaler, continued to manage his business with his sons even during the Holocaust, thanks to two Aryanizers who allowed him a free hand. One of them was Žozi Starinský, wife of Peter Starinský, an important man in the Center for State Security. The factory supplied goods for the camp's workshops and, through its useful connections, contributed greatly to saving Jewish lives.

of spending the coming year dwelling in peace and joy among my people and would have no need to continue writing these pages. May nothing out of the ordinary happen and may the Jewish people go back to being the same ancient nation it once was, performing its mission as a nation among the nations. God only grant that it be so!

I devoted the first workdays of July to cancelling the arrest warrant against Winterstein, who has been in hiding for two months. This was an extremely difficult undertaking, since the warrant for his arrest had been issued by the president himself, and only a person of ministerial rank could cancel this order. Sivák tried to do so a number of times, but without success. On July 3, I appealed to him again. This time I requested that he appeal directly to Tiso, since the person who issued the arrest warrant should be the person to rescind it. Sivák did so. The president did not promise to take specific action to help Winterstein, but indicated he would not take any measures against him or oppose his release. Thus, there was room for hope. The following day Sivák turned to Mach and obtained a promise that Winterstein would soon be released. I immediately relayed him the heartening news, but, as was his way, he received the news with doubt and skepticism, thus somewhat putting a damper on my joy. Yet one should not be surprised at his reaction, for he has been patiently awaiting this moment for almost two months, and who knows how many promises were made him and not kept. Wednesday was another day off, a Christian holiday, and government offices were closed.

On Thursday, July 6, I went to the Sered labor camp, primarily on business pertaining to supplying huts for Ohel David. Upon my return late that evening, Alizka our housekeeper told me that Dr. Winterstein had left a telephone message in person to say that he was free. I received the joyful tidings with great satisfaction. I had worked hard on his affair and was very glad that Sivák succeeded in the mission. He has proven his loyalty eminently. Without his help Vojtech Winterstein would not have been freed. Blessed is He who releases the imprisoned.[55]

XXVII. Conferring with a Man from the Security Service

During the second week of July, we worked at finding employment and obtaining protection papers for evacuated Jews. The problems of the Jews who escaped across the border to Hungary were no less difficult. The hunts and searches for foreign Jews in Hungary were very serious. Not only have Slovak Jews been returning, but also an ever-increasing number of Hungarian citizens have been crossing into Slovakia. When I visited the 14th Department, I sensed that the situation was becoming progressively graver in the wake of intervention by the German Protector in Hungary, Peselmayer, who was accusing the Slovaks of allowing illegal border crossings and thereby preventing the Jewish problem from being solved. I attributed great importance to conferring with Dr. Pavel Prikopa, head of the political department of the State Security Services, who had just entered office and agreed to meet with me secretly. The meeting was held on July 13 in Senica. "It will be important for us both," I told him candidly, "to find a basis for cooperative action, because, in your position, you will find yourselves in confrontation with those underground circles that are destined to rule when the war is over." Many of these circles help us in rescue operations, and through this connection we shall be able to help them in the future and avail ourselves of their help at the present. I let Dr. Prikopa

---

[55] After the war, when Sivák was put on trial as a member of the Slovak government, Winterstein was his defense attorney. Sivák was sentenced to a prison term which he completed during his detention for interrogation. The Jewish community helped him and his family in their straits after the war.

understand that, precisely because he was new in his position, he must plot his actions and choose his steps carefully and in such a way that, when the time comes, we shall be able to testify to his integrity and assistance during this difficult period.

It appears that what I said surprised him but also made an impact upon him, for after our conversation he took me to his private apartment and introduced me to his wife. This gave me a good opportunity to present her with a nice gift. A friendly atmosphere was established as a foundation for cooperative action. Before parting, Prikopa gave me his telephone number so that I could call him in the event of an emergency.

I returned home full of satisfaction and hope that this acquaintance would enable me to help our brethren who are pursued by the curse of Cain – "a fugitive and a wanderer shalt thou be in the earth" – and quite a number of whom have been caught by police of tie Security Services.

XXVIII. A Meeting with Sivák in Prievidza

We have been feeling in tighter straits and more keenly aware that "when the month of Av comes in, gladness is diminished." The extremist Germans have seen to this, for they persist in demanding that the Jews be concentrated in ghettos and camps, especially those Jews returning from Hungary and those evacuated from the eastern parts of the state. The minister of interior has gone even further, seeking to kick out all the Jews from the Jewish Quarter in Bratislava, from Jews' Street, and from Kapucinská St. and transfer them to abandoned industrial buildings, in a manner similar to what was done in Hungary.

Faced with this difficulty, I decided I must see Sivák, who was on vacation in Prievidza. On July 19, I went to the Nováky labor camp and from there by car to Prievidza. The minister received me warmly, and we discussed the general political situation and our problems – establishing ghettos and rounding up the Jews; the government's plan to use frozen Jewish assets to compensate victims of the bombings for the damages they suffered in the war; and the possibility of establishing contacts with the leaders of the ruling party. I asked the minister to introduce me to the chairman of the parliament, Dr. Martin Sokol, who is deputy chairman of the People's party. The minister of education promised me he would talk with him.

I gave Sivák a full report on an incident of personal interest to him. A certain Jew by the name of Akoš Adler, who was born in Topolčany and whose parents were living in London, studied law in Prague and since 1942 was living in Slovakia under Aryan papers. Adler was arrested by the Center for State Security on suspicion of being an agent and spying for the Czechoslovak government in exile in London, headed by Eduard Beneš. Dr. Karvaš told Sivák that Adler had revealed information to his interrogators about his ties with Karvaš. Since Adler had also had contact with Sivák, the latter was particularly interested in knowing details about the investigation. Sivák requested attorney Weichherz[56] to handle the matter and told him that Adler was already in the Nováky labor camp. I immediately contacted the camp and discovered that the report was erroneous. Our agile intercessor, Alexander Adler, managed to get hold of a copy of the interrogation transcript, which was five typed pages long, and now I was able to pass it on to the minister of education. Sivák was impressed by our connections and swift action and, after looking over the material, was glad to see that he himself had

[56] An ex-Jew and one of Slovakia's finest jurists, protected by immunity papers from the president.

not been implicated in the affair. He was also pleased to be able to present the transcript to Dr. Karvaš and keep him up to date.[57] This service strengthened my position and henceforth gave me more confidence and a better feeling when appealing to these two persons, who at every opportunity championed our side without the least reservation.

After a conversation which lasted three hours, I returned to the Nováky camp to spend the night, and on the morrow, July 20, planned to visit the commissar of the Nové Mesto district to discuss the Ministry of Interior's secret circular with him. Vašek had not kept his promise and had issued an urgent secret circular for immediate implementation, in which he gave instructions to transfer all the state's eastern Jews for whom jobs had not been found and all the Jews who had returned from Hungary, regardless of whether they were Slovak or Hungarian citizens, to labor camps. The provisions of the circular were very serious, and insisting of their implementation was likely to make our situation extremely perilous. Therefore, I rushed over to see Rakovský, who was on vacation in Zlaté Moravce, to sum things up with him on all the affairs pursuant to the new directives. The district commissar (náčelnik) received me cordially, showed me his well-tended vineyard and wine cellar, the fruits of our large "investments," and, in good spirits from the wine, was open to all my proposals regarding the plans to establish a ghetto and concentration point in Nové Mesto.

XXIX. The Three Weeks before the Ninth of Av

On July 25, I was in Bratislava at the 14th Department. The same day the Nové Mesto police received an urgent circular about

---

[57] The transcript of Akos Adler''s testimony is in FYVS, vol. 4, pp. 215-219.

rounding up the state's eastern Jews and refugees from Hungary, and my wife called me home to handle the emergency. In Nové Mesto I reached an agreement with the regional commander of the police on how the searches would be carried out, and the following day we went to District Commissar Rakovský to obtain his approval.

We knew beforehand that the searches would be held on Friday, July 28, the eve of *Shabbat Hazon* ("Sabbath of Vision," preceding the Ninth of Av), and everyone behaved cautiously. The Jews who had come from Hungary disappeared from the scene and the Jews from Šariš-Zemplin were to go into the new huts which we had built in Ohel David, Nové Mesto's ghetto. Actually, most of them returned to their apartments once the official search was over.

* * *

Upon returning home I found an urgent letter on my desk:

Michalovce, July
24, 1944

Dear Reverend Rabbi,

Please forgive me for bothering you with this letter. You have surely heard that last week many people in the transport of Hungarian Jews to Poland jumped off the train near Michalovce. Sixteen of them are under arrest in Michalovce, and 81 of them are injured and incarcerated under guard in the hospital. Last week I appealed to Bratislava, but to this day I have received no response. Therefore, I am turning to you to request that you do something for their sake, for the authorities plan to send them to Poland. Today they gave me the enclosed note to send you a cable, but for obvious reasons I did not send it. For the same reasons I have not signed this letter. Hoping that this letter does not remain without the attention which it deserves, I close

with the blessing
of Peace.

The enclosed note read as follows:

Cable. Reverend Rabbi Frieder, Nové Mesto. Help the survivors from the transport to Poland. Come immediately to the district office. Sender: Bedrich Krakauer, Michalovce.

Some youngsters who refuse to be led to the slaughter have been jumping from train cars. Unfortunately, this only happens in isolated instances, while tens of thousands of our fellow Jews in Hungary sit waiting to be led like sheep to the slaughter in this terrible Holocaust. It is our moral obligation to help these survivors. I also see possible developments here in Slovakia from the same point of view; what is likely to happen if the new directives regarding concentration of Jews are executed?

Sunday, July 30, was the postponed fast day of the Ninth of Av. From 7 a.m. we sat on the floor and recited *kinnot* (elegies) till close to mid-day. The synagogue was almost full. The Jews of Šariš-Zemplin, most of them devout and educated, added their part to the service. The *kinnot* were recited with intent and feeling, for we ourselves were downtrodden: "Coerced and oppressed by the nations, Thou wilt not bear a grudge against us to destroy us forever; Thine left hand repels us whilst Thine right beckons, why wouldst

Thou forget us to eternity?"

In the evening I held a *siyyum* in my parent's home to celebrate concluding the study of Tractate *Gittin*. We sat around the table until the evening hours, family and a number of friends, and discussed the matters of the day in fear and prayer. The Soviet army was advancing along the entire front. Vilna, Lublin, and Lvov were already liberated, and in the south the Red Army was approaching Bucharest. "For God will not cast us off forever, for there is hope and much peace for Thy sons."

August is the month people go on vacation. I went with my family to the Vyhne labor camp, where we spent several restful days. Although I went to Bratislava every week, four days a week I devoted to resting with my family.

On August 24, while on my way from Bratislava to Vyhne, I stopped off at my congregation to be part of a true act of loving kindness. Three elderly residents had passed away in Ohel David, and we made them a joint funeral. Greatly moved at seeing the three coffins before me, I said we were facing the last and decisive stage along our way from slavery to redemption and prayed we would live, not die. These three were fortunate to have the *Hevra Kadisha* give them a proper Jewish burial and recite *kaddish* over their graves; whereas millions of our fellow Jews from all over Europe were killed, suffocated, and burned to death in the death camps, and did not receive a proper Jewish burial, and their ashes lay scattered like dung over the fields of the land of doom. These three deceased, who in their lifetime enjoyed the shelter of Ohel David, will intercede on our behalf as they now come before the Throne of Glory in the World Everlasting. May they pray that this home continue to be a source of blessing and remain a stronghold and place of refuge for all its inhabitants.

Chapter Seven

Suppression of the Revolt and the

"Final Solution" 5705

(August 29, 1944 – April 10, 1945)

*"And ye shall be left few in number, whereas
ye were as the stars of heaven for multitude"*
(Deuteronomy 28:62)

I. Suppression of the Revolt in Southwest Slovakia

On the 10th of Elul (August 29), Dr. Kováč and I visited Vašek to discuss matters concerning us. He spoke in a tone to which we were unaccustomed and, contrary to his usual way, was sharply critical of the Slovaks. He said that they were not worthy of sovereignty and independence and would never be a free people, but would serve others and be enslaved by them, and that he was ashamed of belonging to a people that was incapable of holding its own and maintaining its state.

I did not interject my opinion, nor did I understand the meaning of his words. It was not until we had left that we learned of the insurrection which was afoot against the government. In Trnava the army was in rebellion and the train lines had been blown up. The Germans, it was rumored, were planning to conquer Slovakia and seize all the barracks of the Slovak army, disarming any forces that resisted. Indeed, rebellion appeared imminent, and a liberation movement, patterned after Tito's liberation movement in Slovakia, seemed to be emerging.

I could not reach the Vyhne camp and therefore decided not to return to my family, who were still there, but rather to go to Nové Mesto to be with the people under my protection. With public transportation disrupted, I did not reach my destination until 1:30 a.m. At Leopoldov I met many Jews from the Sered camp. They told me that the gates of the Sered and Nováky camps had been opened and that the guards had joined the insurrectionists. A Partisan army had formed in the Nováky camp; no news had come from the more remote Vyhne camp.

* * *

The Jews of Nové Mesto began leaving the city. Many went underground into "bunkers" in the area and in the surrounding villages. Around thirty young men got together and joined the Partisans.

From Tuesday on, I was cut off from my family. Thursday, after great effort, I finally managed to reach my wife on the telephone. I advised her not to return from Vyhne to Nové Mesto, but rather to move to the Banská-Bystrica region, where the Czechoslovak government in exile, which was organizing the insurrection, was already functioning. But my wife was opposed to being there without me and decided to return home Friday, after midnight. We were glad to be reunited in our home once more and to listen to our children prattling about "Partisania," as they called the territory which had been liberated by the Partisans. The youngsters understood that the developments concerned the freedom for which everyone yearned, even though that was still a long way off and far from assured. Joy over the insurrection was mingled with worry and fear, and, as I looked at my children, I felt an urge to transfer them to a safe and secure place. Rumors reached us that the Germans were likely to capture Nové Mesto on Saturday, and this put on my shoulders the great responsibility and obligation of seeing to the safety of the residents of Ohel David. For the institution could certainly not be left without anyone to direct it. What captain deserts his ship in an hour of danger? I wanted my wife and small four-year old and six-year children to go to a "bunker." But my wife acted as Ruth the Moabite, who told her mother-in-law Naomi: "Entreat me not to leave thee, … for whither thou goest, I will go; … where thou diest, will I die, and there will I be buried; … if aught but death part thee and me" (Ruth 1:16-17). Thus, it was, for the time being, that we remained together.

* * *

On Saturday, the 14th of Elul, 5704 (September 2, 1944), in the afternoon, a small dispatch of German soldiers arrived in Nové Mesto. The next day a larger force followed, and several hundred soldiers entered the barracks. The Germans disarmed the Slovak soldiers and arrested the officers without encountering any opposition. It soon became clear that the insurrection in western Slovakia had failed. Some soldiers had deserted and joined the Partisans, but the vast majority remained indifferent. Many citizens, fair-weather patriots, switched their allegiance within a week. They adapted rapidly to the new circumstances and, just like opportunist Slovaks, became Guardists and good friends of the Germans.

That Sunday I shaved my light-colored beard. I had been growing it for ten years, and parting with it was a difficult act. Removing it under these circumstances was like stripping a captured officer of his rank and decorations. Troubled and depressed, I took my children, Gideon and Gitka, on my knees and asked them if I should shave off my beard. My son said no, my daughter yes. Thus, right in front of them, with tears in my eyes, I began shaving it off. My wife also became emotional. I shaved because I wished to continue my public activity, and with a beard on my face I could no longer move around freely in the conquered city of Bratislava. The following day I went to Bratislava. Tiso set up a new government.

All the ministers who had helped us were replaced. As I held parting conversations with them, I came to the realization that our situation was desperate. The Germans were irate at the Slovaks, had no trust in them, and were penetrating every ministry and taking over the administration of the entire state. There was no longer anyone with whom we could talk; all our strength and influence disappeared, as if it had never existed. I was reminded of the biblical hero Samson, who lost all his might after his seven locks were cut off his head. My strength vanished and my influence waned over the very day during which I felt constrained to remove my beard. We, the colleagues of the Working Group, met for consultation, essentially for the last time. I reported everything I had learned and expressed my deep apprehension about the situation into which we had fallen. Everything, it seemed, had been lost.

I returned to Nové Mesto on September 6. The German

municipal officer, Hilvik, had requested a list of Jews from the district commissar. I assembled all the Jews in the synagogue and advised them to leave Nové Mesto before the day's end and go underground into "bunkers." I said the same to the residents of Ohel David, where I announced that I was sending my parents, my brother and sister, and even my wife and children to places of hiding in villages in the surrounding hill-country, although I myself would remain here, in Ohel David, with those people who were not capable of leaving the institution, and would be at their disposal to advise and help them.

My parents, brother and sister and their families, as well as most of the Jews of Nové Mesto, left the city. Most of them found refuge in the small villages of the surrounding forest-covered mountains, known as Kopanice. These villages, consisting of some 15 to 20 houses each, were inhabited by Evangelist peasants, who opposed the rule of the Catholic party and in exchange for a handsome sum of money gave refuge to the Jews, helped them establish "bunkers" in the forests, and assisted them by supplying food and other essentials. My wife and children remained with me.

* * *

At 8 a.m., on Thursday September 7, 1944, several Jews were arrested in Nové Mesto, among them my friend's brother-in-law Desider Komloš, and the Jewish activist Adolf Rosenberg, who had come to the synagogue and requested that I intercede. By the time I arrived at the lock-up, I also found Rosenberg himself among the detainees. I took all their documents and belongings which might be used as incriminatory evidence against them, such as various "Aryan" papers, all sorts of blank forms signed with official stamps, and 25,000 korunas, and hurried home, expecting my intercession with the authorities to have positive results.

In truth, however, by Wednesday I was already extremely nervous and had told my secretary, Dr. Isidor Ganz, that I feared for my own personal safety. I spent a sleepless night, and in the small hours of the morning my wife awakened and surprised me with the question: "Dearest, do you love me?" I did not understand what was behind her question. Was she having a nightmare? Of course, I nodded my head in assent and, adding several warm and sincere words, reassured her until she fell back asleep. Those were the last words I exchanged with my wife. Several hours later, that same Thursday morning of the 5th of Elul (September 7), on my way home from interceding at the police station I was arrested, never to return home again.

All the material I had taken from Adolf Rosenberg and Desider Komloš was on my person. In the interrogation I maintained that the documents were my own. Since Komloš' photograph on his "Aryan" identity papers was dark and blurred, I proclaimed it was mine and had been intentionally defaced so that I would not be recognized. I did not know at the time into whose hands I had fallen. It was only after I was taken to the army barracks and thrown into a cell that I found out I had been arrested on orders from the Germans. On the way to my confinement, I managed to notify my wife of my arrest and advised her to contact the district commissar and flee with the children immediately.

In the barracks I succeeded in relaying a letter, via a German sergeant, to Adolf Biermann and through him to my wife. Subsequently Biermann came to me in the barracks and handed me a short letter from my wife, which read as follows:

Dearest,

To spare our children suffering. broken-hearted from what has happened to you, I decided to go to the "bunker" of the Head.[58] Lovingly and yearningly I wait to see you soon. But if fate have it otherwise, and we not meet again, dearest, I cease to be your wife and shall only be mother to your children, my children. Bearing up, with everlasting love, yours truly and faithfully,

Roži and the
children.

I managed to answer this letter. I expressed my consent to her important step and requested that she not be downcast, for I myself was feeling quiet and calm. The fact that I had been able to work, to serve my people and faithfully perform my public calling, delegated upon me by Divine Providence, gave me the strength of spirit to continue fighting. Losing one's life is not losing all. Some people die in the fullness of time, some before then. For life not to lose its meaning, its content – that is what counts. Even if I die, my death shall not be worse than my life. For my life's work, the fruit of my steadfast labors, will live on; and many other people will survive. I sealed the letter to my wife with the promise that I would do all I could to remain alive, for her sake and for the sake of our children.

* * *

Rakovský, the district commissar, proved his friendship and sent my family by Red Cross ambulance to the Hrka "bunker" that very evening. Having received word of their safe arrival at their destination, I felt calmer and less anxious in the knowledge that

---

[58] A code word for the district commissar.

Rozi, Gideon, and Gitka were in a secure place. On Saturday, the 21ˢᵗ of Elul (September 9), the Germans transferred me to Bratislava. The guards were hostile and strict, and I could not find out where they were taking me. Various thoughts passed through my mind during the long journey.

The guards handed me over to the police attaché of the German embassy. I found out in a roundabout way the details of the indictment in my personal file, on the basis of which I was to face trial before a military tribunal on charges of having bribed government persons and thus having forestalled solution of the Jewish problem. Likewise, I was accused of directly and indirectly supporting the Slovak revolt, the insurrectionist movement, and the Partisans. The fact that I had shaved my beard allegedly testified to my revolutionary intentions and underground activity. The police attaché handed me over to the *Gestapo,* who cross-examined me using their infamous methods. Afterwards they turned me over to the Center for State Security, and thus it was that I found myself being detained by the Slovaks.

While I was being transferred, I risked sending a message to Adler and Winterstein to inform them that I was on the way to the Center for State Security. Adler, with his usual alacrity and devotion, arrived the same evening, and we talked over the situation. The building of the Center for State Security was full of Jews, and most of them were being sent to Sered.

Trnava, Nitra, and Topolčany were already *judenrein.* The Jews who had not gone underground and had been found in their homes were being rounded up and transferred to Sered, which had become a concentration camp.

The number of Jews in the camp increased from day to day. Great over-crowding made conditions extremely difficult, and no one knew what fate awaited him. I was firmly resolved to do everything possible to prevent being transferred to Sered. I feared this camp was destined to serve the same purpose as the Žilina camp had served in the past – as a terminal for transports to Poland.

II. "Days of Awe" in Prison

All the detainees in my cell on the second floor of the Center for State Security were Jews from Malacky. They told me that my father-in-law Max Berl had been in this cell and had been sent to Sered in the large transport which left from here. I spent three days, the first days of selihot (penitential prayers recited before the New Year), in this cell. We recited the prayers from memory, to the best of our ability, and, with rent hearts, prayed for God's mercy.

With Adler's intercession and in accordance with my testimony in the interrogation, I was turned over to investigator Kukula in the investigations department of the Ministry of Finance. As a suspect accused of financial crimes, I was transferred from there to the national court, which on September 13, 1944 (the 25th of Elul) issued a warrant for my arrest. In this prison I formed a friendship with the jailer, who helped me manage in the cell and eased my life in isolation. I received books and newspapers, and the management approved kosher food for me.

Being severed from my family, to which I was bound heart and soul, and having no word from them, and thinking about my larger family – my congregation and Slovak Jewry in general – all this oppressed me greatly. The days were those of selihot and repentance, and being thus cabined, cribbed and confined, and withdrawn into myself, sunk in my thoughts, memories, and ponderings, I was able to do some soul reckoning. I planned a fixed daily regimen, setting aside time to read, study, write and sing; and, with a little sleep and rest added to my schedule, the days passed by.

New Year's 5705 (September 18, 1944)

On Monday, the first day of the New Year, during the daily morning walk, I was humming the holiday liturgy and, unintentionally, had raised my voice slightly. Suddenly the supervising jailer burst out with torrents of threats and rebukes at me: "You, over there, stop humming and mumbling or else you'll get a thrashing from me straight away!" Angry outbursts such as this, and even worse, were commonplace in the life of the prisoner. After the walk, to my surprise, I was taken to the office. A clerk was awaiting me there and ordered me to come with him. I realized immediately that this was the result of intercession by my friend Alexander Adler, who had managed to obtain my release for several hours so that I could participate in the holiday services. Upon arriving at Adler's house, I found out that the rabbinical court of Bratislava had decided to shorten the New Year's services this year. The minyan, having omitted most of the piyyutim (liturgical poems), had finished praying early, and thus I was left to pray singly. Dr. Neumann, Dr. Winterstein, and Rabbi Weissmandel arrived at the Adler house and brought me up to date on the situation. Rabbi Weissmandel and his family had been caught in the large hunt after Jews in Nitra and had been imprisoned in Sered; but the Working Group had managed to obtain his release for several days on the grounds of his being on the economic committee in charge of supplying food to the camp inmates.

The following day, the second day of the New Year, I left prison to participate in the minyan. In the middle of the service, I raised my eyes and noticed pictures of my two children on the walls. It was only then that I realized the minyan was meeting in a room of my in-laws' apartment.

After services I went to the house of Alexander and Iluš Adler, where I found an allusively phrased letter from Adolf Biermann, saying that my wife and children were with "Julan," from which I gathered they were in the town of Bánovce, in an area under Partisan control. The reason my family had left their previous hiding place had to do with District Commissar Rakovský being dismissed from office; someone had informed on him that he had helped the rabbi's wife escape in a Red Cross ambulance. The district commissar warned Roži in time and advised her to flee with her children from Hrka to Partisan territory, lest they be caught by the Germans, who were on their tail. They set out together with a noble youngster, Ervin Jakobovic, crossed the forested mountain of Inovec and, after a hard, two-day trek, arrived in Bánovce, very worn out. From there the Partisan commander transferred them to Banská-Štiavnica, where they remained until the Day of Atonement. My wife and small children proved what great latent physical and spiritual strength man has, young and old alike, when put to the test.

On the Sabbath of the scriptural reading of Va-Yelekh, September 23, Dr. Winterstein visited me in prison, reported on the situation, and told me there was a possibility of obtaining my release if a fine were paid for "the financial crimes which I had committed."

On September 26, the eve of the Day of Atonement, I was

brought to the head office of the Ministry of Finance to sign an agreement terminating legal proceedings against me in exchange for paying a fine of 20,000 korunas. The sum was paid and I was returned to the Center for State Security. Since I held an Argentinian passport, I was released the same day on condition that I enter the Mariental detention camp, where Jews "with American citizenship" were being held. Of course, I did not go to Mariental, but prayed with the minyan instead, and even gave an emotional sermon on Kol Nidre eve and the next day before the yizkor (memorial) service. I concluded my second sermon with a reference to the prayer of the High Priest: "May it be Thy will that our homes not become our graves, that they not be left abandoned and empty of man, uninhabited and still as graves. Our Father and King, seal us in the book of life."

I led the congregation in the afternoon service and ne'ilah (special concluding service of the Day of Atonement). The prayers on this Day of Atonement were not like other years; they were supplications, full of wailing and sighing. Never had I felt so keenly the danger of death hovering over the entire congregation. I did not know where my family was, and I prayed that they would find a safe harbor in the area which had been liberated from the murderers and that the entire House of Israel would be sealed in the book of life. I was told about the service led by Rabbi Dov Michael Weissmandel, who prayed for the congregation in the synagogue "Temimei Derekh." This righteous man, who through the years of the war and Holocaust devoted his entire life to saving lives, prayed with such meaning and intent and with such fervor that the entire congregation wailed and sighed the whole time. "May He who hears the sound of our cries save us from all cruel decrees."

III. Sered – A Camp of Horrors under the Command of the SS

My colleagues' reports on the situation in the Sered camp were horrifying. While I had been under arrest the number of inmates had increased to 4,000. They were entrusted to the dangerous hands of SS troops. The commissar of the camp was an SS officer by the name of Knollmayer, a beastly man, infamous for his cruelty. At his behest the Jews were beaten mercilessly and subjected to all sorts of torture. Every person who arrived in the camp was robbed of his valuables and money and then severely beaten. The inmates had wounds, bruises and fractures all over their bodies, their faces were swollen with welts, and their eyes were black and blue. After every interrogation the Jews left the rooms of the SS thugs, beaten, swollen, and bleeding, for no fault of their own. Curfew was at 8 p.m., and whoever was late to his hut was mercilessly beaten. Many Jews were shot.

Shots were heard day and night. When the huts were closed, the SS men threw in grenades; and when they were open, they entered and beat everyone inside. At night they would burst into the huts and order the women, naked or dressed in no more than a nightgown, out for roll-call and would scoff at them and abuse them. So crude and cruel was the behavior of the SS buns, it is difficult to describe. The men they tortured with blows and the women they humiliated, treating them with contempt and raping them.

Cruelest of all was the Slovak captain by the name of Zimmermann, who in 1942 had gained an infamous reputation for torturing Jews by whipping and beating them. Now he had the rank of SS Obersturmfiihrer. On Saturday night after the scriptural reading of Nitzavim, the eve of the New Year, he orchestrated a night of frightful horror. At 10 p.m., under the command of this savage, his drunken officers burst into the camp's huts and, shooting, hitting, shouting and cursing, shoved out all the men, women, and children into the camp yard, just as they found them, in their nightgowns and barefoot, and made them run around in a circle. Those who fell behind were prodded on with clubs, whips, the buts of rifles, and even with shots from pistols and guns. Six victims fell during this cruel "amusement" of the SS animals, who continued indulging their lust for Jewish blood until after three a.m. The men, who at the risk of their lives remained in the inner circle to shield the women, elderly, and children, received fractures and bruises all over their bodies from the blows which the murderers, standing in the middle of the circle, inflicted on them with whips, lashes, and clubs. Their eyes and faces were swollen and gashed beyond recognition. The camp hospital was filled to the brink and could not take in all the wounded. The following day everyone had to show up for work at 6 a.m.

Such was the situation in the Sered camp, as I heard from Rabbi Weissmandel and, when later incarcerated there myself, from the camp inmates, as well.

IV. Alois Brunner Aspires to the "Final Solution"

Every day more Jews were captured in the cities and concentrated in the Sered camp. SS Hauptsturmführer Alois Brunner, who came to Slovakia with the German units brought in to suppress the revolt, headed the hunt; his task was to solve the Jewish problem. This cynical, cruel, and devious man, Brunner – who had commanded the deportations of the Jews in Vienna, France, and Greece – negotiated with Dr. Kováč and Gisi Fleischmann and proposed transferring the Jews of Bratislava to the Sered camp, which, he said, would become a ghetto modeled after Theresienstadt. The "voluntary" evacuation would start in another fortnight, he said.

* * *

Dr. Winterstein and Gisi Fleischmann told me about visits by Dr. Neumann, Dr. Kováč, and engineers from the Jewish Center to the Sered camp, together with Brunner, who toured the camp and stated unequivocally that the place was suitable for establishing a ghetto. I was dumbstruck. The camp, originally planned for 1,000 to 1,200 people, now had approximately 4,000 Jews crowded into it, with barely air left to breathe; yet, according to Brunner's plans, another 6,000 Jews were to be concentrated in it. This meant starvation, epidemic, and worse. Oppressed by this prospect, I fell into an agonized depression.

Gisi was just as downcast and depressed as I. She saw the approaching Holocaust, but did not want to speak about it or reveal her fears, lest that lead to panic. For who was this Brunner, who was trying to fool us? A mass murderer, who had already wiped-out Jewish communities in a number of countries and whose hands were stained with the blood of millions of Jews. His speech was always well-mannered, but his every word was devious. He plotted out all his deeds in advance, and their clear objective was to annihilate what remained of the Jewish community. Our lobbyists were not acquainted with his deviousness and did not fathom his mind, for everything he said was calculated to mislead and deceive.

On Thursday after the Day of Atonement, September 28, I went to see Gisi Fleischmann and found her so distressed that she had tears in her eyes. She had believed Brunner, who had promised to extend Rabbi Weissmandel's leave, when he invited the latter and Dr. Kováč to go with him to Sered; Brunner, however, had lied, as it soon became clear. People began whispering about preparations for a chytačka – a hunt of the Jews – which would take place that night. I was still not in tune with recent developments and could not assess the situation correctly. Gisi and Oscar were both of the opinion that there was nothing to fear yet, and, believing this, we all went home. En route I had second thoughts and decided to evacuate my mother-in-law and sister-in-law from the house, but remained there myself, for I felt a moral and public duty not to abandon my colleagues. A short while later, after I had gone to bed, there was a knocking at my door. The time was 10:45. I did not open. I heard voices, shouting, and the echo of heavy boots; but still, I did not open. Suddenly the door was forced, and the troops burst in, shouting and carrying cocked guns. Pagač, from the Hlinka Guard, and three of his soldiers entered the bedroom. Without saying a word, Pagač raised his hand and struck me with his whip. The soldiers ordered me to dress quickly and come with them. In the yard a terrible sight was revealed before my eyes. The entire house had been occupied by German and Slovak soldiers of all kinds – SS, SA, Voluntary Defense Squads, and Hlinka Guardsmen. Soldiers encircled the entire Jewish quarter, the former ghetto, and guards were stationed by every gate and entrance. They had broken into the yards and all the apartments and rooms, had removed all the Jews by force, and had led them to the offices of the Jewish Center on Kozia Street and Edlová Street. We filed between two rows of SS men and Voluntary Defense Squads, who lined either side of the road, holding cocked guns in their hands, ready to kill and destroy.

Brunner had drafted thousands of German soldiers for this operation, while at the same time negotiating with the Jewish leaders without arousing their suspicions. That night, towards Friday dawn, 1,960 Jews were rounded up. When I arrived at the Center, I saw Dr. Kováč looking tired and pale. He whispered to me that he and Rabbi Weissmandel had not been to Sered at all and that Brunner had received them with the words: "I tricked you; tonight, I shall catch all the Jews, while you at the Jewish Center shall prepare lists of the captured." Brunner kept them under arrest the entire day, until the end of the operation, while himself continued his devious investigations.[59] The Germans harassed us all night long. Finally, at 6 a.m., orders were issued to form five columns and file between two rows of German soldiers standing on either side of the route along which 1,960 Jews – men and women, young and old – marched with their pitiful bundles towards the train station. We stood there until 2 p.m., at which time we were led away, 90 people in a cattle-car. We arrived at Sered, which by now had 6,000 inmates, at 2 o'clock in the night. The terrible congestion and overcrowding broke even the strongest spirits. We were put into the carpentry shop and left to sleep on the concrete floor.

V. Transports are Resumed on the Eve of Sukkot, 5705

At 6 a.m. on Saturday, September 30, the entire transport from Bratislava was lined-up in the yard to check bundles and money. Several hours elapsed, yet the examination was not held. Suddenly we saw that the res idents of the other huts were also lining up and that only the workers in the workshop had remained inside.

---

[59] Several days before the hunt, the offices of the Jewish Center were broken into and the files and lists with the addresses of the Jews were stolen. In response to the complaint which was lodged about the break-in and damages, Brunner politely promised to make a thorough investigation and punish the perpetrators. It had now become clear who had broken into the offices and why. Brunner had prepared the operation secretly and had gotten hold of the addresses of the Jews behind the backs of the leaders of the Jewish Center.

Why was everyone being lined up? We all found it most peculiar and were seized by an uneasy and extremely tense feeling. No one knew what the Huns were plotting to do with us. Today, the thirtieth of September, is a joyous day in my family: it is my son Gideon's seventh birthday. I turned my thoughts to my wife and children, to my family as well as my congregation. Pleasant and not such pleasant thoughts ran through my mind, but above all was a growing fear that Brunner would resume deporting Jews to their death. I had not even had time to communicate my apprehensions to Rabbi Weissmandel and Dr. Winterstein before a camp orderly came running up. I asked him what was about to happen, and he disclosed that 1,000 people were about to be deported and that hut number 7 had been set aside for the people who would remain here. If I wished not to be in the transport, I had better get out of this line.

We, the members of the Working Group, stood there, divested of all influence and authority. We agreed among ourselves that Rabbi Weissmandel would go to the hospital to join his family. Dr. Winterstein decided to go into the electrical workshop, and I chose the carpentry. Only Dr. Neumann had not yet decided where he would go. Meanwhile a list of 1,860 men, women, and children was drawn up, and all were deported the same day. Thus, on the Sabbath of the scriptural reading of Ha'azinu, the 13th of Tishri, 5705 (September 30, 1944), the deportation of the Jews of Slovakia was renewed.

In the afternoon of the same day all the laborers in the workshops were taken out for roll-call. An SS man of the rank of Scharführer arbitrarily sorted out the people who apparently were to be added to the deportees. I considered trying to escape from the line, but the officer suddenly stopped selecting people and ordered Joseph Löwinger, the head carpenter in charge of the camp's carpentry shop, himself to choose several carpenters for his workshop. I hoped that Löwinger, who knew me and had done several jobs for Ohel David, would take me under his protection. Löwinger did not let me down; he took me into the carpentry shop, saying I was a carpenter named Abraham König. Thus, I managed to survive this selection, too.

Brunner planned to dispatch another transport on October 2, the first day of the Feast of Tabernacles. So that I would not be in the camp at the time of the transport, Pokorný, who was in charge of the camp laundry and at the time had an influential position, sent me to work on outside jobs. Adolf Rosenberg, my friend from Nové Mesto, and Ali Adler, a member of the Maccabee movement and an honest and devout man and former social worker in the Jewish Center, were also in my group. We, along with several other Jews, were sent to work in the SS barracks in Sered. Although we were forewarned that we were likely to get a good thrashing from the SS thugs, nevertheless we preferred to go out on the job to avoid the transport. The weather was terrible – it rained all day long – and our job was to load saddles onto carts and transfer them to train cars at the railroad station. We literally worked hard as horses, for we had to pull the carts by hand. Dressed lightly, without overcoats, we were drenched by the pouring rain and chilled to the bone. The ground was wet underfoot and the wheels of the heavily laden carts sank into the mud. Six carts were hauled in a row, each by four men. It took all our strength to move the carts whose wheels had sunk in the mud. The SS man, seeing that the convoy was proceeding slowly, spurred us on with a sound beating. I, too, received several of his lashings; but it is better to suffer a beating than to be among those deported. Thus, we were driven hard, until late into the night.

Upon returning to camp, we learned that the transport would not leave until the following day. We drank the poisoned cup and faced the morrow, when we would have to pass through all the gates of hell. Lord Almighty, it says in the Torah of Moses: "And thou shalt rejoice in thy feast" (Deuteronomy 16:14); Heaven have mercy!

The following day, October 3, 1944, the second day of the holiday, was a very sad day, for on it the hospital was vacated and the Jews recently captured in Bratislava were added to the transport, bringing the number of deportees in that transport to 1,836. Among the deportees were Talmudic scholars, rabbis, and geonim: the Rebbe of Csörcs, Rabbi Spitzer of Kirchdorf; Rebbe Isaiah Kalisch, the dayyan of Bratislava; Rabbi Simeon Haberfeld, the dayyan of Topolčany; Rabbi Reich, the dayyan of Trnava, and his son, Rabbi of Žabokreky; Dr. Eliezer Schweiger, the chief rabbi of the Yeshurun congregation in Nitra; and Rabbi Dr. Lichtenstein of Kremnica. This transport took shohatim, Jewish teachers and instructors from Bratislava, as well as Mikuláš Eichner from the Jewish Center, my good friend Friedl Winterstein, the school principal Willy Fürst of the Working Group, and my father-in-law R. Max-Meir Berl of Bratislava, who was one of the patients in the hospital. I shall never forget the scene of horror in the hospital before the transport left. I also saw Rabbi Dov Weissmandel there, pale and despairing, sitting and looking on beside his large family. I ran towards him and he called out to me, "Rabbi, mine own vineyard have I not kept" (Song of Songs I :6), for he was suffering pangs of conscience, feeling culpable for having neglected his own family and not having provided for their safety. Who could understand him better than I, who also felt remorse for not having been more devoted to my family and congregation.

Rabbi Weissmandel succeeded in keeping himself and his family out of this transport, to everyone's joy. Oscar Neumann remained, too, since he was married to a Christian; and Olga Adler, a courageous woman who worked as a clerk in the camp, saved Vojtech Winterstein by claiming that he was her fiancé.

It was truly a terrible, awesome day, a day of fearful wailing. One thousand eight hundred and thirty-six Jewish souls were taken and are as good as gone. They were taken from all circles, from all ranks of society, men of degree along with simple folk.

Although we prayed, "May the All-merciful raise up for us the fallen Tabernacle of David,"[60] additional traumas lay in store for us during the festival of Sukkot, traumas which destroyed the greater part of the camp; on Simhat Torah, the Rejoicing of the Law (October 10, 1944), another transport, carrying 1,890 people, rolled from the Sered train station. The selection began three days before the transport, on the intermediate Sabbath of the festival (October 7, 1944). Brunner himself took charge of the line-up and divided us into three groups, single males on the right, families in the center and on the left. No one knew what he was planning; he always acted secretively and deviously. Whoever tried to move from one group to another was beaten mercilessly.

I did not know what to do. Not having anyone with me, it was easier for me to get around and, when I discerned that Joseph Löwinger, the chief carpenter, was in the center group, I instinctively followed him, for logic seemed to dictate that he would not be deported. My reasoning proved correct. The two end groups were rounded up separately, and their fate seemed sealed. However, the selection was not over yet. On Monday,

---

[60] A prayer traditionally recited on Sukkot, the Feast of Tabernacles. Translator's note.

Shemini Atzeret,[61] the middle group was dragged out for another line-up. This time SS Hauptsturmführer Brunner divided us into two groups – for a gruesome fate or for mercy, for life or for death. A bitter fate awaited me, for I stood in the group of the unfortunate. It was only with the help of the engineer Emanuel Cohen, the Jewish Elder at the time and a man who helped many Jews, that I escaped deportation and remained in the camp.

The following day, the Rejoicing of the Law, became, as I have said, a painfully sad day. Among the people deported that day were Rabbi Weissmandel,[62] his wife, his eight children and their grandmother, and the wife of Rabbi Ungar of Nitra and her daughters.[63]

---

[61] The concluding holiday of the Tishri cycle of festivals. Translator's note.

[62] Rabbi Weissmandel knew it was beyond his power to save his family, yet he hoped that if he could save himself, he might succeed in sending aid from abroad. Therefore, after difficult vacillation, he decided to jump from the train car and succeeded in reaching Bratislava. Shortly before the city's liberation he was smuggled out of the "bunker," along with several other Jews, and reached Switzerland. From there he emigrated to the United States, where he and his brothers-in-law founded the Nitra Yeshiva to spread Jewish learning. With blood and tears, a broken and exhausted man, he set about writing his memoirs of the Holocaust, and to this end he turned to the author of these lines, via Dr. Ernest Abeles, and requested a copy of Rabbi Frieder's diary, which request was gladly granted. Weissmandel's health, however, had suffered, and he did not live to see his memoirs' publication. His book, Out of the Straits, was published posthumously by his students, in New York in 1960. In the preface to his book Rabbi Weissmandel wrote: "There were days and years during which, with a tormented soul, like Jonah the prophet, I prayed to the Lord, saying: "Therefore now, O Lord, take, I beseech Thee, my life from me; for it is better for me to die than to live."" On the 10th of Kislev, 5718 (1958), he was released from his suffering, and his pure soul departed while he was in the midst of his writing.

[63] All the Jews of Nitra, including the wife of Rabbi Ungar, her son-in-law and all her family, as well as the residents of the Admor of Nitra's court, were arrested on Elul 17, 5704 (September 5, 1944), and were taken to the Sered camp. The head of the family, the Admor R. Samuel David Ungar of blessed memory, at the time was in a sanatorium on Mt. Zobor, near Nitra. The lads who were with him scattered in various directions in search of hiding places and havens. The Rebbe, his son Shalom Moses, and his disciple Meir Eisler reached Banská-Bystrica, the Partisans' capital. On the High Holy Days, they still prayed with a minyan. Before the city fell to the Germans, they fled to the forest and hid in a "bunker" which they established. The Rebbe took care not to eat the bread of the gentiles or drink their milk. Under these sub-human conditions of abnegation, fasting, and suffering he grew frail and wasted away. His holy and pure soul departed this world on Adar 9, 5705 (March 22, 1945). After the war his bones were laid to rest in the Jewish cemetery of Piešťany. May his merit protect us!

VI. The Jews of Nové Mesto and the Residents of Ohel David Are Sent to Their Death

The tears which we shed when 1,890 Jews were deported to Auschwitz were not our last. The tyrannical regime continued its evil plot of genocide. The butchers fell upon my congregation and wiped it out. The finest members of the Nové Mesto Jewish community were deported in this transport. Among them were the beloved couple, Oscar and Ilka Horvát, whom even a certificate of protection from the President of Slovakia was inadequate to save; the principal, Julius Mészáros; the deputy head of the congregation, Alfred Schlesinger, and his brother and their families; and many other Jews. The hunt for Jews in the area conquered by the Germans continued at full speed, with Brunner leading the way. He annihilated the holders of foreign citizenship papers[64] in Mariental and paid no heed to any sort of protection papers issued by the Slovak authorities; for, according to his words, he hated them no less than the "filthy Jews." Seeing that this was his way, the dread which all the while had been clutching at my heart, lest Ohel David be transformed – God forbid – from a shelter and house of refuge into a prison and house of detention, became a mortal fear.

To my chagrin, my apprehensions were born out; soon individual residents from Ohel David began arriving at Sered, day after day. I hoped that my parents, who had gone into hiding

---

[64] On October 12, some 200 residents of the camp, holders of foreign citizenship papers, left under the heavy guard of SS soldiers, for a long and exhausting trek, carrying their heavy bundles to the Stupava train station, whence they were transported to Sered. Two of the deportees, Paul Seidler and Alexander Eckstein, succeeded in escaping from the transport in the dark of night. A. Eckstein, one of the group's leaders, who was on good terms with the police and to whom much credit was due for obtaining the release of prisoners, with the help of the police reached Bratislava. The following day he visited the government hospital and requested Professor Koch. one of the world's righteous gentiles, to use his good offices to save the Jews who held foreign citizenship papers, however his intercession was to no avail.

in the village of Stare Pole, along with my sister and her two children, would be able to hold out and remain in a safe place. But when my father learned that the elderly individuals were dwelling in Ohel David undisturbed, he longed heart and soul to prayer there on the festival of Sukkot, hoping that he might even find a lulav and etrog there. The righteous are sustained by their faith. On Hoshanah Rabbah (the seventh day of Sukkot), as a new resident of Ohel David he worshipped – without a lulav and etrog – in Ohel David's Eshel Abraham synagogue, named after his son, and prayed, "Save us, we beseech Thee, for the sake of martyrs cast into the fire, save us!"

On the Sabbath of the scriptural reading of Genesis (October 14) we met in Sered. Father was then 63 years old and mother, 56. Realizing that they, too, had been caught, I went into shock but retained my composure and held back my tears. Perhaps they did not fully grasp the situation, or perhaps, like myself, they, too, were holding back their emotions. I, who knew more than they did, lost all hope of saving their lives. Under Brunner's regime there were no miracles.

Three days later, the first day of the new month of Heshvan (October 17, 1944), was another black day, a day of grief and lamentation. Nine hundred and twenty new victims went off to the slaughter, among them elders from Ohel David, residents of Wing A and the new third hut, my dear parents, and also the valorous Gisi Fleischmann.[65] I sank into deep sorrow and sadness,

---

[65] Gisi Fleischmann, nee Fischer, was born in Bratislava and began her public activity in 1925, along with the Zionist couple, Julia and Isidor Knöpfelmacher, by laying the foundations for the Women's International Zionist Organization in Slovakia. When Gisi took over the task of running the organization, along with Hannah Steiner and Miriam Schmulka, she assumed leadership of its social welfare, education, and pioneer training activities. With the rise of the Nazis to power in Germany (1933), she took care of the Jewish émigrés and refugees who came to Czechoslovakia in large numbers, opened vocational training courses for them, and formed contacts with the Joint's office in Prague and its center in Paris. Her Zionist and social

like one who has lost the light of day.

My parents, Rabbi Pinchas and Sarah Frieder – May the Lord Avenge Their Blood (השם ינקום דמם)[66]

My parents, especially Father, were ready to face anything. Strong in his faith and trust in God, he said: "If the Lord desires my death, I shall go and be bound to the altar, for I have fulfilled my role in this life. I have raised sons who have worshipped God and helped His people, I have reached old age and am ready to relinquish my soul to the Creator of the Universe." These were

---

work became increasingly more extensive. In the spring of 1938, refugees from Austria began pouring into Slovakia. Hicem leaders, including Gisi, hurried to extend assistance and rescued a group of Jews from the Burgenland, who were in a boat on the Danube. Several times Gisi went with Oscar Neumann on missions to London and Paris. She also traveled to Budapest to raise money for the Working Group. In London and Paris, she visited the embassies of various countries and requested entry visas for Jewish émigrés and refugees who were staying in Slovakia. Her efforts, however, did not bear fruit. In the summer of 1939, she represented Slovak Jewry at a congress of the Joint in Paris. In 1940 she was elected to the executive committee of Slovakia's Zionist Organization. When the movement went underground, she continued working with redoubled energy as one of the mainstays of the Working Group, which had its office at 6 Edlová Street. It was from here that she and her colleagues in the Working Group sent their letters crying for help. This was also the address from which valuable articles and money were sent to Jews deported to Poland and from which reports were mailed abroad. Her activities and suffering during her arrest are recounted in the earlier chapters of this book.
On September 29, 1944, when all the Jews of Bratislava were captured and transferred to Sered, Gisi Fleischmann and Dr. Kováč remained in Bratislava. Brunner charged them with providing for the maintenance of the camp's inmates, using the Working Group's remaining assets. The two of them were free to return to their homes, but were followed by detectives all the time. The offices of the Jewish Center at 6 Edlová Street were taken over by the Gestapo, who kept an eye on Gisi's office. On October 15, Gisi committed an indiscretion; she responded in writing to a Jew hiding in a "bunker," and was caught by the Gestapo. Brunner ordered her arrest and had her sent to Sered. Dr. Kováč, who heard about the tragedy by chance, managed to escape to a "bunker."
One of the things Gisi had written in the letter which was seized Gisi was, "I am now in the jaws of the lion." Brunner began questioning her. The following day he told her that if she were to reveal the hiding places of the Jews of Bratislava, she would be granted clemency. Whoever was acquainted with this woman of valor knew what her response would be. Several times friends urged her to flee, to go to a "bunker" and work in the underground. But, at the risk of her life, this brave woman had decided to continue working in the open to try to save Jewish lives. Never would she turn traitor. Gisi, who came from an orthodox family, surely knew that Jewish law teaches us to choose a martyr's death rather than transgress certain precepts. This being so, championing her righteousness was of no avail and entreating her was of no use, and Gisi went straight to the fiery furnace of Auschwitz.

[66] Editor's addition (September 30, 2021) השם ינקום דמם

the words of my father, teacher and rabbi.

Father was a wise and learned man, who not only brought up his sons to follow the Torah but also was the spiritual leader of his congregation and kept the flame of Judaism alive in the hearts of the Jews of Prievidza. I trembled at hearing his moving words, but was powerless to save him. My beautiful, good, heroic mother, who bore the yoke of suffering and bereavement nobly, who refused to be comforted for her daughter Etelka – Esther and her family, from whom no sign of life had come from the Opole ghetto for the past two years; mother, the years of whose life were short and difficult, spoke in the words of the patriarch Jacob, who threw himself around the neck of his son Joseph at their emotional meeting, and said: "Now let me die, since I have seen thy face, that thou art yet alive" (Genesis 46:30). She had uttered these words when we first met in Sered, and now, as she departed, she repeated them again: "Now that I have seen you alive and well, I can die quietly, as it is God's will; the main thing is that you, my son, are alive!"

As she had been a brave woman and mother throughout her life, so too, she held up her countenance in the difficult moments before departing along the road from which she would most likely never return. And I, who had dedicated my life to the mission of "saving their souls from death," stood helplessly by, watching with a rent heart. I wanted to cry out but restrained myself and held back my tears. During this emotional crisis, with various thoughts and memories racing through my mind, I began to wonder whether I had fulfilled the precept of honoring one's mother and father, and I decided to join my parents. "It is not within my power to save you," I said to them, "but it is also beyond me to abandon you, therefore we shall go together."

My parents, however, would hear nothing of the kind and made me promise them that I would make every effort to be strong and safeguard my own life. My parents were cheered that their sons and daughters were still alive, although they had informed me that my sister Rosa and her two sons were in Ohel David, which meant that they, too, were in danger. Nevertheless, they felt comforted.

The following day, early in the morning, I went to the hut in which my parents lived, to take leave of them. I asked Father to bless me. He rested his hand on my head and blessed me. On the eve of the Day of Atonement, Mother also used to bless the children. I asked Mother to spread forth her hands and give me her blessings, as well, that they might accompany me and protect me all the days of my life. As she was reciting the traditional priestly benediction, "May the Lord bless you and keep you …," we all burst into tears. This was their last blessing.

R. Moses Aaron, father of my sister-in-law Helenka (née Schwarz), who had also been in Ohel David only about a month, was sent to Auschwitz along with my parents. This righteous man was the father of the first Jewish Elder, the late Elhanan-Heinrich Schwarz, famed for refusing to accept the orders or obey the harsh decrees issued at the Nazis' behest. R. Moses Aaron was 74 years old, a God-fearing man and outstanding Jewish scholar. Also taken from Nové Mesto were Adolf Rosenberg's parents, R. Samuel Moses Rosenberg and his wife, from the Wohlstein family. He was a learned Jew, a man of letters, who drafted all the important epistles of the congregation most elegantly in the holy tongue. Many other dear friends were in this group of 920 deportees. Through the window of the carpentry shop we saw the train, its freight cars loaded with people, slowly chugging off.

As I said, this transpired on the first day of the New Month of Heshvan, at 4 o'clock in the afternoon. I went about mournfully downcast. Adolf tried to cheer me, but I remained heavyhearted and wailed in the elegiac melody of Lamentations, "Remember, O Lord, what is come upon us; behold, and see our reproach … We are become orphans and fatherless, our mothers are as widows … For this our heart is faint, for these things our eyes are dim" (Lamentations 5:1-17).

* * *

Several days later my sister Rosa-Rachel arrived in Sered along with her two sons, Amiel and Egon. Her husband Meir-Max had been taken back in 1942, with the first Jews expelled from Trenčianské Biskupice, and had died in the Treblinka extermination camp. My sister and her two sons spent two years in Nové Mesto, living near our parents as "illegals." They went to the "bunker" together and from there returned to Ohel David, which had become a sort of ghetto. Our meeting was heart-breaking. I suggested that she declare herself an Aryan married to a Jew. Those who proved this to be their status were gathered in hut number 23 and were not being deported. I was convinced she could face the trial successfully and pass Brunner's test. But, alas, after all the hardship and suffering she had been through, she was extremely nervous, and contradictions were found in her testimony under cross examination. She was imprisoned with the people destined for deportation.

One evening, as I was leaving the hut, I heard that six people from Hlohovec had been brought to the camp. "Woe," I thought, for who knows whether my other sister and her family, who lived in that city, were not among them? I rushed over to the dark doorway of the hut and, peering inside, immediately saw my sister Leah-Malwin and her husband Arye Jungleib, their daughter Greta and their son Walter, and another couple from Hlohovec. They had all been captured in a "bunker." Both of us burst into tears. But tears cannot bring deliverance. The following day I saw to it that both my sisters and their families were put into the same room. Leah and her family had arrived destitute of everything, for all their belongings had been stolen from them. I made sure that their basic needs were provided for. On Thursday, the 16th of Heshvan (November 2), both my sisters and their families were deported. As we parted, they expressed their happiness that their two brothers and their families had not yet been deported. This transport took 930 people to Auschwitz. We learned later that the Red Army had already reached the vicinity before the transport arrived at the extermination camp, that the Germans had destroyed the gas chambers and crematoria, and that the prisoners had been sent further west to camps at Ravensbruck, Mauthausen, Bergen-Belsen, Oranienburg, and elsewhere.

Although we were confined in a camp, sealed off from the rest of the world, nevertheless occasionally we received news from the outside. Sometimes newspapers were smuggled in to us, and we could read about developments on the front. Later we even got hold of a radio receiver and could listen to news of the war several times a day.

VII. My Wife's Death (השם ינקום דמה)[67]

"For the waves of Death compassed me. The floods of Belia! assailed me."[68] That is how we felt upon hearing of the fall of Banská-Bystrica, the Partisan's stronghold, on October 28, 1944,

---

[67] Editor's addition (September 30, 2021) השם ינקום דמה

[68] Cf. Second Samuel 22:S. Translator's note.

and of the bitter fate of the fighters who fell into the hands of the Germans, who were reasserting their control over the entire state. Three months had passed from the day I took leave of my family, and I was worried about their fate. Where were they? In the mountains, out in the rain and cold, without a roof over their heads, clothes to keep them warm, or food to eat? My friends and acquaintances tried to reassure me, saying "Your wife is a woman of valor, and in times of stress has repeatedly proven herself shrewd and resourceful. Her great prudence will surely enable her to manage, and her friends will marshal to her side and help her." In such circumstances only faith and hope can sustain man's spirit. Therefore, I put aside my oppressive thoughts.

Arming myself with patience, I passed the dark and dreary days of Heshvan (November) in emotional torment, until on the 27th of Heshvan (November 13, 1944). a group of Jews who had been captured in Banská - Bystrica arrived in Sered. In the evening I ran to the hut where they were imprisoned to see if they had any news of Mrs. Frieder. I intentionally did not call her "Rabbi Frieder's wife," so as not to reveal my identity, in order that I might receive a candid report. "Alas, Mrs. Frieder, the wife of the Rabbi of Nové Mesto?" "Yes, that is whom," I responded. "We heard that she and her children were killed in an air raid over Stare Hory," was their answer. Summoning super-human effort, I managed to hold back my reaction. Trying to keep a rein on my emotions and remain calm, I entered the next room. Here I was told, "Yes, Mrs. Frieder was killed along with her son. Her daughter remained in the forest; gun shots were heard on all sides, and it appears that she, too, perished." My heart sank. Nevertheless, I proceeded to the third room. There I saw a teacher whom I knew and went up to her. Seeing that she did not recognize me, I inquired whether she had heard anything about the wife of the Rabbi of Nové Mesto. She knew about the tragedy which had happened and told me: "The Rabbi's wife and her daughter were killed in the bombing, and her son was lightly wounded and picked up by a Czechoslovak officer, who took him to the village. This was at the end of October." This report, I felt, was accurate and reliable. All the witnesses had confirmed that my dear wife, Rozi, was no longer. The fate of my children was unclear. Broken and spent, I met the camp orderly Bela Rosenzweig outside, and he took me to my hut. I walked in silence, without uttering a word. Not until I had crossed the threshold of my room, did I collapse and burst into bitter wailing, barely able to stammer the bad tidings.

I had a terrible, restless night. My insides convulsed and my heart churned, and I could find no repose. Had my young wife really been taken from me so cruelly and my children plucked in the bud? Woe was unto me, for my dreaded fears had become real.

I could not stop sighing, nor could I find solace. As long as I did not know the precise day of her death, I did not observe the laws of mourning. The following day, November 14, Aladar Wagmann, who also had been captured in Banská-Bystrica, was brought to Sered from Prievidza. Deep in my heart I still refused to believe that this terrible misfortune had indeed befallen me; perhaps they had only been injured, and there still was hope. I approached Wagmann, but he did not recognize me with my face shaven and, when I asked him what he had heard of Rabbi Frieder's wife, responded by pushing me aside, "Lay off of me, Mister!" Only after I entreated him and revealed my identity, did he confirm what I had heard: "Your wife and daughter Gitka were killed on October 27 at 11 a.m., when the Germans bombed Stare

Hory. Gideon was lightly wounded in the leg, and is in one of the villages." "Aladar, is it really true?" I asked him. "If so, I must sit shiv'ah" (seven days of mourning, traditional in Jewish observance). "Yes Rabbi, sit shiv'ah," he said, tears running down his cheeks. Feeling shaken and spent, I returned to my room. One of my roommates made a tear in my clothes, but also my heart was rent in two. "Blessed be the true Judge. The Lord gave and the Lord hath taken away." A minyan gathered around, and I began sitting shiv'ah.

I mourned a noble wife, the finest of women, a devoted mother, slain along with our daughter, adorable Gitoshka, by the sinful hand of a cruel foe. My wife Roži was good-looking and her spiritual endowments made her a noble assistant to me in my public work, always supporting me with love, wisdom, advice, and encouragement. As a housewife she not only cared for her family, but also opened the doors of our home to the poor, the needy, and the persecuted in their hour of distress. She was an outstanding hostess and knew how to instill a pleasant atmosphere in the home. Her demeanor in the home and outside was always pleasant. She was active in philanthropic institutions and women's organizations, and cared for the public welfare. She was a wonderful woman, beloved by all. After being happily married for ten years, I became a forlorn widower. My beautiful rose had been plucked in its prime, my crowning glory felled.

Gitoshka was a four-year old full of charm, unusually precocious for her age. Her light curls, blue eyes, and smiling face commanded the attention of all around her. My dear ones, lovely and pleasant in their lives, even in their death were not parted.69[69] I felt I had lost my wits and was not even moved when

---

[69] Cf. Second Samuel 1:23. Translator's note.

more transports were organized. I did not care whether I was taken for the transport or not. Sometimes depression overcame me, and I thought to myself it would be good to put an end to all this suffering and wondered why I had not gone with my parents. Thoughts of Gideon, who surely was in need of me, alone gave me strength and made me take heart. And thus, I remained in the camp, even after two more transports had departed.

השם ינקום דמם [70]

These were the sixth transport, which departed on the 30th of Heshvan (November 16, 1944), taking 785 souls, and the seventh transport, which left Sered on the 16th of Kislev (December 2, 1944) with 742 people. The transports were no longer sent to Auschwitz, but to other camps. Some individuals managed to escape before the trains reached their destination.

VIII. Sered in the Winter of 1945

On the first eve of Hanukkah 5705 (December 10, 1944), many of the camp's inmates assembled in my room to light the first candle of the holiday, and we held a sad little party. I said a few words to bring to mind the fathers and sons, the men and women, for whom the Hanukkah lights no longer shine and who are enveloped in darkness and gloom. Our youngsters were fighting heroically for their survival, as in the days of yore, during the Maccabean revolt. Each day the number of candles lit increases, but the number of Jews who remain alive dwindles. We all cried. It was a sad celebration of the Feast of Lights; our mirth had turned to mourning, for we knew not what would become of us. On *Zot Hanukkah* (the eighth day of Hanukkah), before the holiday had elapsed, Brunner issued orders to evacuate the entire

---

[70]Editor's addition (September 30, 2021)(השם ינקום דמם

camp. Full of trepidation and excitement, people began packing their belongings. I took everything calmly. My brother could also provide Gideon a warm home; but no one could restore his mother to him.

Suddenly all the men were ordered to line up. Brunner himself selected 110 men, who, it was rumored, would remain in the camp. On the third of Tevet (December 19, 1944), the eighth transport departed, taking 944 men, women, and children to the camps at Oranienburg and Buchenwald. Only 110 men remained in Sered; their wives and children were sent to Theresienstadt.

Jews from all over the state were brought to the camp almost daily. In the region where the Partisans were active, the Germans blasted every house in which they found underground fighters or Jews. Many peasants turned in the Jews, after having extorted all their money from them. Many Jews found themselves forced to wander from "bunker" to "bunker." I thought I might find someone among them who had news of my son Gideon. I looked for a sign of life from him all the time and therefore questioned every person who came from the area of Banská-Bystrica. The first person to bring me tidings was Vilmoš Steiner from Zlaté Moravce, who told me he had seen my son in the village of Buly, a small place between Donovaly and Kalište. I contacted Paškovič clandestinely and requested him to track Gideon down. He did me this favor and, on the eve of the Sabbath of *Va-yehi,* the 13th of Tevet (December 29, 1944), sent confirmation that Gideon was alive and well and was living in the village of Buly. "*Va-yehi* (Heb.: and he lived)," I said, "My son Gideon is still alive!" This was the first ray of light that penetrated the gloom, grief and sorrow enveloping me.

Even during this difficult period, the Jewish Council of Sered continued functioning. The Jewish Elder was a man by the name of Cohen, who tried to help and even succeeded in getting many people out of the transports. Twice he saved me, "the carpenter König," from transports, even though he knew full well that Brunner was particularly eager to find the "dangerous Rabbi" and fervently wished to send him to an extermination camp with explicit instructions ordering "special treatment" or saying "his return is undesirable," as he had done with Gisi Fleischmann. Later Cohen's influence waned, and all activity of the Jewish Council became concentrated in the hands of three people – Alexander Weiss, Desider Komloš, and Desider Müller – who, in performing their difficult office, lacked the mettle to stand up against the mass murderer Brunner and gave in to his dictates.

In contrast to this troika, which sometimes came under sharp criticism, we, the underground troika of Neumann, Winterstein, and myself, continued preparations in anticipation of the war's end, which, with the Red Army advancing westward and the Germans fighting desperately to consolidate their position, appeared imminent. Although our preparations were being made in the utmost secrecy, they almost miscarried, entailing the gravest consequences for us. But we covered our tracks, and the head Jewish attend ant made an earnest show of dutifully searching for hidden arms, but came up with nothing. Keys were made in the smithy for opening the side gates, and saws and other tools were prepared for breaking open fences and train cars, so that people could escape from camp or jump from train cars. The news from all the fronts was encouraging. On January 26, 1945, the Soviet army entered Auschwitz. On February 13, Budapest was liberated; on March 25, the Americans conquered the Saar region and the Red Army began marching on Austria. Šariš-Zemplin was liberated, as well. After Purim large areas of central Slovakia were liberated, and as Passover – the festival of freedom – drew near, the front line approached Sered, where approximately 500 Jews were imprisoned in camp. This news came to us via secret radio broadcasts and also more directly, from the rumble of artillery in the distance. Despite the great risk entailed, I decided to hold a Passover seder in the camp. Taking great precaution, we made matzah in the bakery, doing our utmost to prepare it quickly so that it would be kosher for Passover and would not be spotted by our oppressors. All the other necessary preparations were likewise done surreptitiously. The ceremony was held in a secluded side room of the carpentry workshop. Wooden plates and improvised implements were set on a plain wooden table; at a pinch they served quite well. Several youngsters stood guard outside. In the middle of reading the Haggadah they suddenly signaled danger. The lights went out and we all held our breath, trembling with fear and terror. Had somebody informed on us? Shortly, however, the alert passed and the celebrants resumed their reading of the Haggadah. Several verses from the Haggadah commanded our attention: "This year we are here, next year may we be in the Land of Israel; this year we are slaves, next year may we be free men; for in every generation people rise up against us to annihilate us, but the Holy One blessed by He delivers us from their hands." God grant that it be so.

IX. Exodus from Sered – Passover 5705

On the intermediate Sabbath of Passover (March 31), when the front was some twenty kilometers away from Sered, Brunner ordered the residents of the camp to finish the packing they had been doing for several days. His plan was to transfer all the equipment and goods to the camp at Theresienstadt. At noon, orders came to cease all work and report with our bundles in the camp yard. Bundles in hand, we hastily went to the train. Was this exodus from Sered like the exodus from Egypt? Were we going from slavery to freedom, from bondage to redemption? We boarded the train. We heard the thunder of artillery no more than a few kilometers away; there liberation from the yoke of Brunner beckoned to us. I was firmly resolved not to go to Theresienstadt and tried to convince others to flee with me, but I could not find a willing ear. No one wished to join me. On April 1, we reached Nové Mesto, and the cars were opened to provide us water. My attempt at fleeing was thwarted, and towards nightfall we reached Trenčin. Here the train was held up for nearly two days, until Tuesday at 1:30 p.m. The official reason given for the delay was that the Vlára mountain pass was blocked with trains full of soldiers retreating towards Moravia. Several Jews got off the train almost unhindered and went into town to do shopping. Some even negotiated with their acquaintances from among the train clerks, trying in various ways to persuade them not to provide a locomotive to continue the journey.

The Christians celebrated Easter on Sunday and Monday. I knew that Rakovský, the deposed district commissar of Nové Mesto, had been transferred to Trenčin, and on Monday I decided to pay him a visit, to plan my escape. The meeting in his house was extremely moving. Rakovský was surprised and glad to find that I was still alive, and promised to help me escape. In consultation with him we devised a plan of escape.

My principal concern was for my comrades, with whom I had shared six months of suffering, worry, and common fate in Sered. I did not wish to escape alone; but hoped to organize a group escape, thus saving my friends from entering a new house of bondage. Therefore, the same day I also visited my acquaintance Losdorfer, the head commissar in the criminal department of the Treasury, and requested him to arrest me and 10 to 15 of my colleagues on the pretext that we had committed financial violations and thus get us out of the transport. But Losdorfer was afraid of the *Gestapo* and refused to put himself in jeopardy. I returned to the train and told my comrades that I intended to escape and requested that they join me, but I could not prevail upon them.

On Tuesday, the eve of the last day of Passover, I left the train again. I met a group of Partisans and offered to help them if they attacked our train at the Trenčianská Teplá station and prevented it from continuing along its way. I promised them that if the women, children, and elderly were conducted to safety, the young men would join the Partisans. With this plan in hand, I returned to the train for the third time, hoping to finalize the scheme with my comrades; but I was too late. The train had already pulled out of the station.

At the station I met another three Jews and two SD men who were escorting the transport, all of whom, like myself, had missed the train. When the Germans detected me, again they tailed me, keeping a close watch on me and the three others. I suggested that the three of them join me and attempt to flee at the first opportunity, but the entire plan miscarried. I managed to get away, and they were put on a freight train at Púchov and were returned to the transport. Trenčín and its environs were crawling with German army units. The front line passed through the area, and whoever wandered around the city, without a roof or shelter, placed himself in danger. Therefore, I decided to see Rakovský again and to plan my next step. Rakovský gave me papers signed by Nové Mesto's district commissar and a letter of recommendation to the head of the Franciscan abbey in the village of Beckov, near Nové Mesto. I decided to go there under cover of night, even though the 22-kilometer journey entailed crossing the area where the Germans were deployed. I faced many hardships along the way. I was caught in pouring rain, lightly dressed and without a coat. All along the way there was shooting and bombing; and I was afraid lest I be arrested en route. Finally, close to 9 p.m., I arrived at the gate of the monastery. The gate was not opened for a long time, and, after being questioned by the monk at the gate, I was brought to Father Qardian, the head of the abbey. He read Rakovský's letter of recommendation and unhesitatingly took me into one of the monks' cells. I remained confined in the cell until Saturday, April 7, 1945, when the village was liberated by Rumanian soldiers, fighting alongside the Red Army. I left the cell but remained in the abbey until Nové Mesto was liberated. On Tuesday, the 27th of Nisan (April 10, 1945), I left Beckov and went on foot to Nové Mesto.

Chapter Eight

A Dismal Liberation

Nisan 27 – Iyar 23, 5705

(April 10 – May 10, 1945)

I. Returning to the Ruins of My Congregation

Millions of people fell in this war of Titans. Europe lay in ruins. The rapacious Nazi beast had run wild obstreperously, until at last, its strength was spent. Yet no other nation suffered as much as we, the Jews. In every generation people have risen up against us to annihilate us; we have experienced pogroms, massacres, and expulsions; but what the Nazi beast did to us is unparalleled in the annals of mankind. The Slovaks, too, participated in the atrocities. Tens of thousands of our brethren in this country perished. We remained a decimated few. Can we possibly continue living in Slovakia, according to our Jewish way of life? I pondered over these things as I walked from Beckov to Nové Mesto.

Upon my arrival I found only five Jews in the city, but within a week the number had increased to one hundred. First, I headed for my apartment, which until now had been occupied by strangers. The kitchen and living rooms were empty; every piece of furniture had disappeared. The furniture in the children's rooms had not been taken. Never more shall my dear little Gitoshka live in this room, nor my wife smile at her and stroke her hair. Everything is forsaken, gloomy, abandoned.

Our two thousand and three hundred books remained neatly arranged on the shelves. The library had been a part of my existence. I had collected it, lavishing care on every volume. All the books were bound and catalogued. For tens of years, I purchased books at every opportunity. I used to sit here with my wife in the evenings and tell her of the events of the day. As I looked at the books in their gilt bindings, they once seemed to me to return my smile and talk to me unceasingly. Oh, how much I learned from them! Now they stood row upon row, dumb and silent, no longer speaking to my broken and wounded heart.

Everything was sad, forsaken, bereft. The woman of the house, the mother of our children, who had always been so full of happiness, was lacking. She was no more. How could I live in this house without her? Where was the charm and beauty, where the magical light that used to shine from her countenance? Now only darkness and gloom, loss and bereavement, harbored under my roof.

I went to my second home, the Ohel David Old-Age Home, which was supposed to "deliver their souls from death," until, on the intermediate days of Sukkot, the festival of Tabernacles, this "tabernacle of David," too, began to collapse. And thus, like my wife and parents, the residents of this home, as well, went to their eternal home. A scene of terrible destruction unfolded before my eyes. Everything had been broken and destroyed, doors and windows had been ripped out, and only broken dishes and worn-out clothes had been left by the rabble who plundered and ransacked the place after the elderly had been uprooted from here and deported to the death camps. It was a heart-rending spectacle, how our carefully fostered institution had become an abandoned ruin.

Next, I stood in front of the Great Synagogue on Rabbi Weisse Street. "O wall of the daughter of Zion, let tears run down like a river day and night… See, O Lord, and consider, to whom Thou hast done thus! … Shall the priest and the prophet be slain in the sanctuary of the Lord? The youth and the old man lie on the ground in the streets; my virgins and my young men are fallen by the sword; Thou hast slain them in the day of Thine anger; Thou hast slaughtered unsparingly" (Lamentations 2:18-21). Thus, the prophet bewailed the destruction of Jerusalem and the Temple. Also, our young men and women, our youth and our elderly, fell by the sword, were slaughtered mercilessly. Also, our house of worship was destroyed, bombed, burned, and plundered. The Torah scrolls were defiled, their parchments torn and strewn over the floor covered with straw and dung, for the Huns had turned our sanctuary into a stable for their horses. See, O Lord, to whom Thou hast done thus! Here we cried out, here we prayed; but our prayers did not penetrate the heavy clouds that covered the heavens. "Terror and the pit are come upon us, desolation and destruction. Mine eye runneth down with rivers of water, for the breach of the daughter of my people" (*Ibid.,* 3:47-48).

A meager few returned every day – first those who came out of hiding in the area, later the survivors of the death-camps, saved from the fire. Widows and widowers, orphans and bereaved parents. There was not a home in which someone had not perished.

II. Gideon's Saga

Transportation was scarcely available. All the trains and vehicles were enlisted for the war effort. Traveling to the region of Banská-Bystrica was altogether unfeasible. But some kindly souls, in parallel with my efforts, managed to reach Gideon in Buly and bring him home. Gideon had grown older, taller and skinnier, and looked very neglected. He recounted his story, the gist of which I present below:

"When the Red Cross car brought us to Hrka, we were warned that the Germans and guardists were searching for Jews. Immediately we fled into the forest and, with the help of the local ranger, who gave us some food and two bottles of milk, we reached a cabin where we spent the night. The next morning, we continued along our way and met two Slovak soldiers, who explained to us how to reach the Partisans' territory. For a sum, a farmer working in the fields brought us to the village of Zlatnik. From there we set out by cart for Bánovce but, when we learned that the Germans and Partisans were fighting each other there, we turned back and spent the night in Zlatnik. That was our second night. We reached Bánovce the next day. Two Partisans questioned us and brought us to headquarters. The commander saw to it that we were given food. Then suddenly there was an alarm. They said a large German force was coming, and the Partisans decided to leave the area. We were placed in a broken-down car, tied by ropes to another car. The rope broke twice along the way, and we barely managed to reach Uhrovec. Here, in a castle, were the

Partisans' main headquarters. The following day they sent us to Prievidza with a wounded Partisan, and from there we took the train to Banská-Štiavnica, where we stayed until the city was evacuated and we had to go to Banská-Bystrica. We were evacuated from here, too. The same thing happened everywhere we came – in Staré Rory and afterwards in Yelenec. As we continued towards the mountains, we were attacked by German planes. Mother and Gitka were hit in one of the attacks and killed. A group of twenty-two soldiers, who had fled from Poland and come to Slovakia to fight the Germans, passed through the area, and one of them took me to Buly. There I stayed for seven months."

This was the story of my seven and a half-year-old son, who by his resourcefulness and wisdom managed to adapt to the primitive farm life in Buly and to hide his true identity from the hostile people who combed the area. He told stories of Partisans who roamed the mountains and of Jews in the Russian and Rumanian armies. He talked about the Russian and German soldiers of General Vlasov, who fell prisoner and joined the Germans. Gideon also talked about his mother and sister, without fully comprehending the meaning of their death. Such expressions as "killing" and "death" had become commonplace concepts for him, and he used them with great naturalness, as if he were talking about toys and games – the things that make up the world of normal children of his age. Bitter experience had hardened him.[71]

III. A Mournful Liberation

---

[71] Henry A. Herzog, a Jewish Partisan officer from Poland, handed Gideon over to a village shoemaker by the name of Jozef, strongly admonishing him to protect the boy and promising him a rich reward if he saves his life. Herzog now lives in New York.

The war had drawn to a close. The Nazi monster, which threatened all mankind, had surrendered. Fascist Germany and all her satellites had been defeated. Throughout the cities of Europe there was jubilance and rejoicing over the long-awaited peace. Only we, the survivors of the Holocaust, in which six million Jews had been wiped out, remained vanquished and beaten, unable to rejoice.

* * *

I shall never forget the blessing I received from my parents, may the Lord avenge their blood, when we parted in Sered, before they were deported to Auschwitz. They asked me to take care of myself and to continue working for others. Here in Nové Mesto, where my house of worship was destroyed and my dear ones were no more, I felt I could not possibly carry on. Nevertheless, I decided to fulfill the precept of the Holy One, "And thou shalt choose life." Beaten, bereaved, and orphaned, by no choice of our own, we embarked on a new era, hoping to live as free men.

I have, laid out before me, all the documents and papers which were given me by the Slovak authorities and which were to no avail after the Germans invaded. Perhaps the only benefit that can come of them shall be if they are used as documents for future generations, as testimony to the oppression, dispossession, deportation, and assassination of the Jewish people, performed with bestial cruelty by a nation which is considered civilized. "Remember what Amalek did unto thee … thou shalt not forget!"

Here I conclude the fourth and last section of my diary. The war criminals and murderers of the Jews have disappeared from the scene. Most of them managed to flee the country, and the heads of state have been arrested and will be brought to trial. We must hope that the people who take their place will be harbingers of freedom and equality under the law.

Our martyrs shall never be forgotten. We must study the significance of the Holocaust and learn its lessons. Were these the birth-pains of the Messiah, ushering in our redemption? Or must we continue living here, bearing the yoke of our suffering and exile? Will the conscience of the enlightened world awaken and comprehend the significance of the sacrifice of millions of people? Will we ourselves be able to draw the proper conclusions? In what direction are we to go, and whither are we to direct the surviving remnant? What lies in store for us, and what shall be the fate of our religious precepts and our Jewishness?

The answers lay in developments of the near future. Our questions will be answered by life, the people, the land. We, the eternal wanderers, are called upon to give the answer by returning to our promised land. We can no longer live here, deprived of security and freedom; for without freedom there is no Judaism. As Jews, we have no future in the Diaspora.

* * *

"Independent Slovakia" sent 58,534 Jews to death in 1942, and in the second stage, in 1944, another 9,907 souls[72] were deported from Sered in eight transports. Of all those deported only several hundred returned. The Germans, during their suppression of the insurrection in Slovakia, killed approximately 3,500 Jews. Thus, the total number of Holocaust victims in Slovakia is estimated at 70,000 souls.

---

[72] This figure does not include the 500 Sered prisoners who were transferred to Theresienstadt on March 31, 1944.

The Jews of Slovakia who lived in the regions annexed to Hungary were deported to death camps in the spring of 1944; of these Jews approximately 40,000 souls perished. Ten thousand Jews were all that remained in what was formerly "Independent Slovakia"; of Slovakia's entire Jewish community, which before the annexation numbered 136,737 souls, approximately 23,000 survived; and in all of Czechoslovakia approximately 30,000 Jews were left.

These grim statistics sum up the Holocaust of Slovak Jewry in the Second World War.

Epilogue

The Jewish Underground

in the Slovak Insurrection

"A psalm of David: Blessed be the Lord my Rock,
who traineth my hands for war, and my fingers for battle"

(Psalms 144: 1)

I. The Czechoslovak Government Declares War on the Nazi Invader

The political situation in Slovakia in the summer of 1944 was extremely tense. The Red Army was at the border, ready to cross into the state. The forests covering the mountains of Slovakia were an ideal location for gangs of Partisans, comprised of various groups: Russian soldiers who had escaped from captivity, Slovak soldiers from various units, and Jewish youngsters, whose ranks steadily swelled as the Jews were evacuated from eastern Slovakia. Many Jews by then shared the views of the underground and were among its organizers. Evacuated Jews headed straight for the mountains. The Soviets parachuted experienced commanders into the area and organized terrorist actions in July and August 1944.

In coordination with the German army, Slovakia's General

Malár, commander of a brigade in Prešov in eastern Slovakia, fortified the Lupkov and Dukla mountain passes, while a regiment of German infantry essentially acted as watchguards over the Slovaks. General Jan Golian and his staff planned a mutiny of the army, in which Slovakia's eastern units behind the front lines would join ranks with the Soviet army against the German conqueror. On Black Friday, August 25, 1944, Tiso, feeling that the Slovak army was inadequate to protect his regime, invited the Ger man army to defend Slovakia. On August 28, the Slovak government approved a resolution appointing General Turanec Commander-in-Chief of the Army. For the time being, General Čatloš remained in office as Minister of Defense. Jozef Sivák did not participate in the cabinet meeting in which Slovakia was essentially handed over to the German army. In a speech on the radio, Šaňo Mach admonished the general populace not to collaborate with the Partisans, whom, he said, were all Bolsheviks and Jews whom the German army had come to liquidate. German Ambassador Ludin thanked Mach for his "courageous words." Slovakia's patriots decided their time had come. On August 29, they broadcast a radio announcement from Banská-Bystrica proclaiming a rebellion, and army units in central Slovakia joined the revolt. The Germans reacted swiftly and by August 30, 1944, had disarmed the Slovak units in the eastern part of the country. The Germans also seized the upper hand in Slovakia's western cities. Only the central part of the state remained in the hands of the insurrectionists. Here, in the Tri Duby airport near Banská-Bystrica, the Czechoslovak government in exile – led by Minister František Nemec and General Rudolph Viest, both of whom had just returned from London and were joined by General Golian – landed and declared war on the German invader.

II. The Gates of the Labor Camps Are Opened

The day the rebellion broke out, Metuščin, commander of the gendarmes in the Sered camp, accepted the proposal of the Jewish Council, which was headed by Alexander Pressburger, to disband the camp and join the forces fighting the Germans.[73] The gates of the camp were thrown open, and Metuščin gave ten rifles, a machine-gun, and a large amount of munitions to a group of Jewish youths. Ernest Spitzer, the commander of the Jewish police force in the camp, knew about a case of rifles and munitions cached in the carpentry shop. The arms had been purchased by the Jewish underground and had reached Sered from Nováky by way of people whom the underground had taken into its confidence. Dr. Neumann, assisted by Zvi Fehér, who served as liaison, handled this operation for the Jewish Center. For some reason these valuable arms remained in their cache. When the decision was made to disband the camp, the inmates had to decide hastily in which direction they would head. For, unlike Nováky and Vyhne, which lay in a region liberated by the Partisans, Sered lay in an area under German conquest. Truck-loads of German soldiers were already rolling towards the outlying cities along the Vah River, the closest of which was Sered. Most of the camp's adult inhabitants searched in panic for places to hide in the vicinity of their home towns, and those who were capable of fighting joined the Partisans. About one thousand people dispersed in all directions; but many, who had not managed to leave in time, found themselves under the rule of the SS Huns.

---

[73] See Nir, Akiva, Shevilim be-Ma'agal ha-Esh, Merhavia, 1967, pp. 27-29, 50 (hereinafter, Nir).

Underground activity in the Nováky camp began back in 1942. Zionist-youths maintained contact with the underground outside the camp and even disseminated propaganda inside the camp. On August 30, 1944, approximately 1,500 Jews living in the camp were liberated, and of them around 250 joined the fighters. These groups of fighters liberated the district city of Prievidza, the coal-mining center of Handlová, and the town of Nemecké Pravno. The latter two towns had a large Nazi German population. Many of the Jewish youths, who had been sent poorly armed, untrained, and inexperienced to fight in the front lines against the German tanks advancing from the direction of Topolčany, were cruelly slaughtered. In the village of Nemčice the local residents disclosed the hiding place of 52 Jews from Topolčany, and the SS murderers ordered the Jews to dig themselves a communal grave in an open field and then liquidated them on the spot. This blood-bath took place on September 10, 1944. Wherever the SS Huns found Partisans or Jews in hiding, they massacred them in cold blood.

The SS units advanced rapidly towards the area conquered by the Partisans. The units of Ferdinand Goldstein of Piešťany, one of the organizers of self-defense in the Nováky camp, and Dr. Imrich Rosenthal of Prievidza, a native of Pravno, defended themselves heroically. The two commanders, members of the Maccabee movement, and many others like them, sacrificed their lives, dying a hero's death.

At the conference of *Ha-Shomer ha-Tza'ir,* held clandestinely in Nové Mesto at the end of 1943 in the Ohel David Old-Age Home, the leaders of the movement decided to prepare for an exodus to the forests to fight alongside the Partisans. In the wake of the conference, talks were held with Young Maccabee activists in the Sered camp. People like Moshe Stark and Joseph Korniansky did not agree with the plan and believed that the duty of the Zionist movements was to safeguard the surviving few. "Enough blood has been shed," they maintained, "and venturesome underground activity is likely to jeopardize the Jews prospects of remaining in Slovakia until the liberation." Despite this legitimate argument, members of the Maccabee and B'nai Akiva movements were active in the underground and evinced much personal courage. Many of them joined Partisans units individually and fought the Germans, while others worked in the underground in Bratislava.[74]

It is a historical fact that youngsters from Nováky, from all movements, battled fiercely and heroically in the Nitra River valley. The Jews were sent to arrest the German advance and, despite heavy losses, did not abandon their positions at a time when many Slovak soldiers were deserting in the dark of night. Our boys fought in various Partisan units, and virtually every Partisan unit had some of our young men and women in it.

The Slovak Partisans also had many anti-Semites in their ranks. These were assorted types who, seeing that the tide was about to turn and the Fascist regime be replaced, had only joined for appearances' sake, to wash themselves clean and assure themselves of an alibi. These people made a lot of trouble and hardship for the Jews. When the Germans advanced and purified the area of Partisans, most of the Slovaks went back home, while the Jews continued the struggle and retreated to the region of Banská-Bystrica. Soon there were five thousand Jewish refugees in Banská-Bystrica and its environs.

---

[74] Nir, p. 50.

Parachutists from the Land of Israel landed at the nerve center of the revolt in an attempt to strike at the Nazi foe and assist their persecuted brethren. Theirs is a story of supreme heroism in the Jews' desperate attempt at self-defense. The parachutists tried to help the Jews who fled to the mountains and encourage their fighting brethren, but they were captured by the Germans. Only one of them, Hayyim Hermesh, made it back to the Land of Israel. Havivah Reik, Raphael Reiss, and Zvi Ben-Yaakov, may the Lord avenge their blood, were executed in Kremnička, near Banská-Bystrica. There the SS butchers slaughtered masses of men, women, and children, young and old, in cold blood. The Germans combed the forests and murdered every Jew whom they caught, and German fighter planes, overflying the mountains, shot at the fleeing masses of soldiers and Jewish Partisans.

III. The Insurrection is Quashed

By the end of October 1944, SS General Herman Höfle had quashed the Slovak revolt. Generals Viest and Golian were taken prisoner and executed in Mauthausen, and thousands of insurrectionists dispersed. Partisans, Jews, and refugees retreated and took to the forested mountains in droves. Hundreds of Jews had to seek refuge in "bunkers" in the lap of nature, exposed to the harsh winter weather. Many were killed by marauding gangs of various nationalities who roamed the mountains in search of food and money. This hatred of the Jews compelled many young Jewish fighters to disavow their Jewish identity and equip themselves with forged Aryan papers.

The Germans had stationed a large force in the Carpathian Mountains and mountain passes to forestall the advance of the

Red Army. The Red Army's slow advance was also attributed to political reasons: differences of opinion and lack of coordination between the Czechoslovak government in exile in London and the Czech exiles who were acting under Soviet inspiration. The Jews, of course, paid the price: they were captured by the Germans and either liquidated forthwith or transferred to Sered and from there deported to death camps. According to figures of the German security forces in Slovakia, dated December 9, 1944, a total of 9,563 Jews were arrested, of whom 2,237 received "special handling." Later, 8,975 Jews were handed over to the Germans.[75]

The Jewish underground in Sered was also active during Alois Brunner's reign of terror in the camp. Whenever this tyrant toured the residence huts and workshops, everyone trembled in fear. This was no wonder, for his thugs claimed 44 lives here at his behest, among them Rabbi Ben-Zion Ungar, the head of the Piešťany rabbinical court, may the Lord avenge his blood, who was shot to death after being severely tortured and sadistically victimized. The tension relaxed after Brunner left Sered to perform his satanic work in Bratislava. Without Brunner around, the Jewish guards could risk easing the life of their brethren. The Working Group became involved in clandestine social work and philanthropy. They supplied clothing, medicine, food, money, and various commodities, and the "carpenter-rabbi" Frieder even helped daring youngsters escape from camp, at the risk of his own and the fugitives' lives.

Meanwhile, in Bratislava Brunner was taking charge of the hunt for Jews. He discovered them in "bunkers" and hide-outs, whose existence was often revealed to him by Jews whom he had caught and, by torturing them and making them vain promises,

---

[75] Cf. Anton Ra la, Tiso a povsranie-Dokumenty. Bratislava, p. 57.

had forced to betray their brethren. After revealing what they knew, they, too, were sent to the death camps.

IV. Underground Assistance to People Hiding in Bratislava

In the capital city of Bratislava, a group of clandestine activists, seeking to help people hiding in the "bunkers," came into being. Dr. Tibor Kováč, who had worked of late with Gisi Fleischmann, knew of a large sum of money still available to the Joint and, assisted by Juraj Révész and a group of youngsters from the youth movements, distributed this money among the needy in the "bunkers." They undertook this mission at the risk of their lives, for countless detectives milled about the city, keeping a vigilant eye on all goings-on. More than once the Jewish activists got away at the very last moment, and sometimes they managed to affect an escape after having been caught. Leo Rosenthal and Oscar Krasniansky, activists of the Zionist movement, joined in this clandestine work, and members of the youth movements saw to it that contacts were maintained. When the funds of the Joint ran out, Dr. Révész availed himself of the good services of George Dunand, the International Red Cross's representative in Bratislava, and through him continued receiving stipends from the Joint in Switzerland.

Bumi Lazar, who had escaped from Sered, also turned his hide-out in Bratislava into a center for underground activity and was on good terms with Dunand. Shelly Fürchtgott, a courageous young woman from the Young Maccabee movement, looked like an Aryan and thus came and went freely to and from the "bunkers" with great self-assurance, performing missions and visiting Jews in hiding. Equipped with counterfeit papers, she transmitted money, food, medicines, information, greetings, and encouragement, even at great risk to herself. She was one of many who proved their courageousness and helped their brethren in great suffering, sometimes actually saving them from starvation.[76]

This marvelous work went on in the capital at the same time as the Huns of the SS, the *Gestapo,* the Voluntary Defense Squad, and the Hlinka Guard were being enlisted to purify the city of its Jews and wipe out the "bunkers." Brunner's net was spread out night and day. His men lay in wait in the dark of night to discover the Jews' hiding places and to capture whomever had to leave stealthily to tend to vital errands. Many people were disclosed by sundry detectives and informants, including certain depraved Jews. Others were caught due to lack of prudence. Thus, time and again, more people were discovered in "bunkers" and shipped off to Sered, including Vojtech Winterstein's wife and daughter Margit, and Ernest Abeles' family. Brunner did not let up his roguish behavior for a moment. Nevertheless, more than a thousand Jews lived in hiding in Bratislava, sometimes under sub-human conditions, and waited for deliverance.

In 1944 and 1945, the International Red Cross and representatives of the Vatican tried to intervene to prevent Jews from being deported, but the Slovak government responded that the Germans were transferring the Jews to Germany for reasons of security. According to estimates, approximately 5,000 Jews remained in the underground in Slovakia. The Sered camp had close to 500 Jews left, whom Brunner worked like slaves in workshops producing for the German army, until it was decided to transfer the camp, with all its equipment, to Theresienstadt.

V. The Last Transport from Sered Arrives in Theresienstadt

The train carrying Sered's inmates departed for Theresienstadt

---

[76] See Lazar's essay in FVYS: Arnold-Bumi Lazar, Erinnerungen, Tel Aviv, 1963.

on March 31, 1945. It proceeded slowly towards its destination because the tracks were overloaded with army trains. The journey lasted eight days. At interim stations the cars were opened and people were allowed off the train to tend to their needs. It was quite easy to make a get-away from the train at any of these stations, but the men longed for their dear ones in Theresienstadt or were afraid to take the risk. Of the entire transport, only about a dozen people ran away. Three young men jumped from the train car in Moravia, when the train slowed down. Among them were Berea Klug and Samuel Salomon, members of *Ha-Shomer ha-Tza'ir* who were active in the underground and had been caught by the *Gestapo*. Now they had escaped and returned to Slovakia. On April 7, the eighth day of the journey, the cars were opened and the Jews found themselves in the Theresienstadt ghetto.

Theresienstadt was considered a "model ghetto." The Germans brought transports from many countries here and beguiled visitors to the camp into thinking that here the Jews could live autonomously. Of course, the honorable delegations that came here heard nothing of the thousands who were deported to Auschwitz, the terrible overcrowding, the hunger and starvation, the disease and typhus; nor were they interested in these things. Approximately 20,000 Jews were concentrated here. The men who came here from Sered and became permanent res idents with a *"stand"* (i.e., expertise or a profession, which made them beneficial and therefore protected them from being deported) faced another month of suffering, torment and fear for their fate. By the time they arrived at Theresienstadt, Bratislava had been liberated (April 4, 1945). Prague and Theresienstadt, however, were not liberated by the Red Army until the last day of the war. On that day, May 8, 1945, Nazi Germany surrendered, the war came to an end, and the Jews began their return home, their doleful repatriation, from Theresienstadt, as well.

Part Two

Slovak Jewry after the War

5705 - 5709

(1945 - 1949)

Chapter One

An Illusory Liberation

"Return, O my soul, unto thy rest;
for the Lord hath dealt bountifully with thee.
For Thou hast delivered my soul from death,
mine eyes from tears, and my feet from stumbling."
(Psalms 116:7-8)

I. Returning from the Underground

When the SS officer requested a list of the Jews in the city, we (I and my family, that is) decided to leave Nové Mesto and go underground. Thursday morning, the 19th of Elul, 5704 (September 7, 1944), before dawn, we set out on foot for the neighboring village and from there took the train to Stará Túra. Boženka Ondrášková, a woman in the Partisans, brought us by cart to Podkozince, on the slopes of Mt. Yavorina. Several times we managed to slip out of the hands of German soldiers who had come to comb the area and purify it of Partisans and

Jews. A peasant couple, Michal and Eva Klimo, and their son Milan helped us buy food and set up a "bunker" in their cabin. I presented myself as someone from the underground whose apartment in Bratislava had been bombed. My wife Helen and our three-year-old daughter Pirka-Margalit, both of whom were fair-haired and blue-eyed, looked quite Aryan in their peasant dress, and we all had forged documents. Although the inhabitants of the mountain communities were Evangelists, opponents of the regime, they were nevertheless afraid to help the Jews, even for a large sum of money, because the Germans were blowing up every house they found harboring Jews or Partisans. We were in constant danger. The Germans had stationed themselves at the foot of the mountain, in the village of Lubina, a 45-minute walk from Podkozince, and after each time they combed the mountains and exchanged fire with the Partisans, they would march down with their prisoners – suspected civilians and Partisans who were generally Jewish. Nevertheless, a number of families managed to survive nine months underground, sometimes in sub-human conditions, in cold and snow, living in forests inhabited by Partisans and roamed by gangs of deserters of dubious character. Spies and informers also operated in the area. Thus, one had to be cautious and resourceful.

On Saturday, the 24th of Nisan (April 7, 1945), the entire area was taken over by Rumanian forces under the command of the Red Army. The Germans retreated. On Wednesday, the 28th of Nisan (April 11, 1945), we returned to Nové Mesto. Meeting my brother was sad and depressing. He immediately informed me of his intentions to leave Nové Mesto for Bratislava to help restore the central Jewish institutions, and requested me to devote myself to community work. There was no one for whom to open a Jewish school, not even ten children; and, what is more, a new regulation had abolished all parochial and denominational schools. The first activities undertaken by the Jewish community after the war were to renovate the Orthodox synagogue, which had survived unharmed, and to open an office for the community. At Rabbi Frieder's request, I coordinated the affairs of the Jewish community and the Zionist movement. The few Jews who returned were busy trying to find a livelihood; I turned to administrative work and social work in the community. We made repairs to Ohel David and provided Holocaust survivors temporary quarters in its rooms. We opened an orphanage, maintained by the central organization of Jewish communities, in the building in 1946. None of the kosher butchers had returned, therefore we took on Rabbi Avigdor Engel of Sala on the Vah as our *shohet* and *hazzan*.

Classes were resumed for school children in May 1945, and the new supervisor referred me to the state civilian school, whose new principal was my friend Jozef (Jožko) Šucha, a democrat who had been active in the underground. Having no alternative, I accepted the position temporarily and taught Russian. But I found it more than a little distasteful to teach Slovak pupils, some of whom were the children of Fascists whose hands were stained with Jewish blood. The school had no Jewish pupils at all. Even though the principal and teaching staff were friendly and courteous to me, I could not adjust to this atmosphere or continue living in it. I felt I had been uprooted from the soil in which I had been brought up and transplanted into pagan soil. Tens of years of studying Judaism in *yeshivot* had left their mark and had had a greater impact on me than my secular studies which certified me to teach. My job satisfaction lay primarily in teaching Jewish studies, including Hebrew and Zionist education. Now, after the Holocaust, I asked whether I must sever myself from this heritage and teach the children of a foreign people. My answer was no, I could not graze in foreign pastures.

The state school was located in the building of the Jewish community, which once had housed the Jewish secondary school and, in one of its wings, the Jewish elementary school where I had served as principal. Tvrdoň, my predecessor in the state school, had been the county commandant of the Hlinka Guard, which, in its day, issued orders evacuating our school and the offices of the Jewish community from the building. Now he has disappeared.

One day in June 1945 I had an unusual experience. While I was sitting in the teachers' room, the principal came over to me with a grin and invited me to his office, where a man whose business, he said, was "equity and justice," was waiting to see me. In his office I was approached by a tall, young officer – Alexander Deutelbaum from Zvolen, a former student of Rabbi Frieder's – who requested me to come with him. We went out to the street, where a car was parked in front of the building, and in the car sat Anton Vašek, handcuffed. The officer said, "I just took this despicable hunk of flesh out of a "bunker." And where do you think he was? When your brother left the Franciscan abbey in Beckov, this sly criminal sought refuge there." This officer, Deutelbaum, who still went by the underground name of Doman, also arrested Tiso, Tuka, and Mach in Austria and brought them to Bratislava to stand trial in an international court of justice. Now the fortunes of wickedness which these evil men amassed by thievery will be of no avail to them. Has the day arrived that all wickedness shall dissipate like smoke?[77] Very few of the Nové Mesto community survived – approximately 120 people. Only a small fraction were entire families that had managed to hold out in secret hiding places; most were widows, widowers, and single

---

[77] From the liturgy for the Jewish New Year. Translator's note.

men returning from labor camps. David Levy, who had been among the last deportees in 1944, came back from Mauthausen, and his family returned from Auschwitz, bringing my nephew Amie] Schwarz, a five-year-old boy who had managed to hold out, along with them. The story of how he survived Auschwitz and made the difficult and dangerous journey home is not only fascinating but also testifies to the suffering, resourcefulness and heroism of the children of the Holocaust. Our parents perished at Auschwitz; my sister Esther-Malka, as well as her daughter and husband Ernest Klein perished in Opole in 1942. My brother- in-law Meir Schwarz perished in Majdanek in 1942, and my brother-in-law Aryeh Jungleib died the day Mauthausen was liberated, may the Lord avenge his blood. My sisters, Leah and Rachel, each of whom were widowed and had lost a child, returned from the labor camp in Lippstadt, Germany, bringing with them the young Greta Jungleib.

II. National Jewish Organizations Are Restored

While my brother Rabbi Abraham-Abba was still in Sered he had the idea of uniting both organizations of Jewish communities to work jointly to revitalize Jewish life and restore it from its destruction. On the basis of his experience working hand in hand with Rabbi Weissmandel, developing a relationship of sincere friendship, complete understanding, and public decency, and in view of his personal prestige and good relations with all the public bodies and surviving activists of the Jewish communities, Rabbi Frieder hoped that all the activists and movements would be receptive of his idea of unification. Furthermore, the number of Jews who survived in Slovakia did not justify maintaining two Jewish communities in one city, nor two parallel organizations to handle some 22 to 24 thousand Jews dispersed over 135 congregations, including the southern regions which had been restored to Czechoslovakia. The idea was well-received by most of the public bodies, but not by all the Orthodox circles, especially not *Agudat Israel,* which set fundamental preconditions and, on initial first contact, opposed the proposal to unite.

Thus, Rabbi Frieder opened the central office of the Yeshurun congregations on Jews' Street, corner of Fish Square, in Bratislava, and started work. Many complaints began pouring in from the communities of western Slovakia. (Contact with the east was still hampered by difficulties in transportation.) Rabbi Frieder also initiated cooperation with the Orthodox Bureau and the Joint. These three offices began functioning as soon as Bratislava was liberated.

On April 25, 1945, the representatives of these organizations sent a memorandum to the Slovak People's Council in Bratislava, pointing out that broad echelons of the population, as well as senior officials who remained in office in government bureaus, were still discriminating against Jewish citizens because the laws of the Nazi regime, which served as the foundation for unbridled anti-Semitism, had not yet been explicitly repealed.

The organizations submitted a memorandum requesting:

> That it be officially publicized that all laws, ordinances, and edicts issued by the Fascist Slovak State are null and void, and that Jewish residents have equal rights under the law, like all other citizens loyal to the democratic government of the liberated Czechoslovak Republic. This state has been restored and with it the ethical and cultural values that abhorrently reject Nazism and its cruel manifestations – the concentration camps and death camps with their gas chambers, the

reign of terror, and the suppression of freedom – which were fought by the Red Army, the Allied forces, the Czechoslovak brigades, and the Partisans, among them thousands of Jews who joined the battle as comrades in arms and sacrificed their lives and whose blood was spilled for human ideals. And to assure freedom and equal rights to every person who is loyal to the state, without difference of religion or ethnic origin, we request that directives be issued to all government and public offices, to the local, district, and provincial people's councils, instructing them to respect the rights of the Jews and to come to their side with concrete aid in exceptional circumstances when attempts are made to disadvantage them, and to redress the perversions of justice which have taken place of late throughout Slovakia. To wit:

In Hlohovec, it was announced over the city's network of loudspeakers that Germans, Hungarians, former members of the Hlinka Guard, and Jews must register for work with the offices of the municipality.

In Banská-Bystrica, notices were posted congratulating the Red Army for liberating the city, while at the same time expressing satisfaction that the Jews will soon clear out.

In Bratislava, the official in charge of the department allocating apartments declared that Jews who returned to Bratislava and had previously been residents of the city could receive apartments, but only in the city's suburbs, whereas Jews who were new émigrés would be evacuated to their previous place of residence. According to instructions from the Ministry of Interior, Jews have been the same priority as German and Hungarian members of the Democratic party. Hungarian and German Fascists were evacuated from the city and expelled from the state. The Jews have not been permitted to return to their former apartments, even if these were vacant and empty. Jewish homeowners have been unable to retrieve furniture and household items which were taken into the homes of their Slovak neighbors.

In Trnava, a Jew who returned from the camps to find his factory had been nationalized requested to be appointed its "people's manager," instead of the "Aryanizer" who was still in charge; but the authorities preferred to appoint a stranger as the "people's manager" of the factory.

In public offices there is a widespread principle not to appoint Jews to senior positions, and in general there is a tendency not to employ Jews, even at their former places of work. All of these cases, and many similar ones, have occurred because the Government has not made an outright and unequivocal declaration repealing the entire body of anti-Jewish legislation, and because no official directives have been issued to restore civil rights to the Jews. Officials, hostile to the Jews, have taken advantage of the confused situation to continue following racist laws and discriminatory practices. Such actions contravene the international convention which guarantees human rights and liberty.

We do not wish to make exaggerated accusations. We are aware of the difficulties of the early days after the war. We know that everything must be rebuilt and that the populace must be educated to a new way of life in the spirit of democracy, which also grants and assures equal rights to the Jews, who experienced indescribable suffering under the defeated Nazi regime.

Copies of this memorandum were sent to the central government and the Partisans' organization, whose general secretary was a Jewish major by the name of Vladimir Ružanský (now living in Netanya, Israel).

The memorandum was signed by Rabbi Frieder, chairman of the Yeshurun Federation of Jewish Congregations in Slovakia, Dr. Joseph Grünblatt, general secretary of the Central Bureau of Orthodox Congregations in Slovakia, Dr. Juraj Révész, director of the Bureau for Jewish Relief (the Joint), and Alexander Eckstein, a member of the local (municipal) People's Committee in Bratislava.

This was the first memorandum sent after the war, when the government offices were not yet organized. A Slovak People's Council *(Slovenská národna rada – SNR)*, the supreme legislative body in this part of Czechoslovakia, came into being. It was headed by a man from the Democratic party, Dr. Jozef Letterich. A cabinet, or Assembly of Deputies *(Shor poverenikov – SP)*, under the leadership of a Communist named Dr. Gustav Husák, functioned as the Slovak government. Various People's Committees were also established on the local, district, and provincial levels.

A special national court tried Tiso, Tuka and Mach – who had fled to Austria when the Germans retreated and had been caught in Kremsmünster – and the rest of Slovakia's war criminals, including

Vašek, Koso, Konka, Vašina, and others. Captain Martin Kolár-Abeles located the Slovak war criminals in the area under American conquest and brought them to trial. He succeeded, among other things, in capturing Generals Pulanich and Ištok and the Germans Visliceny, Höfle, Goltz, and Ludin, and brought them to trial in Bratislava.

* * *

Our fellow Jews in the United States were the first to come to our aid. The American Joint Distribution Committee opened a central office in Prague, with Israel Jacobson as director and Henry Levy as assistant; and a branch office in Bratislava, under Mr. Ruby and Dorothy Green, with Dr. Juraj Révész serving as administrative director and Leo Rosenthal as his assistant.

Bratislava's Jewish hospital, old-age home, and orphanage were reopened with aid from the Joint. Sanatoria for children and adults were opened in the High Tatra Mountains. Monthly stipends were given by the Joint to the Jewish communities, which established social committees for distributing the funds among the needy.

The leaders of the Zionist movement – the Zionist Organization, youth movements, and sundry parties and factions – who had remained active in the underground, even when conditions were at their worst, began applying themselves energetically to organizational work. A court was established within the movement to purge its ranks, and all suspected collaborators were put on trial. Flagrant traitors and informers from the period of the insurrection had been tried and liquidated by the Jewish Partisans while they were still in the mountains. Others had received their retribution in the Sered camp. For example, Hochberg was tried by the Partisans and executed. An office of *Agudat Israel* was opened under the direction of Rabbi Hayyim Grünfeld, and a bureau of Hias for aiding émigrés was set up under Dr. Tibor Bársony. Oze (Russian abbreviation for The Society for the Protection of the Health of Jews), headed by Dr. Eugen Verný, and Ort, which ran vocational retraining programs, also opened branch offices. Discharged Jewish soldiers and former Partisans were active in two non-Jewish organizations, in which they held important posts: the Union of Partisans *(Sväz partizánov)* and the Union of Anti-Fascist Political Prisoners in Slovakia *(Sväz protifašistických politických väzňov na Slovensku),* which published a weekly entitled *Hlas Oslobodených (The Voice of the Liberated),* a publication which fought openly and valiantly against the Slovak Fascists and printed articles about the atrocities perpetrated by the murderers in the death camps. Both associations contributed greatly to exposing war criminals and bringing them to justice.

III. The Attitude of the Populace and the Authorities towards the Jews

The early days after the war were extremely difficult. The survivors of the Holocaust, returning from the valley of death to their former residences, were bitterly disappointed. The survivors not only included Jews who had suffered in the death camps, in the mountains and forests, in the underground and "bunkers," but also many Jewish soldiers who returned with decorations of honor and war medals, having fought in the brigades of General Svododa on the eastern front or in the forces of the Allies on the western front. All these freedom fighters and many Jewish Partisans were under the illusion that they would return as victors and expected to be enthusiastically received with open arms, just like the freedom fighters of Marshall Tito's units in Yugoslavia, de Gaulle's soldiers in France, and the Czech forces of General Svoboda, all of whom returned to their liberated countries as emancipated citizens and were treated as the nation's most loyal sons, who, aside from honor and appreciation, also deserved first priority in the reorganization of democratic life after the regime of racist discrimination had been defeated and brought to its knees in a war in which they, too, had participated. But in Slovakia both the Jewish fighters and the victims of Nazi persecution quickly realized that their hopes had been dashed like vain dreams against the blind wall of the state administrative apparatus, the vast majority of which was still staffed by the same clerks who had served under the previous regime – except that they had been swift to exchange their Nazi party cards for cards of the Democratic or Communist parties. These two competing political bodies comprised the national coalition and held the reins of the revolutionary government, for they also made up the People's Committees on the local, district, and provincial levels. Neither the Jewish community nor any other Jewish organization was represented on these councils.

What atmosphere prevailed in Slovakia's towns, and how were the few Jews who began to reappear on the streets received? Most of the residents, who had waxed rich from Jewish property, remembered well the propaganda of the Hlinka Guard – the pillagers of Jewish wealth and annihilators of the Jewish communities – who had led a life of luxury and hedonism. They disseminated propaganda that "the Jews, who will return after the war as the allies of Stalin and Churchill, will take over the Czechoslovak state, will avenge their blood, and will take an eye for an eye, repaying the harm done them in kind. What we did to them they will do to us therefore we must beat them wherever they are and do everything we can to assure that they shall not return." These were the words of the murderers who during the insurrection combed the mountains and villages, slaughtering every Jew they caught and burning the cabins of peasants who dared help the Jews. Although these pigs fled with a vast fortune across the border and were taken in by other states, nevertheless their teachings and views remained engraved in the memory of their supporters, who had also benefited from the vast booty which was distributed among anyone who lent the Nazi regime a helping hand.

When the war was over and the first Jews began returning utterly destitute to their former places of residence, their erstwhile good gentile neighbors brought them a fraction of the belongings, the silver and gold, the jewelry and other movable possessions, that they had received for safe-keeping or had robbed and plundered from the homes of the deported Jews. Mostly they did this out of fear, to appease those who were likely henceforth to be influential in the government. However, after a week or two they, too, realized that the Fascists had exaggerated in their propaganda and that there was no need to fear the Jews. For, they discovered, these Zhids were non-violent, and even the Partisans and soldiers from the brigades, who returned with their arms, did not make use of their rifles and pistols. Seeing that the Jews were acting with restraint, the gentiles concluded that there was no urgency in restoring the possessions of the Jews who returned later from the more distant camps of Germany. The excuse commonly given by the gentiles was: "The Rumanian and Russian soldiers of the Red Army who liberated us asked for presents and mementos, and since the Guardists told us you would no longer return, we divided your property among them. The soldiers who liberated us deserve something, after all."

Such was the behavior of the Slovak Christians, who retained the wealth of entire families of which no members returned. They had no guilty conscience, since everything was vested in the law; and even the local authorities turned a blind eye to injuries done to the Jews. Christianity under the Fascist regime had failed in its moral obligation to defend man, and Christianity under the democratic regime had proven itself bankrupt. It did not even attempt to stand up for the commandment of love thy neighbor, which it champions in theory.

The Jews returned in poor health and shaken to the depths of their souls at the loss of their dear ones. Their first aspiration was to go in quest of their kin, from whom they had parted three years ago. They began asking after the fate of their relatives, to see if any survivors remained. Faced with the loss of their dear ones, whom no one could bring back to life, the material losses which they suffered were practically insignificant, and no one took strong measures to restore them.

In this crisis, as well, we stood up to the test and proved our moral rectitude. This time, too, the precept "thou shalt not take vengeance, nor bear any grudge" prevailed over the rightful demand that what had been stolen from us be returned. Vengeance would not bring us consolation; and we hoped only that the war criminals and people who wrought the Holocaust would be brought to justice and punished for their crimes against mankind. Every nationalistic Jew, whether or not he observed the commandments, and even assimilated Jews and converts from Judaism, perceived clearly that, even after the evil Fascist regime had collapsed, the anti-Semites had no fear and continued to walk abroad with their heads held high. We shall have to fight to win our moral and materials rights, "for truth hath stumbled in the broad place, and uprightness cannot enter" (Isaiah 59:14).

* * *

Undisguised anti-Semitism was commonplace in daily life. The populace revealed its true complexion, and even the heads of the revolutionary People's Committees at times displayed a hostile stand.

In Surany, a town in the region that had been annexed to Hungary, the local People's Committee imposed forced labor on the Jews. They took people who had returned from the concentration camps, who were suffering from malnutrition and disease, and instead of sending them to sanatoria, placed them in work gangs with activists of the Hungarian Nazi party, the *Nyilas*. This practice became routine. The Committee apparently believed that the Jews could always be penalized.

The Jews in Bánovce, Prievidza, and Topolčany were deprived of their civil rights, and their petitions were rejected on the grounds that they were of Jewish origin, plain and simple. And this was done in accordance with the racist anti-Jewish legislation which was still in force in the local governments.

A policeman in Topolčany witnessed Jews being forced off a public bus and did nothing to defend them. Posters, graffiti, pamphlets, and anti-Semitic pictures made their appearance in Banská-Bystrica, the capital of the insurrection, in Nové Mesto, whose inhabitants were relatively tolerant, and in other cities, as well. Various newspapers, such as *Tatran* and *Čas (The Times)*, as well as periodicals and local leaflets, published articles besmirching the Jews. The old accusation against the Jews, that they are disseminators of the German language and culture and that many others are adherents of Hungarian culture and speak this language, gained currency once more. The assailants seeking our ill were not prepared to accept the explanation that the adults in the Jewish population had received their education in these languages, which had been the local languages in the time of Austro-Hungarian domination, and that therefore the Jews speak German and Hungarian – because they had no alternative, and not because of any national affiliation to these peoples. The fact is that their children, and the entire younger generation, were educated in Slovak public or parochial schools and use nothing but Slovak as their spoken language.

The local People's Committees in Senica and Liptovský-Svätý-Mikuláš refused to issue Jews certificates attesting their national-political probity, even if they had declared Slovak nationality in the past. (During the early months after the war, citizens were required to enclose with their petitions a document which confirmed that the petitioner had not collaborated with the Nazi regime and that his political past was untainted. The political probity of citizens was examined by special committees, established in government offices in all sectors and in all public organizations. Of the various national minorities, only Hungarians and anti-fascist Germans who remained in Slovakia were eligible for these documents.)

A blood libel was fabricated against a 12-year-old Jewish lad in Žilina, who was seen playing with a gun; and rumors were started that he had shot his Christian friend. Former Jewish factory owners in Bratislava and Bánovce were arrested on a number of pretexts, while the Aryanizers, Nazi collaborators running their factories, went undisturbed. In many places Jews were imprisoned together with Fascists and members of the Hlinka Guard, without being interrogated and without being informed of the reason for their incarceration. Government representatives and party leaders were not ashamed to declare that their anti-Jewish policies stemmed from the will of the people. Others proclaimed that they had received instructions from above. Such assertions were made in a public lecture by Jožo Zvonár-Tieň in Piešťany, and by Committee Chairman Repka in Bánovce. Jews who returned from the camps did not receive apartments, despite explicit directives. The Jews of eastern Slovakia and of Komárno and Krupina complained that they had not received UNRRA rations, even though, according to the international convention, this aid was intended first and foremost for repatriates.

Riots broke out in Topolčany and almost turned into a massacre. The Jews encountered difficulties everywhere; the Aryanizers, vexed that the Jewish owners had "dared" return to their homes, did not want to give back what they had stolen from the Jews. In 1944, aided by the Germans, the Guardists in Topolčany did all they could to prevent Jews from returning to their homes and businesses and employed the cruelest of means, even murder, to achieve their ends. Now that the Jews had returned, they continued using intimidation tactics and threats, hoping to chase them away by use of violence. To this end they staged a libel, which served as the pretext for the riots which erupted in the city on September 24, 1945. The first victim was

Dr. Karol Berger, who was vaccinating children in the state-run elementary school, previously a Catholic parochial school where the children of the most radical members of the Hlinka Guard studied. The same day a group of rioters organized and accused the Jewish doctor of poisoning their children and demanded that he be tried and punished. The libel spread like wildfire. Rioters broke into the doctor's clinic, dealt him a fatal beating, and incited the rabble to a pogrom against the Jews. They broke into Jewish homes, attacked men and women, humiliated them, and broke their housewares. Approximately 50 Jews were wounded and extensive damage was done to their property. Soldiers who had been sent to maintain order and protect the Jews actually joined the rioters, who were demanding that the Jews be kicked out of the city. The Jews were also attacked in localities around Topolčany and were forced to flee for their lives. Personal intervention by Dr. Letterich, chairman of the Slovak People's Council, put an end to the riots. The Czechoslovak press refrained from mentioning the riots, but foreign newspapers publicized the scandalous affair.

This attitude on the part of the local authorities and the populace left their mark on the Jews. Reality had to be faced and the proper conclusions drawn.

The world is all the same. The situation was not different in other cities. In Nové Mesto, too, when it came to the attitude of the populace and the authorities towards the Jews, our path was hardly lined with roses. The commanders of the Hlinka Guard – Pavel Holec, Stephan Vlášek, Jozef Albert, Gašpaník and Benko – disappeared from the scene; but the rest of the activists, such as the Hlinka Guardist Faro Hurtik and the entire gang that had extorted, robbed, pillaged, harassed and threatened the Jews all the years of the Independent Slovak State and had actively participated in all the actions and campaigns against the Jews, including the *chytačka* – capturing and deporting Jews – remained in the Jews' apartments, which they had come to view as their own, and kept hold of the Jews' possessions. Whenever they saw a Jew walking down the street, they did not hesitate to hurl out a curse. As for regrets or feelings of guilt, they had none of these!

Yet the world goes its way. The city notables continued to patronize the barbershop of the courteous Guardist Hurtik, who, along with his colleagues, now began to curry favor with the new rulers, and the rulers, on their part, saw to it that Hurtik and his cronies came to no harm. There is nothing new under the sun. The boot-licking opportunists stashed away their black Hlinka Guard uniforms and accustomed themselves to red. Everything remained as before; only the mayors had changed.

* * *

The local revolutionary government, known as the People's Committee, was controlled by two parties, the Democrats and the Communists, in a parity coalition. In Nové Mesto the Evangelists in the Democratic party had the upper hand. The Jews knew from experience that the ranks of the Evangelists were filled with duplicitous people who, while speaking kindly, bore hatred in their hearts. The Nové Mesto branch of the Communist party had at one time had Jewish activists in its ranks, but they had been the first to be deported, and not one of them survived. The Communists were represented on the People's Committee by a man of dubious character and an unsavory past. Now that he had been appointed deputy chairman, he came out with the view that the Jews whom Hitler wiped out had been the good Jews, and that those who were left were capitalist Jews who had collaborated with the Nazis and were to blame for the war because they had used their money to finance the Nazi war effort for six years and, on top of this, had bribed and paid-off the local rulers. With aggressive persistence, this man managed to take control of the municipality. The two parties began competing for popular support and, in order not to "arouse the fury of the people," were not the least bit responsive *to* Jewish requests. The difference between them was that the Democratic chairman phrased his refusals politely, whereas his Communist deputy rejected the Jews crudely.

Because of their distrustfulness and mutual suspicion of one another these representatives sat at first in the same room. The first time I was given a reception as a representative of the Jewish community I managed to make two requests: that the repatriated Jews be given representation in the People's Committee, and that part of the equipment which had been plundered from the Ohel David Home be returned so that temporary quarters could be set up for the repatriates until they could settle in their own apartments. The deputy chairman immediately burst out sharply against Rabbi Frieder, saying, "Does your rabbi lack funds? Where did he get the money necessary to establish and run the institution? After all, he supported hundreds of people, and bribed and collaborated with the Fascists! The equipment in the old-age home was distributed among the people, to the old folk in the city, and will not be returned. We are not going to rouse the wrath of the people over such a trifling matter!" The Democratic chairman was embarrassed and, to extricate himself from the predicament, referred me to Jožko Šucha, an active member of the People's Committee, who had tried to help the Jews during the Holocaust.

Several days later Šucha gave me a letter, dated April 19, 1945 and signed by the chairman, Eduard Tvarožek, appointing me to the Social Committee of the municipality. I was never invited to meetings of the committee; the appointment was fictitious, solely for appearances' sake. All the decisions, including social problems, war indemnities to all residents, etc., were made privily. Rehabilitating the Jews and their community, with its demolished institutions, and restoring the rights of Jewish residents were not issues which perturbed the city fathers. Even a month later, when it became clear that the deportees to Poland would no longer return from the death camps and that 90% of the city's Jews had for a certainty been annihilated, the new city fathers still did not raise an outcry of shock and horror, or express solidarity with the Jews, or admonish the German murderers and the Slovaks who had been drawn along with them and still had not shown the least sign of regret for their actions nor given any indication that the horrors of the war had left them with the slightest pangs of conscience.

IV. The Association of Persecuted Persons

There were Jews during the Holocaust who, wearing the yellow star of David, said that the badge of calumny sewn on their garments should be safeguarded as an object which some day would be valuable. These Jews naively believed that after the war every Jew would become *persona grata* in the liberated state and that their rehabilitation would be spontaneous and immediate. Others were not so overly optimistic and did not openly identify themselves as Jews for fear that their Jewishness would be a burden to them. There was also a third group converts from Judaism, who rejected the mold from which they were made and who had only come under the common cover of "Jew" because of racist legislation. The converts were convinced that they would not even have to mention whence they came; they hoped their new religion would defend them and that by Christian charity they would be restored to their former glory.

As all these groups became disabused of their illusions, they came to the realization that they would have to fight to right the wrongs and redress the injustices done to them, that they would have to work to enact special laws to restore their property and rights, legislation which would rescind the extensive and complex legislation of the Nazi regime in Slovakia. Therefore, it was decided to establish an umbrella organization for all Jews, as defined by the racist legislation and not by one's affiliation with a specific Jewish community. The initiative for this move came from the Yeshurun Federation, at the suggestion of its general secretary, Dr. Winterstein, who was joined by the leaders of the community and its finest lawyers, engineers, doctors, and other professionals, as well as farmers, former industrialists, and members of other vocations. The organization was called the Association of Persons Racially Persecuted by the Fascist Regime in Slovakia *(Sdruženie fasistickým režimom rasove prenasledovaných na Slovensku - SRP)*. Dr. Eugen Verný was its chairman, and Mr. Lipshitz, Arthur Skála, Rabbi Frieder, and general secretary Dr. Winterstein were its deputy directors. An executive committee was also elected, as well as a legal committee comprised of excellent jurists and charged with the paramount task of drafting the laws necessary for a new constitution righting the wrongs done to the Jews. Egon Gold was chairman of this committee.

The Slovak People's Council, the supreme legislative body, actually promulgated an edict in 1944, published in the codex of orders of the People's Council in Banská-Bystrica and known as edict number 1/44, abrogating all the laws of racial discrimination, with the aim of providing in one sweeping law a comprehensive solution to the problem of discrimination against the Jews. Although the legislature proved its good intentions – significant in and of itself – the law was never actually implemented and remained an idealization on paper; discrimination had only been done away with in theory. Therefore, the legal committee of the Association of Persecuted Persons drafted a memorandum on the restoration of rights and property to persons considered Jews pursuant to the Jewish Codex (edict # 198/4l, dated September 9, 1941). In so doing, the representatives of the Jewish organizations hoped to hasten the abrogation of the discriminatory legislation. It should be noted that the edict on abrogation of racial discrimination did not specify the date the law came into effect. Jurists' opinions were divided over this date, some claiming it to be the date of publication in the official law journal, others claiming it to be retroactive to the date the discriminatory legislation was introduced *(ex nunc vs. ex tunc)*. The authorities, however, found to the disadvantage of the weak Jewish minority and proclaimed the law to be effective as of the day it was published. This meant that the Jews did not have to bear the mark of calumny, but that the wrongs and damages which had been done to them over the course of close to six years – not to mentions the loss of life of their dear ones, which has no earthly restitution – would go without compensation, since these damages had been done under the law of the Nazi state, which had not been retroactively abrogated. The legal conclusions and their implications for society were extremely serious and far-reaching. The result was an absurd situation in which the legal norms in the Czech Republic were totally different from those in Slovakia. The difference was especially prominent with respect to the law on nationalization of agricultural property. Edict number 12/45, issued by the president, prevented discrimination against the Jews in the Czech Republic; but in Slovakia, pursuant to the Slovak law on nationalization, which made it possible to perpetrate the dastardly injustice of proclaiming the Jews, who spoke German and Hungarian, to be "Germans or Hungarians, traitors to and enemies of the Slovak people," Jewish agricultural property was nationalized along with property belonging to Germans and Hungarians.

The seventeen-page memorandum was submitted in July 1945, jointly by the Association of Persecuted Persons and the two central organizations of the Jewish community – the Yeshurun Federation and the Orthodox Bureau – and was sent to President Beneš, Chairman of the Slovak People's Council Dr. Jozef Letterich, as well as the ministers of the central government in Prague, the ministers of Slovakia, the party leaders of the National Front, and the heads of the trade unions.

Part I of the memorandum reviewed the condition of the Jews to the present and listed all the worrisome facts testifying to continued racial discrimination in contravention to the constitution of the state and the president's edict of May 19, 1945, which explicitly applied *de Jure* and *de facto* to the area of Slovakia, although for unknown reasons was not recognized in this part of the country.

The second part of the memorandum included suggestions for redressing this perversion of justice as quickly as possible by enacting legislation to restore the Jews' rights and property, elaborating on these rights from a variety of angles: moral, political, legal, economic, commercial, social, and ideological.

The memorandum concluded with a request that the Jewish organizations be given representation on the Slovak People's Council, not only to stand up for the equitable rights of formerly persecuted persons, but also to explain and clarify the situation, which at the time needed to be brought to the attention of the Council. As loyal citizens of the state, the Jews wished to fulfill their duties yet also requested that they be granted their full rights.

V. A Year after the Insurrection

At the end of August 1945, a year after the outbreak of the Slovak revolt, ceremonies and celebrations were held throughout the state. Our congregation in Nové Mesto marked this event in the renovated Orthodox synagogue and invited local government officials to join in the celebration. I quote from parts of my speech on this occasion:

During the latter days of August 1944, approximately thirty Jewish youths were working in the Ohel David Old-Age Home. Upon learning of the army's insurrection in the barracks, they were filled with enthusiasm and immediately enlisted to fight the German conqueror. Their jubilance, however, was short-lived. The lads were dressed in uniform and had already taken up guns when orders suddenly came to release the Jewish youths and disarm them. The Guardists went into action and wrote down the names of the Jews who had volunteered. But the enthusiastic young men refused to remain passive. Knowing that their friends in the labor camps were secretly amassing arms and preparing to launch an armed struggle when the time was ripe, they expressed their desire to join the fighters. They turned to the Jewish community in an organized bloc, and I, acting on behalf of Rabbi Frieder, gave them a sum of money. The anti-Jewish propaganda in the Nazi Slovak state was based on a pack of lies but was accurate about one thing – that many "Zhido-Bolsheviks" were participating in the insurrection – and therefore, the Nazi Slovaks claimed, the Jews must be wiped out as enemies of the people. Today, strangely enough, there is a tendency to overlook the contribution which the Jews made to the insurrection. It is hard to say how many Jews took part in the Slovak uprising, how many fell in battle, how many fell captive and were executed by the Germans and the Guardists, how many fought and lost their lives in the brigades on the eastern and western fronts. Recent studies are gradually revealing that Jewish participation in the insurrection was several times higher than the relative participation of the non-Jewish Slovak population. This has been confirmed by the Ministry of Defense and the Partisans' Union. Many other Jews, who lived underground, would have gone to battle had someone been available to care for their families and see to it that they not be left to the dogs, to be deported and annihilated.

We commune with the memory of the martyrs of the Holocaust, and the valiant fighters who rallied to the cause and ignited the flame of revolt, among them the Jewish Partisans from Nové Mesto on the Vah: Tibor Bauer, Laco Guttman, lgnac Weiss, Stephan Mészáros, Erich Polizer, Oscar Fiala, Vojtech Friedman, Albin Kornhauser, Ondrej Rotman, and many others whose fate is unknown to us, may the Lord avenge their blood. They fell in the fight for freedom, that we may live as citizens with equal rights, without suffering discrimination. We, on our part, shall fight for the victory of democracy in the spirit of Masaryk, whose watchword was "the Truth shall win."

VI. Evacuating Communal Graves

When, in 1944, the *Nyilas* (the Magyar SS) were terrorizing

Hungary and expelling Jews to death camps, transports were also sent to a labor camp in Petržalka, a suburb inhabited by Germans and separated from Bratislava by the Danube River. Petržalka had been annexed to Germany in 1938.

After the war, when Petržalka was restored to the jurisdiction of Bratislava, the Nazi atrocities against the Jews incarcerated in the camp came to light. Conditions here were similar to the concentration camps in Germany. The SS maltreated the inmates, Jews from Hungary, subjecting them to violence, back-breaking labor, humiliation, starvation and torture. Only faith that the end of the war was near gave the few who remained strength to survive.

In March 1945, approximately 800 people were living in the camp. The inmates heard the canons rumbling on the approaching front at night and rejoiced over every bomb that came crashing down in the vicinity. Salvation was close at hand. On April 4, Bratislava was liberated by the Red Army. On the other side of the Danube the persecuted prisoners heard echoes of the jubilant cries of Bratislava's liberated citizens. As the hours passed, they sat in fearful expectation, in prayer and hope, awaiting the moment they, too, would be liberated. Then, on the verge of liberation, terrible disaster befell them. At the last moment before the liberating army arrived, the goose-steppers ordered the inmates to evacuate the camp and flee the Russian advance.

This fateful flight became the inmates' death march. The SS man Koch, in charge of the commando, decided, along with six of his fellow murderers, to wipe out all the inmates as they marched along, and gunned them down from behind. Over five hundred Jews were slaughtered by the Nazis in this insane and beastly deed. The local residents covered the bodies of the victims with earth where they had fallen, in the ditches along the road. Six months later the bodies were exhumed and properly buried in the local cemetery.

In 1946, in the national court in Bratislava, an undertaker named Prepelica testified against the 33-year-old SS man Koch, who was found guilty and punished. His six colleagues were brought to trial in Vienna. According to testimony of the few survivors, approximately 1,600 inmates passed through Petržalka; most of them either died of starvation and hard labor, or were shot in the death march on their way to Mauthausen or murdered in the camp itself.

The plot where these martyrs were buried belongs to the Jewish community of Bratislava. Many of them were removed from their graves and transferred by relatives to Hungary. In cooperation with the Budapest Jewish community, the martyrs' relatives built a memorial on the site, and every year, on the 20th of Sivan, the Jews of Hungary and Bratislava hold a joint memorial ceremony for the martyrs of the Holocaust. Thirteen individual graves and a large communal grave containing the bodies of five hundred martyrs cry out from the ground: Remember, and do not forget!

Many cities had cemeteries with communal graves which the Jews themselves had been forced to dig before they were murdered. Mass graves were discovered in areas where battles were fought between the Partisans and the German army in cooperation with the Hlinka Guard. The task of exhuming these graves was begun in the summer of 1945. Most of the victims buried in the two hundred or so communal graves which were dis covered were Jews; but the authorities did not stress this fact. Moreover, it was difficult to identify the bodies. Of the 372 victims found in Kremnička, 69 were children, some of them with pacifiers still in their mouths. The bodies of the paratroopers from the Land of Israel – Haviva Reich,

Raphi Reis, and Zvi ben-Yaakov, may the Lord avenge their blood – were also found there. After the war they were brought to a proper burial on Mount Herzl, in Jerusalem. Also found in Kremnička were the bodies of Rabbi Frieder's wife, Roži Frieder, and their daughter Gitka. They were given a Jewish burial in Bratislava. The corpses of 21 children were found in Turčiansky-Svätý-Martin. Many victims were found in Bánovce, Topolčany, Prievidza, Zvolen, Ružomberok, Rimavská Sobota, and elsewhere.

In his book, *Tiso and the Insurrection – Documents,* Colonel Dr. Anton Rašla, the government prosecutor in the national court, states that the Slovak villages of Klak, Ostrý Grúň, Hažlín, and Tokajik shared a similar fate to the Czech village of Lidice, where most of the men in the town's peasant population were shot by the Germans because they had helped the Partisans. He accuses Tiso and his collaborators of crimes against humanity on account of the hundreds of Slovaks who were killed, but makes no mention of the seventy thousand Jewish victims. In his speech for the prosecution his only allusion to the Jews was an oblique and slightly scoffing remark that "there is still a large group of people who would like to send other citizens, who have slightly different shaped noses or different political views, to the crematoria. These people are preparing for a Third World War. But the Slovak people has suffered enough from the atrocities of war and condemns these opportunists."

The tendency to disregard the Jewish people and to attribute the suffering and sacrifices of the war to all nationalities, in this case the Slovaks, found expression immediately upon conclusion of the war and has been growing steadily with the passage of time, so that the world will eventually forget that back in the far distant past Slovakia once had Jewish communities, as well. To give an example, in 1968 the municipality of Nové Mesto on the Vah published a pamphlet on the history of the city, which made no mention of a Jewish community. The old Jewish cemetery is mentioned in the list of historical sites; but it has since been destroyed. Thus, the next edition will no longer mention the word Jew at all, and there will certainly be no need to express regret for the crimes against humanity that were perpetrated by the Slovaks, crimes that were committed on the instigation of major war criminals. True, the latter have been sentenced to death, but many of their collaborators have come out clean, and some of them, even ahead.

VII. Uniting and Rehabilitating the Jewish Communities

Several months after the Holocaust the leaders of the Jewish communities came to the realization that it was both pointless and unfeasible to maintain two, small, separate Jewish congregations in every city, and that the congregations must be united and joint institutions established to provide for the religious needs of the community. This necessitated reorganizing the structure of the Jewish communities and changing the legal status of the congregations in Slovakia, following the example set by Hungary. The Czech Republic had always had a single central organization for all the Jewish communities. The legal authority to decide on a merger of the communities rested with the Ministry of Education and Culture. Minister Ladislav Novomeský expressed his support for this practical and logical proposal, and on September 15, 1945, issued an ordinance regarding organization of the Jewish communities in Slovakia, which was approved by the government, the Assembly of Deputies. According to this resolution, the two central Jewish organizations would cease functioning and would merge into a single center, to be called the Central Union of Jewish Communities in Slovakia (Ústredný *sväz židovských náboženských obcí na Slovensku,* henceforth the Union of Jewish Communities or Central Union). Likewise, all the congregations in the cities of Slovakia, which previously belonged to one or the other of the two central organizations, would merge into single congregations, under the title of Jewish Religious Community.

The property of all the congregations, whether extant or defunct, as in localities whose Jewish residents had either been wiped out or had left, would revert to the Union of Jewish Communities, which was delegated to reorganize the Jewish communities and to assist in reestablishing and maintaining their institutions. The union was given exclusive power to ratify election of Jewish community representatives and decisions of the communities. The congregations were not entitled to sell or transfer immovable assets without the union's approval. The union was charged to prepare by-laws for the new central organization and the congregations forthwith and to hold democratic elections for the offices of the Jewish community.

Chief Rabbi Armin Frieder was appointed president of the Union of Jewish Communities and was requested to set up an executive committee of 18 members from all factions of Slovak Jewry.

The representatives of the Orthodox community in Bratislava, Rabbi Mordechai Lebowitz and Chairman of the Orthodox Bureau Salomon Weber, appealed this resolution to the supreme court, but their appeal was rejected. The ordinance became law upon its publication in the law books.

In Bratislava the Jewish quarter and the center of the city remained without a synagogue. The Great Synagogue on Zámocká Street had been badly damaged in the bombings, and the neologist synagogue on Jews' Street had become a storehouse for books. After the 1942 deportations, tens of thousands of holy books owned by Jews who had been deported to Poland were collected in this synagogue. A number of learned men were employed cataloging Torah scrolls and ritual objects and storing them away, and by virtue of this work they were spared from deportation. The authorities were well aware of the value of this treasure of books and therefore supported the storage effort, with the intention of one day taking advantage of the vast wealth incorporated in the collection. The librarians, however, skillfully maneuvered their handling of the books in such a way that the books remained on the shelves and, when the war was over, were handed out to anyone who requested. Thousands of books were transferred overseas by rabbis, *yeshiva* students, and religious émigrés, and many Torah-scrolls and religious objects were brought to Israel by immigrants from Slovakia. The books that remained were given to the Great Orthodox Synagogue.

In 1945, Rabbi Armin Frieder went to London to raise the necessary funds to finance the restoration of Slovakia's synagogues. He decided to revamp the former neologist synagogue and redesign its interior along the lines of Hungary's Orthodox synagogues, as he had done in other Jewish communities. A platform for Torah-reading was built in the center of the prayer hall and a partition was set up to separate the women from the men. A plaque commemorating Slovakia's 70,000 martyrs, victims of the Holocaust, was hung in the synagogue's corridor. (Both synagogues in the Jewish quarter were destroyed in the 70's.)

By 5706 (1946) the Jewish communities had been rehabilitated, and Jewish organizations functioned in every city. A vast amount of social work had been accomplished by the Joint, which established a special fund to provide loans and reinstate incomes so that the Jews, who had to rebuild their lives again from the very beginning, were assured a minimal level of subsistence. The Zionist movement reactivated its branches, and the Land of Israel Office appointed deputies to the Jewish National Fund. Once more Slovakia became a transit station for repatriates from Germany and Poland, making their way to the Land of Israel.

The Central Union of Jewish Communities was run by Rabbi Frieder, Dr. Winterstein and, representing the Orthodox, Dr. Ernest Abeles, who served as treasurer and chairman of the finance committee. Work was organized according to the guidelines agreed upon on January 27, 1946, at a symposium which was held in the Ministry of Education and Culture and in which the representatives of the Orthodox and Yeshurun congregations participated. However, even after these deliberations, certain articles remained a bone of contention. It became evident that the ultra-Orthodox had not changed their position, and another round of negotiations was required to smooth over differences. Nevertheless, this controversy did not prevent the Jewish congregations in Slovakia's cities from solidifying.

Every congregation that held services on Sabbaths and Jewish festivals and maintained a *shohet* and coordinator for Jewish community affairs was considered viable. There was a great shortage of teachers, rabbis, and *shohatim;* hence courses to train kosher butchers and teach religious subjects were planned. Jewish schools, however, were not opened because there were too few children and because the reform in education had abolished all parochial schools and henceforth only allowed for state schools. Every community was responsible for its own religious education. One of the central problems of the Jewish communities was to provide instruction in Hebrew, prayers, and religious subjects. The World Jewish Congress offered enrichment programs for teachers in Jewish studies, but these programs had no subscribers; for the general atmosphere in the Jewish communities was to recover from the trauma of the Holocaust and leave Slovakia. The Jews waited with bated breath for the day that the gates of the Land of Israel would be thrown open. Thus, the problem of Hebrew and Jewish studies instruction remained unsolved.

VIII. Rabbi Frieder's Death

Although the Central Union of Jewish Communities grappled with the difficult problems swamping it, solutions to these problems were not found, and they continued weighing down upon the leader of Slovak Jewry, who was unable to answer all the needs of the community. In the spring of 1946, Rabbi Frieder went to London to raise money and request assistance from the British Jewish community. In the middle of his trip, he was taken ill and hospitalized in London. After three weeks he returned home and resumed work but never fully regained his strength. On the Feast of Weeks, 5706 (1946), in the synagogue, which was filled to the point of overflowing, he delivered his last sermon, dedicated to the memory of Slovakia's seventy thousand Jewish martyrs. The rabbi called on the Jews of Slovakia to band together and. prepare themselves for immigration to Israel. "We live by the merits of the martyrs who sacrificed their lives; but life in the Diaspora lacks significance," he said, and concluded with a rallying call: "Next year in Jerusalem!"

On the 20th of Sivan, 5706, he was operated on, but his heart had grown weaken, and on the eve of the Sabbath of the Scriptural reading of *Shelah,* the 22nd of Sivan (June 21, 1946), he returned his soul to his Maker. Sivan 22 is also the anniversary of the death of Rabbi David Deutsch of blessed memory, the eponym of Ohel David. On this day, all the years he officiated in Nové Mesto, Rabbi Frieder used to hold a commemorative celebration, timed to coincide with the conclusion of studying an order of Mishnah or a tractate of Talmud. His soul departed that day, ten days before his 35th birthday. His death came as a shock to the community, and it was even rumored that some treachery had been committed during the surgery, since the rabbi was scheduled to testify in court against war criminals in the Nazi Slovak government. These rumors were totally unfounded. The surgeon was Professor Koch, one of the world's righteous gentiles, a friend of the rabbi, who had done much to save Jewish lives during the Holocaust.

The Slovak press and radio paid tribute to Rabbi Frieder, praising his personality, and *ha-Aretz* published a full article on his person and works, written by his friend and colleague in the movement and fellow worker in rescue operations during the Holocaust, Dr. Oscar Neumann.

His funeral, held on Sunday the 24th of Sivan, 5706 (June 23, 1946), was attended by many public figures, foremost Chairman of the Slovak People's Committee Dr. Jozef Letterich, representatives of the Jewish communities, and vast numbers of people. Dr. Paul März eulogized him in the name of the Zionist movement, Dr. Winterstein took leave from the rabbi in the name of the central organization of Jewish congregations, and I parted from my brother in the name of the family and the Nové Mesto Jewish community.

On the first anniversary of the rabbi's death, an unveiling ceremony was held at his graveside. The tombstone was erected by the Central Union of Jewish Communities. The vice-chairman of the union, R. Jacob Hoff, who was the representative of the ultra-Orthodox Jewish community, gave a eulogy on behalf of the union. I eulogized the rabbi in the name of the Nové Mesto congregation; Dr. Spitz of Brno represented the Council of Jewish Communities in Bohemia and Moravia *(Rada Židovských nábožensých obč v Čechách a na Morave);* Dr. Vojtech Winterstein gave a eulogy on behalf of the Union of Persecuted Persons; Alexander Pressburger spoke for the Bratislava community, Moritz Seidmann for the Zvolen community, and Dr. Paul Valach for the workers in the Central Union of Jewish Communities. Cantor Samuel Landerer led the prayer for the deceased, and the rabbi's son, eight-year-old Gideon, who was preparing to immigrate to Israel with his stepmother, recited *kaddish.*

Chapter Two

The Jewish Community

Works in a United Front

(5704-1947)

"That they may all form a single band to do
Thy will with a perfect heart"
(From the High Holy Day service)

I. Activities of the Union of Jewish Communities under United Management

After my brother's death, Dr. Winterstein offered me the chairmanship of the Central Union of Jewish Communities. Dr. Winterstein was a successful lawyer and performed his public duties in the community and in all the other Jewish organizations as a volunteer. The Central Union of Jewish Communities was not only supposed to provide religious services but also to fill an important organizational, social, and political role in the life of Slovak Jewry. Therefore, the void left by the death of Rabbi Frieder, the first mover towards the idea of unification, had to be filled without delay.

My candidacy for this office was rapidly publicized, and several congregations invited me to participate in various activities. Among the invitations to which I responded was a request by Dr. Leo Révész, head beadle of the synagogue on Jews' Street in Bratislava, that I deliver a sermon on topical matters, in Slovak, at the *Kol* Nidre service. Since then, the Bratislava community has also invited me to speak at its special services on national holidays, which were attended by representatives of the regime.

On Sunday following the weekly Scriptural reading of *Lekh lekha,* 5706 (October 27, 1946), four Partisans who had fallen in the vicinity of my home town of Prievidza were brought to a Jewish burial, and I obliged the community by taking part in the funeral service at their request. The following day, Czechoslovakia's Day of Independence, the renovated Prievidza synagogue was inaugurated. In this house of prayer my father and teacher – may the Lord avenge his blood – brought me and all the youth of the area up to be devout, God-fearing Jews. The speeches and prayer for the state were delivered in Slovak. After the war the community numbered around 80 people, and on the High Holy Days Jews from the entire area used to assembly here for public worship. Several new Jewish families, who worked in the local industries, had also settled in the city.

During the winter I joined the negotiations to establish a directorship for the Central Union of Jewish Communities which would be comprised of a coalition of the various factions and would be acceptable to all. Three people were elected to the board: I, as the candidate of the Zionist movement, was elected chairman; Eugen Hoff, secretary of the Orthodox community in Nitra, was made vice-chairman; and Dr. Vojtech Winterstein became general secretary.

Eighteen people were elected to the executive committee, nine from the Yeshurun Federation and nine from the representatives of the Orthodox communities, among them five members of *Agudat Israel* and four members of the Mizrachi movement. It was agreed that the sole authority to rule on matters of *kashrut,* personal and marital status, and *halakhah* in general would rest with a rabbinical court recognized by the Board of Orthodox Rabbis. A committee for strengthening the faith would be set up under the aegis of the Central Union of Jewish Communities. This committee would be in charge of the administration of religious services and would be subject to instructions from the Board of Rabbis. There would be only one united congregation in any Slovak city, and if a congregation decided to call itself Orthodox, the central organization would honor this decision and approve it.

According to the agreement, I took office in Kislev 5706 (December 1946), and on the 14th of Shvat, 5706 (February 4, 1947), the new executive committee held a festive meeting, attended by representatives from the Jewish organizations and many guests.

All the congratulatory remarks stressed the importance of unity and cooperation between the various trends of Slovak Jewry and took note of the great contribution made by Rabbi Frieder of blessed memory, whose dreams of unity dated back to his labor camp days.

Later in the meeting the following committees were elected: social work and supply, headed by Oscar Krasniansky; finance, headed by Dr. Ernest Abeles; economics, headed by Alexander Pressburger; committee for strengthening the faith and providing religious services, headed by Rabbi Mordechai Lebowitz, whose responsibilities included seeing to all religious services: kosher slaughtering of meat, ritual baths, *eruvin* (ways of extending the limits on movement and carrying on the Sabbath), religious education in the state schools, establishing *Talmud Torah* institutions, yeshivas, battei midrash, and synagogues, supplying matzah, etrogs and lulavs, wine for *kiddush,* philacteries, *mezuzot,* and Torah scrolls, and establishing rabbinical courts. The executive board also decided to set up a committee, headed by Attorney Dr. Singer, to draft by-laws for the Central Union of Jewish Communities.

The executive board was granted an interview with Minister of Education Ladislav Novomeský the same day. Unifying all the factions and actually getting them to coordinate their efforts with the Union of Jewish Communities ushered in a new era in the history of Slovak Jewry.

The Union of Jewish Communities and the Association of Persecuted Persons maintained close cooperation and even had an overlap of personnel: both organizations had the same general secretary; the chairman of the Union of Jewish Communities was vice-chairman of the Association of Persecuted Persons; and several members of the Union of Jewish Communities' executive committee were active in both organizations. Thus, the two organizations fully coordinated their political work and lobbying, sending joint memoranda and delegations to government offices.

The Union of Jewish Communities assisted in the documentation campaign set up on the initiative of the Jewish Agency for the purpose of collecting documentary material on the Holocaust. This was an undertaking of paramount importance. The officials of the Nazi regime, who were interested in covering up and obscuring their heinous deeds, had destroyed a large part of the archives in government offices. Many documents had disappeared, especially those which dealt with the "final solution" of the Jewish problem and were likely to incriminate the Nazi rulers. Great efforts were made to obtain either originals or copies of those documents which remained. Quite a few private individuals, as well, had collected material during the war. Now it was necessary to search for, discover, and get hold of important documents, including numerous photographs, held by the Nazis, Germans, and Slovaks.

Official bodies wished not only to dwarf the extent of the Holocaust and the seriousness of the crimes committed then but also to minimize the importance of the struggle by the Jews, who took part in the insurrection and, as volunteers in the legions of free Czechoslovakia, fought in the war against Germany. Nevertheless, this documentation campaign succeeded in gathering thousands of documents attesting to the persecution of 136,000 Slovak Jews, including Jews in the southern realms which has been returned to Czechoslovakia, and to the annihilation of 110,000 of these Jews.

This undertaking was headed by Bedrich Steiner, who edited a documentary book, *The Tragedy of the Jews of Slovakia*,[78] published by the Union of Jewish Communities in the spring of 1949 and containing pictorial and photographic testimony to the Nazis' crimes and atrocities, beginning with their anti-Semitic propaganda and ending with the "final solution."[79]

When most of Slovak Jewry immigrated to Israel, in 1949, Dr. Steiner transferred all the documentary material to Israel, where he gave it to the Yad Va-Shem Archives in Jerusalem.

Our efforts to train teachers in Jewish studies proved unsuccessful. The small number of pupils in outlying cities made the problem all

---

[78] Tragedia Slovenských Židov

[79] The Central Union also published a volume of sketches on the Holocaust by František Reichental. All the revenues from the sale of this book went to maintaining sanatoria for children who survived the Holocaust.

the more, difficult to solve. Therefore, I proposed that we publish a monthly magazine for the youth, entitled *Ha-Lapid (The Torch),* in the hope of giving our pupils a Jewish education, one subject at a time, in monthly installments. Alexander Mittelmann, former principal of the Jewish school in Pieštany, became editor-in-chief. The magazine was enthusiastically received by the youth, and, with the aid of their parents, we tried to impart a basic knowledge of Jewish values to our children.

In April 1947, the Association of Persecuted Persons founded a weekly called *Tribuna,* which served as a mouthpiece in our struggle for equal rights and against overt and covert anti-Semitism. The publication was aimed, first and foremost, at a Jewish audience, although it was also intended to reach political and economic public bodies, to apprise them of our position on current issues. No other means of communication were available to us, and it was important that we make our stand heard and bring it to the attention of anti-Semitic circles and government bodies.

A committee of three – Dr. Jan Steiner presiding, myself, and Dr. Bedrich Steiner – was charged with handling all problems connected with publication of the paper and with serving as liaison between the executive board of the Association of Persecuted Persons and the editorial board of the paper. The paper, edited by Dr. Jan Steiner, began appearing in May 1947. One year later, in May 1948, the paper ran into financial difficulties, and the Union of Jewish Communities was requested to take over its publication. Since overt anti-Semitism had abated, making it no longer necessary to devote much space to the legal column, we now had an opportunity to alter the contents and spirit of the paper so that it would meet with the approval of all circles in the Jewish community. On condition that these changes be made, the Union of Jewish Communities agreed to cover the deficit – close to 600,000 korunas per annum – making it possible for the paper, which had a circulation of 4,000, to continue appearing. Henceforth the content of the paper was exclusively Jewish. More coverage was given to developments in the Land of Israel and Jewish communities of the Diaspora. Dr. Eugen Verný, chairman of the Association of Persecuted Persons, even proposed that a page in Yiddish or Hebrew be added, according to the demand.

The framework for coordinating the activities of the various organizations comprising the Union of Jewish Communities proved itself, and the united body developed and worked in the right direction. There were, in the beginning, some "prophets of wrath" who said that the union would be short-lived because extremists on both ends would not find a common language and the abyss between them would grow deeper and deeper. All these predictions of doom proved false. The Union of Jewish Communities became the supreme institution of Slovak Jewry. The cooperation between the Orthodox and the free-thinkers, on the one hand, and *Agudat Israel* and the Zionists, on the other, was straightforward and decent. All the organizations and movements found a willing ear in the directorship, and every issue was discussed on its merits and solved with mutual understanding to the benefit of all.

The department of religious services, headed by Jacob Eugen Hoff, vice-chairman of the union, worked to satisfy the religious needs of all the congregations that had formed in outlying cities. The union saw to it that matzah, baked in Bratislava, Košice, and Zlaté Moravce, was made available. Flour was still being rationed at the rate of 1,800 grams per person. The Jewish communities collected ration cards for flour and distributed matzah in return, according to the number of cards they collected. Matzah which the Joint sent from the United States was distributed among the needy. In cooperation with the board of rabbis, the department of religious services saw to it that kosher margarine and kosher-for-Passover food products were produced. Stipends were given to institutions of Jewish study, rabbinical courts in Bratislava and Košice, and authors of sacred books. We saw to it that etrogs and lulavs were available for the feast of Tabernacles and provided ritual articles. In both large Jewish communities, the department set up classes to train scribes and kosher butchers. We approved grants for renovating and maintaining synagogues, ritual baths, and cemeteries. The department in charge of immovable assets, headed by Alexander Pressburger, managed the property of abandoned Jewish communities, which according to the law reverted to the union, and also supervised the assets of existing congregations. The congregations were entitled to sell off lands only with the union's permission and were required to pay a levy of 20% of the sale price. The department employed two assessors, a building contractor by the name of Eugen Fischer from Liptovský-Svätý- Mikuláš, and a builder called Weissberger from Prešov, who visited sites and assessed buildings and other property, compiled files, reported on the condition of synagogues and cemeteries, which had largely been destroyed, and photographed them as necessary, to preserve their memory. By May 1947, the property of 122 defunct rural congregations had been assessed at 34,034,500 korunas, and receipts from the sale of buildings and lots had come to 2,390,000 korunas. Receipts from the sale of synagogues and houses of study were handled separately and were earmarked solely for charitable and philanthropic purposes. In 1947, the sum of 500,000 korunas was allocated to restoring cemeteries which had been defiled.

In February 1949, Eugen Fischer, the chief assessor, reported the department's assessment of property belonging to 217 abandoned congregations and 41 existing ones. After the wave of immigration to Israel some of these congregations were reduced to no more than three or four families, to wit: Ilava, Kremnica, Halič, Filakova, Sered, Vrotke and others. About twenty congregations faced liquidation, essentially leaving only ten other congregations, and even these could not maintain assets worth close to 30 million korunas. Aside from the buildings of the Jewish schools – valued at approximately 15 million korunas – which the government had nationalized without compensation, according to the Fischer report the Jewish communities of Slovakia still owned over 100 million korunas worth of property which was up for sale. Over a three-year period following the war, assets totaling 20 million korunas had either been sold or in were the process of being sold. This raised the question of whether the existing apparatus would be able to complete these sales and of how the proceeds should be used.

The food and clothing department, headed by Oscar Krasniansky, distributed goods received from UNRRA and the Joint, according to guidelines from the board. The supplies went primarily to Vlasta and Sylvia, institutions in the Tatra Mountains that took in children needing recuperation; the institution of the World Jewish Congress in Tatranská Lesná; the Ohel David orphanage in Nave Mesta; the *Agudat Israel* home in Bratislava; the Enzian sanatoria run by Oze in the Tatra Mountains; the Jewish hospital, old-age home and soup-kitchen in Bratislava; the soup-kitchen in Galanta; training centers of the Zionist movements, and other community institutions. Aside from matzah for Passover, packages of expensive foods for the holidays were distributed to children under 16 and elderly over 60. Clothing, linens, blankets, and diapers were distributed as well, on recommendations from welfare supervisors in the Jewish communities.

In March 1947, Mr. Ruby, the American representative of the Joint, suggested that the entire apparatus and all activities of the

Joint be transferred to the Union of Jewish Communities, along with complete jurisdiction over social work and monthly stipends to the Jewish communities. The apparatus was headed by Hugo Kollman and, upon being attached to the Union of Jewish Communities, became exceedingly important.

The finance department operated in accordance with the resolutions of the finance committee, headed by Dr. Ernest Abeles. This committee also acted as a social work committee, deliberating all requests for welfare. The following financial report was submitted at the committee's meeting of December 3, 1947, and reflects the activities of the Union of Jewish Communities over a ten-month period in 1947.

Financial Report for the Period 1/1/1947 - 10/31/1947

korunas
1. Grant from the Joint, until 6/30/1947
   1,100,000.00
2. Grant from the Joint, 7/1/1947 – 10/31/1947
   (Via the Jewish National Fund)
   8,236,200.00
3. Grant from the Ministry of Education and Culture
   50,000.00
4. Grant from the Central British Fund
   902,686.00

Total Receipts I10, 288,886.00

Receipts II
5. Net from real-estate sales
   646,510.00
6. Net from real-estate sales
   1,626,185.00

7. Net from matzah sales
417,832.50

8. Miscellaneous revenues
334,271.10

9. Transfers
393,545.60

Total Receipts II
3,418,344.20
Total Receipts I and II
13,707,230.20

Expenditures

1. Stipends (to the ill, brides, students, etc.)
445,350.00

2. Grants to congregations (3 months support)
5,167,291.00

3. Children's institutions
1, 135,116.40

4. Grants to hospitals and institutions
1,164,834.30

5. Religious services
1,204,072.05

6. Association of Persecuted Persons and Documentation
Campaign   228,000.00

7. Investments and loans
199,713.50

8. Expenses for supplying food
18,002.70

9. Salaries
824,930.55

10. Office and administrative expenses
420,834.10

11. Congregational administration (3 months)
235,488.00

Total Expenses
11,043,632.60

Special Grants

In 1947-1948 the Union of Jewish Communities made several special grants. On June 5, 1947, Akiva Lewinsky, Youth Aliyah's European director, visited our office and informed us that a school for youngsters immigrating to Israel was being opened. The union approved a grant of 100,000 korunas, to be paid in monthly installments, to support a ten-month term of the school.

In the summer of 1947, a group of *ma'apilim* ("illegal" immigrants to Israel, in excess of the British quota) organized, among them approximately 300 young men and women from Slovakia. In July 1947, the union approved a grant of 120,000 korunas to cover their expenses. On July 16, 1947, we approved 100,000 korunas to the Association of Persecuted Persons to cover current expenses and joint work with our organization.

In February 1948, we allocated 500,000 korunas to the Haganah fund drive. In March 1948, we approved 100,000 korunas to an agricultural training group of 40 members of the Gordonia – Young Maccabee movement which had formed in Verekna. We requested them to respect the sanctity of the Sabbath and keep a kosher kitchen. In May 1948, we gave a grant of 100,000 korunas to the weekly, *Tribuna.* The Union of Jewish Communities helped maintain the Beit Ya'akov school for girls, run by *Agudat Israel,* and participated in the cost of training counselors for B'nai Akiva. A grant of 20,000 korunas was also approved for Agudat Israel to produce a Jewish calendar for the year 5708.

In September 1948, a grant of 20,000 korunas was given to

Ha-Shomer ha-Tza'ir in Bratislava for the movement to renovate its meeting-house. Oze received continuous grants totaling tens of thousands of korunas to maintain a kosher kitchen in the Enzian sanatorium in Upper Smokovec, in the High Tatra Mountains.

The Union of Jewish Communities assisted in completing construction of the Hatam Sofer burial vault. The new road, the Slavic Way, which passes over the graves, was scheduled to be inaugurated in July 1949, and all work on the sepulchre had to be completed by then. Our Union allocated 300,000 korunas to complete the task. The opening to the sepulchre was covered with a reinforced concrete slab and a rung of stairs were built to provide access to an illuminated burial vault. Since the memorial stone over the grave of the Hatam Sofer was so high, it had to be transferred and erected next to the wall of the burial vault. The cover or entranceway is locked, and the key to it is kept in the offices of the Bratislava Jewish community.[80]

The board of directors handled current political issues, local and international. There were times when several places encountered problems concerning kosher slaughtering of meat. The veterinarian in Lučenec forbade the slaughter of cattle. A similar development occurred in Prešov, but the affair was set straight with the local authorities. We also addressed the Minister of Agriculture Styk on this issue and received satisfaction.

In January 1948, we requested that the Council of Jewish Communities in Prague transfer 4,000,000 korunas from the Terezin

---

[80] The graves of the following rabbis are preserved in the Hatam Sofer Sepulchre:
1. Rabbi Mordechai ben Isaiah (The Ashkenazi Castigator; 1714-1729).
2. Rabbi Moses Lwow-Lemberger (The Sharp; 1730-1758).
3. Rabbi Akiva Eger (1758).
4. Rabbi Isaac Halevi Landau-Dukla (1758-1761).
5. Rabbi Meir be-Rabbi Halberstadt (1764-1789).
6. Rabbi Meshullam Eger (of Tismenitz; 1794-1801). s
7. Rabbi Moses Schreiber (1806-1839), the Hatam Sofer.

Fund *(Terezinská Podstata)*[81] to the Union of Jewish Communities in Slovakia in monthly installments of 500,000 korunas. Since October 1947, the Council of Jewish Communities had been receiving 4,000,000 korunas per month from this fund. The Council of Jewish Communities denied our request on the grounds that the money being released from the fund was not even sufficient to cover the budget of the Jewish communities in the Czech Republic.

We appealed against Jews being fined for shutting their stores on the Sabbath. Difficulties arose in this regard when a commercial enterprise was under "people's management."

II. Cooperation with Czech Jewry

In January 1947, the Czech Council of Jewish Communities and the Central Union of Jewish Communities in Slovakia signed an agreement establishing a committee to coordinate political action on current issues in the Czech and Slovak Jewish communities. This agreement provided for a coordinating committee comprised of six members and six alternates, three of each from each organization. The coordinating committee would elect a chairman from one of the organizations and a vice-chairman from the other organization for a term of one year and would rotate the chairmanship every year. The committee would convene as necessary, at least once every three months. The place would alternate between Prague and Bratislava, and the time would be either a Sunday or a national holiday. Resolutions required unanimous approval by the Council of Jewish Communities and the Central Union of Jewish Communities. Memoranda and requests would be submitted in the name of both organizations and would be signed by the chairman and vice-chairman. Representing the Council of Jewish Communities were: Arnošt Frischer, chairman;

---

[81] A fund originating from money expropriated during the Holocaust from Jews living in the Protectorate.

Fuchs, for Prague; and Spitz, for Brno. The Central Union of Jewish Communities elected me vice-chairman, and Eugen Hoff and Dr. Winterstein fellow members. Dr. Kurt Wehle, the general secretary of the Council of Jewish Communities, was also made secretary of the committee. Dr. Ernest Abeles, Oscar Krasniansky and Desider Reisner were chosen as alternates representing the Central Union of Jewish Communities.

The founding meeting of the coordinating committee was held in Prague in the offices of the Council of Jewish Communities on March 16, 1947. At this meeting the committee's current joint actions were outlined and interviews were planned with Czechoslovakia's president and prime minister and other government ministers, to be held the same week. During these interviews a memorandum of the Association of Persecuted Persons and the Central Union of Jewish Communities on expropriation of agricultural land belonging to Jews was submitted, as was a proposal for a restitution agreement which would apply to Jewish agricultural property. A memorandum was also submitted requesting that factories which had formerly belonged to Jews and had not been restored to their former owners but rather had been placed under "people's management" be removed from such management.

We decided to turn to the highest echelons of the central government since all our efforts to resolve these issues on the level of the autonomous Slovak government had proven barren. In the agricultural sector all Jewish property had essentially been expropriated on the pretext that the Jews were either Germans or Hungarians, and the compromise proposal which was submitted to the Assembly of Deputies (the Slovak government) had not even been brought up for consideration. A second issue concerned a serious infraction of the legal right of Jews who had owned medium-sized factories to have their enterprises restored to them. Even after the court issued rulings in favor of the Jewish owners, the factories had still not been returned. Various government offices, disregarding the laws on restitution, had imposed "people's management" on these factories, and thus the situation which pertained under the Nazi regime essentially persisted, except that the Jewish enterprises were now run by "people's managements" instead of Nazi "Aryanizers." *Plus ça change, plus c'est la même chose.* Another reason, and perhaps the most important, for us turning to the central government in Prague was that several circles, including official ones, which were fighting to improve the social and economic condition of the Slovak population, relying on their experience in the not-so-distant past, were trying to achieve their goals the easy way, i.e., at the expense of the Jews. These circles hoped to change the restitution law (returning to Jews their property) and to introduce in its stead amendments detrimental to the Jews. It was imperative that this be prevented.

One case of scandalous injustice, which became known after the Jewish industrialist who was hurt – Baer of Varensdorf – occurred in the Czech Republic. But in Slovakia thus far some 15 Jews, former factory owners, had suffered, and if hostile circles were to succeed in changing the law, under the guise of instituting a social reform, many Jewish families would be left with no source of livelihood. As Jews we had no desire to put-the-breaks on social progress. We were all for social reform, but not at the expense of the Jews, who sought to have their property returned. Therefore, it was essential for us to appeal to the central government in Prague, along with the Czech Jews. And so it was that the interviews with the prime minister, the cabinet and the president began.

On March 17, 1947, the Jewish delegation was received by

Prime Minister Clement Gottwald. Eugen Hoff and I represented the Central Union of Jewish Communities, Oscar Krasniansky represented the Zionist Organization, and Dr. Egon Gold and Dr. Vojtech Winterstein represented the Association of Persecuted Persons. The representatives of the Council of Jewish Communities were A. Frischer, Kurt Wehle, P. Fuchs and Spitz. The interview lasted close to an hour and a half. Its duration, substance, and outcome testify to its importance and success. Dr. Winterstein brought up the principal problems worrying the Jews of Slovakia. We received the impression that the prime minister was shocked to hear about the behavior of the Slovaks, who were contravening the law of the land, and we had to tell him time and again that 90% of the Jews' agricultural property had been expropriated, not by the former Fascist Slovak state, but by the authorities of the Republic after the liberation. The prime minister promised to intervene immediately and support our proposals for solving the problem. His impact was noticeable, and upon our return to Bratislava we learned that the matter had at long last come up on the agenda of the Assembly of Deputies.

As for doing away with "people's management" of Jewish factories and restoring them to their owners, Baer's case in the Czech Republic and 15 similar cases in Slovakia were discussed. The prime minister promised that a solution in favor of the original owners would be found in 80% of the cases. In the remaining cases, which for one reason or another were exceptional, such as a factories which were destroyed during the war and had been reestablished by the workers on their own initiative, ethically one also had to take the demands of the workers into account and seek a compromise solution. These exceptional cases would be discussed by special commissions, that would hear both parties. The Prime Minister expected that in these exceptional cases all the interested parties would show flexibility and would arrive at a mutual understanding. These commissions would come under the aegis of the Office of the Prime Minister in Prague and the Chairman of the Assembly of Deputies in Bratislava. The problem of the citizenship of subjects who had declared Jewish nationality would be solved in a legal manner and in accordance with our stand, so the prime minister assured us. Likewise, he confirmed that he was aware certain circles wished to add amendments to the law of restitution but said he personally was opposed to any changes in this regard.

The delegation was also received by Foreign Minister Jan Masaryk the same day. Besides general issues, we also discussed the option given the Jews of Carpatho-Russia and requested his diplomatic intervention. Regarding the gold of Hungarian Jews, which had been transferred to the area under German occupation, Masaryk promised us his fullest assistance and support for our equitable demands. In the government's deliberations, once again Masaryk proved his friendliness towards the Jews.

On March 18, Deputy Prime Minister Zdenek Firlinger received the delegation and informed us that the law on restoration of rights would not be changed or innovated. This had been decided by the National Front of Czechs and Slovaks. In his opinion, there was also no need to introduce innovations, since Article 6 of the law was sufficiently flexible and could answer anyone's needs. This interview was extremely cold and did not live up to our expectations.

The delegation was also received the same day by Dr. Srb in the Ministry of Justice, in the absence of Dr. Drtina. The delegation expressed its gratitude for the position taken by the Ministry of Justice in defining an "important public matter," a concept often used as an argument to justify failure to properly implement the law on restoring rights. This competent source informed us that even though the Slovaks used the excuse of an "important public interest" in most of the problematic cases of restoring factories to their owners, the Ministry of Justice in Prague had not approved their position in a single case. The interview afforded us an opportunity to clarify several legal questions with respect to implementation of the restitution law. The delegation's jurists, Dr. Winterstein and Dr. Gold, found to their satisfaction that Dr. Srb, the expert jurist and highest authority on the matter, identified with their position on all the controversial questions in Slovakia. Dr. Srb promised that the Ministry of Justice in Prague would give its fullest support to see to it that justice was duly administered.

On March 19 the delegation was received by Minister of Industry Laušman. In this interview we aired our complaints regarding the Slovak authorities' delay in issuing Jews licenses to run businesses and factories and in restoring them their factories, returning them their homes, and abolishing "people's management" of Jewish enterprises. The minister confirmed what we had already heard from Prime Minister Gottwald – who interceded just as he had promised – namely, that these cases would be heard by commissions to which we could present our arguments. Laušman promised he would talk with his counterpart, Deputy Púl, when he visited Bratislava, and would try to redress the injustice which had been done to the Jews of Slovakia. He also promised his assistance in setting up cooperatives for small industry and expressed his opposition to introducing changes and innovations in the law of restitution.

Deputy Prime Minister Ursínyi, in an interview held with him the same day, expressed the opinion that agricultural property belonging to citizens of Jewish origin, who registered as being of Jewish or other nationality, should not be expropriated provided they know a little

Slovak. But also, other Jews, who speak Hungarian and German, were entitled to hold 50 hectares of agricultural land. Therefore, he said, all the questionable instances of expropriation should be re-examined. The deputy prime minister, himself a Slovak, promised to come to Slovakia in the near future to stand up for his views and to work there for implementation of the agreement which had been reached between the Ministry of Agriculture in Bratislava and the Association of Persecuted Persons but had not yet been carried out.

The delegation was received by Minister Hála, instead of Deputy Prime Minister Dr. Šrámek, and he, too, promised his support and assistance in redressing all these wrongs. Similar assurances were received from the general secretary of the Social-Democratic party, member of parliament Vilím, who announced that the representatives of the Jews may turn to him at any time and that he would work to help them through his party, among his friends in Slovakia, as well.

The well-known negative attitude of the chairman of the trade unions, member of parliament Zápotocký, stood in sharp contrast to the favorable stand taken by these key personages. Confirming his negative position, in his interview with the representatives of the Council of Jewish Communities he stressed that no changes must be made in factory management during the two-year economic plan and that "people's management" therefore not be abolished. He also rejected the Czech Jews' protest regarding the case of Baer of Vahrensdorf and claimed that this incident had nothing to do with the Jews.

In the Ministry of Propaganda our representatives obtained a ban on showing Ivan Olbracht's anti-Semitic film, "Nikola Šuhaj," in Slovakia. This ministry, too, was informed of the problems we were encountering in Slovakia.

The climax of our visit was on March 20, when our delegation was received in the Office of the President, Dr. Eduard Beneš, in Hradčany Castle. This was the first time since the war that a delegation of Czechoslovak. Jewry had been granted an official reception by the president with full pomp and ceremony. Arnošt Frischer greeted the president in the name of the Jews of the Czech Republic, and I greeted him in the name of the Jews of Slovakia. During a cordial conversation with the president, we handed him memoranda on our problems, which we further expounded to him orally. The delegation was comprised of the coordinating committee. The president expressed interest in our problems, and said among other things: "I am all in favor of preserving law and order, for I see their preservation as the safeguard of our existence. I realize that implementation of the laws is not always fair and decent. Sometimes a norm is put into the legislation, then people look for a way to circumvent it. But such things happen to other people, as well. I shall continue fighting and shall advocate your position to the prime minister. Please send my office a copy of any memoranda which you send the government ministries."

At the plenary board meeting of the Association of Persecuted Persons, held on March 26, 1947, Dr. Winterstein reported on the delegation's visit to Prague and summed up his report in the following words:

We stormed the key offices of the government and set public bodies into action. We aroused public opinion, initiated a revision in the law on land expropriation, and shall be party to deliberations on abolishing "people's management" in factories which have not been returned to their owners. We brought influence to bear to prevent innovations from being made in the law on restoration of rights and saw to several other matters.

Although our achievements appear impressive, we must not be overly optimistic or complacent. We are still in the thick of a difficult battle. Anti-Semitism exists and may even increase, not only here, but in the Czech Republic, as well, and in all the lands which came under Nazi conquest. We are fated to have to fight unceasingly against anti-Semitic attacks. Although we are not strong, we shall be able to persist in our defense efforts because we are fighting for the rights of man in a democratic society, and our arms are truth, justice, and equity. There still exist some men of valor, people with a high sense of morality, who recognize and respect these values. We succeeded in putting through the law on restitution, despite the organized "will of the people"; we have been succeeding at transferring Jewish enterprises back to their owners even in specific, difficult cases; and we shall continue to fight for our rights. We must strengthen our faith and our will to stand up and fight for our survival.

III. A European Conference of the World Jewish Congress Meets in Prague

A European conference of the World Jewish Congress, attended by delegations from most of Europe, met in Prague from April 22-29, 1947. Only four countries were not represented: Italy, the Soviet Union, Greece, and Rumania.

The conference discussed the problem of the refugees who, aided by *Berihah,*[82] had fled their homes after the Holocaust and were now waiting in camps in various occupied areas of Germany, Austria, and Italy, and in transit camps in Czechoslovakia for the gates of Palestine to be opened. Other important subjects on the agenda included: rehabilitation and restoration of rights to Jews, reparations

---

[82] *Berihah* (Heb. "flight"), an underground operation moving Jews out of Eastern Europe into Central and Southern Europe between 1944 and 1948, as a step towards their mostly "illegal" immigration to the Land of Israel. Translator's note.

from Germany, disposing of abandoned Jewish property, and creating constructive resources for rebuilding Jewish communities. The conference also discussed documentation projects on the Holocaust and Jewish-Christian cooperation in the war on anti-Semitism.

The Czechoslovak regime deserves mention for its role in hosting the conference. At the festive opening ceremony, the delegates were greeted by Deputy Chairwoman of the National Assembly Hodinová-Spurná, and Mayor of Prague Dr. Vacek. Representatives from the Ministry of Interior, the Foreign Ministry, and the Ministry of Propaganda, as well as high-ranking members of the clergy and the legislature, also attended the opening. I extended words of welcome in the name of Slovak Jewry and proclaimed that even though the constitution of the Democratic People's Republic of Czechoslovakia guarantees equal rights to all its citizens, regardless of religious affiliation, one could not say that the scourge of anti-Semitism, which the Holocaust visited upon us, has disappeared or been wiped out. Quite the contrary, this blight was returning like a pernicious weed among cultivated plants, and, like poisonous mushrooms after a rain, was harming society and spreading its venom among mankind. We must fight unceasingly to redress the wrongs which were done us and to restore to the Jews their full rights, without discrimination; for our martyrs and heroic fighters laid down their lives for the sake of human values and the rights of man. The leaders of the congress were granted an interview with President Eduard Beneš, which lasted an hour and a quarter. The question of Palestine was on the agenda of the United Nations General Assembly at the time, and therefore the president's statement to the members of the congress carried great political significance. The president said that he saw the establishment of an independent Jewish state in Palestine as a reasonable solution into the problem of the Jews and that Czechoslovakia supported the Jews' demands in this regard.

The Council of Jewish Communities in Prague and the Union of Jewish Communities in Bratislava also sent a memorandum to Prime Minister Gottwald and Foreign Minister Masaryk, requesting them to support the resolution to establish a Jewish state in Palestine.

The Czech press covered the deliberations of the congress and the interview with the president, and thus his important declaration received worldwide publicity. In contrast, the media in Slovakia ignored the existence of the congress and did not even give one sentence of coverage to the events of the conference.

It should be noted that the Union of Jewish Communities in Slovakia affiliated with the World Jewish Congress, save *Agudat Israel,* which would have nothing to do with the congress. The Congress had its bureau in the offices of the Central Union of Jewish Communities, and its coordinator, Marta Tochten, was also in charge of the children's recreation center which the Congress provided in Tatranská-Lesná.

IV. Achievements and Failings of the Association of Persecuted Persons

The third conference of the Union of Persons Racially Persecuted by the Fascist Regime, held on June 29, 1947, in the lecture hall of the Bratislava municipality, gives an indication of the association's activities, its successes and failures.

Dr. Eugen Verný, speaking on behalf of the executive committee, gave the opening remarks. He appealed to the association's membership, requesting them to behave with mutual respect in cases of claiming inheritance rights over the property of Holocaust victims and not to cause quarrels or hostility, nor to desecrate the memory of the departed by holding hearings in the state courts, but rather to try to settle their differences through compromise and peaceful means. I, as spokesman for the Union of Jewish Communities, said:

Our organizations, the Union of Jewish Communities and the Association of Persecuted Persons, are fraternal associations, working hand in hand. The difference between us is that the Association of Persecuted Persons was founded after the war as an inherently temporary organization with the purpose of obtaining complete rehabilitation and restitution; and when it achieves its objective it will cease to exist. The Union of Jewish Communities, in contrast, works to maintain and foster eternal Jewish values within the setting of the Jewish community. President Beneš has said to us that the survival of the Czechoslovak Republic depends on maintaining law and justice in this state. We are true to the tradition of our Rabbis, who formulated the principle that the law of the land is binding and must be obeyed, and shall not let our enemies – those who violate the law, who covet and seize Jewish property, who still adhere to the idea of racial discrimination from the era of the Nazi regime – undermine the foundations of our democratic society, on which our liberated state is built.

In his address, general secretary Dr. Vojtech Winterstein said:

After a laborious struggle, for the time being we have achieved publication of the Law of Restitution, number 255/46, which among other things grants priority to persons who suffered from Nazi persecution. But while restoration of rights to Jews is proceeding according to the law in the Czech Republic, in Slovakia this process has still been meeting opposition and has been progressing dilatorily, and in some regions, discrimination actually persists in contravention to the laws of the land. When it comes to actual implementation of the law, there is a large discrepancy between the two parts of the state. In the Czech Republic, for example, the Welfare Department released 60,000,000 korunas of the Terezin Fund's frozen assets to provide for the welfare of the Jewish community; this was during the term of the Slovak minister, Dr. Šoltés. This same Dr. Šoltés, Slovakia's Minister of Welfare, could not manage to give the Slovak Jewish community a grant for social welfare and philanthropic undertakings. Our budget for social work comes from magnanimous Jewish organizations abroad. Take another example: nationalization of parochial schools. In Slovakia the authorities took Jewish school buildings away from the community but left the burden of taxation on these buildings on the Jewish community. Such things do not happen in the Czech Republic. Quite the contrary, we see how attempts are made there to bridge the gap which developed between the two parts of the population during the Nazi conquest and to heal the moral and material wounds.

The world over, representatives of the Jewish community, as well, are generally invited to attend state and public functions. This is so in the Czech Republic, too. In Slovakia, however, the representatives of the Jewish community were not even invited to the reception given the president, although representatives of other religious and ethnic groups were invited. This is not a question of honor, but a clear indication that something is wrong not only with respect to material concerns but also with respect to moral values. Little wonder that the Slovak people has not yet shown a positive attitude towards solving problems concerning the Jewish community, when the representatives of the people do not exert their influence or give any moral or psychological direction. It is not a question of legislation, but of putting the law into practice. Much work lies ahead of us in this regard.

Aside from these criticisms, however, we must extend our most heartfelt thanks to the Soviet and Czechoslovak armies, who liberated us from Nazi subjugation, thus saving our lives, and who assure our survival and security in our democratic state. We thank the government for its positive and friendly stand in the United Nations' deliberations of the Palestine issue. We also thank the government for its humane and liberal position regarding the thousands of Jewish refugees who have been crossing from neighboring states. The border with Poland has been opened, enabling refugees to continue their way westward or southward. Representatives of the government have been helping them, allowing Jewish organizations and institutions to direct them so safely to their destination. We also wish to thank the Government for opening its most important ministries, as well as the Presidential Palace, to us, allowing us to meet with government officials, who have shown good will and are prepared to help us solve our problems. We also thank the Deputy of Interior, General Ferienčik, for his efforts to guarantee our safety and for the firm stand he has taken against manifestations of anti-Semitism. Counterbalancing the requests and grievances that I have stated, I could list many things that deserve praise and thanks, and this fact will encourage us to continue the fight, working through the Association of Persecuted Persons, a valuable political tool in the hands of Slovak Jewry.

Dr. Winterstein concluded his speech by thanking the members of the board and the association's officers.

Among the resolutions passed by the conference was a decision to establish local branches of the Association of Persecuted Persons in 127 Jewish communities of Slovakia. These branches would be obliged to forward a graduated monthly tax to the central office.

All the resolutions of the conference dealt with achieving rehabilitation and restitution, remedying shortcomings and faults in implementation of the law, abolishing discrimination and achieving full equality of rights in all walks of life, fighting anti-Semitism, and integrating into the social and economic life of the state. One of the resolutions concerned the moral demand, not only of Slovak Jewry but also of the entire civilized world, that the property of Holocaust victims who left no heirs be used for rehabilitation and constructive assistance to Jews who survived the Holocaust.

This demand was included in the resolution of the World Jewish Congress, which called on all states concerned to acknowledge this moral imperative and act accordingly. Resolutions in this spirit have already been adopted by Greece, Hungary, and Italy. Other states, as well, have not objected to this moral request, and the Association of Persecuted Person has been delegated to take the necessary steps to see to it that the government and legislature in Czechoslovakia accept this natural principle and vest it in the law, in accordance with

Article 16 of the Law of Restitution.

The conference concluded with the election of officers: Arthur Skala was elected chairman, Dr. Arnošt Frischer, Dr. Eugen Verný, and I were elected vice-chairmen, and Dr. Vojtech Winterstein, general secretary.

On April 8, 1947, the full executive board of the Association of Persecuted Persons met to discuss the association's financial crisis, which had become so grave that the association could no longer pay its workers' salaries. They decided to hold a referendum on whether or not the association should continue functioning another year. All in favor were required to pay membership dues by August 15. After this date another meeting would be called to decide whether to continue or disband the association. The board also decided to launch a public relations and fundraising campaign.

I stressed that the Association of Persecuted Persons had not yet finished its public mission and that its continued existence was essential. I suggested that a long-term loan of 10,000 korunas be requested from the Union of Jewish Communities and further proposed that the chairman of the organization of Jewish communities request the leaders of the community to make annual grants, arguing that if the association were to cease functioning, we would have to establish a similar apparatus within the framework of the Jewish communities and cover all its expenses from the communities' budgets. The motion was accepted, and the head of the Bratislava Jewish community, Alexander Pressburger, promised to collect membership dues through the community's collector and proposed that other Jewish communities do likewise.

The Association of Persecuted Persons continued to exist and even publish its periodical, *Tribuna.* The organization of Jewish

Communities knew that the association's existence was not only justified but essential, and when the Association of Persecuted Persons was in financial straits, the Union of Jewish Communities came to its assistance with loans which it converted into grants to enable the Association of Persecuted Persons to fight for the rights of its members.

On August 20, 1947, Dr. Martinček, the director of the Office of the President of the Slovak People' Council, sent the Union of Jewish Communities and the Association of Persecuted Persons several strongly worded letters regarding "the desire to preserve the Slovak character of our city." He wrote:

> Our office has received complaints about Jews and gypsies, who go about the streets of Bratislava and the provincial cities loudly speaking Hungarian and German, much to the displeasure of the Slovak population. In various places throughout Slovakia, repatriates have been appearing in public places, coffee-shops, restaurants, hotels, health resorts and vacation spots, and by their provocative behavior have been creating the impression that the State has again been inundated by Hungarians and Germans, the self, same enemies who led to the state's disintegration. These elements have posed as Slovaks, and to this end have even assumed Slovak names; but after receiving back their property and establishing themselves financially, they have revealed their true colors, continuing to disseminate the language of those nations who, in the not so distant past, brought unforgettable calamity upon them and us. It is undeniable that such behavior in Bratislava, Košice, Prešov, the High Tatra Mountains,

Sliač, and elsewhere arouses hatred of the Jews and encourages anti-Semitism. The state authorities have transferred the minorities to their homeland, yet we still have a Jewish minority that finds it difficult to part from the language of its former overlords and continues to disseminate an alien culture among the Slovak people. This is an intolerable situation.

The authorities hope that the central Jewish organizations will give serious consideration to this distressing problem and expect to hear what the steps the Jews propose to take to stop this Hungarianization, to redress these wrongs and correct the errors in their ways, which have caused such strong reverberations and elicited such a negative reaction.

In responding to these charges, we took exception to the style of the letter as a whole and to its generalizations and exaggerations, so reminiscent of the shameful past when we were the object of humiliation, false accusations, and incitement. In the name of all Jewry, the Union of Jewish Communities and Association of Persecuted Persons lodged a protest against the manner in which we had been addressed and the exaggerated claims, which smelled suspiciously of racial discrimination.

We explained to the authorities that in the southern cities, which had been temporarily annexed to Hungary, the Jews had been forced to speak Hungarian. The Jews have always been victimized; the Hungarians accused them of disseminating Slovak culture. Language is not the sole factor determining a citizen's national affiliation, nor is it an index for measuring the Jews' unimpeachable loyalty to the democratic state, even if a negligible number of them speak

Hungarian. The alleged German-speakers are actually none other than Yiddish-speakers. The anti-Semites who wrote the complaints will always find some excuse for hating Jews. We also stressed in our response that the younger generation of Jews was brought up with Slovak as its mother-tongue and, with the outbreak of the revolt, enlisted enthusiastically in the war against the Nazi invader, risking their lives to liberate the state and preserve democracy.

Concurrently we sent a circular to the Jewish communities, requesting that their official bodies use language of the state and that the Jews speak Slovak when in public, so as not to provide any grounds for complaints against the Jews. The Jewish leaders were requested to make it clear to their communities that this issue was of the utmost importance. We also recommended that Slovak language instruction be provided for adults, to remove this stumbling block and not open the way for our adversaries to attack us.

On January 29, 1948, Dr. Winterstein reported to a plenary meeting of the board of the Association of Persecuted Persons that, after prolonged effort, arrangements had finally been made to liquidate the Fund for Jewish Emigration. Jewish money confiscated under the former Slovak state had been put into this fund, which had grown to 240,000,000 korunas. The Fascist state spent approximately 75% of this sum, leaving close to 60,000,000 korunas under the control of the Ministry of Commerce and Industry, which now, after wearying negotiations, finally agreed to liquidate the fund and return the money to its owners. Fearing lest the burden of work on the ministry be too great and slow down the process of liquidating the fund, the association agreed to establish a special apparatus to carry out this task.

We discussed the issue and settled on the basic guideline that if and when the Ministry of Commerce and Industry decides to hand over the money in the fund to the Jews, we would deduct 20% from every sum returned, of which 5% would be used to cover the expenses of the administrative apparatus and 15% would be devoted to general Jewish purposes. Two committees were set up to handle further negotiations. One was charged to work out the administrative and technical procedures for liquidating the fund and bringing negotiations with the government to a conclusion. The other was charged to manage the fund of 15% to be deducted from compensation recipients and used for the Jewish community, charity, and public welfare.

These decisions marked an important culmination of two meetings, in which many aspects of restitution in various sectors were discussed and concrete achievements were reached; and the committee dispersed with a sense of satisfaction, expectation, and hope that the Government had indeed come towards us on the issue of rehabilitation. In the meantime, however, a Communist revolution took place in Czechoslovakia in February 1948, and a short while thereafter, on the 5th of Iyar 5708 (May 14, 1948), in Tel Aviv, Ben Gurion proclaimed the establishment of a Jewish state. These two historic events led to unexpected developments and a radical reform in the structure of society. Consequently, while the Association of Persecuted Persons was discussing routine matters still on the agenda, by December 22, 1948, many of the Jews eligible for compensation had already left Czechoslovakia and were concerned with finding their place in the State of Israel, which was fighting for its survival.

Dr. Egon Gold, who replaced Dr. Winterstein as general secretary of the Association of Persecuted Persons, reported to the committee on an agreement with the Office for Agrarian Reform regarding the restoration of land to Jewish farmers. Thus far 65% of the exceptional cases had been handled and had been solved by mutual consent. However, no progress had been made towards resolving the issue of compensation from the funds which had been taken over by the government.

Dr. Verný elaborated on a bill being drafted by the association to establish a special fund, acting on the assumption that the Czechoslovak state would not wish to enrich itself from the vast wealth of property – real estate, buildings, factories, jewelry, securities – left by Jews who had perished in the Holocaust and left no heirs. This property and the balances in the various accounts and funds came to a vast fortune, which the draft law proposed channeling into a "restitution fund" for the general use and social welfare of the Jewish community.

The heads of the association also reported on various lobbying efforts, including intercession in the Ministry of Propaganda with regard to an anti-Jewish broadcast sent over the Slovak radio on October 19, 1948. The Ministry of Propaganda acknowledged our claim and sent a warning to the director of the radio, and even requested him to prepare a program to counter chauvinistic and anti-Semitic trends.

Life is full of irony. While an untapped fortune of Jewish property and wealth was being discussed, the *Tribuna* had a deficit of 300,000 korunas as of December 31, 1948, and the Association of Persecuted Persons was in financial straits. The weekly, as had recently been proven, according to general consensus was still performing an important role in our day to day struggles, and hence its continued publication was deemed essential. The committee of chairmen – Dr. Verný, myself, and Krasniansky – was requested to assume responsibility for the paper. On my suggestion, we decided to cut back *Tribuna's* expenditures so that the monthly grant of 25,000 korunas from the Union of Jewish Communities and the Zionist Organization would suffice to assure its publication.

The committee dispersed with mixed feelings. The government was keeping it hands on a vast Jewish fortune, while a Jewish organization struggling for its very survival was left utterly destitute.

Those very days Horský's department in the Ministry of Interior – the passport office – was packed: the Jews were leaving Czechoslovakia.

V. Memorials to Martyrs and Soldiers

In 1947-1948, many Jewish communities erected monuments and memorial plaques in their cemeteries and renovated synagogues. The ceremonies unveiling these memorials were generally held on Sundays and were attended by representatives of anti-Fascist organizations and the government. These ceremonies were conducted in Slovak. Few congregations, however, had rabbis; and for the most part these ministers of the religion were not fluent in the language of the state. Therefore, I often agreed to speak at these ceremonies.

The unveiling of the tombstone of Ferdinand Goldstein, a leader of the Maccabee movement in Piešťany, took place on the 21st of Iyar, 5707 (May 11, 1947). Ferdinand (Nandy) was an activist in the Nováky underground. "Everyone with one of his hands wrought in the work, and with the other held his weapon" (Nehemiah 4:11). When the insurrection broke out, he went to fight the Nazi foe. He and his comrades, armed only with guns, took on the Germans with their tanks and aircraft, and fell heroically in battle.

On the 7th of Tishri, 5708 (September 21, 1947), ceremonies were held in four communities. In Zvolen I took part in the unveiling of the tombstone of 118 Holocaust victims, whose bodies were removed from Kremnica and buried in a communal grave. The bodies of three hundred and seventy-two martyrs, men women and children, young and old, were identified in this field of slaughter in Kremnica and were brought to a proper Jewish burial in various towns in Slovakia.

In November 1949, the Trnava Jewish community erected a memorial to Holocaust victims next to its synagogue. General Svoboda from Prague represented the government at the official unveiling ceremony and praised the Jewish soldiers in the brigade of which he had been commander-in-chief. Dr. Winterstein spoke for the Association of Persecuted Persons and I for the Union of Jewish Communities.

The Rabbinical Council declared the 20th of Nisan a day of mourning in memory of Slovakia's Holocaust victims and enacted a public fast of half a day. *Minhah* services were held after mid-day, as is the practice on fast days, and were followed by a memorial service and a lesson in Mishnah. All those assembled joined in *kaddish*.

On Sunday, the 20th of Sivan, 5708 (June 27, 1948), at the inauguration of its newly restored synagogue, the Jewish community of Trenčín commemorated the city's 1,600 martyrs who perished in the Holocaust. The leaders of the new community continued the tradition begun by Rabbi Dr. Benjamin Fischer, who in 1917 laid the foundations of the Zionist movement in Trenčín. Dr. Adolph Süss headed the movement for many years, and Gabriela Levy and Charlotte Kalmar were among its more prominent women members. R. P. Singer from Ipolske Šahy participated in the ceremony. The community published a booklet edited by Alexander Mittelmann in memory of its Holocaust martyrs.

Under the leadership of Julius Salvendi, the Jewish community of Rimavská Sobota restored its synagogue and on the walls of the new buildings commemorated martyrs of the Holocaust, among them R. Singer, may the Lord avenge his blood.

VI. The Zionist Movement After the War

In spring 1946 a worldwide Zionist conference convened in London. Czechoslovakia was represented by the chairman of its Zionist movement, Dr. Oscar Neumann, then on his way to Israel. At this conference preparations were made for the 22nd World Zionist Congress. The national conference of the Czechoslovak Zionist Organization took place in the summer of 1946 in the resort city of Luhačovice. This was the first such conference since the war and the last held in Czechoslovakia. The general secretary of the movement was Ervin Steiner, and the movement's main office was in Bratislava, at 18 Markovič Street. At the Luhačovice conference the Zionist Organization elected its officers. Oscar Krasniansky was made the head of the organization, Eugen Fischgrund was made director of the Land of Israel Office in Prague, and Leo Rosenthal was put in charge of the Slovak office and of coordinating immigration to Israel, Jewish fund drives, and public relations and propaganda work. The Zionist Organization published a bi-weekly for its members, called *Spolkové Zprávy (The Movement News)*. Contributions to various fund drives, including a fund for planting a forest in memory of Czechoslovakia's martyrs, were published in this paper. In 1946 half a million korunas were raised for the Jewish National Fund alone.

The Zionist shekel (membership card and fee of the Zionist movement) was raised with great success, and preparations were made to send a large delegation to the 22nd World Zionist Congress in Basel, the last one held outside of Israel, from Kislev 16-Tevet 3, 5707 (December 9-24, 1946). The keynotes of the Congress were the Holocaust and the armed struggle against the British, ruling over Palestine. Dr. Desider Ehrenfeld, Rafi Friedel (Ben-Shalom), Dr. Alexander Goldstein, Dr. Meir Gordon, and other figures from Czechoslovakia were among the 385 delegates to the Congress.

The Congress ratified plans to establish a Jewish state and decided not to participate in a British-Jewish-Arab conference on Palestine. The Revisionists rejoined the Zionist Organization.

On the 21st of Av, 5707 (August 7, 1947), representatives of Czechoslovakia's Jewish organizations – the Council of Jewish Communities of the Czech Republic, the Central Union of the Jewish Communities in Slovakia, the Zionist Organization, and *Agudat Israel* – convened in Prague to discuss recent developments in Palestine and drafted the following protest:

1. The *Exodus,* with 4,500 Jewish refugees on board, was captured on the high seas by the British navy. In a clash with British soldiers in Haifa port 125 refugees were wounded, 25 seriously and 5 mortally. All the refugees were forcibly removed to other boats and exiled to France.

2. Jacob Weiss, born in Czechoslovakia, was tried by a British military tribunal and executed, along with two of his comrades.

   While expressing our sorrow, we also wish to express our surprise that the Mandate authorities have not heeded appeals by Jewish and non-Jewish organizations and institutions in Czechoslovakia, by the Jewish Agency, and by the *Yishuv* in the Land of Israel not to impose the death penalty.

The Mandatory government did not exercise its prerogative to pardon these young men and proved that it has no consideration for the principles of supreme justice.

3. British soldiers shot and killed five innocent citizens in the streets of Tel Aviv in retaliation for terrorist action taken against two British sergeants. The Jews of Czechoslovakia join the peace - loving residents of the Land of Israel, who are vehemently opposed to murder and bloodshed, in condemning the fact that members of the military, whose duty it is to preserve order and safeguard the population in accordance with the principles of democracy and humanity, have reacted by willfully murdering innocent people.

In the name of the Jews of Czechoslovakia, we appeal sincerely to the authorities of the British Mandate to open the gates of Palestine to the survivors of the Holocaust, to permit Jewish refugees, who are living in camps under difficult conditions and whose only aspiration is to reach a safe harbor, to immigrate.

This protest was sent to the UN Secretariat and the British Government by way of her ambassador in Prague. A copy was sent to the Foreign Ministry in Prague.

Extensive Zionist activity and favorable political conditions were certainly among the considerations leading to the decision to hold the European Zionist conference in Czechoslovakia. The conference took place from the 27th to the 30th of Av, 5707 (August 12-16, 1947), in the Pope Hotel in Karlové Vary (Karlsbad).

The 22nd World Zionist Congress in Basel in 1946 ratified the plan to establish a democratic Jewish state in the Land of Israel, and in 1947, the 50th anniversary of the founding of political Zionism, this dream faced the moment of truth.

The Zionist conference in Karlsbad opened at 8:30 p.m., with an impressive memorial ceremony. The podium was decorated to reflect the Zionist activities of the past year: from Holocaust to resurrection.

It was a moving experience to see the Jewish national flag flying beside the flags of European states, to see the leaders of the *Yishuv* in the Land of Israel, the delegates to the congress, the discharged soldiers in uniform, the masses of participants, guided by youngsters from the youth movements – and all this after the terrible Holocaust. Sitting beside the presidential table were the leaders of the Zionist movement, representatives of the government and representatives of the Jewish organizations.

Eliyahu Dobkin opened the conference by lighting candles in memory of the victims of the Holocaust, and after him candles were lit by representatives of the Jews in various countries of Europe.

After commemorative remarks and benedictions, Eliyahu Dobkin reported on the fate of 40,000 "illegal" immigrants, the affair of the *Exodus,* which had aroused world-wide attention, and the bitter lot that befell the "illegal" immigrants in the *Salvador,* the *Patria,* and the *Struma.* He declared that the struggle would continue until the gates of Palestine were opened to the 200,000 Jews waiting in refugee camps in Germany, Austria, and Italy and to the masses of Jews in the Diaspora who aspired to immigrate to the land of their forefathers.

The main speech was delivered by Nahum Goldmann, who gave

a political overview of the Zionist movement, the condition of the Jews, and the United Nations – an organization with a membership of 55 nations, 5 of them Arab, whose representatives, holding a variety of views and positions, were soon to vote on a resolution deciding the fate of Palestine. Petroleum, the importance of which has been steadily growing since the war, is one of the decisive factors in the Middle East. The time has come to demand that a final decision be made to establish a state comprising all of the Land of Israel. Twenty-five years ago, the Jewish people would not have dared make such a demand, but now our sons have shown that they are capable of building houses and working the land with their own hands. The Mandate government in Palestine does not support these endeavors. Arab might is increasing, and time is working against the Jewish people. Today there are five Arab states in the United Nations, and in time there will be more. The Jews can no longer suffer patiently under a foreign regime. They must insist that a Jewish government be established in the Land of Israel, and there is a chance their demand will be met. The *Yishuv,* which was wise to fight against the White Book, is sufficiently strong to continue the struggle and to carry out the will of the people to build its homeland. If the Jewish people show determination and fight in a united front, they will succeed in opening the gates of the Land of Israel in the near future.

The following day Moshe Shertok, head of the political department of the Jewish Agency spoke: "After investigations before international commissions, our unequivocal demand to establish an independent Jewish state in the Land of Israel has been submitted to the United Nations General Assembly. Until then we shall continue our struggle for free immigration and for masses of immigrants to be taken in to build our homeland."

Dr. Ehrenfeld and Dr. Winterstein were chosen to represent

Slovakia in the 13-member presidential committee.

The present regional conference, the third in Karlsbad, was of special significance. The conference delegates represented some 350,000 members of the Zionist movement from 14 countries of Europe, survivors of the Holocaust who were prepared to leave this continent and immigrate to the Land of Israel, if only they were given the opportunity.

The conference succeeded in strengthening the Zionist organization in Europe both internally and externally. It united sundry movements and par ties with different outlooks, bringing them together to fight for their common goal: to raise all the material, human, and moral resources necessary to face the great test of achieving independence for a persecuted people, wandering exiles who wished to live as a free nation in their ancient new homeland.

The Zionist conference made a deep impression, contributing to a greater Zionist-nationalist awareness. The many activists who participated received encouragement and information and passed on the word of the Zionist movement to their home communities. Dozens of Jews everywhere expressed their preparedness to leave their homes and immigrate to the Land of Israel to strengthen the Yishuv in Palestine. Dozens of participants in immigration preparatory programs were waiting for the signal to immigrate and settle in the Land of Israel. Czechoslovak Jewry, steeped in a culture which combined the heritage of East European Jewry with the general culture of Western Europe's Jews, has always been ready to contribute its share to the Zionist settlement effort, to defend and build the Land of Israel; now it did so with redoubled energy.

Czechoslovakia became a center of intense activity in support of Israel. Many emissaries were engaged in various missions in Prague and Bratislava – agents of *Berihah* and the organization for "illegal" immigration and delegations purchasing technical supplies and arms – making Czechoslovakia an important source of arms for the Haganah. The Czechoslovak airline opened a direct flight from Prague to Lod, used by exporters and importers from the Land of Israel, and lively trade relations developed between the two countries. Former Czechoslovak *kibbutz* emissaries purchased equipment for industry and through a variety of transfer agreements took Jewish property out of Czechoslovakia, sometimes under difficult circumstances. Especially good work was done by Irma Polák, a WIZO emissary, and Dr. Paul März, who made public appearances in the larger cities and lectured about the Land of Israel, its development, and the struggle to open its gates. Being from Czechoslovakia, they knew how to establish rapport and inspire the Jewish community.

On Saturday night, November 29, 1947, the eve of the 17th of Kislev, 5708, the United Nations General Assembly convened and ratified the right of our people to national independence in its own land. The General Assembly decided to adopt the partition plan and to establish separate Jewish and Arab states in Palestine. Thirty-three nations voted for the resolution and only 13 against it. The Jewish community in Palestine was jubilant, and Jews the world over joined in their joyous exultation.

On behalf of the Union of Jewish Communities and in coordination with the Rabbinical Council we issued a circular to all the Jewish communities to hold a festive service of thanksgiving on Sunday, the 24th of Kislev, 5708 (December 7, 1947).

In Bratislava the festive service was held in the Great Synagogue, which was decorated with Israel's blue and white flag and the flag of Czechoslovakia. I gave the keynote address.

On December 9, 1947, the eve of the 27ᵗʰ of Kislev, 5708, the Zionist Organization in Bratislava held a Hanukkah party, the tone of which was set by the UN resolution establishing a Jewish state. The public, showing great interest and enthusiasm, came out in force.

On Sunday, the first day of the month of Tevet (December 14, 1947), in the Bratislava National Theatre, the Zionist Organization and the central organization of the Jewish communities held a public rally in honor of the UN resolution. Representatives of the government, foremost Deputy Chairman of the Slovak People's Council Anton Granatier, as well as army officers, diplomats, and representatives from the political parties and the press, attended the rally.

Chapter Three

The Jewish Community After the Communist Revolution

"Strengthen ye the weak hands, and
make firm the tottering knees"
(Isaiah 35:3)

I. Political Changes in 1948 – Social Upheaval

The Communist revolution in Czechoslovakia, in February
1948, took place quietly and without bloodshed. The Communists
raised a militia of about a thousand laborers, armed with sticks and
hoes, and staged a demonstration in Prague. Then in the factories,
plants, and government offices they set up action committees
which pressed strongly for change, causing serious unrest. On
February 25, 1948, President Beneš finally gave in and approved
the establishment of a new government. Jan Masaryk remained in
office as foreign minister; but on March 10, 1948, he was found
dead in the yard below his office. His death is believed to have
been a political assassination, staged to look like a suicide. The
new regime did not wish to make an inquest. Vladimir Klementis
was appointed to replace Masaryk. The Social Democrats were
forced to join the Communist party and the new constitution
made Czechoslovakia into a people's democracy. Beneš resigned

on June 7, 1948. Clement Gottwald was elected president, Antonin Zápotocký was appointed prime minister, and Rudolph Slanský became general secretary of the Communist party. Most of the opposition were arrested, and many fled abroad.

Among those who hastily fled Czechoslovakia were Arnošt Frischer, chairman of the Council of Jewish Communities in Prague, and Kurt Wehle, the general secretary. A Communist action committee took over the Jewish community and the Council of Jewish Communities and appointed a new board, comprised of members of the Communist party and headed by Dr. Ungar, commissioner of hospitals in the Ministry of Health in Prague.

One of the tasks of the action committees was to purge enterprise managements of undesirable "reactionary" elements. Since the Zionists in the Union of Jewish Communities had not fled, but rather had remained in office, the action committee of the Council of Jewish Communities intervened and used the trade union in Bratislava to apply pressure to remove our "reactionary management." As a result, the committee of clerks and workers of the Union of Jewish Communities elected an action committee consisting of Joseph Lipa, Alois Nissel, Marta Tochten, Ladislav Fehér, Salomon Guttman, and myself. A. Nissel, an active person in the trade union and a member of the Communist party, a trustworthy and decent man, was chosen as committee coordinator. In a cable to Prime Minister Gottwald we pledged our loyalty to the new government. Similar cables were also sent to the ministers of the Slovak administration, the head of the administration Dr. Gustav Husak, Minister of Education Laco Novomeský, and Minister of Interior Dr. Daniel Okályi.

On April 22, Dr. Ungar informed us that he had been elected chairman of the Council of Jewish Communities and expressed his hope for close cooperation between the two umbrella organizations of the Jewish communities. In our response we congratulated him and agreed to cooperate in matters that concerned all the Jews of Czechoslovakia.

In post war years the Jewish community was deeply involved in the administration and maintenance of the Jewish hospital in Bratislava, to the extent that this item was almost always on the agenda. The Bratislava Jewish community and the Union of Jewish Communities delegated committees to see to these affairs, until the decree came to nationalize the hospital and turn it over to the government.

On May 25, Ludevit Mayer, chairman of the *Hevra Kaddisha,* and I went to the Ministry of Health in Prague to speak to Dr. Ungar, hoping to win the government's consent for the state's only Jewish hospital to preserve its Jewish character and continue being run in accordance with the *halakhah.* Dr. Ungar took the opportunity to discuss the common problems of the two Jewish umbrella organizations and invited the board of the directors of the Council of Jewish Communities – Dr. Schwarz, R. Feigel, Kisch, and Širnková – to participate in this conversation. I sensed that a trap was being laid for us. The Council's board spoke hypocritically to obtain what they wished in a circuitous way. At first, they asked for advice on providing religious services, then they asked for financial assistance, and by the end they proposed that the community organizations merge and have their main office in Prague, making the Bratislava union a branch office. This far-reaching proposal came as no surprise to me. I rejected it cautiously, saying that I would bring it up before the officers of the Union of Jewish Communities.

The following day I paid a visit to the deputy chairman, Eugen

Hoff, in the Ministry of Education and Culture in Prague, where we talked with Prof. Eckhart, the commissioner of religious affairs. The latter told us that the Central Action Committee of the National Front of Czechs and Slovaks had invited the representatives of the churches and religious communities in the Czech Republic to attend consultations on transferring the churches to the hands of the government and making clergymen into civil servants. The representative of the Council of Jewish Communities in Prague had also participated in these consultations and had raised the question of merging the two central organizations of Jewish communities. After telling Prof. Eckhart about the character, composition, purpose and development of the Union of Jewish Communities, and about the ideological differences between the Jews of Bohemia-Moravia and the more conservative Jews of Slovakia, he declared that the government would not intervene in internal organizational questions of recognized religions. The commissioner of religious affairs assured us that whenever representatives of the churches in Slovakia were called for a meeting the representatives of the Union of Jewish Communities would also be invited, because he viewed our union as the supreme independent institution of the Jewish communities of Slovakia and identified with us on this issue.

On May 26, 1948, we issued a circular requesting that in the upcoming elections to the National Assembly on May 30 the Jewish communities vote for the single list of the National Front *(Národná Fronta),* headed by the Communist party. We said, among other things:

> Only enemies of the regime will put a white slip in the ballot box. These elections will not determine the victory of the National Front, but rather will measure the strength of the forces of reaction. We must take

part in these elections and back the National Front and its program, whose platform promises equality for all citizens of the state, without distinction of race or religion, and whose victory will assure that the regime of anti-Semitic discrimination shall never return and that there shall be progress and social justice for all citizens of the State.

In July 1948, we participated in the meetings of the World Jewish Congress in Montreux. The Union of Jewish Communities was represented by Dr. Winterstein, Oscar Krasniansky, and myself, and the Council of Jewish Communities was represented by Dr. Ungar, Feigel, and Širnková. The Czech delegation joined the Communist bloc and Dr. Ungar requested to act as spokesman for both delegations. We were opposed to such a move as a matter of principle and remained independent. High-placed persons in the Congress advised us to be cautious and guard our words, saying we would do well to remember that "speech is silver, but silence is golden." Dr. Ungar tried again to persuade us that for political reasons it was essential that the two organizations merge and present a unified delegation.

We had decided from the outset not to participate in the general debates, but when England's delegate, Dr. Löwenberg, asked in his speech why the delegations from the Democratic People's Republics were all so homogeneous, Dr. Winterstein saw fit to request the floor and proclaim that the Czechoslovak delegation was not homogeneous, but rather represented various groups in Judaism. He declared that the Czechoslovak government's attitude towards our problems was in the spirit of the democratic presidents, Masaryk and Beneš, and the current president, Clement Gottwald. He also spoke critically of the shortcomings of the leaders of the Jewish Congress during the Holocaust.

Dr. Ungar was displeased by our position and during the congress convened both delegations to point out that we were the only ones in the bloc of People's Democracies whose forces were split and to say that this was an intolerable situation. He warned us again to give serious consideration to his proposal for a merger of the two organizations.

We returned from the Congress extremely concerned about what lay in store for us politically. Dr. Winterstein disclosed to me that he intended to leave Slovakia in the near future to accept an offer made him by Dr. Nahum Goldmann to direct the office of the World Jewish Congress in Brazil.

Upon my return from Montreux, I called an urgent meeting of the executive committee and representatives of the Jewish communities throughout Slovakia, for the 17th of Tamuz (July 22, 1948), to discuss the proposal to merge the two organizations. In my meetings with the leaders of the Council of Jewish Communities in Prague I received the impression that the wishes for a merger were not simply ideologically motivated, but were also designed to take control of the property of the Jewish communities in Slovakia. The Council of Jewish Communities supported its communities with money from the Terezin Fund. Each month two million korunas were released from the fund, but this sum was insufficient to cover the communities' expenses. Therefore, the Council was proposing a merger with the Union of Jewish Communities, to enable them to draft a joint budget and organize the Czech communities along the lines of Slovakia's self-supporting communities. Another pretext which they gave for a merger was their wish for our guidance in matters of religion and tradition, in which they were not so expert.

In addition to the executive committee, representatives of 14 Jewish communities throughout Slovakia participated in the deliberations. The following resolution was adopted unanimously:

> The Central Union of the Jewish Communities in Slovakia, the merger of the former Central Bureau of Orthodox Congregations and the Yeshurun Federation of Congregations, represents only those Jewish communities in Slovakia which are organized in it, according to the principles and laws of the Democratic People's Republic and in conformance to the laws of the Torah and the religious precepts, according to the customs and traditions laid down by our rabbis in Slovakia. Slovak Jewry, true to the Jewish tradition, is not interested in intervening in the affairs of communities beyond the borders of Slovakia and is opposed to other bodies intervening in the religious and organizational affairs of its communities, which are under the sole jurisdiction of the Union of Jewish Communities in conjunction with the Council of Orthodox Rabbis in Slovakia. The Union of Jewish Communities expresses its allegiance to the State and supports the endeavors of the government of the Democratic People's Republic in Czechoslovakia.

Later in the meeting I reported on the deliberations of the World Jewish Congress in Montreux. That evening we sponsored a lecture in Bratislava by the general secretary of Yad va-Shem, Mr. Shenhavi, from Jerusalem. The union's resolution, sent to our counterpart in Prague, did not pass without reverberations. Various messages were sent us in roundabout ways. We felt as if we had put our lives on the line. But the snares which were put in our path were to no avail. We continued our line of action, which was determined by developments in the Land of Israel.

A great historic event took place on the Sabbath eve of the scriptural reading of *Emor*, the 5th of Iyar, 5708 (May 14, 1948), three years after the end of the Holocaust of European Jewry. On that day the leaders of the *Yishuv* met in Tel Aviv; David Ben-Gurion proclaimed the establishment of the State of Israel to the Jewish people and the entire world, and everyone present signed Israel's Declaration of Independence. We stood proud and tall. Establishing the State – for which we in the Diaspora had worked, as well, both openly and underground – opening the gates of the land, and in gathering of the exiles all heralded the beginning of Redemption. The elegy of the Holocaust gave way to the joyous ode of rebirth, and thanksgiving assemblies and festive services were held in many Jewish communities.

On Sunday, the 14th of Iyar, 5708 (May 23, 1948), in Lučenec I participated in a regional celebration of southern Slovakia, marking three closely connected events: the inauguration of the renovated Lučenec synagogue, the unveiling of memorial plaques for victims of the Holocaust, and the birth of the State of Israel. Rabbi Hillel Unsdorfer, a colleague and friend of my rabbi and mentor, Rabbi Moses-Asher Eckstein of Sered, used to pray, preach, and guide his flock in this synagogue. Both men devoted their lives to the goal of settling and building the Land of Israel, and both perished in the Holocaust, may the Lord avenge their blood. At this large gathering we launched a fund drive for the Haganah in Israel and raised close to one million korunas from the Jews of Lučenec.

The Jews of Slovakia did not remain apathetic. The mood of exodus and emigration mounted. Those who were still sitting on the fence, undecided where they would go, should have realized that emigrating from one gentile country, where our parents and brethren were annihilated and thrown to the dogs, to another alien state did not guarantee that the same opposition and hatred towards us would not be brought there in our baggage, that the seeds of anti-Semitism would not be planted there, too, by our very arrival. Therefore, the only constructive solution was to return to the land of our forefathers.

At this stage the Czechoslovak government, as well, viewed Jewish immigration to the State of Israel with favor. It understood the motivations for immigration and supported them. The cable from Foreign Minister Vladimir Klementis to Israel's Foreign Minister Moshe Shertok (Sharett) attests his friendly attitude:

"The Government of Czechoslovakia appreciates the efforts of the Jewish people for the sake of peace and social progress and is convinced that the establishment of an independent Jewish state will contribute to bringing peace and security to the Middle East." By his practical assistance in every sphere, Klementis continued in the footsteps of his predecessors Jan Masaryk and Presidents Beneš and Masaryk, who viewed Zionism as the movement which would bring revival and rebirth to the nation of Israel. Thanks to the full understanding between the Union of Jewish Communities' action committee and its board of directors, we could carry on without changing our political line, maintaining a united front in our dealing with all bodies, according to the needs of the hour and in strict adherence to the laws of the state. We knew that our counterparts in Prague were lying in wait for us, looking for an excuse to dismiss our board, which was working hand in hand with the Zionist Organization and with *Agudat Israel,* neither of which, as the leaders in Prague stressed at every opportunity, belonged to the forces of "progress."

Both central organizations – the Union of Jewish Communities and the Zionist Organization in Bratislava – worked together on many levels: raising money and seeing to it that it reached its designated recipient, assisting the organization for immigration to Israel, and giving public political support to emissaries from the Land of Israel to help them carry out their various missions, including drafting manpower and acquiring arms and equipment.

The Land of Israel Office ran a successful fund drive for the Jewish national funds and various missions. The Jews contributed generously. Many congregations in Slovakia, encouraged by the Union of Jewish Communities and acting with its approval, sold off real-estate and contributed the proceeds to the Haganah and to planting a forest in memory of Czechoslovakia's martyrs. When our request to transfer the contributions to Israel via the Czechoslovakia National Bank was rejected, the money was deposited with the Union of Jewish Communities. A figure of eight and a quarter million korunas appears in the 1947 financial report of the Union of Jewish Communities,[83] and the receipts column in the balance sheet of July 1949 shows an entry of over 11,000,000 korunas in the miscellaneous category. The lion's share of these receipts came from the fund drive. The Union of Jewish Communities resubmitted requests to transfer funds to the State of Israel several times, but to no avail. Our requests having been rejected time and again, we decided to use the money for social welfare and at the same time arranged with the Joint for them not to forward the monthly stipends which it had been allocating us for welfare. "Giving up" dollars which had previously been transferred to the Union of Jewish Communities through a branch of the National Bank in Bratislava, however, became a source of trouble. [84]

---

[83] See p. 257.

[84] See "The Arrest of Zionist Activists," in chapter four, pp. 293-299.

On the 11th of Av, 5708 (August 16, 1948), we held a reception for Ehud Avriel, Israel's first ambassador to Czechoslovakia. Ten years earlier Ehud had visited Bratislava on a secret mission. In March 1938, when Austria was annexed to Germany and thousands of Jews were either expelled or fled from Vienna to Bratislava, Avriel came to arrange for Austrian Jewish refugees to remain in the Patronka camp until such time as they could be sailed to Palestine along the Danube, an international waterway. From then on, Bratislava became a center for thousands of refugees and émigrés. Activists in the Jewish community and the Zionist movement, who came to the aid of the refugees, persuaded the authorities to help the refugees emigrate and to let them stay temporarily in transit camps in Czechoslovakia.

The operations of Vienna-born Ehud Avriel and his colleagues working for *Aliyah Bet* ("illegal" immigration to Palestine) saved many European Jews from perishing in the Holocaust. In the post-war period the office of *Berihah* in Prague was an important center underground activity directed at helping Jews reach Palestine. When the State of Israel was established, Ehud played an important role in the crucial operation of arms acquisitions for the War of Independence. With the assistance of Foreign Minister Jan Masaryk and his deputy, Vladimir Klementis, Czechoslovakia supplied armaments vital to the newborn state, fighting for its survival.

At a festive luncheon I praised the great merits of our ambassador and, speaking in the name of Slovak Jewry and the Union of Jewish Communities, promised that we would continue our Zionist activities with redoubled energy, using all the ways and means at our disposal: encouraging fund drives for Israel, helping organize *aliyah,* and assisting needy immigrants and refugees from neighboring countries.

When Israel's gates were opened to Jewish immigration, special administrative departments were established in the offices of the Zionist Organization. These departments, working in conjunction with the Jewish Agency's Immigration Department, were in charge of seeing to it that passports were issued, cargos inspected by customs officials and shipped to Israel, departure dates set and group travel arrangements made. Jews were required to submit detailed lists of all items they wished to take, down to the last spool of thread and shoe-lace, and obtain export permits from the authorities. Transferring merchandise was forbidden, and sometimes even permission to export home appliances was difficult to obtain. The treasury official in Prague in charge of issuing these permits was a Jewish communist by the name of Otto Fischel, who for ideological reasons was inclined to rule strictly and make things as difficult as possible.

Before Jews received their exit and emigration visas, they were required to sign a declaration giving up their Czechoslovak citizenship and stating that they had no claims against the State, including pensions and other social benefits.

According to the Joint's statistics, in 1948 approximately 1,000 Jews immigrated to Israel via Prague and close to 500 via Bratislava. The first to immigrate from Prague were the Carpatho-Russian Jews, who settled temporarily in cities of the Sudetenland, a region whose inhabitants had been deported to Germany. In November 1948, Jews who had fought in the Czechoslovak Brigade left: 300 from Prague and 1,000 from Bratislava; in 1948 another 500 Jews immigrated from Prague and 300 from Bratislava and enlisted in the Haganah. In April 1949, a group of 1,800 members of the Brigade left via Prague and 700 via Bratislava. In 1949 the Jews began exiting en masse, and by July 4,840 Jews had left via Prague and 5,660 via Bratislava. By 1950 approximately 19,000 Jews had immigrated legally to Israel from Czechoslovakia. This figure does not include Hungarian refugees who passed through Bratislava in 1949.[85]

After 20 years of active public service, Dr. Winterstein decided to accept the offer which had been made him to head the bureau of the World Jewish Congress in Brazil. At a farewell meeting on behalf of the union, on Elul 4 (September 21, 1948), the vice-chairman, Jacob Hoff, paid tribute to Dr. Winterstein's great contribution to strengthening the status of the Union of Jewish Communities and to his genuine cooperation with all factions: "He knew how to fight for our rights with governmental institutions and to defend the generality. As a man of many talents, he shall surely excel in his new undertaking, as well." Dr. Winterstein responded that, along with Rabbi Abraham Frieder of blessed memory, he had always aspired to unity, and expressed satisfaction that all the different factions had united in mutual trust. He cautioned against new members who might be put on the board by hostile elements interested in hurting the unity which existed in the Union of Jewish Communities and in the Jewish congregations in Slovakia, and recommended that the board of the union continue pursuing its present policies.

Later in the meeting the following new members were appointed to the board: Dr. Henrich Lax, Judah Weiss, and Prof. Ižo Rosa. The office of general secretary was left vacant.

The following day Dr. Winterstein was given a public farewell party, attended by leaders of the Jewish community and government officials.

II. Renewed Debate on the Structure of the Jewish Community

In the wake of the Communist revolution provincial action

---

[85] See sections on the flight from Hungary, pp. 299-311.

committees were established alongside the government's offices in the provinces. Religious committees, comprised of representatives of all the recognized religions in the state, functioned in conjunction with these action committees. A list of our representatives in the provinces was sent to the central action committee of the Slovak National Front with a request that a representative of ours be put on the central committee. The steadily diminishing Jewish community, however, was not the foremost concern of the authorities. The religious committees were aimed primarily at the well- healed Catholic Church and the Evangelist Church. The communist Slovaks neither interfered nor showed any interest in the affairs of the Jewish community. Our brethren, the communist Jews in Prague, caused us greater concern.

In August the Council of Jewish Communities again proposed holding a joint meeting of representatives from both Jewish community organizations and requested that we send a delegation authorized to make decisions in crucial questions of joint concern. Our board elected the following people to represent us: Eugen Hoff, Dr. Henrich Lax, Alois Nissel, Prof. Ižo Rosa, and myself.

The meeting took place on November 1, 1948, in the offices of the Jewish Council in Prague, which was represented by Dr. Schwarz, Feigel, and Šimková. On the agenda was an issue of paramount importance to them: a merger of the Union of Jewish Communities with the Council of Jewish Communities.

In talks which lasted five hours they presented us a long list of all our sins. In their opinion, a change was called for in our policies. They began the deliberations speaking obliquely but by the end said outright that the organizations of the Jewish communities had been charged to preserve the integrity of the Jewish communities and to oppose *aliyah* and the Zionist movement. Money must not be wasted on these purposes, they said, but should be allotted to build a solid foundation for future Jewish life in a community of a progressive character. This, they argued, could be assured if the Jewish communities and organizations were headed by suitable persons, desirable to the ruling Communist party, and were run jointly by a single body based in Prague. They argued further that no other democratic people's republic had two central organizations representing the Jewish community. One of the spokesmen stressed the need to act in accordance with the interests of the state and expressed his surprise that the Union of Jewish Communities had given up its dollar stipends from the Joint, since Czechoslovakia was badly in need of foreign currency. This, he said, proved that the Union of Jewish Communities had not acted in the interests of the state.

On hearing these things, I thought of our colleague Krasniansky, who had been arrested several weeks earlier and interrogated by treasury officials, although none of us knew why. After consultation, our delegation presented its final stand, roughly along the following lines:

The Central Union of Jewish Communities in Slovakia, we maintained, is the supreme organization representing the religious Jewish community in Slovakia and is run according to the *halakhah* and Orthodox Jewish practice. The Association of Persecuted Persons in Slovakia handles questions of restitution and rehabilitation, working in parallel with the Union of Jewish Communities. Both Slovak organizations and the Council of Jewish Communities established a coordinating committee to discuss issues of common concern to the Jews in both autonomous parts of the republic. We agreed to have a single delegation represent us at international conferences, in accordance with the by-laws of the coordinating committee, which stipulated that the leadership of the delegation alternate. Our delegation proposed that a Central Jewish Committee comprised of the heads of all the independent nationwide Jewish organizations in the Czech and Slovak Republics be established.

The representatives of the Czech council did not agree to our proposal and warned that if a solution to this problem was not found in the near future they would turn to the government. Dr. Ungar's aspirations simply exceeded all bounds.

In November 1948, the American Joint held a conference in Paris, to which representatives of numerous Jewish communities and organizations, such as Ort, Oze, Hias, Alliance, the Jewish Agency, Youth Aliyah, etc., were invited. After speeches by the director of the Joint, Edward Warburg, and its European director, Dr. Joseph Schwarz, the delegates of the various countries were requested to submit their reports. Our delegate, Eugen Hoff, had had difficulty obtaining an entry visa and therefore was late to the conference. When Mr. Hoff was requested to report on conditions in Slovakia, Dr. Ungar came forward in Mr. Hoff's absence and announced that he was competent to speak for Slovak Jewry, as well.

At the December 15th board meeting of the Union of Jewish Communities the position taken by our delegation was approved unanimously, and Eugen Hoff reported on the deliberations at the Joint conference in Paris. The purpose of the conference was "to work cooperatively with all Jewish organizations to spare the Jews suffering, to guarantee children who had survived the Holocaust an education, and to help rehabilitate the sick and the injured. We must use all means to help any Jew who wishes to immigrate to Israel and settle in his old-new homeland. The aid which the Joint gives should not be viewed as philanthropy, but as a sacred moral obligation to help our suffering brethren, wherever they may be."

III. Riots in Bratislava

On August 20, 1947, the Slovak authorities came out sharply against Hungarian - and German - speakers. To not invite trouble, even Jews who were not fluent in the language of the country tried to speak Slovak. Ceremonies and official events were conducted solely in Slovak. Although we did our best to cool things down, on August 20, 1948, exactly one year after the warning was issued, violent demonstrations, reminiscent of the pogrom in Topolčany immediately after the war, broke out in the capital.

The spark that set off the hostilities was lit by the rabble in Bratislava's municipal market in Stalin Square. That Wednesday, before noon, a woman by the name of Emilia Prášilová accused the owner of a fruit and vegetable stand of selling to a "stinking Jewess" (Aliza Frank) out of turn and thereby supporting the cheek of the "damned Jews." Aliza Frank answered back and the ensuing quarrel developed into a fist fight. The police made no attempt to prevent crowds of women from stepping in and hitting Aliza, accusing her of striking at a pregnant Christian woman. The instigators added all sorts of trumped-up accusations, and the masses shouted things like "A Jewess caused a premature stillbirth," and "A Jewess killed a Christian baby!" The police arrested both women. After a brief investigation the pregnant woman was released in fine health; but Aliza Frank, who had a baby and a young child, as well as an infirm elderly mother at home, was kept under arrest and accused of attacking a pregnant woman. The investigating officer said to her, "If you had done this to my wife, I would have killed you."

Meanwhile, in front of the market building, the fires of hatred were being fanned. The rabble, incited to a high pitch, turned the quarrel into a blood libel and called "Revenge on the Jewess who has killed a Christian child." As the few Jewish housewives who had been shopping for the Sabbath were hurrying to leave the scene and get help, the crowds jumped on and attacked another Jewish woman, P. Cohen, right in front of a policeman's eyes. Another Jewess, Livia Eckstein, a local shopkeeper who had dared to defend Aliza Frank and the Jews, was also attacked and, after being accused of all sorts of fabrications, was arrested. The police detained her for three days, even though she had a six-month-old child at home.

The apathy of the police encouraged bums and street gangs, who organized a mass demonstration under the banner of "Death to the Jews, murderers of the Christians." They marched on the town hall and, in violation of the law, demonstrated in front of 50 policemen, who collaborated with them. The demonstrators were not dispersed until the Jewish community intervened through the Ministry of Interior, and even then, the demonstration was only broken up for several hours. In the afternoon the rabble gathered again in Stalin Square. The security forces only put on a show of intervening. Several policemen actually led the rioters and spurred them on. The police warned the crowd in a polite and restrained manner, calculated to make the rioters, who sensed that the police were sympathetic, very bold. By five o'clock there were two thousand demonstrators in Stalin Square. When reinforcements arrived and the masses began to be dispersed, the rallying call was heard: "Let's march on the Jewish Quarter!"

The police did not take any effective measures to prevent the demonstration from spreading. The offices of the Jewish community had been forewarned and had locked their gates; but the old-age home, the Jewish hospital, and the boys' and girls' orphanages were essentially thrown to the dogs. Their residents, who had been following developments in the city with fear and apprehension, appealed to the police for protection but received no response. Rioting mobs broke into the Jewish soup-kitchen on Zámocká Street and plundered and broke anything they could lay their hands on, causing close to 100,000 korunas worth of damage. From there they marched on the central offices at 29 Markovič Street. Since the gates were locked, they shattered the windows unimpeded and then proceeded to 6 Podjavorinská Street, where they also broke the windows. The riot was not quelled until 11 p.m., at which time the security forces finally intervened and the rioters went home.

The following morning, at 10 o'clock, crowds gathered in the market- place again. This time the demonstrators came up with another slogan: shortage of food and supplies due to the rich Jews who were buying everything up. The authorities realized that the game was becoming dangerous and was likely to develop in an undesirable direction. Hence the gathering crowds were dispersed before the rabble-rousers had time to incite the mob.

In the wake of these demonstrations the two Jewish organizations submitted a memorandum to the chairman of the Communist party, William Široký, who was also deputy prime minister in Prague. A delegation comprised of Dr. Eugen Verný, Dr. Egon Gold, Dr. Jan Steiner, and myself gave the memorandum to the head of the Slovak administration, Dr. Gustav Husák, and to Minister of Interior Dr. Daniel Okályi, both of whom promised to take the necessary measures.

The riots were eminent proof that ranks of the security forces were still filled with Fascists, traitors, and people who abused their office, people who were willing to deny citizens protection and to lend a hand to destructive forces jeopardizing the democratic regime. These forces prevented, and are still preventing, the moral and material rehabilitation of the state's Jewish citizens. One aim of the demonstrations was to perpetuate this state of affairs and make life still more difficult for the Jews, scaring them and hastening their exodus from the country. Indeed, this technique was shown to be quite effective and encouraged the Jews to flee Czechoslovakia, emigrate, and move to Israel.

As the flood of Jews exiting from Czechoslovakia mounted, dealing with converts out of the faith became an issue. Hoping to help solve the problem, on December 8, 1948, we sent a circular to all the Jewish communities of Slovakia about issuing affidavits of affiliation to the Jewish faith. The circular stated:

> Under the Nazi regime many Jews left the Jewish community, some only in outward appearance by acquiring forged baptism papers, others by proper conversion to Christianity. These Jews have recently been returning to their communities and requesting affidavits of their Jewishness, a necessary document for receiving emigration assistance from the central institutions.
>
> The Jewish communities should refer these "repentant Jews" to rabbinical courts in Bratislava and Košice, because only these bodies are authorized to bring them back into the lap of Judaism and to issue them the certificates they seek. Only after presenting a document from the rabbinical court is the Jewish community entitled to list them in the books of the community and to issue them affidavits of Jewishness.

IV. New Year's 5709

The prevailing mood among Slovak Jewry on the High Holy Days of 5709 was that this would be their last New Year in exile. The demonstrations against the Jews at the end of August accelerated their exodus. Everyone was busy making preparations and purchases and arranging official documents and material affairs prior to their departure. The longing to be out of Czechoslovakia grew stronger from day to day. In the spring of 1948, I left Nové Mesto and moved with my family to the building of the Jewish community in Bratislava. Henceforth I could devote the entire week to public work in the Union of Jewish Communities; for with the rise in the number of people leaving and immigrating to Israel there was much more work to be done. The union helped organize services for the High Holy Days, 5709, in all of Slovakia's congregations. In Bratislava services were held in the two large synagogues, on Haidokova Street and Jews' Street. Most of the synagogues did not have rabbis. Thus, I was asked to give a sermon before the shofar service in the Great Synagogue at Jews' Street.

My sermon conveyed yearnings for the day we would immigrate to the liberated State of Israel. The blast of the shofar heralds the beginning of the ingathering of the exiles, as the prophet Isaiah said: "And it shall come to pass in that day, that a great horn shall be blown ... "(Isaiah 27: I 3). For us there is no other way but to make haste and immigrate to Israel, and see each other next year in Jerusalem.

The tide of *aliyah* grew steadily. Many families applied to the Union of Jewish Communities for assistance in covering their expenses. According to a decision of the board, every family immigrating to Israel was given a grant of 15,000 korunas; thus, we laid out close to 400,000 korunas. A large budget was required to cover all the applications, and we found it hard to meet the demands. At first the Joint had reservations about these payments, but after discussing the matter with Henry Levy, the Joint's general director in Prague, we persuaded him to give collective grants to the youth movements, whose requests had not yet come up for consideration, so that no one would be discriminated against.

The employees of the Union of Jewish Communities and of other Jewish organizations established a work gang of 50 men, which spent six days working on paving the Slavic Way. The gang worked exceptionally well and won the "wandering banner." Trade union members belonging to the Union of Jewish Communities ran a fund drive for the French miners who were on strike and gave the money they raised - 42,000 korunas - to Minister František Zupka.

Communist party members of the Union of Jewish Communities, together with Communist party members in other Jewish organizations, formed a professional cell and elected comrade Alois Nissel as their leader. The cell called on the office-holders of the union to join the ranks of the Communist party.

The Ministry of Propaganda cancelled the license for allocating paper to print *Ha-Lapid (The Torch),* a periodical for Jewish youth, published by the Union of Jewish Communities with the objective of imparting religious values to Jewish children, teaching them Torah and religious laws, stories of the Bible, and the meaning of the Jewish holidays.

According to the new directives, the Union of Slovak Youth became the sole body authorized to publish young people's periodicals. We tried to reinstate the license, but the Union of Slovak Youth was not "interested" in religious publications. We had no alternative but to pay our deficit of 26,000 korunas, and at the end of 1948 *The Torch* died out.

The tenth congress of the World Maccabee Organization convened in Israel, December 21-31, 1948. Czechoslovakia's representatives to the congress were Rabbi Dr. Hanoš Rezek, Ervin Diamant, Mikuláš Kanner, and Ervin Steiner. All of them, save Steiner, set out for Tel Aviv on December 21, on board the *Theodor Herzl,* an El Al airplane. The plane crashed over Greece and Dr. Rezek, Diamant, and Kanner were killed along with the rest of the passengers. The fourth delegate, Ervin Steiner of Bratislava, had already arrived in Tel Aviv and participated in the congress. The Zionist Organization communed with the memory of our dear departed colleagues, men of great merit in the Zionist movement. May their memory be eternally blessed.

Attorney Dr. Julius Reiss was delegated to draft uniform by-laws for the Jewish congregations and the Union of Jewish Communities. Prior to then the authority to approve congregational boards of directors rested with the Union of Jewish Communities. In 1948 new boards were elected in many Jewish communities.

Chapter Four

The Year of Aliyah

5709 (1949)

"And the ransomed of the Lord shall return,
and come with singing unto Zion,
and everlasting joy shall be upon their heads"
(Isaiah 35:10)

I. Arrest of Zionist Activists

Our colleague Oscar Krasniansky was released at the end of December 1948, after having been detained for three months by the Felony Department of the State Revenue Administration of the Ministry of Finance. The law provides that a suspect may not be kept under arrest for more than three months when there is insufficient evidence for a conviction. Since Krasniansky's arrest we, the leaders of the major Zionist organizations, feared that a similar fate might await us. Yet I did not expect to receive an unpleasant "visit" at dawn. On Friday night, Tevet 20 5709 (January 21, 1949), there came an insistent knocking on the door of my Bratislava apartment. I opened the door, and three men dressed in long leather coats came in. One of them kept guard on me, watching my every step. Before I got dressed, he searched my clothes. The other two went into the library and immediately set about searching thoroughly through every corner of the house. They asked me about foreign currency and searched for money and valuably jewelry which might arouse their suspicion. To their disappointment, they came up with nothing. They rummaged through the large bookcase and in one of the books found a $10 bill which I had not known about.

One thing worried me. Several days earlier Zvi Fehér, who was in charge of the supplies department, had given me a book for keeping records of the sale of non-Kosher food supplies which we received from UNRRA, such as shortening, dehydrated ground meat, and the like. Given the atmosphere in the state and the pressure which was being applied by the action committee of the Council of Jewish Communities in Prague, Fehér was afraid to keep unofficial documents in the union's offices. Dr. E. Abeles, chairman of the finance department, was in charge of these funds, which were deposited in a special bank account. Before having had a chance to peruse the book, I had put it in a desk drawer among the school books of my daughter Margalit, then in the third grade. The desk opened from above by raising its cover; and I was afraid, with such a thorough search, that the book would be discovered. Although I could not shake off the detective, somehow, I managed to cover the desk with coats and other clothing, without his noticing. After that I relaxed, because there was no other suspicious material in the house.

The plainclothesmen took me with them, assuring my wife that this was being done only to "take a deposition." By the time I reached the investigation department of the Ministry of Finance, the director of the Land of Israel Office, Leo Rosenthal, and the administrative director of the Joint in Bratislava, Dr. Juraj Révész, were in the adjacent rooms. All three of our offices had been searched simultaneously, and the books of the Union of Jewish Communities had been taken for a thorough review.

We were detained until the afternoon and then were informed that our depositions would be taken in the Prague office. Each of us was assigned a private detective, and at midnight we got off the train in Prague. The three of us traveled in the same train car, but were not allowed to exchange a word.

A Black Maria transported us to the gates of the Karl Prison. First all my personal effects, down to my shoelaces and watch, including my philacteries and prayerbook, were taken from me; then I was put in a small, stinking cell. It was 2 a.m., Saturday morning. The three inmates in the cell awoke, curious to discover the nature of the new criminal. Was I in for political or financial crimes? Was I a robber, or a murderer? I refrained from making any response. "Have no fear," they assured me, "we here are all in for financial offenses." The truth was that I myself did not know why I had been thrown into prison, since no warrant had been issued for my arrest.

One of the men, a Slovak merchant named Piovarči from Trnava, said: "I've been in here over a year, and I still don't know why they suspect me of violating foreign currency regulations. So don't be too hopeful; the people here have lots of time." This man gave me my first lesson in prison procedure, the inmates' daily routine and various ways one could manage in prison – tips that only an experienced person like him could conceive of. Later he also helped me inform people on the outside of my condition.

The cell was intended for two prisoners, but the jail authorities had added two bunk beds. I climbed up to the empty bunk and lay down on the straw mattress. The man lying across from me raised his head, looked at me, but did not say a word. I thought through the events of the day and my current situation, thought about my home and my family. How would my wife know where I was? I thought about my children -- Margalit and my 11-month-old Ariel. I knew I was innocent and that I had done nothing illegal, although even our counterparts on the board of the Council of Jewish Communities suspected us of transferring money via underground channels to Israel. Who could prove it? In this regime, however, things do not need to be proven. Nevertheless, I took courage, trusting that Providence protects those who are sent to perform good deeds.

A ray of light from a bulb in the hall shone into the cell through a slot in the door. It was time to recite the *shema*. Straightening myself, I stretched out on the bed and sighed. Two words, *shema Yisrael,* came out of my mouth in a whisper; but in the still of night; they reached the ears of the man lying across from me. He raised his head and, addressing me in an undertone, said in Hebrew: *"Shabbat shalom.* Do you speak Hebrew? Who are you?" "Greetings to you, and who are you?" I responded. This was a pleasant encounter, for such unpleasant circumstances. I was glad I had had the good fortune to be put into this cell. After several questions and answers, the man with whom I was talking concluded, "Don't be sure you'll remain here. On weekends, however, nothing happens here and there are no interrogations." Then he addressed Piovarči in Polish: "Let's try to make sure this chap is not transferred to a different cell." The man presented himself as Shlomo Berman, an emissary of the Zionist Worker. He said he had been in my office in Bratislava, but that I had been busy. He was planning to produce a film in the Barandov laboratories, but had gotten involved in foreign currency transactions and had been arrested. He had been awaiting trial for six months now. In prison he made friends with Piovarči, a well-to-do businessman accused of smuggling merchandise. Piovarči had bribed all the jailors and had become a "privileged" prisoner, allowed out now and then to see the dentist or tend to other medical needs. On such occasions he saw his wife, and through her, after I had spent three days in prison, I managed to transmit a message to my wife.

The cell was quite crowded and the sanitary conditions very primitive. Regimen was strict; searches were frequent, and once a day the prisoners were taken to an inside courtyard, surrounded by the fort-like building, and marched rapidly around in a circle, single file, room by room. Sometimes I saw Rosenthal, but it was impossible for me to communicate with him, even by sign language, since the jailors reacted immediately, hurling curses and threats at us. The cell was dim because the well-barred opening for light was small. During the morning walks we climbed up on the beds to peak through the opening at the famous veteran inmates, each of whom had a story of his own. I learned that Dr. Marcus Gordon, director of the JNF office in Prague, was also here. In my conversations with Berman, he described in Hebrew what it was like living in Israel.

Two weeks after my arrest I was taken to 31 Celetná Street for interrogation. Interrogator Procházka read the warrant for my arrest, which had been issued by the State Revenue Administration, Felony Department: "The American Joint is accused of violating foreign currency regulations in the millions. These violations were committed in collaboration with the Union of Jewish Communities in Slovakia, of which you are Chairman and responsible for its financial activities. To not hamper the investigation, we have issued a warrant for your arrest." The interrogator tried to confuse me with a battery of questions and cross-examination. How had I transferred these millions abroad illegally? What part had the Joint played in this transaction? Why had the JNF given me the money they collected? Why were we not receiving dollars from the Joint? What Jewish capitalists were involved in the affair? And a stream of similar questions which kept on recurring. "If you tell us the truth, you shall be able to spend the Sabbath with your family." Procházka tried hard to convince me that he knew I was not to blame, that the principal people being accused were the Joint and its agents, and that all I had to do was testify and sign a confession, since there was no point in my suffering. The fine would be paid by the Joint, which, he said, had a great deal of money at its disposal.

My answers were plain and simple: "We never had anything to do with financial transfers. The Union is an umbrella organization of the Jewish communities which takes care of religious affairs and is also involved in philanthropic and social work. When the National Bank would not approve the foreign transfer of JNF funds, which the Jews of Czechoslovakia had raised for the State of Israel, we accepted the money and used it for philanthropy in the Jewish community; and when the Joint saw that the Union had enough money for its welfare activities, they stopped sending us grants."

Three weeks later Rosenthal, Révész, and I were transferred to Pankrác Prison, a large, more modern jail. I was put in a cell with a political prisoner, a young Czech accused of spying for the United States. There were many prisoners of his ilk in this jail, and this gave me cause to fear lest we also be accused of political crimes.

On Tu bi-Shvat, my 36th birthday, for the first time, to my great joy, I received two encouraging letters, one from Henry Levy, general director of the Joint in Prague, and the other from Dorothy Green, the regional director in Bratislava. Both letters had been sent on the same date, February 10, 1949. I took this to be a good sign, betokening a turning point in the investigation. Mr. Levy wrote about the efforts my friends had been making to prove my innocence and informed me that my request to receive kosher food and three books had been approved. He also sent me regards from my wife and family and expressed his hope that my affair would soon be settled. Dorothy Green wrote that she sometimes saw people from the Union and that she did not need to stress how sorely my absence was felt. Now, especially, she was conscious of my influence and the great trust that all the people who had dealings with the central community organization placed in me. She also expressed her hope that I would be able to return to my family and my important work in the near future.

The following day kosher food arrived and I was allowed to receive three books: a prayerbook, a Bible, and a book on Hebrew grammar. This was a big relief. One day I was visited by Leo Engelsmann from Nové Mesto, commissar of the political department in the prison. I was glad for the visit itself and appreciated his courageousness, since his office required him to behave with the utmost caution, for the Communist party also kept its eyes on him like a hawk. He promised to relay regards to my family in person, which meant a lot to me. He did so immediately, repaying me the kindness we had done for him and his brother at the end of the war. Upon returning from my second interrogation, I could not escape the impression that the entire affair could be traced to the Jewish communists in the Council of Jewish Communities and that it had been instigated by a member of the Council of Jewish Communities who held a senior position in the Ministry of Finance. The investigation hinged on the question of why the Union of Jewish Communities had ceased requesting and receiving dollars at a time when the Council of Jewish Communities in Prague was adamantly calling for increased subsidies from the Joint. The fact that the Union of Jewish Communities continued reporting monthly to the Joint on its social welfare activities was taken as clear proof of a criminal conspiracy. I continued to withstand the interrogator's threats and vehementlysdenied all his suspicious conjectures.

On Sunday, February 20, we were surprised by a visit from our spouses. They had traveled all night to see us for ten fleeting minutes. We were very moved. With the police watching we could only talk about the family; otherwise, our visit would have been cut short immediately. Nevertheless, the policeman did not hear the question that I whispered to my wife as I hugged her, nor the answer she conveyed in her allusive remarks during our conversation and as we parted. I asked about the public's reaction to our arrest and about getting a lawyer. The answer came in several words interlaced in a story about the children: fear, trust, and concern for my release. The slice of cake my wife gave me had deliberately been wrapped in a piece of Hebrew newspaper, which I managed to fold up and tuck in my hat. Two weeks later I had the good fortune to receive another visit from my wife. Her eyes looked sad, but she did not reveal that it was because she had left a sick baby at home. Quite the contrary, she encouraged me with the hope that I would be released soon. Dr. Révész and Rosenthal got a message through to me that a lawyer, Dr. Alexander Lorian, was working intensively on our case.

The lawyer visited the prison several days before Purim. He told us about the negotiations that were under way and said he hoped we would be released in time to "send portions one to another, and gifts to the poor" at home, in celebration of Purim. I hinted to him that I had not broken down, even during my third interrogation, and that, as I had said in the notes which I managed to sneak out earlier, they should not rush to give in to extortion or pay exaggerated fines to ransom me. The financial authorities had no clear evidence against us; everything was based on conjecture and slander. However, the Joint's experts were afraid a maximum fine, ten times the sum mentioned in the indictment, might be imposed, and their experience in Communist countries pushed them to work for a compromise settlement and good will.

I had hoped that on Purim I would be able to hear the Scroll of Esther read in public, as is alluded therein: "relief and deliverance will arise to the Jews from another place." ... but the holiday went by, and I remained in prison. On the Fast of Esther, I expressed my belonging to the Jewish people, alluded to by Haman as a "certain people scattered abroad and dispersed among the peoples," by abstaining from food, but I was unable to perform the commandment of exchanging gifts.

We were released on Saturday night, the 18th of Adar, 5709 (March 19, 1949). "When Adar comes in, gladness is increased."

Our rejoicing was great indeed, when I and my friends Leo Rosenthal, Dr. Révész, and Dr. Gordon, who had also undergone days of torment and torture, all met on our way to the office of the warden releasing us. Efforts to obtain our release had been made by Henry Levy and Atty. Alexander Lorian, who signed an agreement on behalf of the Joint and the Union of Jewish Communities providing as follows: A) The American Joint would pay the state treasury 2,000,000 korunas in exchange for which the four detainees suspected of foreign currency violations would be released without being brought to trial. B) To restore friendly relations between the Czechoslovak offices and the American Joint, by the end of March 1949 the latter would pay the Council of Jewish Communities in Prague the sum of 2,548,366 korunas, equal to 50,000 dollars, from the Joint's dollar account in the Merchants' and Workmen's Bank. Dr. Glos signed the agreement on behalf of the Ministry of Finance.

I should add further that several days after my release Mrs. Piovarči visited me and handed me a letter from Solomon Berman, who was still incarcerated with her husband in the prison on Karl Square in Prague. Berman, the emissary from Israel, was requesting a loan of 35,000 korunas, which would enable him to get released.

I was in a dangerous position because, on the one hand, giving money to a foreign citizen without receiving authorization from the National Bank was a violation of the law, but on the other hand, I felt morally compelled to help release a prisoner. I decided to send the money on condition that its source not be revealed. That was the last I heard of Solomon Berman.

II. The Exodus from Slovakia and Hungary

Arresting the leaders of the Jewish organizations in Bratislava, at that time the center of Zionist activity for all of Czechoslovakia, was one of the signs of the government's new policy. We had feared this turn of events, but had also known that it would come, especially because of initiatives by high-placed Jews in the Communist party ruling in Prague. These Jews in the government were not interested in other Jews leaving Czechoslovakia and opposed immigration to Israel. Rumors circulated about restrictions being placed on issuing passports, exit visas, and export permits. Compounding the difficulties, however, only stepped up the mass immigration to Israel.

My deputy, Jacob Hoff, took over for me during my absence from the Union of Jewish Communities. He spared no efforts to obtain my release, since, as he said at the board meeting on February 23, 1949, he was convinced that I had not broken the law. At that meeting the board expressed its confidence in the chairman and authorized the management to continue its lobbying efforts to restore the board to its full complement as quickly as possible.

At the end of March, by the time I returned from prison and could resume running the union, most of the members of the board and the administration had left the country, the majority of them for Israel.

Now my deputy made haste to leave, as well.

He deserved public recognition, but time was pressing, and whoever had managed to set his affairs in order made haste to leave Czechoslovakia. Jacob Hoff was no exception. Having performed his duties faithfully, meticulously, and devotedly, he parted from his community in Nitra and from the few staff members in the Union of Jewish Communities who still remained with me to complete the work of arranging for *aliyah*, and left Slovakia.

At the board meeting of the Union of Jewish Communities on May 11, 1949, we appointed new board members: Rabbi Hayyim Grünfeld and Margaliyot Glück for *Agudat Israel,* and Dr. Alexander Friedrich and Ludevit Indich, replacing Desider Reisner, Emil Herzl, Alexander Pressburger, Dr. Ernest Abeles, Koloman Ulmann, Zdenek Stern, Dr. Leo Révész, Oscar Krasniansky, and Leo Rosenthal, all of whom had left for Israel. The board thanked all the activists who were immigrating and wished them success in integrating into life in Israel.

From 1945-1948, with the encouragement of the *Berihah* organization, over four million Jews left Eastern Europe for temporary refugee camps which had been set up in Austria, Italy, and Germany. From here several thousand immigrated secretly to Israel, with the assistance of the *Mossad* and *Aliyah Bet,* but the vast majority crowded together and waited for the State of Israel to open its gates. Thousands of these uprooted people passed through Czechoslovakia. From Poland via Náchod and Broumov and westward through Prague, and from passes in the Slovak Tatra Mountains via Poprad and Žilina towards Bratislava. Here the State Welfare Department ran a hostel for repatriates in the Jeleň Hotel, where the dis placed persons were put up for several days, as necessary. A warmhearted and pious Jew named

Jacob Samek, a senior official in the Welfare Department in charge of repatriation, worked laudably to help Jewish refugees.

From Bratislava homeless Jews traveled to Devinská Nová Ves, where they crossed a wooden bridge over the Danube and continued to the Marchegg border crossing into Austria and from there to Vienna, to the Rothschild Hospital. The biggest convoys of refugees passed through in the summer of 1946. The Czech government supplied most of the food, hostels, and special trains, in cooperation with UNRRA and with assistance from the Joint in Prague, whose energetic director at the time was Israel G. Jacobson. Through the American Ambassador in Prague, a Jew by the name of Laurence Steinhardt, Jacobson established contact with Foreign Minister Jan Masaryk and his deputy Vladimir Klementis, and together they initiated an inter-ministerial agreement on everything pertaining to repatriation. Minister of Welfare Zdenek Nejedlý, Antonin Zápotocký, and Clement Gottwald, leading figures in the Communist party, who themselves had suffered from the Nazi conquest, lent a helping hand to the mass exodus of Jews from Poland by way of Czechoslovakia in 1946.

According to this agreement the authorities did not hamper Jews from crossing the border en masse or homeless persons from staying in Czechoslovakia for several days until they could cross into neighboring counties. *Berihah* opened its main office in Bratislava, which in 1946 was presided over by Levy Argov. He was assisted by devoted and trustworthy young men, who showed great resourcefulness and ability to cope with danger in crossing many European borders. Organizationally *Berihah* was associated with the *Mossad* office in charge of *Aliyah Bet,* whose European center was in Prague, under the command of Shaul Avigdor.

In February 1947, as a result of political changes, the Poles closed the border; nevertheless, 9,315[86] Jews were transferred from Poland in that year. Some went via Aš, on the western border of the Czech Republic, although the majority chose the better-known route via Bratislava to Vienna. This exodus was no longer a panicky flight. These refugees were primarily young Zionists, who risked imprisonment should they be caught crossing the border. In 1948, too, around 2,500 Jews from Poland as well as Hungary and Rumania reached Austria by way of Bratislava.

The moment free immigration to Israel became a reality the *Aliyah Bet* office of the *Mossad* had no more role to play. This, ostensibly, should have made *Berihah* a superfluous organization, as well; however, that proved not to be the case. The organization waned but did not cease to exist through 1949, although it did change its framework.

In 1949 any Jew in Czechoslovakia could generally obtain a passport and exit visa for the purpose of emigration, even though the Communists had exclusive control of the government. Things were different, however, under the Communist regime in the neighboring country of Hungary, where, in contravention to the right of self-determination championed by the nations of the world, Jews were not permitted to leave the country and immigrate to the independent State of Israel.

Despite its shut gate policy, Hungary's borders at the time were not yet closed by an iron curtain or even barbed wire fences, and illegal border crossings were still passable. Young Zionists and devout Jews, who felt themselves hemmed in, without any hope of legal exit and emigration, crossed the border illegally, even at the risk of

---

[86] See Judah Bauer, *Ha-Berihah*, 1975, Tel Aviv, p. 276 [Hebrew].

imprisonment in a Slovak jail. They relied not only on miracles but also on the help of Jewish activists in Slovakia, who would ransom captives and give hospitality to guests. These refugees arrived in Bratislava either singly or in small groups and availed themselves of the assistance of former *Berihah* activists to help them reach Austria.

By that time, it should be noted, the "unsuccessful repatriation campaign" had officially been terminated, and crossing the border from Czechoslovakia into Austria was strictly forbidden. Friedman and his colleagues were aware of the change in the law, yet they continued smuggling refugees across the border until they were arrested by Slovak security forces. Of the hundreds of people who reached Slovak territory, several were caught and imprisoned on charges of illegal entry or sent to the Nováky labor camp. After serving their term they still faced the danger of being deported back to Hungary. The Slovak Ministry of Interior was harassed by this problem, and the security forces were ordered to act with an iron hand. On March 12, 1949, the Jewish community of Bratislava received a letter from the Ministry of Interior, essentially addressed to the Union of Jewish Communities. This is what it said:

> In the wake of the termination and proscription of the "unsuccessful repatriation campaign" run by the Ministry of Welfare, many people of Jewish origin who penetrated Slovak territory illegally and were destined to be removed across the border as part of the repatriation campaign have massed in Slovakia. For reasons of state security and in the interest of not interfering with the lawful emigration of Jewish citizens of Czechoslovakia, the presence of large numbers of illegal infiltrators of Jewish origin on Czechoslovak soil is an intolerable situation. Since the Ministry of Interior does not wish

to create difficulties in dispatching refugees illegally residing in Czechoslovakia, we hereby charge you to assemble these people at gathering points in groups of approximately 100 people, in accordance with the accommodations available, by March 15, 1949. At the gathering point which shall be set up in Bratislava, authorized representatives of the Jewish community shall certify the Jewish origins and past (of the refugees), and the security forces, on their part, shall examine them insofar as the security of the state is concerned.

All the Jewish communities of Slovakia, and through them all the Jewish refugees currently residing in Slovakia, must be notified forth with that these refugees must register in the offices of the Jewish communities by March 18, 1949. They shall be assembled gradually at the gathering points so that they can be sent on to the State of Israel. We hereby warn you that the date of the 18th is final and that instructions have been issued that any person whom the security forces shall catch after this date, not having registered and been sent on, shall be taken to court and punished with the maximum sentence, and that after serving his term he shall be deported to his country of origin.

We expect that the representatives of the Jewish community will fully appreciate our lenient approach, which is far less strict than that required by law, and will make every effort to carry out this mission with the utmost responsibility.

- In the name of the Minister of Interior, Colonel Siedmik

The Synagogue in Prievidza

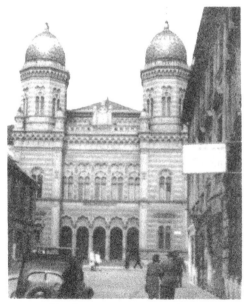

The Synagogue in Bratislava

בע"ה

אֲפָרִיחַ כְּסוּסָה דִיךְ שָׁרָשֵׁי כַּלְבַּתּ הֵהּ הֵרַב הַמֵּאִיר הַגָּדוֹל וְחַרִיף וְשַׁנַן
אַבִּיר מוּפְלָא בַּחוֹכְמָה וּבִינָה יַקִּיר רוּחַ אִישׁ דְּתְבוּנָה
דִּיךְ רַעְיָה פָּר הַתֹּאַר קְרָא הַ שְׁמוּ מוֹהַ"ר **אברהם**
אָבָּא ... רַב הַקָּהָל דְּוָאָקִן הֶלָּא וּמִצְוֹרֵיהוּ פָּרִיסָן
לִקְרִיַת חֹנֶה דָּוִד עַל וַחֲדָשׁ יְיָ

בְּהִתְאַסֵּף רָאשֵׁי עָם יַחַד שִׁבְטֵי יִשְׂרָאֵל זֶמוּ וּבְּחֵיר בְּרוּבָּה דְּאִיתָא קְמָן כְּלַעֲרֵי וּלְעַלֵּי
בְּעַלֵּרֶת צְבִי וְצְפִירֵת תִּפְאָרֵה לִישַׁבּ עַל כִּסֵּא הָרָבְּנוּת בְּעַדְרָתוֹ הַמְּלוֹאָרֵה לְאָשֵׁי
וְכַלְּקֵּים יְסוֹדֵי הַתּוֹרָה... וְלַהֲחֲזִיר עֲטָרֵה בְּקֶהְהֲלָה עֲתִּיקָא קַדִּישָׁא מִקְרָמֵת דְּנָא
לְשְׁאָב מַיִם חַיִּים מִבְּאֵר הַתּוֹרֵה שָׂרִים אַרְבֵּי הַכְּבְּוֹן אַדִּירֵי הַתּוֹרֵה וְהַמְדַּע דְּגוֹל חֵפֵּר
לֵב בַּעֲרֵי יָאָם בְּיִשְׂרָאֵל כִּי שְׁמֹה כְּסֵאֵת לְמִשְׁפַּע כַּסְאוֹת לְבֵית דְּוִיד הָאָן
הַחוֹסִיד רַשִׁכְבָּהּ מַרָן רַ' **דָּוִד דִּי יָשַׁע בַּעַל אוֹהַל דָּוִד יְשָׁהְבָּ**
וְיֵסָף הִיא הַמְּסַבִּיר בִּיאֵר בַּדִּ'הֵ"ם הֵהּ הַגָּאוֹן חֲכָם הַכּוֹלֵל מוֹהֵ' גִוֹסֵף
עֵיר חֲדָשָׁה הַמְעָלֵּרֶה בְּעַלֵּרֶת חֲכָמִים

וּבְּכָן הִתְקַבְּצוּ מַלְאָכִים זָה אַל זֶה מַלְאַכ וְעֵירֵי הָעֵדָה אַלּוּפִים רָאשִׁים וְנִיבִים
וְרוֹזְלִים נִיסְדֵּי יְחַד פֶּה אֶחָד בְּלֵב אֶחָד כְּאִישׁ אֶחָד וִיְבָּחֵרִי אֵת אֲדוֹנֵינוּ מוֹרֵינוּ
וְרָבִּינוּ מוֹהֵ' **אברהם אָבָּא פְּרִיְדֵּר** שְׁלִיטָ"א בְּנַפֵשׁ חָפֵצָה לִכְדִין
פָּאֵר בְּעֲדְרָתֵינוּ כְּהִיוֹת רַב אָב בֵּית דִּין בִּמְהֵלָכְתֵינוּ
וַה' בַּרֵךְ אֵת אַבְרָהָם בַּכָּל וְלָוְנוּ דֵּעָה בִּינָה וְהַשְּׂבֵּל כְּלַהֵ' בַּנֵי עַמֵּינוּ בָּאֵרֵץ
לְחַיִּים וּבְּמֵעַלְכֵּי יֵשָׁר אֲשֵׁר דַּרְכּוּ בָּהּ רָאשׁוֹנִים אַנְשֵׁי שֵׁם כֹּה הֵל בְּיָדוּ יְגַבֵּלִיאֵ
לַגַּדֵּל וּלְהַדְרִיךְ בַּחַרִיסַן צְעִירֵי צֹאן קְדִישִׁים בְּדַרְכֵי הַתּוֹרֵה לַסַּעֵל יְלַמְדֵרִי
לְיִרְאָה אֵת הָעָם הַגָּדוֹל וְהַנּוֹרָא וְלַנְטוֹעַ בַּלְבַב אֲהָבָת יִשְׂרָאֵל וְקָדְשָׁיו

לְכֵן יָאִיל נָא הַגָּדוֹל שְׁלִיטָ"א לָבָא אֵלֵינוּ לְדוּר
עִמָּנוּ בְּמִקוֹמְיְמִינוּ וּלְשֶׁבֶת בְּתוֹכֵינוּ וְאֲדוֹנֵינוּ מוֹכָלִים וּמַחֲמָלִים לְכַבְּרוּ בְּיְתֵּרֶת
הַכָּבוֹד כָּרָאוּי וְכִיאוּת בָּהָקְהֵלֹת הַקוֹדֵשׁ וְכָּפוּנֵהּ אָבָהְתֵנוּ בִּיְרִיאוּ חוֹכְמֵתֵנוּ
נְקַבֵּל בְּאַהֲבָה בַּכָּל מַכֵּי דְּשֵׁפִּיָּא וַיּוֹם יוֹם אֵלֵיוּ יְדְרֵשׁוֹן בַּדְּבָר הַקְּדֵשָׁה בַּנֵי עַמֵּינוּ
וְשֶׁאֲפָתֵּי כָּהֵן יֵשַׁמְרוּ דָּעַת וְתוֹרֵה יְבַקֵּשׁוּ מִפֵּיהוּ לַשְׁפֵּט שֶׁפֵּט בֵּין אִישׁ וּבֵיְן
רֵעֲלֵהוּ וְהֵבָאֵת שָׁלוֹם בֵּין אָדָם לַחֲבֵרִיוּ

צְהָי אַבְרָהָם יָהֵיָה בְּעַזֵּרִי לְהַשְׂבֵּיל וּלְהַנְצֵלִיוֹחַ בַּכָּל דַּרְכַּיוּ וְיַעֲוִיר וְיַן וְיּוֹשֵׁיעַ
אֵת אַדְמוֹיר שְׁאֵילָה הַהַשֵּׁית שְׁאֵילוֹ מַטָּרֵתוּ לֵיַעֵב אֵהָתֵנוּ בַּשָׁלוֹה שֶׁקֵּנֵע וְיַשְׁאֵנֵ מִדְּאוּר
זְהֵ יְרוּחֵיהָ עַל הַתּוֹרָה וְהָעֲבוֹדָה יֵטֵב דְּשֵׁן וְרַעֲנָן יָדֵיל וְיַעֲשֵׁה פְּרִי קֹדֵשׁ
הַלּוּלִים וְהוּא יָשֵׁלַח מַלְאָכוּ לְפָנֵיוּ וִיָבַרַכְהֹ בַּבְּרָכָה הַמְשׁוּלֵשֵׁה בַּתּוֹרֵה. בִּיְמֵיוּ
בִּיְמֵינוּ תּוֹשֵׁע יָהוּדָה וְיִשְׂרָאֵל יֵשָׁכֹּן לָבֵּטוֹח בָּאֵרֵץ אֲבוֹת אָבָת בְּעַל"א וּבִזְמַן קָרִיב
וּבָא לְצָיִּין וְנֹאָכֵל אָמֵן

אֵלֵה הַדְּבָרִים מַבִּיעִים אֲנַחְנוּ אֵל כְּבוֹד הַדִּהֵ' הַדִּ'הֵ"ר שְׁלִיטָ"א בַּשֵׁם אֲקֵרֵיעַ דִּכְּהֵהֲלָתֵינוּ
עֵיר חֲדָשׁ יוֹם ג' לַ_ וְעַל פָּיך יַשֵׁק כָל עַמִי שְׁנָת שִׁוֹ תְּרַוֹחֵן לַ_

_____   _____
         מַזְכִּיר   רָאשׁ הַקָּהָל

כָּתָב רַבָּנוּת שֶׁהֶעֱנִיקָה קְהִלַת נוֹבָה־מֶסְטוֹ לְרַב פְרִידֵר

The Synagogue in Zvolen

The Synagogue in Nove Mesto

Identification card issued by the Central Jewish Bureau in 1941

Michael Dov
Weissmandel

Oscar Neumann

Gisi Fleischmann

Armin Frieder

Tibor Kovač

The members of the underground "Working Group" in Slovakia

Ústavný zákon zo dňa 23 mája 1942 čís. 68/42 Sl. z.

Snem Slovenskej republiky sa uzniesol na tomto ústavnom zákone:

§ 1

Židov možno vysťahovať z územia Slovenskej republiky.

§ 2

/1/ Ustanovenie § 1 neplatí:

a/. na osoby, ktoré sa najneskoršie 14. marca 1939 staly príslušníkmi niektorého kresťanského vierovyznania,

b/. na osoby, ktoré žijú v platnom manželstve s osobou /Židovkou/, uzavretom pred 10. septembrom 1941.

/2/ Osoby, ktorým prezident republiky udelil alebo oslobodenie podľa §-u 255 nariadenia čís. 198/41 Sl. z. /napr. lekári, lekárnici, zverolekári, inžinieri a iné osoby, ak príslušné ministerstvo uzná za potrebné, pomoc ich vo verejnom, technickom alebo hospodárskom živote Slovenska, nemajú byť vysťahovaní, dokiaľ je v platnosti rozhodnutie o ich oslobodení alebo ponechaní.

/3/ Vyňatie spod vysťahovania /ods. 1 a 2/ platí aj na manželku /manžela/, na maloleté deti a v prípade ods.1 písm. a/. aj na rodičov vyňatých osôb.

§ 3

/1/ Židia vysťahovaní a Židia, ktorí územie štátu opustili alebo opustia, strácajú štátne občianstvo Slovenskej republiky.

/2/ Majetok osôb, uvedených v ods.1 prepadá v prospech štátu. Židia radí veriteľom len do výšky hodnoty prevzatého majetku.

§ 4

/1/ Hnuteľný majetok osôb, uvedených v §- 3, ponecháva sa im v držbe a vo vlastníctve. Nárok na vrátenie hnuteľnosti, ktoré im boli podľa doterajších predpisov odňaté z držby pred 15. májom 1942, nemožno uplatňovať žiadne.

/2/. O živom a mŕtvom poľnohospodárskom inventári platia

Text of a "Base Law", dealing with the expulsion of Jews from Slovakia, May 23, 1942.

osobitné predpisy.

§ 5

/1/ Na vykonanie ustanovení §§ 1 a 3, najmä na zlikvidovanie osobných a majetkových právnych pomerov vysťahovaných židov, ako aj židov, ktorí územie Slovenskej republiky opustili, vydá potrebné predpisy vláda nariadením, aj keby Ústava vyžadovala úpravu zákonom.-

/2/ Nariadenia, vydané podľa ods.1 majú platnosť zákona, podpisuje ich predseda vlády a všetci členovia a vyhlasujú sa v Slovenskom zákonníku.-

§ 6

Predpisy o právnom postavení židov, pokiaľ obmedzujú osobné a majetkové pomery nežidovského manžela /manželky/ žida, strácajú účinnosť dňom vyhlásenia tohto zákona.-

§ 7

Tento ústavný zákon platí a nadobúda účinnosť až dňom vyhlásenia; vykonajú ho všetci členovia vlády.

Dr.Tiso v.r.
dr.Sokol v.r.
dr.Tuka v.r.

Mach v.r.   Sivák v.r.
dr.Pružinský v.r.   dr.Medrický v.r.
aj za min.Stana   dr.Fritz v.r.

Čatloš v.r.

Copies of two pages from the original diaries of Rabbi Frieder describing the
transports of Jews from Žilina in 1942. The diaries are kept in the archives of
Jad va Shem, Jerusalem.

streng bewaffnet
verlassen sie das
Lager mit und mit
ihren Nummern
auf den Kopfen
und Jacken in
der Hand gehn
sie zum beruhigt
begleitet von
einem Posten
wenn sie nicht
genug schnell mar-
schieren. Es wim-
melt von Auf-
sichten aus, ob
hohe, es redwine
vertschaffene Men-
schen sind, die
ihren eigenen Volk
herraus der Kon-
lagern.
Es werden sie

JEANE D'ARC

Gisi Fleischmann as Jean D'Arc, surrounded by various activists of the Working Group. In the center Rabbi Weissmandel and Rabbi Frieder. To the right Dr. Oscar Neumann, to the left in the first row Endre Steiner and Wilhelm Fuerst, second row Ernst Abeles and Tibor Kovač.

Workshops in the Sered labor camp

New Year's greeting cards, printed in the Sered labor camp

The Carpentry workshop in Sered

Workshops in the Nováky labor camp

Workshops in the Vyhne labor camp

New Year's greeting from the students of the Yeshiva "Shevet Shimeon".
These were living clandestinely in "Ohel David" under the protection of Rabbi
Frieder

The new building of "Ohel David"

Ohel Dávid — Základina Adolfa Baiersdorfa
nahradzujúca podľa výmeru Prezídia Ministerstva vnútra č. 14-1191-1/43 zo dňa 2. februára 1943

Ústredný židovský táborový starobínec v Novákoch
s prechodným sídlom v Novom Meste nad Váhom.

Číslo: 110/44.   Nové Mesto n/V., dňa 18.mája 1944.

                    Pán

              Izidor L a n d a u nar. r. 1879
              a manž.Šarlota r. Stehrová nar.1890

                         P r e š o v.

              Nakoľko ste vyše 60. ročný, obyvateľ šarišsko-
zemplínskej župy, môžete sa v smysle príkazu pána prednostu
14.odd. Ministerstva vnútra, pána hlavného radcu Dr. Vaška
prisťahovať do Ústredného táborového starobínca v Novom
Meste nad Váhom.-

                                        vedúci starobínca:

Notification of Acceptance to "Ohel David", May 18, 1944.

The tombstone of Rabbi Frieder in the Jewish Cemetery in Bratislava

Children, survivors of the Holocaust, in "Ohel David" 1946-1948

The tombstone of Rabbi Frieder in the Jewish Cemetery in Bratislava

Children, survivors of the Holocaust, in "Ohel David" 1946-1948

Meeting of the representative of the Czechoslovak Jewry with President
Beneš, 1947. Seated, counter clockwise, starting from left: Beneš, Frischer,
Frieder, Spitz, Hoff, Fuchs, Wehle, Winterstein.

The delegation of the Czechoslovak Jewry in the World Jewish Congress in Montreaux, France — 1948. From left to right: O. Krasnansky, V. Winterstein, E. Frieder, Mrs. Šimkova. Missing from the picture is Dr. Ungar.

Meeting of the representative of the Czechoslovak Jewry with President Beneš, 1947. Seated, counter clockwise, starting from left: Beneš, Frischer, Frieder, Spitz, Hoff, Fuchs, Wehle, Winterstein.

Židovská náboženská obec v Lučenci

Vaša značka   Naša značka 1619/48-L.   v Lučenci 31.mája 1948

Titl.

Emanuel Frieder

B r a t i s l a v a.

Veľavážený pán Predseda!

Predovšetkým sa Vám ospravedlňujeme,že sme sa Vám skôr nepoďakovali za Vašu účasť na slávnostných bohoslužbách,ako aj za pekné a úspešné reč,ktorú Ste prednieslii.Chceli sme Vám však referovať o bezprostrednom ďalšom úspechu Vašej reči a Vášho vystúpenia,ktoré nám umožnily aby sme započali ihneď so zbierkou pre Hagana.Vďaka oduševnenému osadníku,ktoré Ste práve Vy pomohli vytvoriť prebieha táto zbierka úspešne a v najkratšej dobe budeme môcť dať k dispozícii patričným činiteľom asi 1,000.000.-Kčs.

Nechceli sme Vám o tomto nepísať,lebo inak by náš dopis nebol úplný.Skrátili by sme Vás o vedomie užitočného kusu práce a úspechu,ktorý Ste dosiahli v úsilíu pomáhať Izraelu.

Ďakujeme Vám ešte raz a prosíme,aby Ste na Lučenec mysleli naďalej a láskou a s vedomím dobre vykonanej práce.

So srdečným členom!

tajomník   Predseda   pod predseda

The Jewish congregation of Lučenci announces successful fund raising for the Hagana, May 1948.

The construction of the Hatam Sofer burial cave, 1948

The tombstone of the Hatam Sofer

Certificate of tree donation for a forest in the Land of Israel, in honor of Rabbi Frieder, 1943.

Festive gathering of the Czechoslovak Zionist Movement to celebrate the declaration of the State of Israel.

The difficult task of transferring the Jews to the border crossing was placed upon the board of the Bratislava Jewish community, headed by Moshe Jacob (Max) Weiss. The board of the community, many of whose leaders had already immigrated to Israel, worked industriously and resourcefully. A gathering point and hostel for one hundred refugees – men, women, and children – was set up in the building of the Jewish school. Many refugees stayed with friends and relatives. The Jewish soup- kitchen provided food. The clerks of the Jewish community prepared the lists, the security and customs officials checked what they had to, and afterwards the refugees were bussed to the border crossing and from there were taken by train to Vienna. Thus, from the 15th to the 31st of March – the arrangement having been extended until the end of the month – 1,088 refugees left Czechoslovakia. Upon my release from prison, I returned to work and fell into the thick of this complex problem. In our attempts to rescue people and help our brethren from Hungary immigrate to Israel we encountered opposition on the part of the security forces and the police, which worsened as the number of Jews crossing the border from Hungary increased. A few days later, when several hundred more refugees had collected again, we managed to persuade the authorities to issue permits for the transit of additional groups. Upon request from the police, I undertook to issue an urgent circular, also in the name of the Bratislava Jewish community, requesting that refugees not be directed to the city because the authorities would not approve the transit of any more groups to Austria and were threatening to return the refugees to their country of origin. On April 7 a group of 310 Jews left for Austria, on April 12 another 409 people departed, and on the 22nd yet another 800 Jews left, bringing the total for the month of April to 1,519 Jews.

Expediting these groups encouraged the Jews of Hungary, and within a week's time the leaders of the communities in Kosiče and the southern cities informed us of an influx of hundreds of people, among them entire families, who had crossed the border. Two approaches began to emerge in the government. The policy-makers were against sentencing these Jews to prison and deporting them back to Hungary. In contrast, the security forces and those in charge of preserving law and order argued that a soft-handed policy was costly and demanded that extreme measures be taken. Since the hard-liners had been entrusted with implementing the government's decisions, we were worried lest they gain the upper hand and put us in a difficult position. They warned me explicitly that they would not tolerate having us, the Zionists, run immigration to Israel from Hungary in this manner.

To clarify this political and humanitarian issue I requested an interview with Slovak Minister of Interior Dr. Okályi. Our delegation was joined by Max Weiss, the head of the community, and Jacob Samek, the official in charge of repatriation. The commissars of state security also attended the interview and put a damper on the humane and open approach of the minister, who was inclined to approve continued repatriation to Israel without the slightest hesitation. "I do not understand my colleagues in Hungary," Dr. Okályi said. "We support the rights of man, including his right to self-determination. If citizens of the Jewish faith identify themselves as Jews and after thousands of years have finally achieved a state of their own, why not enable them to live in this Jewish state? I am prepared to convey this to my counterparts in Hungary at the earliest possible opportunity." With these words the minister backed our position in the presence of the commissars of state security. In the end we won permission to organize one "last shipment" to Austria of around 1,600 people, but the security forces insisted that we warn the Jewish communities in Hungary that the security forces in Slovakia would turn back all people who crossed the border illegally.

On May 5 the Jewish community of Bratislava organized transit for three groups, totaling 1,389 people. The Zionist Organization and the Department of Immigration assisted the Bratislava community in this undertaking, and no one kept watch to prevent people who were not listed in the group charter and had only passed the inspection of the *aliyah* workers from boarding the train at the Devinská Nová Ves border crossing. Among the *aliyah* activists was a certain Jew whom we knew had taken advantage of the refugees' tight position, taking these people "under his protection" and collecting payments from them "to cover their transportation expenses." It is possible that the man, who was also known to be an informer, was not the only crook whom we encountered. Since we could not prevent such things from happening, we looked the other way. All the transportation expenses were covered by the Union of Jewish Communities, despite reservations expressed by officials who had no intention of moving to Israel or of emigrating and who complained behind my back that I was emptying the coffers of the Union of Jewish Communities. Max Weiss, however, was chairman of the finance committee at the time, and his committee approved all the expenditures unanimously.

My friends were apprehensive and asked me to proceed cautiously. The commander of the national security forces also feared what lay in store. In the wake of various warnings, we dispatched a circular to all Slovakia's Jewish communities and cables to the two central offices of the Jewish communities in Budapest and to 20 communities in Hungary and Poland, as we had been requested – but not until May 5. I was obliged to comply with this request, although I did not expect my warnings to be effective.

Throughout May, the Jewish communities forwarded me heart-breaking letters from Jews who had been sentenced to six months imprisonment. Eliyahu David Lichtenstein wrote a letter in Yiddish in the name of 25 men, women, and children in a forced labor camp in Nováky. Abraham Singer and Eugen Rubiczek wrote on behalf of six male friends and two female friends serving six-month prison terms in the Bratislava prison at 9 Radlinská Street. Mordechai Abraham Weiss, the treasurer of the Jewish community in Kis Körös, Hungary, requested that efforts be made to release the head of their community, R. Isaiah Szabolcs, and his wife and brother and their family, who were incarcerated in Nováky[87] and most of whom were religious Jews who had requested kosher food. Great pressure was put on us from many directions.

On May 20, 1949, Max Weiss, leader of the Bratislava community, was called to the Ministry of Finance and presented with a summons for financial violations in connection with arranging transportation for Jews who had crossed the state borders illegally before March 1. The community had had nothing to do with these charters, but the representative of the office in Prague suggested that we pay a "nominal fine" to cover all the financial violations allegedly committed by all the Jewish organizations, which for technical reasons were being subsumed under the name of the "Jewish community of Bratislava." These violations had not yet been investigated but, the senior controller stated, had undoubtedly been committed in Bratislava. Therefore, in exchange for closing the file and ending the affair, he proposed that we pay a nominal fine of one million korunas.

This, another scheme plotted in Prague, made us fear lest the community also be accused of illegally giving money to foreign nationals recently sent on to Israel. Therefore, the Jewish community's officers quickly submitted formal requests to the National Bank to approve the expenditures associated with *Berihah*. After urgent consultation, a committee comprised of the leaders of

---

[87] The Szabolcs family immigrated to Israel and settled in Kefar Gideon.

the union and the community, including Attorney Zoltan Weichherz, was set up and decided to pay the fine. The union agreed to cover 60%, and the other organizations the remainder. The representatives of the community declared that they had had absolutely nothing to do with the charges and that they had taken upon themselves to pay the fine solely for moral reasons. To prevent an uproar and to assure proper functioning of the Jewish organizations, the representative of the Ministry of Finance also signed this declaration and, for the same reason, "contented himself with a nominal fine."

After services on the Feast of Weeks, June 4, 1949, David Weiss, the brother of the head of the congregation, informed me that refugees from Hungary were incarcerated in Nováky. We agreed to go to the minister of interior forthwith and there succeeded in releasing all the Jews with foreign citizenship. Major Haban promised me he would recommend to the national headquarters of the state security services that an exit permit be issued for all the refugees who penetrated Czechoslovakia. So as not to desecrate the holy day, I walked the letter releasing the prisoners over to headquarters, and obtained the permit from Police Officer Devečka. On the basis of these orders all the detainees in Slovak prisons were released, and on June 6 we organized six charters to Austria, transporting a total of 416 people across the border. A report sent by the Jewish community to the customs office on June 20, 1949, claimed a total of 4,412 people had been transferred out of Slovakia, although in actuality the number of refugees was far greater.

In July, the Jewish flight from Hungary accelerated rapidly, increasing the pressure on our community. The position of the police was rather equivocal; the senior officers were hesitant to commit themselves and referred me to the chief commissar in national headquarters. The new commissar of the security forces turned out to be from my home town. Thus, our shared recollections of growing up in Prievidza brought us together. I received the impression that he wished to be helpful in solving the refugee problem.

On July 22, Ilčik requested us to make a list of the refugees from Hungary and from Poland. His letter, which was not to our liking, asked for very many details, which set us worrying about what would happen after we submitted the lists. By drafting the lists would we not be helping the security forces send the refugees back to the country whence they had come? We decided to prepare the lists

but not to submit them until we received authorization to send the refugees through. On the eve of the Sabbath, July 29, 1949, Ilčik handed me a document authorizing the refugees from Hungary and Poland to be sent directly to Israel by the Land of Israel Office on August 4, 1949, and the remaining refugees to be sent by the Jewish community the following day.

To not desecrate the Sabbath, the first group, comprising approximately 500 people, actually set out on August 3, directly for Israel, via Naples. The following day, the Ninth of Av, a large group departed for Vienna, where the refugees were received by the Land of Israel Office. For technical and administrative reasons, it was impossible to send everyone on directly to the port city. Many refugees, who refused to join the charters to Israel, departed for Vienna on August 9. This operation handled the transit of approximately 1,600 people in all.

This relatively large operation, however, carried out under Ilčik's aegis, led to political debate and had repercussions in the Office for State Security. When the Hungarian government protested the transfer of "traitors and reactionary elements" to western countries, the Slovak officers tried to wash their hands of the entire affair. Men from the secret service, including two Jewish communists, called me to the Ministry of Interior, where I was warned to cease my involvement in illegal immigration to Israel. (The two Jewish secret servicemen subsequently immigrated to Israel.) Fortunately, the secret service was not yet like the secret police of the 50's, patterned after the Soviet model. Although I did not make light of the warning, I asked myself how my brother, Rabbi Frieder, would have acted; would he have abandoned the fray in the midst of battle? Rafi Ben-Shalom, the First Secretary at the Israeli Embassy in Prague, who during the Holocaust had been an activist in the underground in Budapest, contacted me periodically. to keep posted on developments in Bratislava with respect to illegal or semi-legal immigration to Israel from Hungary. He begged me not to go to Israel yet because so much work remained to be done, and if I left there would be no one to take my place in the Union of Jewish Communities.

Sending the Hungarian Jews to Israel cost us millions of korunas. On August 2 we received authorization from the Slovak National Bank to spend 2,132,400 korunas to finance the immigration to Israel of Jews from foreign countries. The large Jewish communities of Kosiče and Bratislava enlisted in this endeavor, proving that all Jews indeed stand up for one another. They worked resourcefully and devotedly, with love for the Jews, and, with the assistance of dozens of simple Jewish folk in the outlying communities, for whom welcoming guests was a precept which they accepted as natural and performed without the least hesitation or fear, they rescued many people.

When I called a meeting of the board of the Union of Jewish Communities on the 21st of Av, 5709 (August 16, 1949), to report on the work we had been doing on immigration to Israel, I did not know this would be the last meeting over which I would preside. The meeting was attended by the veteran board members Max

Weiss, head of the Bratislava community, Alexander Schweid, head of the Kosiče community, Mark Weber, chairman of the committee for promoting the religion, Dr. Biss, an engineer and longstanding member of the Yeshurun congregation, and the new board members - Rabbi Hayyim Grünfeld, R. Eliyahu Katz of Nitra, Judah Weiss, Wilhelm Klingenfrau, Dr. Henrich Lax, and Eugen Fischer. Dr. Alexander Friedrich, Ludevit Indich, and Prof. Ižo Rosa were absent. Among the officers who participated were Joseph Lipa, director of the union, and Zvi Fehér, the secretary.

The meeting began with a report on expediting the transit of refugees from neighboring countries. Thus far we had arranged transit for over 6,000 Jewish refugees with authorization from the authorities, who issued them permits to cross the border at Marchegg. The chairman thanked the Slovak minister of interior, Dr. Daniel Okályi, and the Slovak government for enabling Slovakia's Jews to immigrate freely to Israel and for being lenient in enforcing the law with respect to those Jews who had been denied repatriation and were unable to reach their dearly desired destination of Israel from their country of origin. He also thanked the leaders of the congregations in the two large cities, the dozens of other activists in Slovakia's Jewish communities, the members of the youth movements, and the dedicated workers in the Jewish communities and organizations, who came forward to help in this historic undertaking.

Max Weiss and Alexander Schweid added to the report, stressing the efforts made to ensure the operation's success and the large expenditures associated with handling the transit of thousands of refugees.

The board accepted the report, expressing its acknowledgement and appreciation of the work which had been done to rescue these

Jews, and authorized payment of the expenditures, including special grants in the sum of 500,000 korunas to the Jewish community of Bratislava and 300,000 korunas to the Jewish community of Košice, which were given on the recommendation of the finance committee.

Also, a special of 350,000 korunas was approved for expanding the old-age home in Bratislava.

Prof. Ižo Rosa, a member of the board, advised the board prior to the meeting that the secretary of the Slovak government, a Jew by the name of Ladislav Kurták, had warned him that henceforth only "progressive people" were to be appointed to the board of the union. Kurták was critical of the fact that in the past most of the board had come from the merchant class. The board took note of this announcement and affirmed that its members were loyal citizens of the state, and that if for reason of immigration to Israel a place should become vacant on the board, the Jewish organizations would take into consideration the demands of government circles in sending representatives to fill the spot. At the same time the board expressed its hope that the authority to approve new appointments to the board would continue to rest with the Ministry of Education and Culture.

III. The Last Group Departs

Within three weeks another 1,500 refugees had arrived from Hungary. There were essentially no refugees from other countries, and the so-called Polish refugees were only listed as such as a cover-up. At this point things became complicated, for with the Hungarian government's change in policy and their vehement opposition to refugees being sent on to the West, the senior officials in the Slovak Ministry of Interior refused to issue papers going against the official line. Having no alternative, I requested authorization for the transit of refugees from Poland, but the security forces knew the facts and did not dare risk involvement in this deception. I felt I had put up with all I could bear but, with the fate of 1,500 people at stake, I could not give up. I appealed candidly to Ilčik, commissar of the security services, and proposed that the refugees be processed through as Jews from Poland. He did not reject the proposal out of hand, but told me of a heated argument he had had with his rival, Colonel Siedmik, a king-pin in the Ministry of Interior in matters of security, who began accusing him of putting the state in a difficult position because he was suspected of abetting the transit of Jews from Hungary. Ilčik said he was prepared to run the police inspection provided I obtained the requisite official authorization from the Ministry of Interior.

After much vacillation I finally decided to take the matter to the Slovak minister of interior, Dr. Daniel Okályi. I requested an urgent and short interview, and was granted one. He picked up the telephone receiver and, after a brief conversation, referred me to the person in charge of issuing passports, a man by the name of Horský-Stern, a former member of *Ha-Shomer Ha-Tza'ir* and a fine man, who had issued thousands of passports to Jews wishing to emigrate or move to Israel. By the time I saw him, the letter was already being typed: Authorization for the exit of Jews with Polish citizenship and for their transit to the State of Israel.

Very satisfied, I hurried to my office with the letter and rang up Oscar Blaho, the secretary of the Jewish community, and Vlado Turčan, the coordinator of the Zionist Organization's Department of Immigration, who were in charge of organizing transportation to Israel. Sunday, the 10th of Elul (September 4, 1949), was the date we set for the operation, since the customs and police officials liked to work extra hours on Sundays and receive double time from the Jewish community.

Many refugees changed their Hungarian names, and each person invented himself a "Polish" life history, as if he had been born somewhere in Poland. Tension among the refugees ran high when, during registration, the representative of the Polish consul came to check if these people were indeed refugees from his country. The Hungarian Jews could barely speak enough Yiddish to say their birth date and certainly did not know a word of Polish. The visitor was actually glad the people were not Polish citizens and, after receiving a few words of explanation which concealed more than they revealed, intimated that he was not the least bit interested in the entire affair. The incident, however, left us with an uneasy feeling, as if someone were meddling behind the scenes.

On the appointed day I contacted Ilčik in the morning to thank him for his help in everything concerning the group's departure, and he promised to do everything necessary to send the refugees on. However, he requested that in future affairs concerning the transit of refugees we deal with his assistant. The reasons for his request were given in a registered letter.

I followed the procedure of providing transit for over 1,500 "Polish" refugees in awe and reverence. The border control and security checks passed without mishap. Buses took the people to the train, which was scheduled to depart at 2 p.m. We were afraid that this might be the last group allowed out.

That afternoon I went to the Devinská Nová Yes station. Ilčik, too, was there to supervise and see to it that no Czechoslovak citizens or persons sought by the police sneaked onto the train. Our workers requested me to divert his attention, since his presence was somewhat disruptive and was leading to tension. Being Sunday, a non-work day, I tried to persuade him to take off, since everything was in order and his wife had just given birth several days earlier. He seized the opportunity to share his views on Communism with me. What he was doing now fit in with his aspiration to help the poor, the underprivileged. Therefore, he was opposed to the position taken by Palo Heumann, the "capitalist" from Prievidza, and would, if he caught him, send him straight to prison. He told me this several times. A while later we shook hands and parted.

Meanwhile the last bus arrived at the station. The group departing had many religious refugees in it. The leader of the congregation, Max Weiss, came to escort the convoy. I was told that Palo Heumann and other illegal immigrants were also on board the train, and I wished the train would depart already.

Suddenly the station manager came out of his office, hurried over to the locomotive, and turned around nervously. He called me to his office and said, "I regret to have to inform you that I received orders to reverse the position of the locomotive. The train will go in the opposite direction; instead of Vienna, it will go to Budapest. Soon the security forces will be here." The bad news descended on us like thunder out of the blue. To reduce the number of people who could be taken to task I intimated to our administrative workers that they should remove themselves from the scene and, depressed by the magnitude of the disaster, awaited Ilčik's arrival to hear what he had to say.

What I feared had come to pass, but I did not give up hope. I knew that the decree was due to quarrels between rival officials and officers, fighting among themselves at the expense of refugees who, should they be sent back, would be sentenced to long prison terms and forced labor. Ilčik confirmed the bad news, leaving only one course of action open to me – to appeal immediately to the minister of interior and try to avert the decree. I shall never forget the devotion shown by Max Weiss, who refused to let me remain by myself despite my entreaties that he leave the scene so that we should not both end up victims of evil designs. With Ilčik's consent, the station manager agreed to delay the train's departure for two or three hours, for "technical reasons," thus giving us time to appeal the decision.

Somewhat heartened, Max Weiss and I went to Dr. Okályi 's private apartment, but to our disappointment we did not find the minister at home. His wife received us graciously and assured us that her husband had only gone out swimming and would return shortly. I seized the opportunity and, with tears in my eyes, described to her the suffering of the refugees, including were women and children, whose only crime was their desire to realize their dream of immigrating to the land of their forefathers, and for whom, should they not be permitted to continue their journey, a similar fate to that suffered by the Jews during the Holocaust now awaited: imprisonment and forced labor under the harshest conditions. A kind-hearted woman, Mrs. Okályi promised us she would strengthen her husband's resolve and said that if it was true, he had authorized transit for these refugees, he would surely stand by his word and not let us down.

A short while later the man in whose hands lay the power to decide the fate of 1,510 souls arrived. The minister was taken aback: "Who dares intervene and hold things up; I gave my consent, because we are dealing with refugees from Poland, are we not?" Ilčik had intimated to me that the instruction had come from Colonel Siedmik, but I refrained from revealing this, for it is sometimes wiser to keep silent. In my heart I knew that things were not quite so simple and therefore I only praised and encouraged him in his stand, saying that through his humane approach he was making reparations to the Jews who had suffered from the Nazi regime and was helping them realize their yearnings to be united with their families and live faithfully according to their Jewish heritage among their own people. The minister arose and entered the next room, leaving us with the impression that we had found a willing ear.

In tense anticipation I uttered a silent prayer: "By the great power of thy right hand, O set the captive free. Mighty, holy God, in thy abundant grace, guide thy people. Accept our prayer, hear our cry." [88]

Several minutes later the minister handed me a letter to the commander of the police and promised to telephone the manager of the train station immediately and instruct him to take the refugees to Austria. Some people assure themselves a place in the World to Come in one fleeting hour. We had come, bowed down with worry; now we left, heads high in joy. Max Weiss hurried to the office of the Jewish community, and I returned by car to the Devinská Nová Yes station.

When I arrived at the station, I found great excitement there. Overjoyed, the refugees were waving from the windows and cheering. Several people had been allowed off the train, among them two cantors who parted from us singing psalms and saying, "See you later in Israel." Then they reboarded the train, which finally pulled out of the station and took all the refugees to Vienna.

During these days Otto Fischel, a department manager in the Ministry of Finance in Prague, requested an urgent interview with Slovakia's Minister of Commerce and Industry Jozef Schultz, a known friend of the Jews. Fischel, a Jewish communist who opposed immigration to Israel, used his official capacity to delay issuing exit visas and on various pretexts held up passports in his office. (He had

---

[88] A liturgical poem from the Friday evening service. Translator's note.

delayed Dr. Winterstein's departure and now was refusing to give Dr. Gold his passport.) He suspected every Jew of deceit. During the exodus of Czechoslovakia's Jewish citizens and Hungary's refugees he sought a hearing with this decent minister to try to persuade him to stop Jewish immigration to Israel. Schultz preferred to have a third person present during his conversation with Fischel and therefore invited Ferdinand Friedman, who was in charge of the division of foreign trade in his ministry, to attend. (Friedman is now an official in the Association of Czechoslovak Immigrants in Israel.) Fischel argued that Jewish emigration was causing the state great harm, especially due to the transfer of funds without state control, and pointed out that a stream of Jewish refugees from Hungary, among them various elements who were causing great harm to the Democratic People's Republic, was passing through Czechoslovakia those very days. Therefore, he maintained, one should demand that Okályi stop the exodus of these groups.[89]

Fischel was not the only one who intervened in the refugee affair. Ilčik's involvement also had its repercussions. The last Jews who planned to immigrate to Israel made haste to leave. A European conference of the Zionist movement was scheduled to be held in Paris. I had made all the necessary preparations to participate and had already obtained passports for myself and my family and visas to France and Israel.

IV. A Precipitate Departure

On September 6, late in the evening Ilčik showed up stealthily in my apartment and warned me: "Mr. Chairman, the jig is up; the Sword of Damocles is hanging over your head; I advise you to clear out, or else you will be arrested, and that will also be my downfall."

---

[89] Otto Fischel was sentenced to death in the Slánský trial.

We agreed that I would cross the border early Sunday morning. The following day I visited Dr. Okályi and, at Ilčik's request, vehemently denied all suspicions and accusations of bribery and asked him about my personal safety. The minister reassured me, and I took my leave, expressing to him my thanks and appreciation.

On Thursday evening the boards of the Bratislava Jewish community and the Union of Jewish Communities held a modest farewell party for me. Max Weiss, the leader of the community, said a few words of parting and appreciation, and Dr. Lax bid me farewell on behalf of the Union of Jewish Communities, the Association of Persecuted Persons, and representatives of the Zionist movement. I availed myself of the opportunity to praise the dedication of everyone who had worked for the public welfare, to laud the cooperation of all the various groups, and to thank various institutions and individuals for the trust which they gave me in my undertakings during my three years as chairman of the central organization of Slovak Jewry. Thanks to the mutual understanding which we shared through the years we were able to carry out many courageous operations, despite certain well-meaning individuals who had reservations about some of our activities, fearing these would conflict with the state's political line. Yet we always managed to find common ground and smooth over differences, even of late. Thanks to this we were able to help our brethren, the refugees from Hungary, and expedite the transit of close to 10,000 people, either directly or via Vienna, to Israel. The dozens of activists who were involved in this operation showed how truly great love of the Jewish people is; may they all receive their well-merited reward.

On the 17th of Elul, 5709 (September 11, 1949), I left Czechoslovakia by train, accompanied. by my friends Max Weiss and Oscar Blaho as far as the historic Devinská Nová Ves border crossing. There they handed me a farewell letter and a silver *etrog* case as a memento.

In Paris I participated in the Zionist congress. Friends from Bratislava told me that the day after I left the police came in search of me to arrest me. Illegal border crossings from Hungary ceased after many refugees were caught by trickery and, instead of being sent on to Austria, were sent back by the police to Hungary, where they were put in forced labor camps. On the first day of Heshvan, 5710 (October 24, 1949), my family and I disembarked from the *Kedma* in Israel. We settled in Netanya, where our son Raphael Moses Aaron was born. There I have had the privilege of being part of rebuilding the land, establishing schools, working as a principal, and educating hundreds of students.

V. Reinterring Rabbi Frieder and His Family in Israel

From the time I came to Israel I felt a moral responsibility and public duty to bring the remains of my brother and his family from Bratislava to Israel. For many years political circumstances made it impossible to disinter bodies from graves in Slovakia. Aside from the fact that the two states had no diplomatic relations, reinterring Holocaust victims was hampered by the fact that the Jews of Bratislava and Czechoslovakia did not dare undertake any action associated with the State of Israel and by the fact that Israeli citizens were denied entry visas to this communist country. In the late seventies relations improved, and several Jews succeeded in bringing to Israel the bones of their relatives, buried in Slovak cemeteries that the authorities planned to destroy.

In 5734 (1974), before he departed for the United States, my nephew, Prof. Gideon Frieder, gave me a set of *Mikraot Gedolot* on the Pentateuch which had belonged to his father for safekeeping. In 5736 (1976), thirty years since my brother's passing, close to the 22nd of Sivan, the anniversary of his death, I was looking through one of the volumes of the set and chanced to find a slip of paper, written in R. Frieder's hand, saying: "And Moses took the bones of Joseph with him; for he had straitly sworn the children of Israel, saying: 'God will surely remember you; and ye shall carry up my bones away hence with you" (Exodus 13:19); and "And all the years that the Children of Israel were in the desert, these two boxes, the one a burial case and the other the ark of the Divine Presence, went side by side" (Tractate *Sotah* 13).

I became very excited, contemplating the significance of this wonderful note. It is common for preachers and public speakers to jot down verses and homilies to use in their sermons. Yet it seemed most miraculous that this, of all notes, should have survived tucked in a book, and that Gideon should have brought me precisely this book for safekeeping, of all the many books he still had in his possession. Was this not a reminder to fulfill a promise? Should the note be treated as a last will and testament or a Divine sign? I conferred with friends and relatives; and even the chief rabbi of Netanya, the late Rebbe Moses Levine of blessed memory, agreed that the note was a sort of last will and testament. Thus, we decided to undertake the mission. The Association of Czechoslovaks in Israel established a committee consisting of Dr. A. Zevergbaum, Leo Rosenthal, Jacob Samek, Abraham J. Rosenberg and myself, and under the aegis of this committee the bones of Rabbi Frieder, his wife, and his daughter were brought to burial in Netanya.

The funeral ceremony was held in the plaza of the Great Synagogue in Netanya on Tuesday, the 17th of Heshvan, 5740 (November 6, 1979), and was attended by the chief rabbis of Netanya, Mayor Reuven Kligler, public figures, people wishing to honor his memory, Holocaust survivors, and immigrants from Czechoslovakia, foremost the honorary president of the Association of Czechoslovak Immigrants, Dr. Jeremiah Oscar Neumann – all of whom had come to pay homage to the man who had formerly been their chief rabbi, and many of whom had Rabbi Frieder to thank for saving their lives.

The ceremony was opened by the chairman of the Association of Czechoslovak Immigrants in Israel, cantor Jacob Samek, with a reading from the Book of Ezekiel. Eulogies were delivered by the chief rabbis of Netanya, Rabbi David Shalush and Rabbi Israel Meir Lau. Afterwards I spoke on behalf of the family and the Association of Czechoslovak Immigrants. Among the things said by Rabbi Lau were the following:

Our forefather Jacob requested of his son Joseph, "But when I sleep with my fathers, thou shalt carry me [*u-nesatani*] out of Egypt" (Genesis 47:30). *U-nesatani* evokes the idea of *hitnas'ut* – elevation, loftiness; to bring to burial with our forefathers in the Holy Land our exalted martyrs, who sanctified the name of Heaven in life as in death, Rabbi Abraham-Abba Frieder, his wife, and his daughter (may the Lord avenge their blood), the lovely and the pleasant in their lives, even in their death they were not parted. Together, this day, they are blessed to join, to be united with, the land of Israel. This privilege is due to the efforts of R. Emanuel Frieder and his colleagues, the members of the Association of Czechoslovak Immigrants in Israel, and to all those who helped in the performance of this holy deed, to bestow a small kindness on a man who earned himself many thrones in the world of the Almighty – Rabbi Frieder of blessed memory. He sanctified the Lord in his life and was a shining light in the dark days of the Holocaust. For there he appeared as a pillar of fire by virtue of his grace, by virtue of his contacts, by virtue of his finding favor and good sense in the eyes of God and man, and saved many souls from death. Here among us stand Jews who owe their lives to him; and this is something which has no likeness, no equal, in the world of the living. He was a Jew who saved entire worlds, for it says in the Mishnah that "whosoever rescues a single soul . . . is as though he had saved a whole world." Rabbi Abraham-Abba Frieder rescued entire worlds, and of all his fine attributes, of all his merits, of all his graces, this shall accompany him again this day to the world of the Almighty. As a pillar of fire his merit of literally saving souls from the valley of death, delivering them from death unto life, shall proceed before him. Here stand Jews, survivors rescued from the fiery furnace, who have attested to me that to this man they owe their lives, they and their children after them. Rabbi Abraham-Abba Frieder, you devoted your life to instilling faith, teaching Torah, and planting love, true love of the Jews, in many hearts, working under the most difficult of circumstances imaginable. We stand here today to pay you a small fraction of the tribute, the thanks, the appreciation, which we, the entire house of Israel, owe you. May their memory be blessed, for their souls are bound in the bond of everlasting life of martyrs and heroes of the Jewish people, along with the pure souls of the Holy Throne. May your light ever shine upon those returning from the Exile, that they may take you as their paragon and model of a leader of the Jews, a member of the Jewish people who gave his life for the sake of his brethren. We wish to repay at least a small fraction of the holy obligation we owe you. May your memory be blessed.

The ceremony was concluded with memorial prayers led by cantor R. Jacob Samek.

An unveiling ceremony was held on the 26th of Sivan, 5740 (June 10, 1980), beside the grave of Rabbi Frieder and his family. That day the Jews hailing from Nové Mesto held a convention and decided to publish this book.

Appendices

Appendix 1

Excerpt from the Memorandum of the Central Jewish Bureau on Vocational Retraining, Emigration, and Property Transfers[90]

Purpose of the memorandum: to look into Jews' vocational retraining and preparation for emigration, as well as to coordinate, plan and direct various emigration projects.

Many Jews have been dismissed from their jobs and have lost their positions against their will. We note this fact, not to express protest but to explain the reason for our decision to prepare Jews to emigrate and live in other countries, primarily overseas.

Preparation for emigration involves work on the material and physical, as well as the spiritual, level. Since most candidates for emigration are inclined to immigrate to the Land of Israel (Palestine), our office shall deal first and foremost with this problem. The Zionist Organization in Slovakia, in which the pioneering movements *Ha-Oved, He-Halutz ha-Poel ha-Dati, He-Halutz ha-Mizrachi,* and Youth Aliyah are federated, is organizing summer camps and immigration training programs with the assistance of our bureau. Hebrew and background on the Land of Israel and its history are being taught in youth camps. Participants in the immigration training programs and vocational retraining programs are given the necessary preparation to place them in productive jobs as vocational laborers, craftsmen, laboratory workers and other technical experts. The immigration training programs and summer camps are intended primarily for the younger generation. The next, somewhat older, generation is receiving training in various classes organized by our bureau according to need. Jews have been emigrating in groups or individually and with their families. Immigration to the Land of Israel is being handled

---

[90] The original, 8-page memorandum in Slovak, submitted to all government offices, is in the Minutes of the Central Jewish Bureau, FYVS.

by the Land of Israel Office in Bratislava, which receives a number of certificates (immigration permits) annually and distributes these among the candidates for immigration to the Land of Israel. This year more certificates are anticipated than in the past. Certificates are issued to various categories of immigrants: capitalists, craftsmen, agriculturalists, laborers, students, children, and entire families. Candidates for certificates issued to capitalists must prove ownership of capital worth at least one thousand Land of Israel Pounds, and agriculturalists must prove ownership of at least five hundred Land of Israel Pounds. Of course the quota of certificates issued to Slovak Jews far from meets the great demand, and therefore the Jewish public seeks other avenues of immigration.

Emigration to the United States is being handled by Hicem, an international Jewish organization assisting Jewish emigration, which is looking for places to take in Jews the world over and is helping finance emigration expenses for needy Jews of all ages, both individuals and groups, from all countries.

These organizations do not limit their work to vocational retraining and transferring émigrés abroad, but also see to it, through their international organizational ties and ongoing cooperation, that the Jews integrate successfully in their new location. The offices of our bureau are not propagandizing for emigration but are helping organize it, evincing the public responsibility which is required to carry out this difficult and complex undertaking. Emigration possibilities are extremely limited, considering the vast number of Jews who have lost their livelihood and wish to leave Slovakia at the earliest possible opportunity. As a result, emigration offices have been opened by people with initiative and a will to help their fellow Jews, but also by people working on a purely business-oriented basis. Sometimes the offers and promises given by the latter offices are of dubious reliability, and the public has no way of checking their trustworthiness or assuring that they will not become victims of profit-mongering speculators. Two charters of Jews from Slovakia and the Protectorate, bound for the Land of Israel, were stranded on the shores of Greece, causing the refugees - men and women, young and old - untold suffering in their wanderings.

To prevent emigration operations from being inadequately organized, thus bringing tragedy to the émigrés and giving the state a bad name, our bureau, in cooperation with the Jewish organizations for emigration,requests that it be granted exclusive authority to organize, supervise and, as necessary, approve or abrogate the emigration of Jews from Slovakia.

Emigration is closely related to the question of property transfers. Every emigrant needs foreign currency to pay his fare and to ship his belongings to cover his expenses en route and to help him establish a means of livelihood in his new land. Since the emigrants are not in possession of any foreign currency, someone must see to its acquisition. The National Bank grants licenses, in principle, but the cost of foreign exchange for emigration is too high, and therefore general directives and special regulations must be issued.

To enable the National Bank to allocate foreign currency, Jewish emigration must be financed by revenue from exporting Slovak-made goods and by alternative means, so as not to cause a foreign currency shortage or weaken the National Bank's capabilities.

A committee for property transfers shall be established under the Central Jewish Bureau and shall be in charge of organizing the export of goods, using existing connections with Jews and other groups abroad, and shall encourage the export of Slovak-made goods, so that both sides shall benefit. All operations shall be supervised in accordance with explicit instructions approved by the authorities, the purpose of which is to prevent various speculative acts which are likely to harm the émigrés as well as the economy of the state. Therefore, our bureau requests that a directive be issued ordering all transfers related to Jewish emigration to be done only upon our recommendation and with our approval.

In view of the social and moral importance attaching to this memorandum, we look forward to being called for consultations and deliberations to expedite its approval.

The Central Jewish Bureau of Slovakia

Letter regarding Vocational Retraining

Ministry of Interior No. 100 - 16519/9 Bratislava June 26, 1939

The Central Jewish Bureau
3 Ventúrska St.
Bratislava

re. Classes to provide Jewish youths vocational retraining and preparationfor immigration to Palestine.

The Ministry of Interior, Division 9, approves without objection your intention to hold summer camps and vocational retraining classes sponsored by the Central Jewish Bureau in the State of Slovakia. We hereby authorize the programs for 350 people in Vladovce from July 2-31 of this year, for 350 people in Laboče Spas from July 2-31 and from August 1-31, and for 150 people in Ganovce by Poprad from

July 2-31. These programs, which include theoretical and applied studies, are intended for mass vocational retraining of Jewish youth, and the objective of the courses is to enable the youngsters attending them to emigrate from the Slovak Republic.

On behalf of the
Minister,
Dr. Bezak

Appendix 2
Circular regarding Zionist Education

Bratislava,
August 12,
1940

The Zionist Organization of Slovakia
Department for Zionist Education

Circular No. 1

Internal document

To:

Bornstein - Michalovce, Rabbi A. Frieder and Emanuel Frieder - Nové Mesto on the Vah, S. Goldenberg - Žilina, Handelsmann -Labovce, Haya Hammer - Nové Mesto, Julius Herlinger - Trnava, Arnošt Hofstatter - Sečovce, Prof. Imrich Müller - Prievidza, Pasternak - Poprad, Prof. I. Rosenblüt - Bratislava, Mrs. Roth - Trnava, Spitz - Humené, Alexander Schwarz and Joseph Weiser - Bratislava.

The draft committee for organizing the Department of Zionist Education has drawn up the following proposal for activities during the coming school year:

A. The draft committee has decided to nominate you to serve on the committee of the Department of Zionist Education which shall set the guidelines for cultural-organizational work and ways to apply and implement our joint decisions.

B. We propose establishing a larger committee, consisting of one teacher from each school, which shall be responsible for implementing our program.

C. We define our relationship to the Jewish Teachers' Union as follows: The Teachers' Union is a general professional organization of all Jewish educators in Slovakia, whereas we are a cultural association of Zionist teachers.

D. Our plan is to change the pedagogical activity within the Jewish Teachers' Union, including professional editing of the union's publications - booklets and *Chronicle,* the periodical of the teacher's organization - and to introduce more intensive cultural and pedagogical work focusing on Zionist education.

E. To promote our plan we propose to call a general meeting of the Jewish Teachers' Union in October 1940. Personnel changes and union affairs will be on the agenda.

F. We propose the following appointments: Department Chairman - Chief Rabbi A. Frieder, General Secretary -Alexander Schwartz, a teacher from Bratislava. For the secretariat in Eastern Slovakia, we nominate the following members: Bornstein, Hofstatter, Pasternak and Spitz. The teachers' association in Michalovce, in cooperation with the teachers Hofstatter and Spitz, shall undertake editing of the department's periodical. Professor Imrich Müller shall serve as secretary at large to maintain personal ties between the educational institutions and the center. Please inform A. Schwarz, at 19 Reichhardova St., Bratislava, of your position on the matter within three days.

> Dr. O. Neumann and Dr. D. Ehrenfeld
> The Zionist Organization of
> Slovakia

Appendix 3

Letters from the Ministry of Education and Culture

The Ministry of
Education
and Culture Bratislava
August 20, 1942
Number 456131/22 – 4

Mr. Armin Frieder, National Chief Rabbi
Nové Mesto on the Vah

The Ministry of Interior has requested the Ministry of Education and Culture to rescind its decision to exempt certain Jews from expulsion and allow them to remain in the community of Bratislava because, in view of the large number of Jews who have been transferred out of the city, the Ministry of Interior no longer deems it necessary for them to remain active in the public life of the Jewish community.

These are they:
1. Schwarz, Isidor – clerk.
2. Rosenfeld, Adolph – clerk.
3. Dr. Winterstein, Vojtech – clerk.
4. Liebensfeld, Simeon – undertaker.
5. Engel, Aaron – employee of the Jewish Burial Society.
6. Kievsky, Joseph – cantor.
7. Grünberg, Mark – prayer leader.
8. Yoffe, Miriam – secretary of the Jewish Burial Society.
9. Goldstein, Moshe – Jewish studies teacher.

Your urgent consideration and suggestions in this regard are requested.

Na straž ("on guard"),
On behalf of the
Minister,

Revucký

* * *

The Ministry of
Education
and Culture Bratislava
August 20, 1942
Number 45815/42 – 4

Mr. Armin Frieder, National Chief Rabbi
Nové Mesto on the Vah

The Ministry of Interior has requested the Ministry of
Education and Culture to rescind its decision exempting
from deportation the Jews from Vorotky, Samuel Alexander
Oroven and Stephan Yerkeš, officers in the Jewish Burial
Society, since the Jewish Burial Society in Vorotky does not
exist and the above-mentioned persons have not performed
nor are they performing any role in the Jewish community.

I hereby request you to state your position on the matter
urgently and to submit your suggestions to our office.

Na straž ("on guard"),
On behalf of the
Minister,
Revucký

* * *

The Ministry of
Education
and Culture Bratislava
December 22, 1943
Number 47894/43-4

Notice

re.:   Eduard Lichtenstern, Chief Rabbi of Žilina –
Travel Orders

On the basis of Edict no. 377, dated August 26, 1943, regarding restrictions on the travel of Jews, I order Eduard Lichtenstern, Chief Rabbi of the Jewish Religious Community of Žilina, to travel within the limits of the State of Slovakia on business concerning the Jewish religion and community.

This order constitutes a travel permit throughout all regions of the state and is valid until the 15th of February, 1944.

Na straž ("on guard"),
On behalf of the Minister, Revucký

* * *

The Ministry of
Education
and Culture Bratislava
January 7, 1944
Number 42050/44-4

Notice

re.:   Samuel Kellerman, Leader of the Jewish Religious Community in Prievidza – Travel Orders

On the basis of Edict no. 377, dated August 26, 1943, regarding restrictions on the travel of Jews, I order Samuel Kellerman, Leader of the Jewish Religious Community in Prievidza, to travel within the Prievidza district on business concerning the Jewish community.

This order constitutes a travel permit valid for six weeks from the date of issue.

Na straž ("on guard"),
On behalf of the Ministe

Appendix 4

Circulars on Religious Conversions

The Yeshurun
Federation
of Jewish Communities
Bratislava
August 11, 1942

Circular No. 5

To: The Jewish communities in the Federation.

re.:   Jews abandoning the faith.

Of late we have been witnessing the sad manifestation of many Jews, forsaking the Jewish community and going over to another faith. As a religious organization we must take note of this fact and draw the necessary conclusions. Although the motives for this mass psychosis are known to us all, we must express our opposition to and rejection of this manifestation, which in any event does not achieve what it had hoped.

We have been apprised that even individuals holding office in or working for the Jewish communities, in other words, representatives of the Jewish faith, have given in and fallen victim to this psychosis, but have not turned in the white protection paper which they received from the community. We have not the means to prevent the religious conversion of people who have drifted away from the Jewish faith. Their decision is a result of their weakness of character and rests on their own conscience. However, we can under no circumstances tolerate officials or office-holders in the

Jewish community betraying the faith they supposedly represent. Thus, it is our moral imperative to take the following measures against them:

To demand the resignation of these transgressors or dismiss them immediately. Likewise, to inform those among them who hold a certificate of protection from the Ministry of Education and Culture of the abrogation of their certificate, so that it can be given to somebody else. Please advise us of the names of all such activists who have left the Jewish community for any reason.

According to a resolution of the Council of Rabbis the transgressors are to be banned and denied religious services such as participation in prayers, using the ritual baths, burial by the Jewish Burial Society, and the like.

Since the district offices have not been bringing announcements regarding conversions of faith to the attention of the Jewish communities, you are charged to investigate and obtain information on converts from Judaism by any means at your disposal.

For your attention regarding work permits: sections 43 - 48 of the Jewish Codex must be followed. The notice published in the press on behalf of the Central Office for Economy is valid only in Bratislava. Therefore, continue acting in conformance to the existing directive. Bear in mind:

A. A white protection certificate is not a substitute for a work permit.
B. A community leader who holds an honorary position is not consideredan employee of the Jewish community and therefore does not require a work permit.

> Dr. A. Rosenfeld, on
> behalf of the Chairman
> A. Frieder, National
> Chief Rabbi

A Letter to the Perplexed

Office of the Chief Rabbinate of the Yeshurun Federation, Bratislava

To: ; ..

Dear Sir:

It has come to our attention by way of your circle of friends that you are intending to leave the Jewish community and have even been considering converting your faith. We are aware of the motives for such a step on the part of despairing people who have been swayed by the mass psychosis prevailing in Slovakia at this time; but we find it difficult to believe that you, too, are inclined to succumb and would be sorely distressed were such a thing to happen.

Therefore, do not take umbrage that we have decided to interest ourselves in a private, personal affair bearing on your view of the world and your religion. However, as the supreme religious authority we feel obliged to warn you against taking any rash or misguided action which you may never be able to rectify or justify before God or man.

A person's faith and nationality sometimes demand great sacrifice of him. But our lives as Jews, replete as they are with sanctity, have special significance. Until now you have acted as an upright Jew and therefore, henceforth as well, do not shrink from circumstances which put us to the test and cause us suffering on account of our Jewishness.

Need it be pointed out that the other side, as well, views conversion of one's faith as a despicable act, which in any event will not help a single Jew? (Have you taken note of the dates specified, which were fabricated and false?)

We wish to give you strength; and we stress that you belong to us. Therefore, be strong, especially in a time of trouble. You, too, must take courage and think about yourself, your forefathers, our prophets; and do not succumb! Remember, in your actions you bear responsibility not only towards your family, whom you (mistakenly) hope to save, but also towards your people in its darkest hour. Therefore, continue to live according to your ancient faith, in the spirit of your forefathers' tradition, pure and untainted by any reproachable action.

We would like to believe that the information which has reached us was all unfounded and would be glad to hear from you about your position.

Yours truly,
Rabbi Frieder, National
Chief Rabbi

Appendix 5

A letter from Jewish soldiers serving in the Sixth Work Brigade in Slovakia

Zohor
November 18, 1942

Reverend Chief Rabbi!

To begin with, we wish to express our hearts felt and sincere thanks for the information and aid which you have given us. We are grateful to you for your trouble and for the fatherly assistance which you extended to us during these hard times.

Today, victimized by fate in all respects, as every man struggles to provide for himself, we hope and pray that we shall get through the day alive. Today, after we had lost all hope of learning where our dear ones are, you were sent us by Divine Providence, to act as our adopted father, bringing us comfort and hope of salvation, which we need now more than ever.

Forgive us for bothering you with more questions; but is there any possibility of receiving the exact address of our dear ones, whose place of residence alone is known, and how can one send them money or other aid?

Here, in Zohor and the neighboring village of Láb, there are approximately 300 of us young men, and, as I mentioned, we all are in need of encouragement to keep our spirits up and restore our souls; and since we do not wish to trouble you with many letters, we have decided to request that the reverend Rabbi meet with us and talk to us in person.

Three hundred young men, 99% of whom have lost their parents and relatives, desperately need some words of fatherly affection. We look to you in hope, for who knows better than you what a family means to a Jew; who knows better than you that our feelings for family are more highly developed than those of other nations? Therefore, you will surely understand us and our request.

Please let us know how we can meet with you. We thank His Reverence in advance for all his trouble.

As you informed me, my father Moritz Zlatner is in Lublin. My mother Adele (nee Scheimann) and Mina Scheimann are in Sobib6r. I would be grateful if you could ascertain their precise addresses. As for Auschwitz, I shall contact you in approximately two weeks' time, as you told my friend Meisel. I would also like to find out where the following relatives of mine are: Ondrej Feureisen of Trastina, who was deported in the first transport from Žilina, Kati Schumann of Prešov, who was deported in the first transport of girls from Poprad, and Kati Scheimann of Trastina, who was taken with the second transport of girls from Poprad.

We await an answer from you and thank you in advance for everything.

Shalom,
Oscar Zlatner and
Arthur
Steiner 21st Company

Appendix 6

Letters of a young girl from Auschwitz

June 8, 1943

My dear ones,

I am taking the opportunity to write you a longer letter. I am still under the influence of your letters, from Vera and Father, and am very glad that all of you at home are in good health. At long last I heard from you, and can you imagine how I felt? Knowing that Piri is with Micki brightened my day. I was overjoyed at receiving Vera's letter, which gave hope that the illness from which Puntik has been suffering may be cured. I know that one must not lose hope, but it is also not good to live under false illusions. You cannot grasp the full extent or gravity of the situation; only someone who has seen it for himself could, perhaps, do so. The wildest imagination cannot describe this process. They take a person who feels well, and the doctors determine he is suffering from an ailment, which can only be cured in a few cases.[91] Puntik is one such case. It is tragic that in many instances those women who survive will never be able to bear children. But with her that is not the case, although everything depends on luck . . . With older people things are altogether different. They are finished off immediately. I would like to believe that she will hold out. I know that the chances of being hospitalized [in the camp] and ever getting out are very slim.

I know I am writing about sad things; do not imagine that it is easy for me to get these hard words out. I weigh each and every word, and believe me, they are no exaggeration in comparison with the reality. I do not write otherwise to spare you and mislead you. You have surely already heard about the situation, and I want you to know how things are; and, although I do not want to distress you, I must say it

[91] The reference is to medical experiments performed on women's bodies.

vexes me when people arrive here and are surprised and amazed to find that such a thing is indeed possible. I hope you understand now. Please, if you should happen to write to her [Puntik], do not reveal that I have written you anything; just say that you are glad she is in better health, so that she will know you received the letter. Not a moment passes without my thinking of you. My dear ones, in the beginning I used to cry, but by now I have become inured; one becomes apathetic here. You surely are curious to know how I look. I am not skinny and, although I eat little, have remained asI looked before, albeit my clothing is very modest. Do you remember the striped dress I had? My hair is very short, so I do not have to go to the hairdresser – that's the fashion here. I go without a hat but always wear a scarf on my head. Do not send money; I don't need any. The apartment and all the surroundings are similar to those of Oscar D., before he moved in with his brother – you remember, he lived there seven months – except that my apartment is worse. I do not wish to write too much, just give you a general idea, so that you will be able to conjure up a picture in your minds. True, sometimes even the most fertile imagination plays false.

You could send a package; and if I send back confirmation of receipt, send another. I am in contact with Klary P. Klarika S. died of tuberculosis, and the rest of the girls went to live with Piri Frieder,[92] although they did not wish to. Write to me more, for that is my only joy. When did Andor write? Do you know about Edith Z? I must finish this letter. Keep well and do not be sad. I am in good health and that is important. I have been lucky and hope that that continues to be the case in the future. I work in an office and am treated well. Tell attorney Dr. Werner of Bratislava that Juliška, who used to work for him, is here with me and is in good health. Regards and kisses, and write to Piri that I am so glad to hear you are all well and that I have the inner strength to live. Regards to all our friends, especially Marika.

---

[92] Rabbi Frieder's sister, who passed away.

* * *

August 24, 1943

Dear Mother and Father, Aunty and Uncle Arpy,

I have just been reading your letter and am so glad that you are all well. It is very important to me that Aunty to read my letters; perhaps she shall understand them better. It pains me that she has not written; is there any reason why? I do not understand, Daddy, how it could be that after my letter in Slovak you tell me about a package of clothes being sent. For Heaven's sake, do you not understand where I am and that I do not need clothes?! It is food that I need; but there is no point in sending it to the camp, because I shan't receive it anyway. If you can, send things only via the channel that you received my letter of July 24. I never received the package of clothing that you sent to the camp. I wrote you that I have been wearing a striped dress, i.e., camp uniform; but I see you did not understand.

It seems I must spell everything out for you. Please read my letters closely, paying attention [between the lines]. I know it is not easy for you to imagine what sort of a world we live in, when you live in a different world; but you must be apprised of the most important things: the people who came here are no longer alive, save a very few, the exceptions, who still live under such conditions as you can imagine for yourselves. Of course, there are also places where people like us are needed for work. But there are not many like us; and some have it worse, some better, depending on their work. I belong to the latter group. It is my individual good fortune, but there are very few such people amongst us. It would be well for you to understand me right now. When I write in Slovak, my letters do not come from the camp, but via other channels. Your letter sounds as if it was written to Puntik, but never mind. You probably were afraid; but it's better this way. I only want you to understand me and to know everything. So, send packages this way only; I would very much like to eat something from home.

I am so glad that you are all well and that you are at home, my dear ones, although I know that you are miserably worried. Still, be glad that for the time being I am well and that Andor is alive, and that perhaps someday we shall all see each other again. It is only this hope which sustains me. Perhaps, someday Your letters never arrived. Since I left home, I have only received two letters from you, save this special one. I am glad that Micki got married; when I have a chance, I shall write to him and Pirka. You did not write anything about Thomas – is he well? When I heard I had a letter from you, I counted the hours until it wouldbe in my hands; and now that I have it, on the one hand, I am tremendously happy, yet on the other hand, the terrible homesickness it brings arouses indescribable pain. Oh, if only one did not have to think and think. It is terrible that Edith Z. came here; I thought she was with Grandpa in Bb. I am so sorry for her.

Please write to me at camp often, too. Not through the center. Send me a regular letter every week. Some people receive them, so perhaps I shall, too. Only, take care what you write in these letters, because I gamble on my life with them. When you write to the camp do not mention whatI wrote in this letter; but you can write a lot. Dear Dad, I have already sent you a number of congratulations in my postcards from the camp, but who knows if they ever arrived. All the best to you on your birthday, and may we all return home and spend many happy years together.

Give my regards to Marika, as well. I think of her often. Kisses.

Appendix 7

Letters from Survivors of the Deportation Living Underground

September 29, 1943

His Reverence, the Chief Rabbi,

If, for reasons of circumstance, I have remained silent all this time and have not informed you of my existence, it does not mean I have lost my spiritual tie with His Reverence. Quite the contrary, I think of you often, Rabbi, with gratefulness and hope that we shall be able to be in touch once again under better and more joyous circumstances, for you had such a decisive effect on my life. I hope and pray that someday I shall also be able to show my thanks and appreciation in deeds; but now only veiled words can lend expression to my emotions. At this time, on the eve of the New Year, what wish can I extend to a person as great as yourself – a man who has taken upon himself the heavy yoke of working to save his flock from straits and distress, a burden which only a man of vision and supreme devotion can bear on his shoulders. May the All-Merciful keep you in good health and sustain you with the spiritual and physical strength necessary to perform, heart and soul – as you are wont to do – the difficult public mission which has been ordained upon you.

My best wishes to all the family,

Laco

* * *

By the help of God, the 2nd day after the Sabbath of the scriptural reading containing the passage, "and through this thing ye shall prolong your days ... " (Deut. 32:47)

5702, Nitra, may God protect and preserve him.

As the year departs, may he be blessed from On High with
a pleasant life, rich and fresh, the *gaon* and judge in the
holy community of Nové Mesto, his citadel spread over
the state. Wise in secrets, praised in the communities,
and all is by his help; his light illumines and shines as the
noon-day sun; and in the days of mercy, which are come
upon us for good, we shall blow the *shofar* aloud, and may
the Merciful Father open to him the gates of good will
and inscribe him and all his dear family in the book of the
righteous, and may he have the merit of Ahiezer (of being
a helping brother) and Ahisamah (a sustaining brother)
to our brethren the children of Israel, who are in need of
deliverance; until the Lord take pity upon His people
who are in distress and captivity, and bring them out from
darkness unto light, from slavery to redemption, and lead
them in gladness and joy to Zion in song.

Respectfully, as is His· Excellence, gratefully and
humbly,

Israel Abeles

* * *

A letter from Jenny Singer, one of the dispossessed from Bratislava

Nové Mesto,
December 2, 1943

His Reverence, the National Chief Rabbi,

I have taken pen in hand to write to you and thank you. I know that I should come and thank you in person; but the Rabbi must forgive me, for I am not capable of doing so. I fear I should tremble all over from emotion, my legs would give way and I should not be able to stand, my eyes would fill with tears so I should not see, my throat would become choked and I should not be able to speak; yet I have so much to say to his reverend Rabbi and his most venerated wife.

I thank my dear parents and the Rock of Israel, and you, Rabbi, for instilling life in me. You held out your helping, saving hand; were it not for your protection, my fate would have been like that of many of our brethren, and I surely would no longer be among the living.

During the hard and sad days of last year, when my dear parents were taken and exiled, I wished to go after them; but Divine Providence decided otherwise and sent you to me as an angel of deliverance; and my brother and I had the good fortune to be among the many souls which you saved. Not only did you save us, but when we were in despair, you raised us up and provided for all our needs. For in your most respected home, we found everything and lacked nothing. You were like a father to us, in the fullest sense of the word.

I have grown up and reached maturity. At this age parents generally become concerned about marrying off their children. Having no parents, the thought of marrying did not even cross my mind. And again, it was you, the National Chief Rabbi – who is so overburdened with cares of the community, who is always working to help all the Jews of the state – it was you who found time to care for the individual, for this single soul by the name of Jenny Singer. You took care of me as a father would, sparing neither money nor effort to give me a wealth and abundance of all that is good, so that I could enter matrimony with the man whom I loved. At times I have wondered why I deserved the privilege of having Rabbi Frieder's family care for me.

I do not know if I shall ever be able to thank you for all you have given me. All I can do at this time is give thanks and pray for the well-being of our venerated Rabbi and his most respected wife, that you may have a good and happy life in the bosom of your family, for many years, and that you live to a ripe old age.

To you, reverend Chief Rabbi, I wish continued success in your public work; but not only here, for I hope you shall become our National Chief Rabbi in the Land of Israel – God-willing, in our lifetime.

With deep respect and well-merited appreciation, I remain eternally grateful to you,

Jenny Singer-Weiss. [93]

---

[93] Today Jenny Singer-Weiss lives with her family in B'nai Brak.

Appendix 8

Warrant of Arrest

The Ministry of Interior
Bratislava
July 20, 1944
Number 14420/72-
441438-1
Secret - Urgent

re.:   The Jews from Hungary and Šariš-
Zemplín Province Edict

To: General Headquarters of the Gendarmes,
Štubnianska-Teplica
Head of Police in Bratislava and Prešov
The Center for State Security, Bratislava
Police Station, Žilina

I hereby order you to arrest and transfer to the Jewish labor camps in Sered, Nováky, or Krupina:

A. All Jews who were evacuated from Šariš-Zemplín and for whom jobshave not been found. A certificate attesting that a Jew is employed in a certain place does not suffice; rather, you must ascertain whether he is actually working there.

B. All Jews who entered Slovakia from Hungary after March 19, 1944, regardless of whether they are employed, and regardless of whether thy are citizens of Hungary or are former Slovak citizens who by virtue of the laws in force lost their citizenship due to their absence.

All other Jews from Šariš-Zemplín who have

employment shall live together in residences marked by a special sign, from which they may exit only to go to work and return there from by the shortest possible route. Jews shall not be permitted to engage in any work which brings them in contact with the public at large (traveling, working in factories, offices, etc.). Jews shall not be permitted to leave the camp or their place of residence, even in the event of illness. Health care shall be provided either by a resident Jewish doctor in the camp or by [a Jewish doctor] brought in to the camp from the outside.

Na straž ("On guard")
On behalf of the
Minister
Dr. Vašek

Appendix 9

Arranging for the transit of refugees from Hungary

The Ministry of Interior
Bratislava
June 4, 1949
Number 256/71-158

To: The Management of the Camp for Forced Labor Nováky

Re.:   Release of foreign nationals of the Jewish religion who are being held in the camp.

The foreign nationals of the Jewish religion who were arrested for illegally crossing the borders of the State and were put in the forced labor camp in Nováky are to be released.

Please transfer these persons, with all their belongings, to the representatives of the Jewish community in Bratislava, Emanuel Frieder and Desider Weiss, to whom I am giving a copy of this order.

Report back on the order's execution.

On behalf of the
Minister,
Colonel Haban

Copy: The Jewish Community of Bratislava.

For your attention: you must see to transporting, feeding, and housing the people who are released.

On behalf of the
Minister,
Colonel Haban

* * *

National Headquarters
of
the Security Services
Bratislava
June 4, 1949
Number 10-808/1949

The Central Union of Jewish Communities
Emanuel Frieder, Chairman
Bratislava

re.: Transit of people belonging to the Jewish religion

According to orders from the Ministry of Interior, you must see to it that the Jewish refugees who are in Bratislava be transported to the land of Israel (Palestine) by way of Marchegg.

On behalf of the
National
Commander of the
Security Forces,
Devečka

* * *

National Headquarters
of
the Security Services
Bratislava
July 29, 1949
Number 95-01/1949

The Central Union of Jewish Communities
Bratislava

re.: Transit of Jewish refugees

We have no objection to your request that the Land of

Israel Office (Palestine Office) in Bratislava dispatch a charter of Jewish refugees from Hungary and Poland on August 3, 1949.

Likewise, I have noted that the second charter, on August 4, 1949, shall be arranged and run by the Jewish community in Bratislava.

> National Commander of
> the Security Services
> Ilčik

Glossary of Hebrew Terms

Arvit	The evening service.
Beit midrash	A school for the study of the Bible, Talmud and homiletical literature. Also serves as a house of prayer.
Bimah	Platform in the synagogue where the Torah is read.
Dayyan	Rabbinical judge, assistant to the chief rabbi of a community.
Eruvin	Tractate of the Mishnah dealing with rabbinic provisions facilitating performance on Sabbath or festivals of otherwise forbidden acts, e.g., cooking on a festival immediately preceding the Sabbath, extending the limits one may walk on the Sabbath, making it possible to carry within certain limits on the Sabbath.
Gaon, geonim	Illustrious rabbis.
Gemara	Discussions and elaborations on the Mishnah; together with the Mishnah, comprises the Talmud.
Gematria	Method of biblical exegesis assigning numerical values to the letters of the Hebrew alphabet.
Halakhah	Traditional Jewish law.
Hazzan	Cantor.
Kaddish	A doxology, recited during public prayer.
Kinnot	Elegies recited on the 9th of Av, commemorating the destruction of the Temple.

Mashgiah	Kashruth supervisor.
Mezuzah, mezuzot	Parchment inscribed with passages from the Bible, specifically "Hear, 0, Israeli:," and affixed to the doorposts of Jewish homes.
Minyan	A quorum of ten men, required for public prayer.
Minhah	The afternoon service.
Mishloah manot	Purim custom of sending presents to one's fellows.
Musaf	"Additional" service, recited on Sabbaths, Festivals, and the first day of the new month, after the morning service.
Ne'ilah	A special service concluding the Day of Atonement.
Omer	Forty-nine days counted from Passover to the Feast of Weeks. Traditionally a solemn period of semimourning.
Piyyut, piyyutim	Liturgical poems.
Posekim	Scholars who determined halakhah in practice.
Sandak	Godfather at a circumcision ceremony.
Se'udah shelishit	Third meal of the Sabbath, Saturday afternoon.
Selihot	Penitential prayers recited on fast days and on days of special intercession. Also applies to special services from before the Jewish New Year until the Day of Atonement.
Shaharit	The morning service.
Shehitah	Kosher slaughtering of meat.
Shiv'ah	Literally "seven." Refers to seven days of mourning.
Shohet, shohatim	Person in charge of the ritual slaughter of kosher meat.
Siddur	Jewish prayer book.
Siyyum	Literally "completion." A festive gathering and meal in celebration of completing a tractate of Mishnah or Talmud.
Tallit, tallitot	Prayer shawl.
Yahrzeit	Anniversary of a person's death. It is customary to recite kaddish on a close relative's yahrzeit.

Yarmulka	Skullcap, Jewish man's traditional head covering.
Yeshiva, yeshivot	Talmudic academies for advanced study in Torah, Mishnah, and Talmud..

Made in United States
Orlando, FL
17 October 2023

37975082R00343